The Economics of ELECTRIC VEHICLES for Passenger Transportation

SUSTAINABLE INFRASTRUCTURE SERIES

The Economics of ELECTRIC VEHICLES for Passenger Transportation

Cecilia Briceno-Garmendia
Wenxin Qiao
Vivien Foster

WORLD BANK GROUP

1 2 3 4 26 25 24 23

ISBN (paper): 978-1-4648-1948-3
ISBN (electronic): 978-1-4648-1949-0
DOI: 10.1596/978-1-4648-1948-3

Cover and interior design: Chris Phillips, Circle Graphics, Inc.

Library of Congress Control Number: 2023900711

ABOUT THE SERIES

Sustainable infrastructure is a key enabler of economic and social development, as well as environmental sustainability. Quality infrastructure enhances productivity and competitiveness, contributing to economic growth and employment as well as facilitating international trade. Broad coverage of infrastructure services promotes social inclusion and equity and supports the formation of human capital. Green infrastructure safeguards local environmental quality, while contributing to the global decarbonization process. The challenge of delivering sustainable infrastructure services is a complex one that goes far beyond "bricks and mortar" to encompass good policy, sound planning, efficient procurement, smart regulation, transparent governance, affordable finance, and functional markets. The Sustainable Infrastructure Series covers a wide range of policy topics relating to network infrastructure services, including energy, multimodal transportation, information and communication technology and digital development, water and sanitation, and urban and rural infrastructure, as well as irrigation and flood management.

PREVIOUS TITLES IN THIS SERIES

Off the Books: Understanding and Mitigating the Fiscal Risks of Infrastructure (2023) by Matías Dappe Herrera, Vivien Foster, Aldo Musacchio, Teresa Ter-Minassian, and Burak Turkgulu

Laying the Foundations: A Global Analysis of Regulatory Frameworks for the Safety of Dams and Downstream Communities (2020) by Marcus J. Wishart, Satoru Ueda, John D. Pisaniello, Joanne L. Tingey-Holyoak, Kimberly N. Lyon, and Esteban Boj García

Rethinking Power Sector Reform in the Developing World (2020) by Vivien Foster and Anshul Rana

Lifelines: The Resilient Infrastructure Opportunity (2019) by Stephane Hallegatte, Jun Rentschler, and Julie Rozenberg

Beyond the Gap: How Countries Can Afford the Infrastructure They Need while Protecting the Planet (2019) by Julie Rozenberg and Marianne Fay

All books in the Sustainable Infrastructure Series are available for free at http://hdl.handle.net/10986/31290

Contents

Boxes

Figures

Tables

Foreword

Electric mobility is gaining momentum, especially in China, Europe, and the United States, which account for more than 90 percent of the world's electric vehicle (EV) fleet. However, this report, *The Economics of Electric Vehicles for Passenger Transportation*, shows that EVs could be increasingly relevant for low- and middle-income countries (LMICs).

Whereas many advanced countries see electric mobility primarily as a way to decarbonize the transportation sector, the rationale for electric mobility adoption in LMICs is much wider. It brings the potential to reduce local air pollution, improve the quality of public transportation, provide last-mile connectivity, reduce dependence on imported fuels, and provide new opportunities to participate in vehicle supply chains. Electric mobility adoption, however, does not address all aspects of transportation and development, such as road safety, congestion, land management, or urban planning. Therefore, electric mobility adoption must be part of a comprehensive program to promote sustainable and inclusive urban mobility.

EVs will eventually come to dominate the passenger transportation systems of all countries, but the timing of this transition will be determined by the economic and financial realities of each case. For some countries, it already makes economic sense to pursue electric mobility, even though EVs can cost 70 percent more than conventional vehicles. The operating benefits EVs bring to the table—such as lower maintenance and fuel costs—often offset the higher capital cost, making them a feasible option in the medium term.

Factoring in the broader health and environmental benefits makes the economic case even stronger. Regardless of how a country generates electricity, EVs emit less carbon per vehicle-kilometer than conventional vehicles. These reductions become even more pronounced as the power sector decarbonizes. For LMICs with serious urban air pollution problems, the value of local environmental benefits associated with electric mobility adoption exceeds even that of global climate benefits. After performing an analysis based on these criteria, this report finds that, in half of the countries studied, global policy targets aiming for 30 percent of new passenger vehicles to be electric by 2030 makes economic sense for many LMICs.

Efforts to accelerate an electric mobility transition should target the most viable market segments. In view of their relatively low capital cost, the case for electric two-wheelers and three-wheelers is particularly strong in almost every country studied, and the case for electric buses is expected to strengthen as technology evolves and countries adopt efficient procurement and management practices. Currently, for more than half of LMICs studied, the electrification of buses is an attractive proposition when externality benefits are included and vehicles are deployed on busy, high-volume routes.

Once a country decides that accelerating electric mobility uptake makes sense, governments can be proactive in several ways. Accelerating adoption requires coordination across sectors and a combination of strategic, transportation, energy, and financial policies. An evaluation of the timing and chief motivations should guide policy design. Nonmonetary incentives such as promoting leasing and consumer financing all show promise and are cost-effective. But governments also need to invest in robust charging infrastructure, which can be up to six times more effective at encouraging EV purchases than subsidies. Thus, the ultimate success of electric mobility adoption involves additional public investment; in some countries, it also means reductions in fiscal revenues because of the forgone oil taxes. Governments may need to plan to anticipate the fiscal implications.

Although most of the pieces of the puzzle might seem to be in place, making the proposal attractive for users is essential. Doing so might require devising financial and procurement schemes such as pooling demand and transferring power and benefits to buyers rather than to providers or creating financing mechanisms to reduce the risk to new buyers and spread higher capital costs. Electric mobility is an agenda of increasing relevance to LMICs, although each country will need to find its own way. Like many transitions, the trajectory is uncertain but the ultimate destination is clear.

Nicolas Peltier-Thiberge
Global Director for Transport Global Practice
The World Bank

Binyam Reja
Practice Manager for Transport Global Practice
The World Bank

Acknowledgments

This report has been prepared by a core team led by Cecilia Briceno-Garmendia (Global Lead Economist) and Wenxin Qiao (Senior Transport Specialist) of the World Bank's Transport Global Practice, with major contributions from Vivien Foster (Chief Economist, Infrastructure Vice-Presidency) and under the overall guidance of Nicolas Peltier-Thiberge (Global Director, Transport Global Practice) and Binyam Reja (Practice Manager, Transport Global Practice). Other contributing members of the team include Muneeza Mehmood Alam, Fan Zhang, Kristin Panier, Nino Pkhikidze, Annika Berlin, Helena Goetsch, Jevgenijs Steinbuks, Yoomin Lee, and Azeb Afework. The report also benefited from a fruitful collaboration with the Energy Sector Management Assistance Program (ESMAP) and the World Bank's Energy and Extractives Global Practice, including contributions on the energy and transport nexus from Ivan Jaques, Yanchao Li, Tarek Keskes, Henrik Rytter Jensen, and Adam Krzysztof Suski, under the guidence of Gabriela Elizondo Azuela.

A diverse group of consultants and consulting firms contributed to the report. Special acknowledgment goes to Senior Consultants Uwe Deichmann and Shanjiang Zhu for their key contributions to the report and model. The team also appreciates contributions from Cambridge Econometrics, led by Stijn Van Hummelen, Jamie Pirie, and Jon Stenning; Wood PLC, led by Bipin Muley and Moshiuzzaman Mahmud; Chenfeng Xiong, Sadanand Vishwanath Wachche, Gustavo Collantes, Adyasha Mohanty, Jerónimo Callejas, Joshua Linn, Danhui Tian, Huijing Deng, Tali Trigg, Nicolas Oxenford, Jijun Wang, Nathalie Del Valle Barboza Rojas, Vidula Damle, and Elizabeth Font; and the World Resources Institute (led by Ryan Sclar, Pawan Mulukutla, and Krithi Venkat) for their valuable inputs during the research for this report.

The team thanks peer reviewers Bianca Alves, Franck Taillandier, Gerald Ollivier, John Gregory Graham, Pierre Audinet, and Yang Chen for their excellent critiques and suggestions to improve the quality of both the report and the model. The team also appreciates comments received from participants of technical workshops, the quality enhancement review, and decision meetings. The team benefited from additional comments from Ani Balabanyan and her team, led by Tom Remy from the World Bank's Energy and Extractives Global Practice.

Special heartfelt thanks to the World Bank's Transport Global Practice teams from Brazil, Cambodia, the Arab Republic of Egypt, Ethiopia, Ghana, India, Jamaica, Jordan, Kazakhstan, Maldives, Nepal, Nigeria, Poland, Rwanda, Tajikistan, Türkiye, Ukraine, Uruguay, Vanuatu, and Vietnam for their help in providing data, sharing country-specific documents, and fact checking the country studies included in the analysis. Similarly, our thanks go to our World Bank Transport Global Unit colleagues for their continuous feedback and permanent encouragement and to the team from the Office of the Infrastructure Vice-Presidency's Chief Economist's Office for its valuable input.

We appreciate the World Bank's Carbon Price Assessment Tool team members Stephen John Stretton, Stephane Hallegatte, Alexandra Andrea Maite Campmas, Daniel Esteban Bastidas Cordova, Paulina Estela Schulz Antipa, and Dirk Heine for facilitating access to key data.

The team has been lucky to count on the support of members of our Communication and Knowledge Management teams, including Erin Scronce, Xavier Bernard Leon Muller, Jonathan Davidar, Sara Sultan, and Leszek Tymoteusz Zemke.

The team is deeply grateful to Riccardo Puliti (Vice President, Infrastructure) and Pablo Fajnzylber (Director of Strategy and Operations, Infrastructure) for their excellent leadership and invaluable guidance. The team also extends its gratitude to Makhtar Diop (Managing Director and Executive Vice President, International Finance Corporation), Guangzhe Chen (South Asia Regional Director, Infrastructure), and Franz R. Drees-Gross (West Africa Regional Director, Infrastructure) for supporting our initial ideas and launching the underlying research project.

About the Authors

Cecilia Briceno-Garmendia is the Global Lead for Transport Economics, Policy, and Innovation at the World Bank and leads the World Bank's Transport Decarbonization agenda. She also works with the World Bank's operational teams in reassessing the lens through which mobility and logistics are incorporated at country and regional levels to capitalize on synergies between climate action and development. She has conducted research and development projects in over 75 countries spanning Africa, Asia and the Pacific Islands, Europe, and Latin America. Previously, she worked in software engineering, specializing in artificial intelligence and the design of information and organizational systems. She has a PhD in economics from Georgetown University and an MBA from the Instituto de Estudios Superiores en Administración in Caracas, Venezuela.

Vivien Foster is Chief Economist for the Infrastructure Vice-Presidency of the World Bank. For over 20 years she has been advising governments of more than 30 countries across the developing world on a wide range of infrastructure policy issues. Her policy-oriented research has been extensively published, including titles such as *Water, Electricity and the Poor: Who Benefits from Utility Subsidies?*; *Africa's Infrastructure: A Time for Transformation*; *Building Bridges: China's Growing Role as Infrastructure Financier for Sub-Saharan Africa*; and *Rethinking Power Sector Reform in the Developing World*. Most recently, she was Co-Director of *World Development Report 2021: Data for Better Lives*. She holds a PhD in economics from University College London.

Wenxin Qiao is a Senior Transport Specialist with the World Bank, working on analyzing transformative technologies and their impact on global transportation networks and supporting improvements toward sustainable and intelligent transportation networks. She specializes in developing network models to optimize traffic conditions and resource use, including prioritizing public transit systems, predicting travel times, and improving network resilience. She has authored or coauthored about 30 peer-reviewed publications in international journals and conferences and has served as a peer reviewer for several transportation journals. She holds a PhD in transportation from the University of Maryland.

Executive Summary

INTRODUCTION

Electric mobility has garnered growing interest and significant momentum across several major global markets—often motivated by transportation sector decarbonization. Together, Europe, China, and the United States account for more than 90 percent of the world's electric vehicle fleet. For many Organisation for Economic Co-operation and Development countries, electric mobility is seen primarily as a lever for transportation sector decarbonization, given that many of the other relevant policy options have already been exhausted.

This report finds that electric mobility is also increasingly relevant for low- and middle-income countries. As of today, electric mobility for passengers is a comparative rarity across low- and middle- income countries (LMICs). In some of the LMIC leading markets, such as Brazil, India, and Indonesia, electric vehicles account for less than 0.5 percent of total sales. There are signs that this situation is changing. Brazil, Chile, and India are leading the way in electrifying their bus fleets in their largest cities by introducing innovative financing practices and improved procurement practices. Battery swapping schemes are taking off in Asian and East African countries to lower the up-front cost of two- and three-wheelers. Original modeling for this report suggests that established global policy targets, such as 30 percent of new passenger vehicles to be electric by 2030, would make economic sense for many LMICs under a wide range of possible scenarios.

The potential benefits of electric mobility for LMICs go well beyond those associated with decarbonization. Electric mobility for passengers in LMICs can certainly bring significant decarbonization benefits, but it also has the potential to contribute to several other important development agendas—notably inclusive mobility, local air quality, energy security, and industrial policy.

- **Promoting inclusive mobility.** Life-cycle costs for some types of electric vehicles are becoming lower than those associated with conventional alternatives. Moreover, the proliferation of cost-effective two-wheel and three-wheel electric vehicles may bring transportation within reach of lower-income populations. Electric two- and three-wheelers are already popular in many low-income markets for transporting people and goods. In rural areas, low-cost electric motorbikes, in combination with solar photovoltaic systems, reduce dependence on expensive or hard-to-obtain gasoline, facilitate access to markets and other opportunities, and help solve the first- or last-mile problem when using public transit. As electric vehicles move toward capital cost parity with their conventional counterparts, such benefits will be accentuated.

- **Improving local air quality.** Deteriorating local air quality is a serious health issue in many large cities across the developing world and is responsible for 7 million fatalities globally each year. Switching to electric passenger vehicles reduces emissions of the most harmful particulate matter by as much as a factor of 10 per passenger vehicle-kilometer traveled. Not only is electricity sometimes the cleaner fuel, but the fact that it is generated in remote locations also moves remaining pollution away from vehicle tailpipes in crowded cities.
- **Bolstering energy security.** Many countries rely on imported oil products to power traditional gasoline- and diesel-based vehicles. Fuel imports can absorb a significant amount of foreign exchange and often leave balance of payments vulnerable to oil price shocks. To the extent that countries generate electricity from renewable energy, or even other indigenous fossil fuels, introducing electric mobility can bring significant benefits in terms of enhanced energy security and associated macroeconomic resilience. For example, countries such as Ethiopia and Nepal, which import fuels but can generate electricity almost entirely from indigenous hydropower, could significantly reduce their reliance on oil by switching to electric mobility.
- **Democratizing manufacturing.** The manufacture of motor vehicles based on internal combustion engines is relatively complex, and thus not widespread, with just five countries accounting for 60 percent of global production. Although the manufacture of batteries for electric vehicles also remains highly concentrated globally, the greater simplicity of electric vehicles themselves, as well as the considerable commoditization of many key components, suggests the possibility of much greater scope for domestic production (or at least assembly) in many LMICs. An early indication is the innovative start-ups emerging in Kenya, Rwanda, and Uganda, providing affordable alternatives for electric two-wheelers and already exploring lower-cost options for electric buses and trucks.

Despite these potential benefits, the transition to electric mobility raises many complex choices and policy questions, many of which have never been considered from an LMIC perspective. Much of the policy literature on electric mobility takes the perspective of higher-income countries; however, the transportation policy context in LMICs differs sharply from that in higher-income countries in light of the disparities in age, performance, and composition of the baseline vehicle fleet. For the first time, this report undertakes a detailed analysis of the adoption of electric passenger mobility across a broad cross-section of 20 LMICs, and provides a wide-ranging review of emerging country experiences. This executive summary briefly answers some of the most pertinent policy questions and draws out the main policy recommendations. More comprehensive analysis is provided within the report, and the associated original modeling for this study can be adapted and applied to any country to gain deeper customized insights into the most appropriate policy trajectory in each case.

KEY MESSAGES

Policy makers have many questions about the relevance of electric mobility. Using the original research for this report, it is possible to clear up several common misconceptions about the case for electric mobility and to shed light on the many related questions that arise.

Question 1: Is the higher capital cost of electric vehicles compensated by lower life-cycle costs?

Capital cost premiums associated with electric vehicles are substantial, but declining. Electric passenger vehicles are significantly more expensive to purchase than conventional internal combustion engine vehicles. The magnitude of the capital cost premium varies according to the type of electric vehicle. As of the early 2020s, the largest premiums of about 80 percent are associated with four-wheel and two-wheel electric vehicles, and slightly lower premiums of about 60 percent with electric buses (figure ES.1). Some 30 percent of the cost of purchasing an electric vehicle is associated with the battery. Given rapid technological progress, the cost of batteries has been falling on average at 7 percent per annum. As a result, the cost premiums associated with electric vehicles are expected to fall to the 25 to 40 percent range by 2030 (figure ES.1), and will eventually reach cost parity. Nevertheless, uncertainties continue to surround the evolution of battery prices, which are closely linked to the availability and price of the critical raw materials (such as lithium and cobalt) used for their manufacture.

Charging infrastructure is another significant capital cost associated with the adoption of electric passenger vehicles. Although electric two-wheelers can largely be charged from regular power sockets, other types of electric vehicles require more specialized charging infrastructure. This infrastructure includes both private charging points, at home or

FIGURE ES.1 **Vehicle capital markup of BEVs over ICE vehicles, 2020 and 2030**

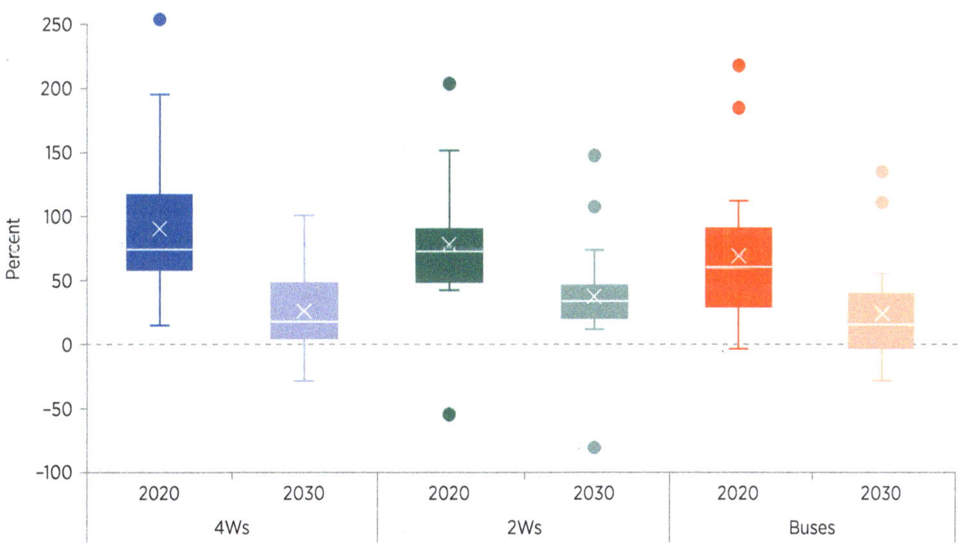

Source: World Bank.
Note: The figure shows vehicle capital markup in the 20 low- and middle-income countries included in the study. The mean of the vehicle capital markups is indicated with an X. The median of the vehicle capital markups is indicated with a horizontal line in the box. Dashed line indicates cost parity. Dots represent data outliers. 2W = two-wheeler; 4W = four-wheeler; BEV = battery electric vehicle; ICE = internal combustion engine.

at work, and public facilities to ensure that electric vehicles can recharge while roaming. The associated investments are largest in the case of electric buses, which require more significant charging infrastructure given their greater power needs. Overall, investments in charging infrastructure typically amount, on average, to some US$2,500 per four-wheel vehicle and US$25,000 per electric bus.

Once purchased, electric vehicles are significantly cheaper to operate given their simpler and more efficient motors. Because much less can go wrong with an electric vehicle than with a fuel-based vehicle, maintenance is more straightforward, amounting to a typical savings of US$5,000 over the life cycle of a typical four-wheel vehicle. Electric vehicles are also less costly to run because they are much more energy efficient than their conventional counterparts (see question 3), amounting to a typical savings of about US$10,000 in the economic cost of energy over the life cycle of a typical four-wheel vehicle. Such underlying economic advantages are accentuated by the fact that many LMICs tax gasoline while subsidizing electricity, generating even larger financial savings for electric vehicle owners (see question 7).

In addition, the ongoing externality benefits resulting from reduced emissions of carbon and various local air pollutants can sometimes be the deciding factor for electric mobility. These benefits bring an estimated economic value of approximately US$5,000 over the lifetime of a vehicle (see questions 3 and 4). For a significant number of countries, electric mobility is attractive solely for the lower operating costs, even without taking externality benefits into account. When these benefits are included, however, the number of countries for which electric mobility looks economically attractive increases significantly.

Question 2: Can consumers afford the capital cost differential associated with electric vehicles?

Until electric vehicles reach capital cost parity, higher purchase costs will be a significant barrier to uptake. In many countries, the capital cost premiums for private two-wheel and four-wheel vehicles do not represent much more than 10 percent of gross national income per capita, suggesting that they might potentially be affordable with some consumer financing. In a significant number of countries, however, the capital cost premium of electric four-wheelers is prohibitively large—ranging from 20 percent to 500 percent of gross national income per capita, which is potentially an insurmountable barrier for many consumers.

Many Organisation for Co-operation and Development countries have tried to offset higher capital costs with vehicle purchase subsidies, but financing mechanisms are likely to be a better solution in the developing world. Subsidies for the purchase of electric vehicles, mainly four-wheel, are widespread in many market-leading countries. These subsidies have proved to be very costly, about US$12,000 per induced vehicle purchase. Moreover, such subsidies are likely highly regressive, given that four-wheel electric vehicles are expensive and have been adopted mainly by higher-income consumers. As a result, such subsidies are unlikely to be a good use of public funds in LMICs, particularly because those higher capital costs often pay for themselves over time as consumers enjoy lower operating costs. What may prove more cost-effective and scalable for LMICs is to develop financing mechanisms to allow consumers to spread the higher capital costs of electric vehicles over time. These mechanisms could be consumer credit lines or adoption of vehicle (or battery) leasing models. For instance, in India, the government offers a first-loss partial credit guarantee to financial institutions to unlock commercial financing availability at concessional rates for the purchase of electric two- and three-wheelers.

Leasing electric vehicles can be effective in mitigating ownership risks faced by consumers and transferring them to leasing companies, which may be better equipped to manage them. "Battery as a service" is one of the emerging business models in which the purchase of the battery—the costliest component of electric vehicles—is decoupled from the vehicle itself, and a combination of battery leasing and swapping reduces the up-front vehicle cost, a key barrier to electric vehicle adoption for low-income populations. This model has been observed in China, India, Thailand, and, increasingly, Africa. Similarly, leasing schemes have been introduced to make the adoption of electric buses more palatable. In Chile, the business model for electric buses separates service provision from fleet ownership, with the utility becoming an asset owner and investor that leases buses to operators. The use of "mobility as a service" models in the context of electric vehicles provides a practical way of shifting the burden of higher capital costs to firms with potentially easier access to credit and having consumers pay gradually per trip or via monthly subscriptions.

Question 3: Does it make environmental sense to electrify transportation before the power grid is fully decarbonized?

Electric vehicles offer a major energy efficiency advantage, particularly in the context of LMICs with highly inefficient fleets of conventional vehicles. Electric motors are much more efficient than internal combustion engines, which lose a great deal of energy in the form of heat and noise. This advantage remains, even accounting for significant energy losses in the generation, transmission, and distribution of electricity. When it comes to LMICs, the efficiency advantage is accentuated by the low baseline efficiency in the motorized fleet due to the prevalence of older vehicles and the relatively lax fuel efficiency standards. When all these factors are accounted for, electric vehicles require only about a quarter to a third of the energy needed by existing internal combustion engine vehicles to move one passenger vehicle-kilometer.

Given its greater energy efficiency, electric mobility is typically advantageous in carbon terms even before the power grid is fully decarbonized. Countries vary greatly in terms of the current carbon intensity of their power generation mix. Because of the much higher level of energy efficiency associated with electric vehicles, however, electric vehicles are almost always less carbon intensive than their conventional counterparts *per vehicle-kilometer traveled* (figure ES.2). Of course, this advantage only intensifies as the power sector pursues the necessary decarbonization trajectory over time. For example, countries like Kazakhstan and Poland, which generate electricity primarily from fossil fuels, can increase the externality benefits of electric mobility by 50 percent and 90 percent, respectively, as a result of shifting toward renewable sources of electricity.

Question 4: How important are local environmental benefits in relation to global ones?

Electric mobility also carries a huge advantage in the reduction of local air pollutants. Electric vehicles emit just a fraction of the local air pollutants—NO_x (nitrogen oxides), SO_x (sulfur oxides), PM_{10} (particulate matter with a diameter of 10 microns or less)—associated with internal combustion engines per unit of energy consumed. This advantage increases to about an order of magnitude when the energy efficiency differential is considered. In addition, local air pollutants associated with power generation are typically emitted at relatively remote locations where power plants are situated. The associated

FIGURE ES.2 Comparative carbon intensity of gasoline and electricity

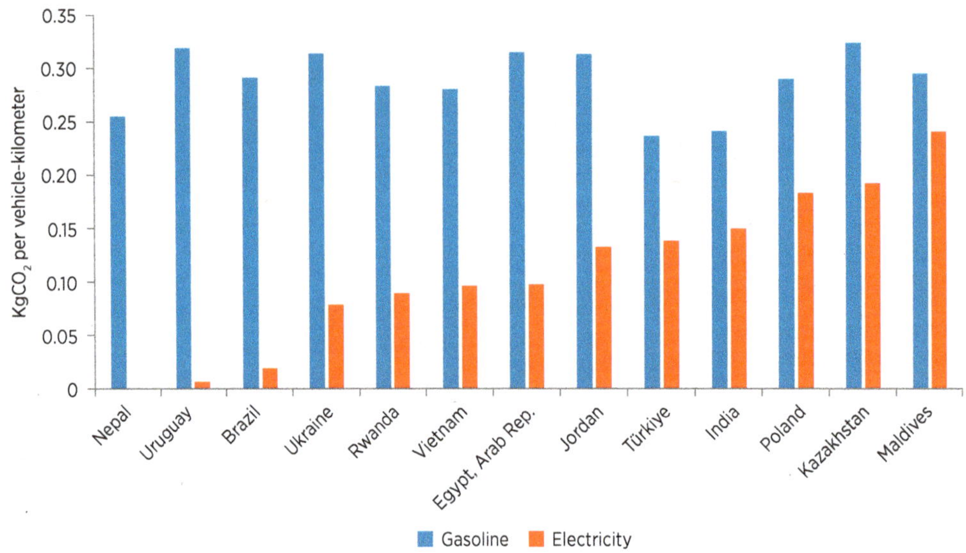

Source: World Bank.
Note: CO_2 = carbon dioxide; kg = kilograms.

human health damage factor is therefore much lower than when the equivalent pollution is emitted from a vehicle tailpipe on a congested urban street.

For some emerging economies, the environmental benefits associated with reducing local air pollution are even more significant than those associated with mitigating global climate change. The relative importance of local and global environmental benefits of switching to electric mobility varies considerably across LMICs (figure ES.3). For countries such as the Arab Republic of Egypt and Türkiye, which still rely significantly on fossil fuels for power generation and face major urban air pollution challenges, the environmental benefits associated with electrifying passenger transportation are primarily local in terms of improved urban air quality. Conversely, for countries such as Ethiopia and Nepal, which have exceptionally clean hydropower and less pressing urban air pollution problems, the environmental benefits associated with electrifying passenger transportation are primarily global in terms of reduced carbon emissions.

Question 5: Should countries prioritize electrification of certain vehicle categories, and, if so, which categories?

The case for electric vehicle adoption varies significantly across vehicle categories, with vehicle capital cost and lifetime mileage being critical factors. Passenger transportation electrification is evolving in very distinct ways for two-wheelers, four-wheelers, and buses. As a result, in any given country, electrification may make sense much sooner for some types of vehicles than for others, suggesting the importance of a differentiated approach. Broadly speaking, vehicle types with relatively small absolute capital cost differentials and/or relatively high lifetime mileage are likely to be the most attractive. Because the disadvantage of electric vehicles comes from higher capital costs, it follows

FIGURE ES.3 **Environmental benefits of switching to electric mobility**

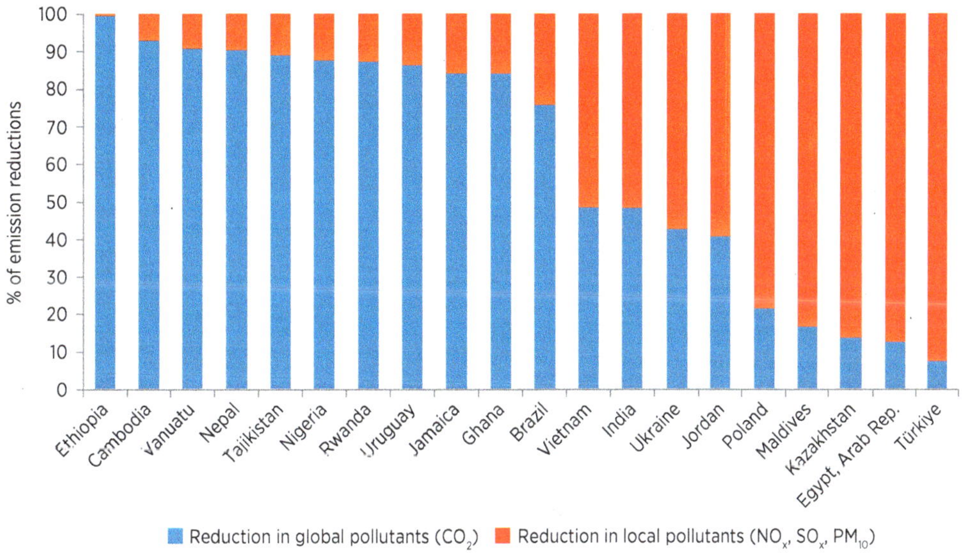

Source: World Bank.
Note: CO_2 = carbon dioxide; NO_x = nitrogen oxides; PM_{10} = particulate matter with a diameter of 10 microns or less; SO_x = sulfur oxides.

that the least expensive vehicles may be among the first to become attractive. Similarly, because the advantage of electric vehicles stems from operating cost savings, it follows that the most intensively used vehicles are those likely to present the most favorable balance of costs and benefits.

Thus, electrification of transportation is particularly attractive for two-wheelers, electric buses, and possibly high-use four-wheel fleets such as taxis and equivalents. In just about every LMIC studied for this report, two-wheelers were advantageous to electrify, in view of their relatively low capital cost. Furthermore, for a majority of LMICs studied, the electrification of buses was also an attractive proposition, particularly once externality benefits were included. The case is strongest for electric buses deployed on routes that involve intensive usage of the vehicle, to allow operating cost savings to accumulate. By contrast, the case for electric four-wheelers was compelling in only a handful of the LMICs studied, albeit slightly better for intensively used commercial fleet or passenger vehicles, such as taxi or ride-sharing services, which may capture higher operating cost savings.

Vehicle fleet compositions vary hugely across LMICs, and this variation needs to inform the adoption strategy. Whereas four-wheel vehicles tend to dominate passenger fleets in many high-income countries, the story can be quite different across the developing world (figure ES.4). In many Asian countries—such as Cambodia, India, Nepal, and Vietnam—two-wheel vehicles account for as much as 60 to 80 percent of vehicle-kilometers, making their electrification particularly relevant. Across African countries—such as Ethiopia and Nigeria—buses account for some 40 percent, which again may be a good case for electrification. By contrast, in many upper-middle-income countries—such as Brazil and Türkiye—four-wheel vehicles account for more than 80 percent of vehicle-kilometers traveled, leaving the case for electric mobility not so strong.

FIGURE ES.4 Prevalence of types of vehicles

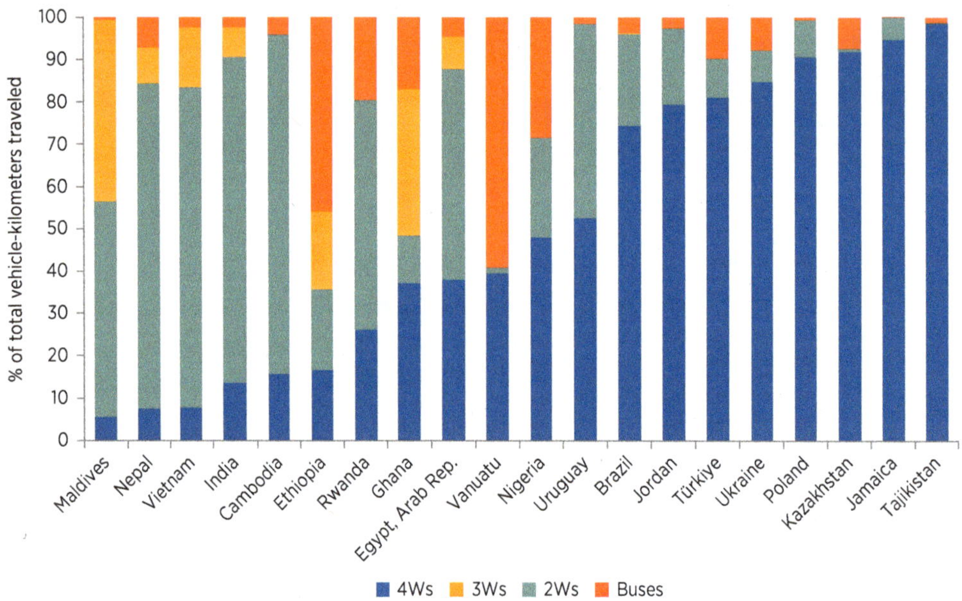

Source: World Bank.
Note: 2W = two-wheeler; 3W = three-wheeler; 4W = four-wheeler; CO_2 = carbon dioxide.

These differences underscore the importance of understanding a country's vehicle fleet composition when designing a vehicle electrification strategy.

Question 6: What impact will electric mobility have on the electric power system?

The overall energy demand associated with adopting electric mobility is not large relative to the scale of the power system in most countries. Electrification of passenger transportation will certainly create additional demand for electricity. Yet demand growth is expected to be quite manageable in most cases because of the energy-efficient nature of electric vehicles and the relatively slow transformation of the vehicle fleet. Across the 20 LMICs studied for this report, the adoption of a 30 percent target for new vehicle electrification by 2030 was found to boost electricity demand by no more than a fraction of 1 percent. Nevertheless, exceptions may arise in some low-income countries where power infrastructure is embryonic. Simulations conducted for several countries in the Sahel suggest that modest electrification of the two-wheel fleet could already place pressure on scarce electricity supplies.

The time profile of electric vehicle charging could potentially exacerbate peak demand. More concerning than the aggregate effect on electricity demand is the time profile associated with vehicle charging. For private vehicles at least, charging will quite likely take place at home at the end of the day, carrying the risk of increasing the evening demand peak. This need is potentially costly to accommodate, given that peak demand for electricity—rather than total energy needs—is the main driver for power infrastructure investment. Moreover, many power utilities lack the pricing tools to incentivize a shift in charging behavior toward off-peak periods, such as the middle of the night.

Question 7: How do taxes and subsidies affect incentives for the adoption of electric vehicles?

Energy taxes and subsidies materially affect the operating cost savings associated with electric mobility. Many countries either tax energy (because of negative environmental externalities) or subsidize energy (because it is a basic need). Moreover, different kinds of energy, notably liquid fuels and electricity, may be treated quite differently from a fiscal perspective. As noted, one of the main advantages of electric vehicles is reduced energy consumption and associated costs. This underlying economic advantage will be distorted by the presence of taxes and subsidies for liquid fuels and electricity.

Most LMICs studied tend to heavily tax gasoline and diesel while generously subsidizing electricity, to the point of overincentivizing electric vehicle adoption. Typical tax rates on gasoline range between 40 percent and 140 percent over cost; subsidies to electricity amount to about 40 percent of the price (figure ES.5). Such a fiscal regime favors the adoption of electric vehicles by widening the cost differential between liquid transportation fuels and electricity. Although pricing gasoline and diesel more expensively than electricity may be legitimate, given related larger environmental costs, analysis suggests that the price differential is often larger than what would be warranted economically by the different environmental impact. Of course, a fiscal regime that taxed electricity while subsidizing gasoline would have the opposite effect of disincentivizing the adoption of electric vehicles and could represent the situation in some oil-exporting countries that heavily subsidize fossil fuels.

The fiscal regime affecting vehicle purchase also plays a role in shaping incentives for uptake. Whereas many Organisation for Co-operation and Development countries have introduced significant subsidies to encourage the purchase of electric vehicles, these subsidies are a rarity across LMICs. In about half of the countries studied, the fiscal treatment of electric vehicles and their conventional counterparts does not differ. In the other half of the countries, vehicles based on internal combustion engines are penalized with a surcharge of about 20 percentage points above their electric equivalents, based on a combination of taxes and import duties. Nevertheless, fiscal incentives—even where they exist—are not typically large enough to reverse the capital cost disadvantage of electric vehicles.

FIGURE ES.5 **Tax and subsidy rates for gasoline and electricity**

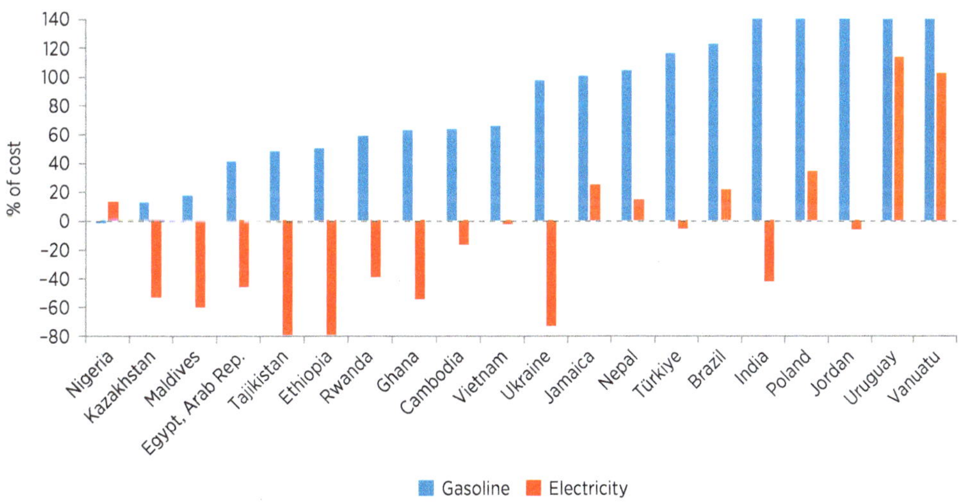

Source: World Bank.

Question 8: What are the fiscal implications of an accelerated transition to electric mobility?

Absent any fiscal reforms, adoption of electric mobility is expected to reduce net fiscal receipts. As noted, internal combustion engine vehicles and associated liquid transportation fuels are generally more heavily taxed than electric vehicles and associated electricity usage. The inevitable consequence is that a shift toward electric mobility will decrease tax receipts from conventional transportation and increase subsidies to the electricity sector (figure ES.6). This shift could be expected to lead to some overall deterioration in public finances, particularly for countries that rely on fuel taxes as a significant source of fiscal revenue. The transition might also prejudice the financial sustainability of power utilities—already precarious in many LMICs—if these utilities are not fully compensated for providing additional electricity to vehicle owners at below-cost recovery rates. In addition to its negative impact on the net fiscal position, the electric mobility transition will also give rise to public expenditure needs (see question 9).

Question 9: What are the investment needs associated with electric mobility, and who bears them?

The investment needs associated with the transition to electric mobility are significant. Broadly, two types of investments are needed to support adoption of electric mobility. The first is the incremental capital cost associated with the purchase of electric vehicles, which is currently substantial but can be expected to decline toward zero over time. The second is the charging infrastructure needed to support the use of electric vehicles, comprising a range of facilities, from private chargers located in homes and offices to public charging

FIGURE ES.6 Relative fiscal impact of electric mobility, by tax stream

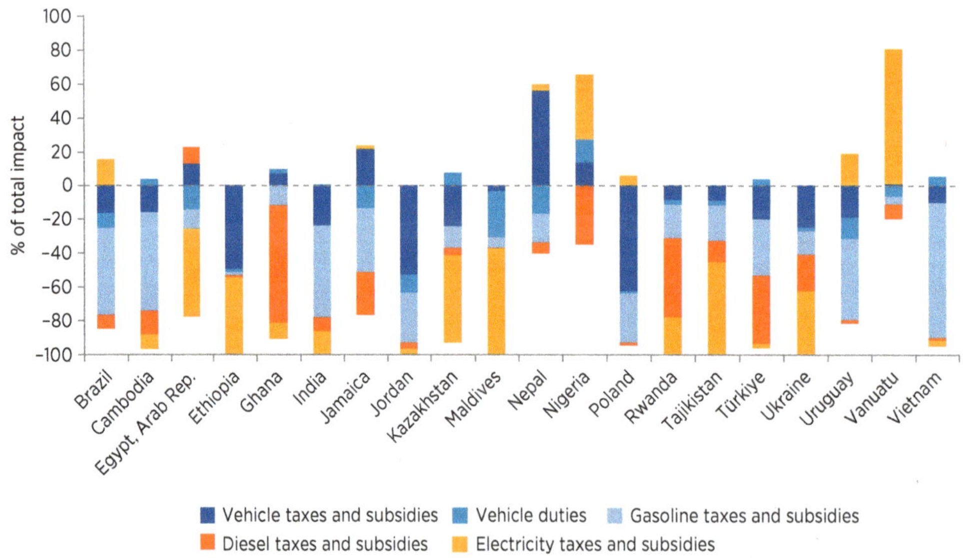

Source: World Bank.
Note: Data in the figure presume a scenario in which electric cars and buses reach 30 percent of the new sales by year 2030, and two- and three-wheelers 70 percent, as compared with business as usual, that is, no new policies for electric mobility and purchasing decisions reflect historical trends.

stations on the road to specialized charging arrangements at bus depots. Despite considerable variation in the magnitude of investment needs across countries, a figure of about 0.25 percent of gross domestic product per annum is representative.

The burden of investment falls mainly on the public sector in some countries and mainly on the private sector in others. The incremental investment cost of personal two-wheel and four-wheel electric vehicles and associated home charging infrastructure will fall on private individuals, whereas the public sector must bear the additional cost of purchasing electric buses and their associated charging infrastructure, as well as provision of public charging facilities for private users of electric vehicles. The relative size of public and private investments needed varies hugely across countries (figure ES.7). In countries where public transportation is dominant, the investment burden falls primarily on the public sector. Elsewhere, most of the investment needs to be undertaken by private actors. Understanding these differences is critical in designing a suitable financing strategy.

Question 10: Could carbon finance play a role in financing the electric mobility transition?

Electric mobility can sometimes provide a cost-effective means of carbon abatement. In almost half of the countries studied, electric mobility can deliver carbon abatement at negative cost—meaning that its adoption is more than justified by the other associated benefits, so that carbon savings essentially "come for free." In many other countries, however, adopting electric mobility would make economic sense only if the price of carbon exceeded US$100 per ton. The relevance of electric mobility as a carbon abatement strategy, then, depends heavily on context.

FIGURE ES.7 **Additional investment needs, by public and private shares**

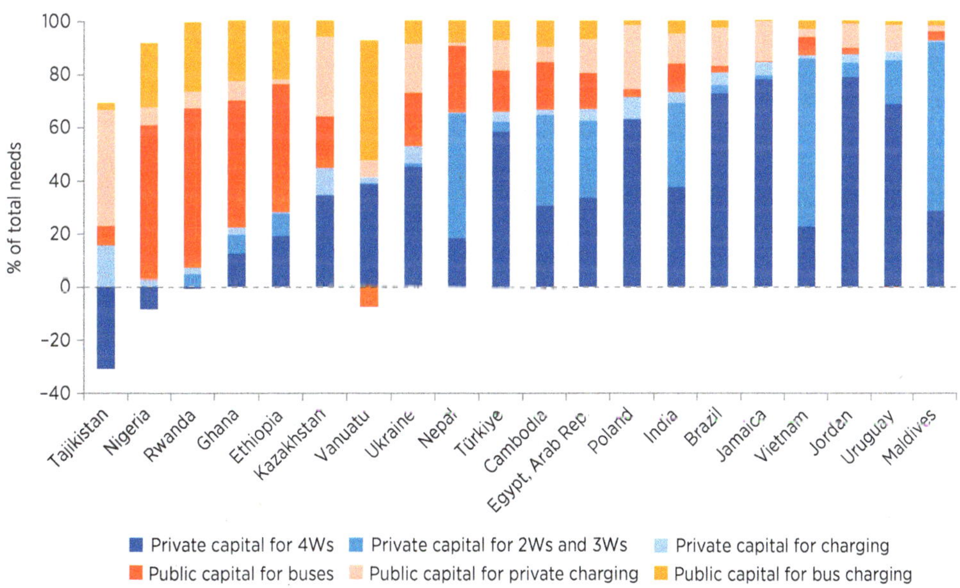

Source: World Bank.
Note: Data in the figure presume a scenario in which electric cars and buses reach 30 percent of the new sales by year 2030, and two- and three-wheelers 70 percent, as compared with business as usual, that is, no new policies for electric mobility and purchasing decisions reflect historical trends. 2W = two-wheeler; 3W = three-wheeler; 4W = four-wheeler.

Carbon financing could potentially cover a significant portion of public investment needs. At present, there is little or no experience with harnessing carbon finance to support electric mobility. If it were possible to capture such finance at a price of US$40 per ton, however, simulations suggest that the resulting revenues would be enough to cover a substantial percentage (about 25 percent) of the associated incremental government investment needs in electric buses and public charging infrastructure. The same cannot be said for private investment in four-wheel vehicles, for which carbon finance is not able to contribute a material share of the incremental investment.

RECOMMENDATIONS

Several useful policy recommendations flow from the answers to the questions posed. These recommendations fall into several categories: strategic context (recommendations 1 to 4), pertinence to the transportation sector (recommendations 5 to 9), pertinence to the energy sector (recommendations 10 to 13), and relation to financing (recommendations 14 to 16).

Strategic Recommendations

Recommendation 1: Identify the primary motivation for pursuing electric mobility. As noted at the outset, reasons for pursuing electric mobility are numerous, particularly in LMICs. These reasons include promoting inclusive mobility, improving local air quality, reducing carbon emissions, bolstering energy security, and democratizing the manufacturing of vehicles. In any given country, one or more of these objectives may weigh more heavily than others. Countries need to articulate why they are adopting electric mobility, because doing so will help to guide and inform their strategic approach. For example, a country motivated by industrial policy may need to press ahead sooner than otherwise to gain a first-mover advantage in manufacturing, whereas a country motivated by decarbonization need advance only once the associated implicit carbon price drops below a certain level.

Recommendation 2: Position electric mobility within an integrated national strategy for sustainable mobility. Even when decarbonization is an important reason for pursuing electric mobility, countries need to recognize that electric mobility is just one of several approaches to decarbonizing the sector and of a wider national strategy for sustainable mobility. Transportation decarbonization will generally require a combination of measures to *avoid* emissions through demand management, to *shift* traffic to less carbon-intensive transportation modalities such as public transportation and railways, and to *improve* the carbon footprint of all transportation modes. Electric mobility is just one way to *improve* the sector's carbon footprint and may not necessarily be the most cost-effective one. It will need to be considered alongside other *improve* measures, such as motorization management to improve the overall fuel efficiency of the conventional fleet, as well as combined with other measures designed to *avoid* and *shift* emissions.

Recommendation 3: Evaluate the case for and timing of electric mobility at the country level. A strong conclusion from this study is that the economics of electric mobility for passenger transportation depend on context. The balance of benefits and costs varies substantially across countries in line with their characteristics. For example, in general, the case looks to be stronger in countries that are net oil importers, enjoy relatively low-cost purchase of vehicles, and have vehicle fleets that are not dominated by four-wheelers. Furthermore, the case for electric mobility is generally improving over time because of technological change, and the moment when it starts to make economic sense will differ from one country to another. The original model developed for this report provides an agile and practical way to conduct a first-order assessment at the country level. More detailed analysis for the 20 countries covered in the report is provided in the appendix.

Recommendation 4: Establish mechanisms for institutional coordination. The transition to electric mobility is complex, calling for coordination across a wide range of institutions, which may not necessarily have any history of close collaboration. For a start, the transportation and electricity sectors need to work closely together to ensure that power infrastructure is increasingly aligned with transportation demands. Further, although electric mobility may be a national policy objective, much of the implementation will need to take place at the city level. For instance, an urban municipality's decision to electrify transportation may reduce national revenues from gasoline taxation, whereas a national decision to accelerate electric mobility may impose significant investment needs at the local level.

Transportation Sector Recommendations

Recommendation 5: Target adoption of electric mobility toward the most promising vehicle segments. Countries should avoid blanket approaches to electric mobility and consider instead the electrification of each vehicle segment individually, because the strength of the case may vary substantially. Two-wheelers (with their relatively low capital costs and negligible charging infrastructure requirements) are typically the first vehicle category for which electric mobility becomes attractive, followed by buses and last four-wheelers. Taking this variation into account, countries may wish to sequence transportation electrification efforts accordingly. Further, because the benefits of electric mobility stem from operating cost savings, the crucial issue is usage. The more intensive the vehicle use, the sooner electric mobility is likely to become attractive, which points to a case for prioritizing, within each vehicle segment, those sections of the fleet associated with the most intensive usage. For instance, taxis, ride-sharing vehicles, and other commercial four-wheel fleets may become suitable for electrification before less-intensively used private family cars.

Recommendation 6: Prioritize use of public funds for subsidization of charging infrastructure. The expansion of electric mobility is subject to a coordination, chicken-and-egg type of problem: demand for electric vehicles depends on the availability of charging infrastructure, and the case for building charging infrastructure depends on demand for electric mobility. Breaking out of this vicious circle is therefore a high-priority area for public intervention. Clear economic evidence indicates that subsidizing construction of public charging stations is a far more cost-effective approach to encouraging the uptake of electric vehicles than subsidizing the purchase of those vehicles directly. Indeed, the subsidy cost per additional electric vehicle sale induced is just US$4,000 for charging stations, versus US$12,000 for vehicle purchase incentives.

Recommendation 7: Facilitate battery swapping models. A simple way of keeping down the cost of electric vehicles and the associated battery charging activities is to swap batteries in and out of vehicles, exchanging depleted batteries for fully charged ones. Associated business models are already springing up across Africa and Asia, but the scale-up of this promising approach calls for further regulatory standardization to ensure widespread compatibility between types of batteries and electric vehicles.

Recommendation 8: Facilitate recycling of batteries for electric vehicles. The most critical bottleneck for the development of electric vehicles is batteries. Batteries not only remain relatively costly to produce but also are subject to a high degree of market concentration and are hostage to bottlenecks in the supply chain of the critical raw materials (such as lithium, nickel, and cobalt) from which they are made. As the stock of electric vehicle batteries in circulation starts to expand, it will become increasingly feasible to recycle batteries extracting further value from their mineral content. Doing so, however, depends on a suitable policy environment being in place to facilitate recycling through the establishment of regulatory standards and procedures at the national and international levels, as well as associated manufacturing facilities jointly set in place with regulations that extend producer responsibility to battery recycling.

Recommendation 9: Adopt demand pooling mechanisms to reduce procurement cost of buses. Similar challenges arise for public transit authorities, which may struggle to afford the capital cost premium associated with electric buses. In these cases, experience shows that the aggregation of demand across multiple urban jurisdictions to form larger procurement lots can be an effective way of reducing the unit cost of purchasing electric buses. India, for example, has achieved cost reductions of up to 30 percent. Achieving such reductions may involve national-level coordination of electric bus procurement across cities, or in smaller countries even supranational coordination, potentially facilitated by regional or multilateral institutions.

Energy Sector Recommendations

Recommendation 10: Integrate demand for electric mobility into power sector planning. As electric mobility becomes increasingly widespread, its implications for the power sector will become more material. Given the long lead times involved in power sector investments, it is important to start integrating projected transportation demand into the planning process along the entire electricity supply chain, starting with generation, moving on to transmission, and focusing on local distribution, where hotspots and bottlenecks are likely to arise. Doing so should provide a clearer sense of the cost implications of electrifying transportation for the power sector.

Recommendation 11: Adopt electricity demand management measures to shift charging demand away from peak periods. The cost implications for the power sector of electrifying transportation depend on charging behavior and the extent to which it is concentrated in existing system peak periods, which highlights the importance of adopting measures to manage electricity demand, with a view to shifting the timing of vehicle charging. The many ways of doing so include simple measures such as providing consumers with information to encourage more efficient behavior and introducing battery swapping arrangements to spread charging activity over time (recommendation 7). Ultimately, smart charging infrastructure that allows the grid operator to influence when vehicles charge, and potentially even integrate vehicle batteries as energy storage resources at the system level, can resolve this issue—though not without significant investment. In the meantime, one of the most powerful demand management tools available is energy pricing (see recommendation 12).

Recommendation 12: Reform electricity tariff structures to provide incentives for more efficient charging behavior. Electricity tariff structures can be complex, and across the developing world are dominated by time-invariant rising block tariff structures. Such schemes can penalize electric vehicle ownership by pushing charging into higher-priced consumption bands. At the same time, they do nothing to encourage vehicle owners to charge during off-peak periods. Greater reliance on time-of-use pricing, where flat linear tariffs vary by time of day, would be better suited to systems in which electric vehicles make up a growing portion of demand. However, implementing such pricing schemes calls for significant investments in smarter metering infrastructure.

Recommendation 13: Reform energy prices to ensure suitable incentives for electric vehicle adoption. The absolute level of electricity prices relative to that of liquid transportation fuels will have an important impact on the incentive for electric vehicle adoption in the first place. As noted, taxing gasoline and diesel while subsidizing electricity may overincentivize electric vehicle adoption, and vice versa. Ideally, the relative prices of transportation and electricity should reflect the relative burden of environmental pollution associated with each of them.

Finance Recommendations

Recommendation 14: Support creation of financing mechanisms to spread higher capital costs. Capital cost premiums for electric vehicles may persist into the medium term, making them difficult for private consumers to afford, especially low-income consumers who might otherwise benefit from electric two-wheelers. Rather than introduce relatively costly and potentially regressive subsidies for the purchase of electric vehicles, LMICs would be better advised to support creating financing mechanisms so that the higher capital costs can be spread over time. They could do so in several ways, from providing credit lines on relatively soft terms to introducing leasing arrangements for vehicles and/or batteries, to adopting innovative models in which an intermediary bears the cost of vehicle purchase in return for a share in the operating cost savings.

Recommendation 15: Tap into carbon finance to offset public investment needs. Depending on the country context, electric mobility could in some cases prove to be a zero- or low-cost approach to carbon abatement. Moreover, analysis suggests that carbon credits could in principle cover a material proportion of the incremental investment cost, particularly well-suited to critical areas of public investment, such as the development of charging infrastructure or the purchase of higher-cost electric buses. As of today, however, there has been little or no experience with designing carbon transactions in a manner suitable for supporting the development of electric mobility. Claiming carbon credits via results-based climate financing could be an option to explore more systematically.

Recommendation 16: Examine fiscal implications of electric mobility and make adjustments as needed. As noted, given the shifting patterns of demand for vehicles and associated fuels, the transition to electric mobility is unlikely to be fiscally neutral. On the contrary, given prevalent patterns of taxation and subsidization for vehicles and energy, the electrification of the transportation sector is likely to erode established fiscal revenue bases, notably fuel taxation. Although a certain amount of fiscal incentive may be helpful to catalyze the transition in the early stages, over time the fiscal architecture will need to adapt to this new reality.

Like many transitions, although the trajectory is uncertain, the ultimate destination is clear. Electric mobility is an agenda of increasing relevance to LMICs given its potential to contribute to multiple development challenges. However, each country will need to find the right moment and the right reasons for electrifying its transportation sector. Many factors will shape the electric mobility transition in each country, including the nature of the vehicle fleet and the wider energy supply situation. But for most countries it will make sense to target smaller or higher-use vehicles first, channel scarce public resources toward development of charging infrastructure, provide mechanisms for consumer finance, and coordinate closely with the electricity sector.

Abbreviations

BEV	battery electric vehicle
CO_2	carbon dioxide
EU	European Union
EV	electric vehicle
FAME	Faster Adoption and Manufacturing of Hybrid and Electric Vehicles
GNI	gross national income
HOV	high-occupancy vehicle
ICE	internal combustion engine
ICEV	internal combustion engine vehicle
IEA	International Energy Agency
LMICs	low- and middle-income countries
NO_x	nitrogen oxides
$PM_{2.5}$	particulate matter less than 2.5 microns in diameter
PM_{10}	particulate matter less than 10 microns in diameter
R&D	research and development
SO_x	sulfur oxides
TOU	time of use
TWh	terawatt-hour
V1G	unidirectional vehicle-to-grid integration
V2G	bidirectional controlled vehicle-to-grid integration

1

Why Is Electric Mobility a Development Issue?

INTRODUCTION

Mobility is essential for economic and social development, but in its current form the transportation sector in most countries is not sustainable. Pollution is among the most severe problems brought on by this sector, causing an estimated 7.8 million years of life lost annually, which translates into about US$1 trillion in health damages globally (Annenberg et al. 2019). Transportation is also a major driver of global warming, responsible for about a quarter of global greenhouse gas emissions from burning fossil fuels (IEA 2020). Given the vast vehicle stock in industrialized countries and continued rapid motorization in low- and middle-income countries (LMICs), the need to decarbonize transportation is urgent. Electric vehicles (EVs) will contribute toward this goal, complementing other sustainability priorities such as a modal shift to nonmotorized and public transportation. Like other major technological changes, EVs will be disruptive—triggering major changes in transportation-related sectors, which are a large economic force and major employer in most countries. These disruptions will certainly play out over the next few decades. Good public policy can ensure a smooth transition. Countries should therefore prepare for and promote the electric mobility transition as one critical element in an overall shift toward a sustainable transportation and energy system. For the purpose of this report, "EV" refers to a battery electric vehicle or a plug-in hybrid electric vehicle. It does not include hybrid electric vehicles that cannot be plugged in.

Almost 130 years after the earliest EVs emerged, the electrification of transportation is approaching a tipping point (Sperling 2018). Numerous automobile firms have announced a shift to producing EVs mostly or even exclusively, and they face stiff competition from newly formed electric-only companies. Countries, regions, and cities have announced bans on the registration or operation of internal combustion engines in the near future (Wappelhorst 2020). Further technology advances and scale economies are quickly reducing the cost of key components in

EVs—notably the battery pack. For some vehicle types and in some markets, EVs already have a lower total cost of ownership than internal combustion engine vehicles (ICEVs). Examples are fleet vehicles or two- and three-wheelers that provide essential shared transportation services in many lower-income countries. Effective policies can accelerate these trends.

Like any major technological change, the electric mobility transition will create winners and losers. It will shrink a massive and complex fossil fuel–based infrastructure built over more than 100 years that delivered unimagined mobility for people and goods. The shift will affect how vehicles are built and traded and how they are fueled and serviced. Opportunities for smart entrepreneurs and businesses will be numerous. Many firms, though, will experience painful adjustment or leave the sector, and turnover in the labor market could be considerable. Jobs will likely be lost in automobile production beyond those already lost to automation. In other areas, such as building a charging infrastructure, new jobs will be created. Whether these disruptions will cause widespread social hardship will depend on the effectiveness of public policies that can mitigate harm.

Electrification is only one of the ways to decarbonize the transportation sector. EVs address the pollution problem but not other transportation sector externalities, such as congestion, road safety, or the large amount of land that transportation infrastructure requires. Electrification is therefore only one element in a comprehensive, sustainable transportation policy that involves such measures as reducing unnecessary travel; making nonmotorized travel and public transit safer, cheaper, and more convenient; and shifting goods transport from trucks to rail or ship where possible.

This chapter discusses the broader development implications of the electric mobility transition. It argues that electric mobility will have important environmental, economic, and social impacts in LMICs where EV uptake has so far been low or absent (see, for example, Dane, Wright, and Montmasson-Clair 2019). The focus, as in the report overall, is on passenger road transportation. The electric mobility transition will take time, although major technological shifts often occur more quickly than anticipated. Not all countries will or should immediately make EVs a priority. Waiting for technology to advance and costs to come down will sometimes make sense. But all countries should develop an electric mobility strategy. The following chapters in this report will discuss when is an appropriate time to start implementation and how to facilitate the transition to electrified transportation with effective public policies.

RAPID MOTORIZATION, ENVIRONMENTAL CONCERNS, AND TECHNOLOGICAL CHANGE DRIVE THE ELECTRIC MOBILITY TRANSITION

Mobility is a fundamental need and, all else equal, people prefer personal transportation. Owning a vehicle makes it easier to access services, jobs, and other opportunities. A vehicle is also an aspirational purchase and status symbol. More than 1.2 billion vehicles—passenger cars, buses, motor coaches, trucks, and tractors—were in use globally in 2018.[1] Most years, the car population grows by more than 4 percent, with the largest increases in the East Asia and Pacific region. Because vehicle ownership in high-income countries is close to saturation levels, two-thirds of the increase in car ownership will occur in countries that are not members of the Organisation for Economic Co-operation and Development (Sims et al. 2014). This rise in the global fleet could be enormous. If China (166 vehicles per 1,000 population in 2018) were to reach motorization rates like those of Australia or Poland (about 720), 770 million vehicles would be added. India (about 25 vehicles per 1,000) reaching the same level would add another 940 million.[2] In principle, increased vehicle ownership could yield enormous personal and societal benefits, which is why many governments encourage car ownership. Those benefits come with considerable social costs, however.

Vehicles using internal combustion engines cause local pollution that has immediate effects on the health of the local population and climate pollution that contributes to global warming. Local air pollution from transportation is associated with health conditions such as heart and lung disease, cancer, complications during pregnancy, and adverse birth outcomes (Health Effects Institute 2010). Specifically, burning gasoline or diesel fuel releases nitrogen oxides (NO_x), carbon monoxide, ozone, sulfur oxides (SO_x) and volatile organic compounds. NO_x and the volatile organic compounds combine to form coarse (PM_{10}) and fine ($PM_{2.5}$) particulate matter. Exposure to particulate matter can also affect mental health (Braithwaite et al. 2019). Although severe health impacts are cumulative and not immediately felt, the visibility of air pollution has helped motivate governments to tighten air quality controls, most prominently in urban China (World Bank and Development Research Center of the State Council, the People's Republic of China 2014; World Bank and EV100, forthcoming). Commuters, cyclists, pedestrians, and residents living near busy urban roads or transportation corridors are most affected by air pollution (Cepeda et al. 2017). One estimate puts the global annual deaths from traffic-related $PM_{2.5}$ and ozone exposure at 385,000 in 2015, which equates to 11.4 percent of total deaths attributed to such pollution (Annenberg et al. 2019). Poorer countries with older vehicle stocks and lax emission controls experience higher air pollution exposure, as do households with low socioeconomic status. Poorer households are more likely to live near pollution sources, including heavily trafficked roads. Poorer children spend more time outside, and their households cannot afford mitigation options such as air purifiers. Satellite data analysis in Dar es Salaam, Tanzania, for example, suggests that areas of high traffic volume and associated air pollution tend to coincide with low-income neighborhoods (Dasgupta, Lall, and Wheeler 2020). Higher air pollution exposure, combined with higher susceptibility to poor health, results in major health disparities driven by environmental factors (Hajat, Hsia, and O'Neill 2015).

Combustion of fossil fuels also produces carbon dioxide (CO_2), which is the main contributor to global warming, as well as other pollutants with high warming potential, such as NO_x or black carbon. In 2019, oil supplied more than 90 percent of the total energy consumed by the transportation sector, generating almost 8.5 gigatonnes of CO_2 (emissions fell to 7.0 gigatonnes of CO_2 in 2020 during the COVID-19 pandemic) or about a quarter of all global greenhouse gas emissions (IEA 2021a). These emissions have been rising fast as improvements in fuel efficiency are more than offset by more and bigger vehicles and higher travel volumes. In fact, the transportation sector is the only major sector whose greenhouse gas emissions have steadily risen during the last decade (figure 1.1). In 2019, they were almost three times as high as in 1970, 70 percent coming from road transportation, which grew even faster than transportation overall (Jaramillo et al. 2022).

Electrification of transportation, using clean, renewably generated electricity, is possible today because of major improvements in several technology sectors. Three are especially important: vehicle technology, especially batteries and electric motors; digitalization of production and management of vehicles and charging infrastructure; and electricity production and the shift from dirty to clean power. Powerful and efficient batteries are the most important technology advance. Batteries account for about one-third of the total price of an EV (König et al. 2021), but their cost is rapidly falling. Learning rates—how much the price falls with a doubling of production—are between 20 percent and 27 percent (Ziegler and Trancik 2021). The real price of lithium-ion cells (scaled by energy capacity) has declined by about 97 percent since their commercial introduction in the early 1990s. Batteries, in combination with highly efficient motors and regenerative braking, allow for a far better use of energy inputs.

FIGURE 1.1 Annual carbon dioxide emissions, by sector, 2010–19

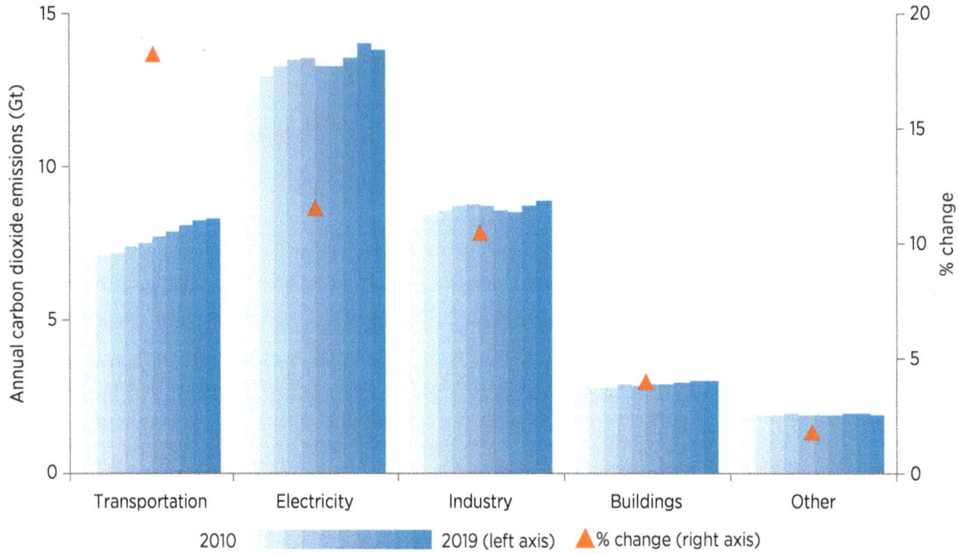

Source: IEA 2021a.
Note: Gt = gigatonne.

More than two-thirds of the energy used by ICEVs is wasted as heat, whereas EVs use more than three-quarters of the power delivered through the grid (US Department of Energy 2011).

Digitalization is the second relevant area of technological change because EVs are much simpler in terms of their mechanical components but rely on more complex electronics. An EV may contain more than 100 semiconductors to manage batteries, sensors that control power train and drivetrain management, and various safety and communication components. Digital technologies are also essential in new vehicle production facilities. Because EVs are fundamentally different, car companies have built new, highly automated factories. Electric charging infrastructure also relies on information and communication technology—from automatically matching a connected car to the driver's charge account to making EVs part of the electric grid of the future by allowing them to draw and supply electricity depending on demand, electricity prices, and owner preferences.

Finally, massive innovation has also benefited the greening of electricity production. Powering EVs with clean energy is one of the most important factors in determining how climate-friendly an EV will be. Fueling mobility with electricity could eventually make a complex supply infrastructure for fossil fuels obsolete. Getting gasoline or diesel to the pump requires exploration, extraction, transportation, refining, and distribution of oil products, which all happen over large distances across the globe. Historically, according to the International Monetary Fund, the fossil fuel industry has been able to offset some of these high costs with large subsidies—US$5.2 trillion, some 6.5 percent of global gross domestic product in 2017 (Coady et al. 2019; see also Mahdavi, Martinez-Alvarez, and Ross 2020). Costs of renewable electricity generation have fallen sharply (table 1.1). Learning rates for wind and solar equipment are particularly steep and costs per kilowatt are now often lower than those for fossil fuel–generated power (IRENA 2020b). Rather than annually burning through more than a million years of photosynthesis embedded in fossil fuels, ways to produce most of the world's annual energy use—including for mobility—from just a year's worth of solar radiation are now realistic scenarios (Carbon Tracker 2021).[3]

TABLE 1.1 **Power generation cost reductions from solar and wind power technologies, 2010–21**

Percent

Concentrated solar	Photovoltaic	Onshore wind	Offshore wind
79	88	48	19

Source: IRENA 2020a.

THE ELECTRIC MOBILITY TRANSITION WILL HAVE ENVIRONMENTAL, ECONOMIC, AND SOCIAL IMPACTS

Because turnover of the vehicle stock takes time, the impact of the electric mobility transition will be felt gradually in all areas of the transportation sector. This transition is under way in many high-income and some emerging economies and will eventually also gather momentum in middle- and even low-income countries. The transition will need to be largely market driven, although policies will initially facilitate and accelerate the switch to EVs. As the electric mobility transition unfolds, it will affect three areas critical for LMICs: the environment, the economy, and social welfare. These areas are also three pillars of development: sustainability, growth, and inclusion. Sustainability is the main driver of the transition, but the economy will be central to its success because the electrification of transportation affects several important supply chains and markets: for vehicles and parts, for raw materials, and for fuels that will be phased out and those that will replace them. Changes and disruptions in each of these markets can have social implications, especially in relevant labor markets, where some types of jobs will disappear and others be created.

Environmental Impacts

The prospect of lowering the transportation sector's environmental footprint is the main motivation for increasingly ambitious policies to promote EVs. For developed countries, and from a global perspective, reduction of CO_2 emissions is a chief priority and a motivation strong enough to pursue rapid adoption of EVs. For developing countries, however, the most pressing and evident motivations are linked to reduction of local pollutants, improvement of the associated health issues, and more generally the need for better air quality and noise reduction. Expected lower costs of owning and operating an EV constitute a useful side effect that will reinforce the electric mobility transition.

Local air pollution (principally NO_x, PM, and sulfur dioxide [SO_2]) and global climate pollution (CO_2) are both generated along the entire vehicle-related supply chain, from vehicle production to fuel supply and vehicle operation and eventual disposal. Well-to-tank emissions occur in the production of fuels such as gasoline and diesel and in electricity generation. Fossil fuels require extraction, transport, refining, and distribution. Electricity generation also still depends largely on fossil fuels. Operation of ICEVs causes tank-to-wheel emissions that are strictly regulated in many countries, for instance, through the Euro standards in the European Union. These emissions can be estimated using information about the age of the vehicle stock and average distances traveled per year. Industry life-cycle analyses have generated estimated emissions from production and disposal of vehicles (European Commission et al. 2020). Absolute emission reductions from increased use of EVs depend on the size of countries and vehicle fleet composition. For instance, under a realistic EV adoption scenario, as described in chapter 2, India could achieve average annual CO_2 emission reductions of 87 million tons, and Vanuatu could avoid 18,000 tons. The power generation mix determines local pollution. The Arab Republic of Egypt and India both depend heavily on fossil fuels. Egypt, though, would see large reductions in SO_x emissions because it uses natural gas for 70 percent of its electricity generation, whereas coal-dependent India would see growing SO_x emissions with increased generation to power EVs. In relative terms, Vietnam would see the greatest average annual CO_2 emission reductions—about 28 percent. Other countries with large emission reductions are Nepal and Uruguay, both of which use renewables for power generation almost exclusively.

For economic analysis, air and climate pollution estimates are converted to monetary costs. For climate pollution, this monetary cost is the social cost of carbon—formally, the discounted cost of damages that will be caused by, say, a ton of CO_2 equivalent. A more practical way to think about this cost is as an estimate of the price or tax on emissions that would be required to trigger sufficient changes to achieve climate goals such as those in the Paris Agreement. The High-Level Commission on Carbon Prices and World Bank guidelines recommend a carbon price of US$40 to US$80 per ton of CO_2 equivalent in 2020, rising to US$60 to US$100 by 2030 (World Bank 2017). Local air pollution has more immediate effects on human health. An extensive literature on health impacts details a range from reductions in productivity to increased mortality. Damages are most severe in lower-income countries (Roy 2016; World Bank 2022). The economic costs of such impacts are typically estimated using the concept of the value of a statistical life, which quantifies essentially how much, on average, people are willing to pay to reduce their mortality risk. Average annual savings (reductions in damage costs) from lower CO_2 emissions are highest in India, at more than US$2 billion, and in Egypt from PM_{10} reductions, at almost US$1.8 billion.

Economic Impacts

For well over 100 years, automobile manufacturers have built internal combustion engines. As both policies and economics start to favor EVs, manufacturers have begun to retool their production facilities. The industry is highly concentrated. In 2019, 61 percent of global motor vehicle production—more than 56 million vehicles—happened in just five countries: China, Germany, India, Japan, and the United States (OICA 2019). The top 10 countries account for 80 percent. Brazil, Mexico, the Russian Federation, Thailand, and Türkiye also have large automobile production sectors. Most production facilities are owned by large, multinational companies. The top 5 global manufacturers produced 43 percent of vehicles, the top 10 more than 65 percent. Five Chinese car companies are the only manufacturers from a middle-income country among the top 20.

Vehicle Supply Chains

These manufacturers have the deep pockets needed for the research and development to design complex vehicle components and build large production facilities. EVs, however, have fewer moving parts and do not require components such as transmissions, fuel systems, or catalytic converters. These differences have several implications. The impact of the shift will be large for firms building complex gas or diesel engines, but perhaps even greater for suppliers of parts and components that are not needed in EVs. International firms have built local supplier networks in countries where they manufacture or assemble vehicles. Thus, a drop in demand for car components could affect suppliers in countries such as Mexico or Türkiye. Production of key EV components such as motors and batteries, in contrast, is still highly concentrated. Most lithium-ion battery cells today are manufactured in China, although additional large manufacturing is done in Hungary, Japan, the Republic of Korea, and the United States.

As vehicle manufacturing shifts from complex engine systems to assembly of mostly standardized electric motors and battery packs, value added in vehicles will come from clever integration of components. This shift leaves scope for new entrants that may be competitive even with smaller production runs and could be an excellent opportunity for manufacturers or assembly plants in LMICs. In fact, the big auto manufacturers and powerhouse technology firms are already teaming with local car assemblers in Africa, Asia, and Latin America to bolster EV assembly lines (Arroyo-Arroyo and Vesin 2021). Innovative start-ups are emerging in Kenya, Rwanda, and Uganda to come up with affordable EV alternatives, particularly for two-wheelers but also affordable options for buses and trucks in which the vehicle body is repurposed and an electric power train installed. Kenya's Opibus is an example of such a start-up.

Stricter climate policies will favor manufacturing locations with access to cleaner energy. EV battery production is a good example. The smaller its carbon footprint, the greater will be the environmental benefit of an EV relative to an ICEV. The production of a conventional gasoline car produces about 5 metric tons of CO_2 emissions and consumes approximately 100 gigajoules of energy, whereas the production of a battery electric vehicle (assuming a 24 kilowatt-hour battery) produces more than 8 metric tons of CO_2 emissions and consumes about 180 gigajoules of energy. The lithium-ion battery alone accounts for an average 3 metric tons of of CO_2 emissions (Helms, Kämper, and Lambrecht 2015). Given the current power mix in different countries, battery cell manufacturing in China currently generates 1,106 grams (g) of CO_2 equivalent per kilowatt capacity, 745 g in Japan, 663 g in the United States, 634 g in Korea, and 468 g in the European Union (EU) (Meyer et al. 2018). Battery production with a higher share of renewables in the power mix will have an advantage in places with strict climate policies, including possible border tax adjustments on the embedded CO_2 content of imports.

A quick transition to electric mobility in industrialized countries could accelerate exports of used ICEVs to LMICs. The volume of such exports is already large (UNEP 2020). In 2018, the EU, Japan, and the United States exported almost 4 million used cars, of which more than 80 percent went to LMICs. The EU was the source of more than half of the total, including 1 million exported to Africa, followed by Japan (27 percent) and the United States (18 percent). Africa, where used light-duty vehicles account for 60 percent of the total growth of the vehicle fleet, was the largest importing region (40 percent), followed by Eastern Europe (24 percent), Asia Pacific (15 percent), the Middle East (12 percent), and Latin America (9 percent). Among countries, Serbia, the United Arab Emirates, and Nigeria imported the largest number of used cars from the three major exporting regions (see table 1.2).

Used vehicles are not necessarily more polluting or less safe than the existing vehicle fleet in an importing country. For instance, Japan has strict vehicle inspections and many drivers replace their cars after only about four years of service (UNEP 2020). But many of the exported cars are older or poorly maintained and sometimes emission controls have been removed to recover valuable metals from catalytic converters. By sending such cars to lower-income countries, wealthier regions clean up pollution at home by shifting it to other parts of the world rather than reducing it overall. Doing so increases local pollution in poorer countries and makes no contribution to limiting global greenhouse gas emissions, similar to shifts in heavy industry in the 1990s and 2000s (Peters et al. 2011).

TABLE 1.2 The 10 largest import markets for used vehicles, 2018

Rank	Market	Number of imports
1	Serbia	260,078
2	United Arab Emirates	238,810
3	Nigeria	238,760
4	Ukraine	173,011
5	Libya	161,814
6	Bosnia and Herzegovina	132,586
7	Tanzania	125,845
8	Georgia	125,745
9	New Zealand	101,034
10	Chile	91,827

Source: UNEP 2020.

Adoption of EVs should therefore be complemented by efforts to keep highly polluting cars off the road elsewhere. Many countries already use a range of policy tools to manage the used vehicle trade. Of 146 countries analyzed in the United Nations Environment Programme report, 18 ban used-car imports outright (UNEP 2020). Most of these are middle-income countries with significant domestic vehicle manufacturing, including Brazil, China, India, Indonesia, South Africa, Thailand, and Türkiye. If those vehicles are produced to low standards, however, import bans may well keep cars built to higher standards elsewhere out of the market. Age limits are used by 66 countries to keep older vehicles out, and 28 countries have modest vehicle emission standards; however, 100 countries have no emission standards for imports. Some countries use selective bans (such as of diesel vehicles), some require labeling of emission performance, and many use fiscal tools such as age-based taxation or progressive excise taxes based on greenhouse gas emissions or engine size. Finally, some countries have exceptions for hybrid electric or electric cars. That report concludes that 81 of 146 countries have weak or very weak policies, and that 47 have good or very good policies to manage used vehicle imports (UNEP 2020). As results from the analysis in this report suggest, high shares of cheaper used ICEV imports can slow down the adoption of EVs. Policies of the type listed here can help accelerate the electric mobility transition.

Supply Chains for Batteries

A successful transition to electric mobility implies a sharp rise in the demand for raw materials required to produce EV components, which raises the question whether a sufficient, secure, and sustainable supply of critical raw materials will be available at a price that ensures at least cost parity between EVs and ICEVs. Essential raw materials to produce current EV batteries include lithium, nickel, cobalt, manganese, and graphite. Other raw materials are important inputs for fuel cells (such as platinum), for electric motors (rare earth elements), and for expanding electric grids and charging infrastructure (copper). Global known resources of these materials exceed projected demand significantly, even when considering a parallel rise in demand from other uses (NOW 2020a). Global reserves—the share of resources that can be economically extracted—generally also appear sufficient under current scenarios. The projected demand increases may strain supply chains, however. In the International Energy Agency's "sustainable development" scenario, the demand for lithium, graphite, cobalt, nickel, and manganese for EVs will see a growth of between 16 times and 42 times—42 times, 25 times, 21 times, 41 times, and 16 times, respectively—between 2020 and 2040 (IEA 2021b).

Reserves of key raw materials are concentrated in a small number of countries, most of which are developing countries (table 1.3). The Democratic Republic of Congo accounted for about 70 percent of global cobalt production in 2019, and Brazil and South Africa have 60 percent of the world reserves of manganese (IEA 2021b; USGS 2021). Most of these raw materials are not refined and processed locally. More than 50 percent of global refining of copper, cobalt, lithium, and nickel is located in China (NOW 2020a). The country also produces about 80 percent of refined rare earth minerals. With such levels of concentration, disruption of mining or processing operations in a single country has global repercussions.

A second concern relates to the social and environmental impacts of mining operations. This concern is particularly important because a significant portion of the mining reserves are in developing countries with poor governance, weak environmental and social safeguards, and a deficient track record of enforcement of existing policies. When poorly managed, revenue from resource extraction comes with high hidden costs. Cobalt mining in the Democratic Republic of Congo has raised substantial environmental, community, and human rights issues (Amnesty International 2016). Much of cobalt is extracted in so-called artisanal mines where miners have no access to protective equipment and basic social protections. Reports about child labor have also been made. Major global customers have reacted and try to ensure that cobalt used in their products was mined under socially responsible conditions. Other parts of the supply chain remain less discriminating. Mining almost always raises environmental concerns, and mining for materials that are essential for the energy transition is no exception (Sovacool et al. 2020). Lithium mining, for example, consumes large amounts of water. In South America, it occurs in areas that are water stressed, creating potential conflicts between industrial and community use (see Liu and Agusdinata 2020).

Finally, recycling and reuse of batteries present both a challenge and an opportunity for developing countries. The disposal of used batteries can be an environment hazard. Their recycling and reuse offer an opportunity to recover expensive and scarce rare minerals and minimize the social and environmental impacts of mining operations. It would also open business opportunities when setting in place battery recycling facilities and leasing and repurposing schemes. A main challenge is to enact and enforce directives to promote battery recycling, which might call for international regulations and agreements. Unfortunately, the global experience on country-specific regulations and directives to promote battery recycling is limited.

Supply Chains for Maintenance and Fueling

Beyond vehicle cost and fuel, the third major cost factor for vehicle ownership is operations and maintenance. These costs include insurance, taxes and registration, fuel or electricity, and servicing and repairing a vehicle. In modern vehicles, repairs typically involve swapping entire

TABLE 1.3 Major sources of raw materials for batteries and fuel cells

Raw materials	Source countries
Cobalt	Australia; Canada; Congo, Dem. Rep.; Cuba; Philippines; Russian Federation
Copper	Australia; Chile; China; Congo, Dem. Rep.; Peru; United States
Graphite	Brazil; China; Türkiye
Lithium	Argentina; Australia; Bolivia; Chile; China; Russian Federation; United States; Zimbabwe
Manganese	Australia; Brazil; South Africa; Ukraine
Nickel	Australia; Brazil; Canada; China; Cuba; Indonesia; New Caledonia; Philippines; Russian Federation
Platinum	Russian Federation; South Africa; Zimbabwe

Sources: NOW 2020a; USGS 2021.

component groups. The automotive aftermarket includes the manufacturing, sales, and installation of additional or replacement parts by original equipment manufacturers, specialized automotive suppliers, and generic manufacturers. One estimate put the global size of this market at US$760 billion in 2015 with expected growth rates averaging 3 percent per year (Breitschwerdt et al. 2017). An increase in EVs will reduce the size of this market. EVs have fewer moving parts and fewer parts overall. Service intervals are longer. Complex and repair-intensive parts like radiators, pistons, or fuel pumps are absent. Regenerative braking reduces wear of brakes and brake pads. Only tires tend to wear out more quickly because of the greater weight of EVs and the greater torque of electric motors. Overall, both battery electric vehicles and plug-in hybrid electric vehicles are expected to incur about half the maintenance costs of ICEVs (Harto 2020).

The transition to electric mobility will also change the business model of the fueling infrastructure, especially gas stations, which number well over 100,000 each in the United States and China and about 40,000 in Brazil. EVs can in principle be charged anywhere grid access is available (24/7 Wall St. 2020; Deloitte 2019). Private charging happens at single or multifamily homes or at the workplace, including for commercial vehicle fleets. Public charging includes charge points at public parking lots such as at retail locations, at decentralized charge points along urban streets, and—as with current gas stations—at charging hubs within towns and cities or along major transportation corridors.

The split between public and private charging depends on many factors. One study predicts that, by 2030, private charging in Germany will account for 76 percent to 88 percent of the total (NOW 2020b). On that basis, the study expects a required ratio of EVs to public charging points that will rise from 11:1 in 2021 to 20:1 in 2030 as private charging infrastructure expands. These ratios are place specific. Areas with large apartment buildings will require a larger share of public chargers than less dense suburbs. A larger proportion of public chargers will also be needed in countries where electricity access is not universal. The EV charging business model also includes the battery-as-a-service approach in which the private sector of LMICs can engage in providing battery leasing and swapping services. This approach will, first, keep demand on the power grid under control and the provision of charging stations decentralized; second, it can significantly reduce the capital cost of EVs when separating the cost of the vehicle from that of the battery, transferring the cost of obsolescence and depreciation from users to the private sector that can mitigate by economies of scale.

Changes in maintenance costs and fueling infrastructure directly affect the economics of EV adoption. Lower maintenance needs directly reduce the total cost of ownership for EVs. Estimates derived from the analysis in chapter 2 suggest that annual per vehicle savings depend on local factors, including the vehicle fleet composition, and could be on the order of US$977 for Ethiopia and US$864 for Ghana. The shift away from gasoline and diesel requires investments in private and public charging facilities. The scenarios estimate that India will need to build more than 2 million chargers by 2030 at a cost of US$4.4 billion. Vietnam will need to spend about US$275 million and Nigeria about US$175 million. These costs are at least partially offset by cost savings in the fossil fuel supply chain. Savings are highest for buses, so countries like Ethiopia that have a larger proportion of buses in new vehicle registrations see the largest annual per vehicle savings of about US$11,650.

Fossil Fuel Supply Chain

As electricity replaces oil as a transportation fuel, demand for oil should in principle drop—along with its price—leaving only the lowest-cost producers in the market. How quickly this transition could occur is uncertain. A range of factors affect the uptake of alternative fuels, including technology, policy, and consumer preference. Even in the most ambitious climate mitigation scenarios, such as the International Energy Agency's "net zero" scenario (IEA 2021a), oil demand does not drop substantially in the near future because oil will be used for nonenergy purposes; with carbon capture, usage, and storage in industrial applications; and in applications like aviation.

In fact, many forecasts predict that oil demand in passenger transportation will remain flat or decline only modestly in the next 10 to 20 years (Hensley, Knupfer, and Pinner 2018; Kah 2018). In 2017, passenger vehicles accounted for only 23 percent of global oil demand. Trucks, ships, and planes, for which electric options are limited, consume 29 percent of all oil used. Industry, petrochemicals, power, and other sectors account for the remainder. Biofuels are an alternative but are expensive and come with their own environmental drawbacks. As economies grow, increasing demand for industry and other modes of transportation could more than offset the amount of oil displaced by electricity in the passenger vehicle market. Furthermore, even if the share of EVs increases, a rapid growth of the vehicle fleet in countries with rising incomes may well lead to a net increase of ICEVs and higher emissions in the short to medium term, especially if the vehicle-kilometers traveled also rise.

Once EVs eventually start to reduce oil demand, public revenue could decline in oil producing countries. Many small oil and gas producers in Latin America, the Middle East, North Africa, and Sub-Saharan Africa did not significantly contribute to climate change historically but are economically the most vulnerable to such income losses. Countries can pursue two broad strategies to reduce their risk (Peszko et al. 2020). The first is to use current resource revenue to diversify economic activities by investing more in education, innovation, and ecosystems services, and boosting their social capital and institutions. The second is to foster climate cooperation within the international community to enable a more comprehensive structural transition toward a low-carbon economy and to compensate the most vulnerable population groups that are negatively affected by the transition. Oil-importing countries will experience positive impacts because large oil imports can have disruptive effects on current account balances and heighten macroeconomic uncertainty when prices fluctuate (Yalta and Yalta 2017). A study for the United Kingdom predicts that replacing imported oil products with domestically produced renewable energy for mobility will benefit household incomes and promote gross domestic product expansion and employment (Alabi et al. 2020).

Electricity Supply Chain

Although demand for fossil fuels for transportation should eventually fall, the shift to EVs will increase electricity consumption. Analysis for this report confirms other estimates that EVs are unlikely to cause a substantial increase in electricity demand in the near to medium term. Assuming a 30 percent share of sales by 2030 for electric cars and buses and of 70 percent for electric two- and three-wheelers, electricity demand will increase by less than 1 percent for most countries studied—a small increase that can be absorbed by existing power systems or by modest capacity increases. In some countries with severe power generation constraints, such as the Sahelian countries, the impact on power generation can be massive and not feasible in the short term even if only two- and three-wheelers shift to electric.

EV adoption, however, could have a significant impact on the shape of the electricity load curve if charging is uncoordinated and mostly occurs during early evening peak hours. This load can threaten the stability of the power grid, require more reserve capacity, and increase overall system costs. Chapter 4 of this report reviews policies to prepare power systems to cope with these impacts.

Although EVs produce zero tailpipe emissions on the road, upstream emissions could be substantial. EVs will be greenest where damage from ICEVs is high and the electric grid is relatively clean. Where electricity is generated from coal, electric cars and buses can sometimes cause more harm than ICEVs (Holland et al. 2016). This concern does not apply to electric two-wheelers: even when using electricity from fossil fuels, such as coal, they have 20 to 30 percent lower climate impacts than conventional motorcycles. When powered with renewable energy, their climate change impact is reduced by 60 to 80 percent (Cox and Mutel 2018). More generally, when powering EVs with electricity derived from fossil fuels, pollution is shifted from densely populated urban areas to areas around large power plants, mines, and waste disposal sites (Cropper et al. 2021; Hendryx, Zullig, and Luo 2020). Coal burning emits more harmful pollutants than any other fuel source; further, disposal of coal ash, which is often poorly regulated, exposes nearby residents to heavy metals that can contaminate drinking water supplies. The burden is often on the poorest. But electrifying transportation still makes sense even when much of the power comes from fossil fuel sources. Vehicle electrification in China does not currently reduce CO_2 emissions because of the country's coal-intensive grid (Peng et al. 2018). More than 41,000 premature deaths, however, would still be avoided annually by shifting air pollution from dense urban to sparsely populated rural areas. Any reduction of coal in the power mix increases the number of lives saved.

Social Impacts

The electric mobility transition is a significant technological change, and such shifts are often accompanied by some degree of social impact. Disruptions in the markets for vehicles, fuels, and transportation-related services will affect labor markets in these sectors. The magnitude of these impacts is uncertain because the electric mobility transition will have ambiguous macroeconomic effects and play out over a long time, especially in lower-income countries, where vehicles tend to stay on the road for 15 to 20 years. Published studies therefore show mixed results, some expecting net job gains and some predicting employment reductions. The overall sense is that job losses in some areas will be offset by gains in others. The extent of these adjustments is unknown, but even significant churning in the labor market can create social hardship for many.

The clearest labor market consequences will be in vehicle manufacturing and mostly in high- or upper-middle-income countries. An early estimate by Ford found that simpler EV assembly could reduce capital investments by half and labor input by 30 percent compared to ICEV manufacturing (Ford Motor Company 2017). These estimated job losses match those predicted in a detailed study for Germany, where the automobile industry currently employs more than 800,000 people. The study expects a baseline fall of employment of 27 percent between 2017 and 2030 simply due to productivity increases. A 25 percent share of EVs would result in overall labor force reductions of 37 percent; a 40 percent share, a reduction of 40 percent; and an 80 percent share, a reduction of just over half of current employment (NPM 2020). Additional job losses are likely in vehicle maintenance and services and in the fossil fuel supply chain, all of which are also large employers in LMICs (see table 1.4).

Battery-related employment will not compensate for losses in manufacturing traditional power trains and components. Cell production is highly automated. Only an estimated 40 jobs per gigawatt of battery capacity are created in battery cell and module production, but more than 200 additional jobs are in the upstream value chain including materials, research and development, and manufacturing machinery (Thielmann et al. 2020). Job gains can be expected in the electricity supply sectors and in construction, the maintenance of charging infrastructure, and continued digitalization in the transportation sector (Pek et al. 2019). Additionally, as the

TABLE 1.4 Potential employment impacts in the transition to electric mobility

Driver	Mechanism	Employment impact
Vehicle production	EVs have fewer parts, and new EV manufacturing capacity will maximize automation potential, as will battery cell production, which will be highly automated and concentrated in a few places.	Decrease
Maintenance	Frequency and cost of maintenance and service will be lower than for ICEVs. Smaller aftermarket.	Decrease
Fuel	Gasoline and diesel supply activities, refining, and gas station operations will decrease.	Decrease
Charging infrastructure	Investments to increase electricity supply and construction, installation, and maintenance of charging stations could compensate for the loss of jobs in the fossil fuel sector.	Increase
Purchase price	Initially higher purchase price could reduce demand for cars; however, EVs are expected to become cheaper than ICEVs, which could increase vehicle demand.	Ambiguous
Lower per km costs	Increased vehicle usage could have positive employment impacts, especially in transportation-intensive sectors.	Increase
Total cost of ownership	Savings from car usage could increase demand for other goods and services.	Increase
Reduced pollution	Fewer health effects reduce demand for health services, yield health care cost savings, and increase productivity and demand for other goods and services.	Small increase

Source: World Bank, adapted from FTI Consulting 2017.
Note: EV = electric vehicle; ICEV = internal combustion engine vehicle; km = kilometer.

costs of purchasing and operating EVs are expected to fall below those for ICEVs, savings by consumers and commercial vehicle owners could increase expenditures for goods and services in other sectors.

Regardless of the net impact on jobs, LMICs will buffer the impact of the EV transition by embracing early interventions that encourage training in newly demanded technologies. Growing the renewables sectors requires local labor and creates jobs in construction and routine maintenance; thus it presents an opportunity for low-skilled workers. Fewer than 20 percent of workers in clean energy production and energy efficiency in the United States have at least a bachelor's degree (Muro et al. 2019). Public renewables investments have high employment multipliers: 24.6 jobs created per US$1 million invested in low-income developing countries, 15.6 jobs in emerging economies, and 6.6 jobs in advanced economies (Moszoro 2021).

Although the greatest development benefits of the electric mobility transition relate to sustainability and growth, the transition can also contribute to inclusion. Electric mobility will benefit the poor and other marginalized or disadvantaged population groups if it can make transportation cleaner, more accessible, more affordable, or more convenient. Most directly, reductions in local pollution will benefit people living near high-volume transportation corridors. Prioritizing electric bus operation in congested, low-income areas can reduce exposure to air and noise pollution for poorer people (Sclar et al. 2019). If costs of EVs can be reduced below the cost of gasoline or diesel vehicles, as many expect, mobility can also become more affordable. Electric two- and three-wheelers are already popular in many low-income markets for transporting people and goods. In rural areas, low-cost electric motorbikes, in combination with solar photovoltaic systems, reduce dependence on expensive or hard-to-obtain gasoline, facilitate access to markets and other opportunities, and help solve the first- or last-mile problem when using public transit (Rajper and Albrecht 2020). Although support for EVs in industrialized countries currently favors already well-off residents, targeted policies can promote benefits for the poorer parts of the population by focusing electric mobility support on smaller, cheaper vehicles and the infrastructure that supports them.

A SUSTAINABLE TRANSPORTATION SYSTEM REQUIRES MORE THAN ELECTRIFYING VEHICLES

The shift to electric mobility is a core element of strategies to mitigate global warming and reduce local pollution. Simply replacing ICEVs with EVs, however, does not address other persistent transportation-related problems such as congestion, safety, and access. Residents in cities globally suffer from traffic congestion. According to INRIX, US drivers lost an average of 97 hours because of congestion at a cost of US$1,348 per driver, some US$87 billion in total (INRIX Research and Cookson 2018). Congestion is often worse in LMICs, where road construction and traffic management have not kept pace with motorization. Drivers in Bogotá, Colombia, lost 254 hours and those in Moscow lost 210 hours in traffic during 2018. Additional losses and environmental impacts come from fragmentation and inefficiencies among transportation operators in many markets that cause delays and poor use of capacity.

Road safety is another costly transportation externality. Traffic accidents cause more than 1.4 million deaths and 50 million serious injuries every year, 93 percent of which are in developing countries (World Health Organization 2018). The World Bank estimates that these deaths and injuries reduce the gross domestic product of LMICs by between 1 percent and 5 percent.[4] Ensuring equitable access to transportation options is another critical goal of sustainable and inclusive transportation strategies. An estimated 1 billion people live more than 2 kilometers from an all-weather road, and one in six women avoids searching for a job because she fears harassment during transit. Switching to EVs will not address any of these issues.

More fundamental shifts in how transportation is organized must therefore accompany the electrification of vehicles. Avoid-Shift-Improve is a simple sustainability framework used in the transportation sector. The first priority is to make the overall transportation system more efficient, primarily by avoiding unnecessary or unnecessarily long trips. In urban areas, land use planning that creates mixed-use neighborhoods reduces the trip to work, shopping, or entertainment, which also promotes local economic development. Moving more activities such as work or education online, as was done involuntarily during the COVID-19 pandemic, also reduces commuting and therefore congestion.

The second priority is to increase trip efficiency by encouraging modal shifts: from energy-intensive modes such as personal cars to nonmotorized transportation or mass transit. Residents will dispense with personal cars only if convenient and affordable alternatives are readily available. Wide and safe sidewalks and bike lanes encourage nonmotorized travel for shorter distances. Efficient public transit gives commuters incentives to use buses and light rail. Transit-oriented development is now used by progressive cities around the world to increase the use of public transportation. It involves planning and design of urban areas that create compact, mixed-use, pedestrian- and bicycle-friendly developments around public transit hubs (Salat and Ollivier 2017). Singapore plans to have 80 percent of the population living within a 10-minute walk from a train station by 2030, which would allow 75 percent of peak-hour trips to be made by public transportation (Singapore Land Transport Authority 2013).

The third priority is to improve the efficiency of vehicles across transportation modes. ICEV engines have become ever more fuel-efficient, but more people buy bigger cars, offsetting these gains. Because electrification will take time, climate goals cannot be achieved without major additional efficiency measures for the ICEV fleet. In the International Energy Agency's net zero emission scenario, such measures contribute more emission benefits by 2030 than electrification of vehicles (see figure 1.2). So far, the trend toward larger, heavier vehicles is also evident in the EV market, with many EVs replacing relatively fuel-efficient ICEVs rather than heavily polluting clunkers. One study for the United States

FIGURE 1.2 Energy consumption and avoided demand in the transportation sector, NZE scenario, by mitigation measure

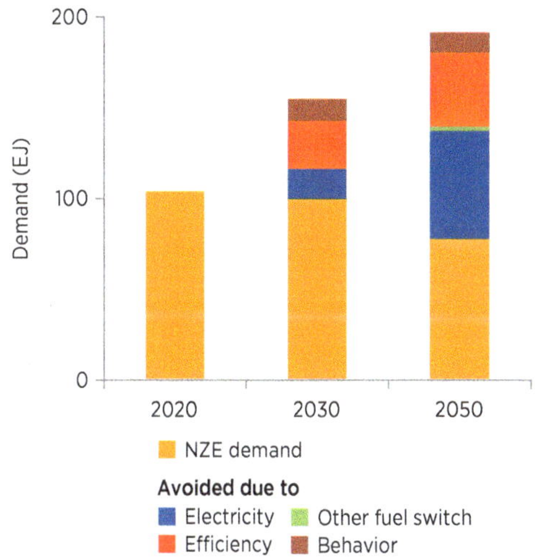

Source: IEA 2021a.
Note: "Other fuel switch" includes switching to hydrogen-related fuels, bioenergy, solar thermal energy, geothermal energy, or district heating. EJ = exajoule; NZE = Net Zero Emission.

found that EVs replaced ICEVs whose fuel economy was 4.2 miles per gallon better than average, and 12 percent of EV buyers replaced hybrid vehicles (Xing, Leard, and Li 2021).

According to United Nations estimates, behavioral changes triggered by avoid and shift strategies—traveling less and switching to more sustainable modes—can reduce about 15 percent of the CO_2 emissions required to meet the Paris Agreement climate target of limiting global average temperature rise to 1.5°C (UNFCCC 2020). Although the behavioral contribution to CO_2 emission reductions seems minor, by 2030 it can more than halve the share of EVs in the global vehicle fleet that would be required to get to net zero emissions—from 45 percent to 20 percent (IEA 2021a). Further, these behavioral changes will deliver many additional social and environmental benefits, including lower congestion, greater road safety, more equitable access to transportation, and decreased land consumption.

Transportation sustainability has many aspects, and decarbonizing the transportation sector in a way that supports global climate goals will require a multidimensional approach that involves all aspects of the Avoid-Shift-Improve framework. An efficient and well-planned transition to electric mobility will play an important role. Industrialized countries have the financial and technical resources to promote a quick shift, but it will be much more difficult for lower-income countries to develop an effective and affordable electric mobility strategy. When to embark on this transition and how to design and implement an EV strategy are discussed in the chapters that follow.

NOTES

1. Data in this section are from the World Road Statistics 2020 database, International Road Federation, Geneva, Switzerland, https://worldroadstatistics.org/.
2. World Bank staff estimate based on World Road Statistics data.

3. With the exception of geothermal, practically all renewable energy is ultimately produced by incoming solar radiation that powers pressure gradients generating wind as well as the hydrologic cycle.
4. See the World Bank's "Transport: Overview" web page (last updated September 29, 2022), https://www.worldbank.org/en/topic/transport/overview.

REFERENCES

24/7 Wall St. 2020. "How Many Gas Stations Are in U.S.? How Many Will There Be in 10 Years?" *MarketWatch*, February 16, 2020. https://www.marketwatch.com/story/how-many-gas-stations-are-in-us-how-many-will-there-be-in-10-years-2020-02-16.

Alabi, Oluwafisayo, Karen Turner, Gioele Figus, Antonios Katris, and Christian Calvillo. 2020. "Can Spending to Upgrade Electricity Networks to Support Electric Vehicles (EVs) Roll-Outs Unlock Value in the Wider Economy?" *Energy Policy* 138: 111–17.

Amnesty International. 2016. *"This Is What We Die For": Human Rights Abuses in the Democratic Republic of the Congo Power the Global Trade in Cobalt.* London: Amnesty International.

Annenberg, Susan, Joshua Miller, Daven Henze, and Ray Minjares. 2019. *A Global Snapshot of the Air Pollution–Related Health Impacts of Transportation Sector Emissions in 2010 and 2015*. Washington, DC: International Council on Clean Transport. https://theicct.org/publications/health-impacts-transport-emissions-2010-2015.

Arroyo-Arroyo, Fatima, and Vincent Vesin. 2021. *Pathways to Electric Mobility in the Sahel: Two and Three-Wheelers in Bamako and Ouagadougou*. Washington, DC: World Bank. https://openknowledge.worldbank.org/handle/10986/37046.

Braithwaite, Isobel, Shuo Zhang, James B. Kirkbride, David P. J. Osborn, and Joseph F. Hayes. 2019. "Air Pollution (Particulate Matter) Exposure and Associations with Depression, Anxiety, Bipolar, Psychosis and Suicide Risk: A Systematic Review and Meta-Analysis." *Environmental Health Perspectives* 127 (12): 126002. https://doi.org/10.1289/EHP4595.

Breitschwerdt, Dirk, Andreas Cornet, Sebastian Kempf, Lukas Michor, and Martin Schmidt. 2017. *The Changing Aftermarket Game—and How Automotive Suppliers Can Benefit from Arising Opportunities*. Washington, DC: McKinsey & Company. https://www.mckinsey.com/industries/automotive-and-assembly/our-insights/the-changing-aftermarket-game-and-how-automotive-suppliers-can-benefit-from-arising-opportunities.

Carbon Tracker. 2021. *The Sky's the Limit: Solar and Wind Energy Potential Is 100 Times as Much as Global Energy Demand.* London: Carbon Tracker. https://carbontracker.org/reports/the-skys-the-limit-solar-wind/.

Cepeda, Magda, Josje Schoufour, Rosanne Freak-Poli, Chantal M. Koolhaas, Klodian Dhana, Wichor M. Bramer, and Oscar H. Franco. 2017. "Levels of Ambient Air Pollution According to Mode of Transport: A Systematic Review." *Lancet: Public Health* 2 (1): e23–e34. https://doi.org/10.1016/S2468-2667(16)30021-4.

Coady, David, Ian W. H. Parry, Nghia-Piotr Le, and Baoping Shang. 2019. "Global Fossil Fuel Subsidies Remain Large: An Update Based on Country-Level Estimates." Working Paper No. 19/89, International Monetary Fund, Washington, DC. https://www.imf.org/en/Publications/WP/Issues/2019/05/02/Global-Fossil-Fuel-Subsidies-Remain-Large-An-Update-Based-on-Country-Level-Estimates-46509.

Cox, Brian L., and Christopher L. Mutel. 2018. "The Environmental and Cost Performance of Current and Future Motorcycles." *Applied Energy* 212: 1013–24. https://doi.org/10.1016/j.apenergy.2017.12.100.

Cropper, Maureen, Ryna Cui, Sarath Guttikunda, and Xiao-Peng Song. 2021. "The Mortality Impacts of Current and Planned Coal-Fired Power Plants in India." *Proceedings of the National Academy of Sciences* 118 (5): e2017936118. https://www.pnas.org/doi/10.1073/pnas.2017936118.

Dane, Anthony, Dave Wright, and Gaylor Montmasson-Clair. 2019. "Exploring the Policy Impacts of a Transition to Electric Vehicles in South Africa." Trade & Industrial Policy Strategies, Pretoria, South Africa.

Dasgupta, Susmita, Somik Lall, and David Wheeler. 2020. "Traffic, Air Pollution, and Distributional Impacts in Dar es Salaam: A Spatial Analysis with New Satellite Data." Policy Research Working Paper 9185, World Bank, Washington, DC. https://openknowledge.worldbank.org/handle/10986/33445.

Deloitte. 2019. "The Transformation of Gasoline Retailing in China." Press release, May 27, 2019. https://www2.deloitte.com/cn/en/pages/about-deloitte/articles/pr-china-gasoline-retailing-development-trends-report-2019.html.

European Commission, Directorate-General for Climate Action, N. Hill, S. Amaral, S. Morgan-Price, et al. 2020. *Determining the Environmental Impacts of Conventional and Alternatively Fuelled Vehicles through LCA: Final Report.* Brussels: European Commission; Ricardo Energy & Environment. https://op.europa.eu/en/publication-detail/-/publication/1f494180-bc0e-11ea-811c-01aa75ed71a1/language-en.

Ford Motor Company. 2017. "CEO Strategic Update." Ford Motor Company. http://s22.q4cdn.com/857684434/files/doc_presentations/2017/CEO-Strategic-Update-12.pdf.

FTI Consulting. 2017. "The Impact of Electrically Chargeable Vehicles on the EU Economy: A Literature Review and Assessment." FTI Consulting, London.

Hajat, Anjum, Charlene Hsia, and Marie S. O'Neill. 2015. "Socioeconomic Disparities and Air Pollution Exposure: A Global Review." *Current Environmental Health Reports* 2 (4): 440–50. https://doi.org/10.1007/s40572-015-0069-5.

Harto, Chris. 2020. "Electric Vehicle Ownership Costs: Today's Electric Vehicles Offer Big Savings for Consumers." *Consumer Reports,* October 2020. https://advocacy.consumerreports.org/wp-content/uploads/2020/10/EV-Ownership-Cost-Final-Report-1.pdf.

Health Effects Institute. 2010. *Traffic-Related Air Pollution: A Critical Review of the Literature on Emissions, Exposure, and Health Effects.* Boston, MA: Health Effects Institute.

Helms, Hinrich, Claudia Kämper, and Udo Lambrecht. 2015. "Carbon Dioxide and Consumption Reduction through Electric Vehicles." In *Advances in Battery Technologies for Electric Vehicles,* edited by Bruno Scrosati, Jürgen Garche, and Werner Tillmetz. Cambridge, UK: Woodhead Publishing.

Hendryx, Michael, Keith J. Zullig, and Juhua Luo. 2020. "Impacts of Coal Use on Health." *Annual Review of Public Health* 41 (1): 397–415.

Hensley, Russell, Stefan Knupfer, and Dickon Pinner. 2018. "Three Surprising Resource Implications from the Rise of Electric Vehicles." *McKinsey Quarterly*, May 23, 2018. https://www.mckinsey.com/industries/automotive-and-assembly/our-insights/three-surprising-resource-implications-from-the-rise-of-electric-vehicles.

Holland, Stephen P., Erin T. Mansur, Nicholas Z. Muller, and Andrew J. Yates. 2016. "Are There Environmental Benefits from Driving Electric Vehicles? The Importance of Local Factors." *American Economic Review* 106 (12): 3700–29.

IEA (International Energy Agency). 2020. *Tracking Transport 2020.* Paris: IEA. https://www.iea.org/reports/tracking-transport-2020.

IEA (International Energy Agency). 2021a. *Net Zero by 2050: A Roadmap for the Global Energy Sector.* Vienna: IEA.

IEA (International Energy Agency). 2021b. *The Role of Critical Minerals in Clean Energy Transitions.* World Energy Outlook Special Report. Paris: IEA. https://www.iea.org/reports/the-role-of-critical-minerals-in-clean-energy-transitions.

INRIX Research and Graham Cookson. 2018. *INRIX Global Traffic Scorecard.* Kirkland, WA, and Cheshire, UK: INRIX Research. http://assets.dmagstatic.com/wp-content/uploads/2018/02/INRIX_2017_Traffic_Scorecard_Final_2.pdf.

IRENA (International Renewable Energy Agency). 2020a. "How Falling Costs Make Renewables a Cost-Effective Investment." IRENA, June 2, 2020. https://www.irena.org/newsroom/articles/2020/Jun/How-Falling-Costs-Make-Renewables-a-Cost-effective-Investment.

IRENA (International Renewable Energy Agency). 2020b. "Renewable Power Generation Costs in 2019: Latest Trends and Drivers." IRENA webinar, June 9, 2020. https://www.irena.org/events/2020/Jun/Renewable-Power-Generation-Costs-in-2019-Latest-Trends-and-Drivers.

Jaramillo, P., S. Kahn Ribeiro, P. Newman, S. Dhar, O. E. Diemuodeke, T. Kajino, D. S. Lee, S. B. Nugroho, X. Ou, A. Hammer Strømman, J. Whitehead. 2022. "Transport." In IPCC, 2022: *Climate Change 2022: Mitigation of Climate Change: Contribution of Working Group III to the Sixth Assessment Report of the Intergovernmental Panel on Climate Change,* 1049–160. Cambridge, UK: Cambridge University Press.

Kah, Marianne. 2018. "Electric Vehicles and Their Impact on Oil Demand: Why Forecasts Differ." Center on Global Energy Policy, Columbia University, New York. https://energypolicy.columbia.edu/sites/default/files/pictures/CGEP_Electric%20Vehicles%20and%20Their%20Impact%20on%20Oil%20Demand-Why%20Forecasts%20Differ.pdf.

König, Adrian, Lorenzo Nicoletti, Daniel Schröder, Sebastian Wolff, Adam Waclaw, and Markus Lienkamp. 2021. "An Overview of Parameter and Cost for Battery Electric Vehicles." *World Electric Vehicle Journal* 12 (1): 21. https://doi.org/10.3390/wevj12010021.

Liu, Wenjuan, and Datu B. Agusdinata. 2020. "Interdependencies of Lithium Mining and Communities Sustainability in Salar de Atacama, Chile." *Journal of Cleaner Production* 260: 120838. https://doi.org/10.1016/j.jclepro.2020.120838.

Mahdavi, Paasha, Cesar B. Martinez-Alvarez, and Michael L. Ross. 2020. "Why Do Governments Tax or Subsidize Fossil Fuels?" Working Paper 541, Center for Global Development, Washington, DC.

Meyer, Kerstin, Hinrich Helms, Claudia Kämper, Kirsten Biemann, Udo Lambrecht, and Julius Jöhrens. 2018. "Lifecycle Analysis of Electric Vehicles: Determining Factors and Improvement Potential." Agora Verkehrswende, Berlin.

Moszoro, Marian. 2021. "The Direct Employment Impact of Public Investment." Working Paper 2021/131, International Monetary Fund, Washington, DC. https://www.imf.org/en/Publications/WP/Issues/2021/05/06/The-Direct-Employment-Impact-of-Public-Investment-50251.

Muro, Mark, Adie Tomer, Ranjitha Shivaram, and Joseph Kane. 2019. "Advancing Inclusion through Clean Energy Jobs." Metropolitan Policy Program at Brookings, Washington, DC. https://think-asia.org/handle/11540/10116.

NOW. 2020a. "Factsheet: Electric Mobility and Raw Materials." Nationale Leitstelle Ladeinfrastruktur, NOW GmbH, Berlin. https://www.now-gmbh.de/wp-content/uploads/2020/10/EN_Factsheet_RohstoffeEmob_2020.pdf.

NOW. 2020b. "Ladeinfrastruktur nach 2025/2030: Szenarien für den Markthochlauf" (Charging infrastructure after 2025/2030: Scenarios for market development). Nationale Leitstelle Ladeinfrastruktur, NOW GmbH, Berlin.

NPM (Nationale Plattform Zunkunft Der Mobilitat). 2020. "Zwischenbericht zur strategischen Personalplanung." NPM, Berlin. https://www.plattform-zukunft-mobilitaet.de/wp-content/uploads/2020/03/NPM-AG-4-1-Zwischenbericht-zur-strategischen-Personalplanung-und-Entwicklung-im-Mobilit%C3%A4tssektor.pdf.

OICA (International Organization of Motor Vehicle Manufacturers). 2019. "2019 Production Statistics." OICA, Paris. https://www.oica.net/category/production-statistics/2019-statistics.

Pek, Alyssa, Giorgia Concas, Janne Skogberg, Lucien Mathieu, and Oddvin Breiteig. 2019. "Powering a New Value Chain in the Automotive Sector: The Job Potential of Transport Electrification." EuropeOn Electrical Contractors Association, Brussels.

Peng, Wei, Junnan Yang, Xi Lu, and Denise L. Mauzerall. 2018. "Potential Co-Benefits of Electrification for Air Quality, Health, and CO_2 Mitigation in 2030 China." *Applied Energy* 218: 511–19. https://doi.org/10.1016/j.apenergy.2018.02.048.

Peszko, Grzegorz, Dominique van der Mensbrugghe, Alexander Golub, John Ward, Dimitri Zenghelis, Cor Marijs, Anne Schopp, John A. Rogers, and Amelia Midgley. 2020. *Diversification and Cooperation in a Decarbonizing World: Climate Strategies for Fossil Fuel-Dependent Countries.* Washington, DC: World Bank. https://openknowledge.worldbank.org/handle/10986/34011.

Peters, Glen, Jan C. Minx, Christopher L. Weber, and Ottmar Edenhofer. 2011. "Growth in Emission Transfers via International Trade from 1990 to 2008." *Proceedings of the National Academy of Sciences* 108 (21): 8903–08.

Rajper, Sarmad Z., and Johan Albrecht. 2020. "Prospects of Electric Vehicles in the Developing Countries: A Literature Review." *Sustainability* 12 (5): 1906.

Roy, Rana. 2016. "The Cost of Air Pollution in Africa." OECD Development Centre Working Papers No. 333, OECD Publishing, Paris. https://doi.org/10.1787/5jlqzq77x6f8-en.

Salat, Serge. and Gerald Ollivier. 2017. *Transforming the Urban Space through Transit-Oriented Development: The 3V Approach.* Washington, DC: World Bank. https://www.worldbank.org/en/topic/transport/publication/transforming-the-urban-space-through-transit-oriented-development-the-3v-approach.

Sclar, Ryan, Camron Gorguinpour, Sebastian Castellanos, and Xiangyi Li. 2019. *Barriers to Adopting Electric Buses.* Washington, DC: World Resource Institute. https://www.wri.org/research/barriers-adopting-electric-buses.

Sims, Ralph, Roberto Schaeffer, Felix Creutzig, Xochitl Cruz-Núñez, Marcio D'Agosto, Delia Dimitriu, Maria J. Figueroa Meza, Lew Fulton, Shigeki Kobayashi, Oliver Lah, Alan McKinnon, Peter Newman, Minggao Ouyang, James J. Schauer, Daniel Sperling, and Geetam Tiwari. 2014. "Transport." In *Climate Change 2014: Mitigation of Climate Change: Contribution of Working Group III to the Fifth Assessment Report of the Intergovernmental Panel on Climate Change,* 599–670. Cambridge, UK: Cambridge University Press; New York. https://www.ipcc.ch/site/assets/uploads/2018/02/ipcc_wg3_ar5_chapter8.pdf.

Singapore Land Transport Authority. 2013. *Land Transport Master Plan 2013.* Government of Singapore. https://www.lta.gov.sg/content/dam/ltagov/who_we_are/statistics_and_publications/master-plans/pdf/LTMP2013Report.pdf.

Sovacool, Benjamin K., Saleem H. Ali, Morgan Bazilian, Ben Radley, Benoit Nemery, Julia Okatz, and Dustin Mulvaney. 2020. "Sustainable Minerals and Metals for a Low-Carbon Future." *Science* 367 (6473): 30–33.

Sperling, Daniel. 2018. "Electric Vehicles: Approaching the Tipping Point." *Bulletin of the Atomic Scientists* 74 (1): 11–18. https://doi.org/10.1080/00963402.2017.1413055.

Thielmann, Axel, Martin Wietschel, Simon Funke, Anna Grimm, Tim Hettesheimer, Sabine Langkau, Antonia Loibl, Cornelius Moll, Christoph Neef, Patrick Plötz, Luisa Sievers, Luis Tercero Espinoza, and Jakob Edler. 2020. "Batteries for Electric Cars: Fact Check and Need for Action." Fraunhofer Institute for Systems and Innovation Research ISI, Karlsruhe, Germany. https://www.isi.fraunhofer.de/content/dam/isi/dokumente/cct/2020/Fact_check_Batteries_for_electric_cars.pdf.

UNEP (United Nations Environment Programme). 2020. *Global Trade in Used Vehicles Report.* New York: United Nations. https://www.unep.org/resources/report/global-trade-used-vehicles-report.

UNFCCC (United Nations Framework Convention on Climate Change). 2020. *Climate Action Pathway: Transport: Action Table.* New York: United Nations. https://unfccc.int/sites/default/files/resource/Climate%20Action%20Pathway%20Transport.%20Action%20Table.pdf.

US Department of Energy. 2011. "All-Electric Vehicles." US Department of Energy, Washington, DC. https://www.fueleconomy.gov/feg/evtech.shtml.

USGS (United States Geological Survey). 2021. *Mineral Commodity Summary.* Washington, DC: US Geological Survey.

Wappelhorst, Sandra. 2020. "The End of the Road? An Overview of Combustion Engine Car Phase-Out Announcements across Europe." International Council on Clean Transportation, Washington, DC. https://theicct.org/publications/combustion-engine-car-phase-out-EU.

World Bank. 2017. "Guidance Note on Shadow Price of Carbon in Economic Analysis." World Bank, Washington, DC. https://documents1.worldbank.org/curated/en/621721519940107694/pdf/2017-Shadow-Price-of-Carbon-Guidance-Note.pdf.

World Bank. 2022. *The Global Health Cost of $PM_{2.5}$ Air Pollution: A Case for Action beyond 2021.* International Development in Focus. Washington, DC: World Bank.

World Bank and Development Research Center of the State Council, the People's Republic of China. 2014. *Urban China: Toward Efficient, Inclusive, and Sustainable Urbanization.* Washington, DC: World Bank. https://openknowledge.worldbank.org/handle/10986/18865.

World Bank and EV100. Forthcoming. "Accelerating E-Mobility for Decarbonizing Road Transport: Experiences and Lessons of Policy-Making in China." World Bank, Washington, DC.

World Health Organization. 2018. *Global Status Report on Road Safety.* Geneva: WHO. https://www.worldbank.org/en/topic/transport/overview.

Xing, Jianwei, Benjamin Leard, and Shangjun Li. 2021. "What Does an Electric Vehicle Replace?" NBER Working Paper 25771, National Bureau of Economic Research, Cambridge, MA. https://www.worldbank.org/en/topic/transport/overview.

Yalta, A. Yasemin, and A. Talha Yalta. 2017. "Dependency on Imported Oil and Its Effects on Current Account." *Energy Sources, Part B: Economics, Planning, and Policy* 12 (10): 859–67.

Ziegler, Micah S. and Jessika E. Trancik. 2021. "Re-Examining Rates of Lithium-Ion Battery Technology Improvement and Cost Decline." *Energy & Environmental Science* 14 (4): 1635–51. https://www.worldbank.org/en/topic/transport/overview.

2

The Economics of Electric Mobility

INTRODUCTION

Although electric mobility of passenger transportation holds considerable promise for the future decarbonization of the transportation sector, many policy makers are trying to understand whether it makes sense for their countries and, if so, when and how to pursue such a transition. The economics of electric mobility entails several important questions. Is the higher capital cost of electric vehicles (EVs) compensated by lower running costs? Would it be preferable to wait until technological change and global scale further bring down the costs of EV technology? Should countries prioritize electrification of certain vehicle categories, such as two-wheelers or buses? Does it make sense environmentally to electrify transportation before the power grid is fully decarbonized? Can the move toward electric mobility be justified purely in terms of mitigating local air pollution? To what extent do the wide array of taxes, import duties, and subsidies levied on vehicles as well as on transportation fuels and electricity services materially distort consumer choices between EVs and vehicles powered by internal combustion engine (ICE vehicles, or ICEVs)? Even if EVs are socially desirable, will private actors have the incentive or the financing capacity to adopt them without explicit public mandates?

This chapter introduces a simple economic framework for answering all of these questions based on an understanding of the costs and benefits of the transition toward electric mobility. The framework examines this issue at a national scale, while exploring how conclusions may differ across vehicle categories. Specifically, it evaluates the net social cost of reaching an illustrative national EV target of 30 percent of cars and buses entering the national fleet being electric by 2030 and more than 70 percent of two- and three-wheelers—known as the 30×30 scenario. Net social costs are calculated as the difference between the lifetime (public and private, capital and operating) cost of the vehicle fleet that meets the EV policy, compared to the lifetime cost of a baseline scenario—called business as usual (BAU)—in which the passenger vehicle fleet continues to evolve according to historical trends without any explicit policy to mandate EVs.

Most of the discussion focuses on the central 30×30 scenario, but sensitivity analysis is also presented for several alternative scenarios. In the "green grid" scenario, a country's power generation mix undergoes further decarbonization by accelerating deployment of renewables in line with what the International Renewable Energy Agency's Global Renewables Energy Outlook takes to be technically feasible.[1] This use of renewables increases the externality benefits—reductions in both local air pollutants and global emissions—associated with the adoption of electric mobility. In the "scarce minerals" scenario, the cost of batteries declines more slowly than anticipated because of global shortages of critical minerals and associated higher prices, a mounting concern among industry analysts. In turn, the "fuel efficiency" scenario explores to what extent the case for electric mobility is diluted by efforts to improve the fuel efficiency of ICE vehicles. The "efficient bus" scenario explores the possibility of further optimizing municipal management of bus fleets to secure savings in procurement and extend bus mileage to maximize operational benefits in line with industry best practices. Finally, the "taxi fleet" scenario explores the implications of focusing electrification of four-wheelers on intensively used vehicle fleets such as taxis, as opposed to private family cars.

The economic nature of the analysis calls for stripping out all taxes, duties, and subsidies to examine the true underlying costs. In addition, the impact on both local environmental externalities relating to urban air pollution and global externalities associated with carbon emissions must also be incorporated to provide a full economic picture. However, comparing the economic results with those from a parallel financial analysis that does not make either of these adjustments is nonetheless instructive. Throughout, results are further disaggregated by vehicle category to shed light on how the net costs or benefits of EV adoption may vary across types of vehicles. The overall framework is microeconomic and does not consider wider macroeconomic repercussions.

The economic framework developed in this chapter is simultaneously applied to a diverse sample of 20 low- and middle-income countries to shed light on how the answers to the fundamental economic questions of electric mobility differ across country contexts. Furthermore, a typology is used to permit a wider generalization of results to countries outside this sample based on their characteristics. In particular, the economics of electric mobility are found to be quite sensitive to various country attributes including the prevalence of four-wheelers in the national vehicle fleet, whether a country is a net fossil fuel exporter, and the relative cost of purchasing vehicles in a country.

Overall, the results suggest that the economic case for the electrification of transportation is already strong in close to half of the countries studied and is improving over time as technological change brings down the cost of vehicles. In general, electric two-wheelers are economically advantageous in almost all of the countries studied, but electric four-wheelers do not make sense in all but a handful, even when they operate in commercial fleets. Electric buses also offer economic and financial advantages in about three-quarters of the countries studied, which increase when more efficient management practices are adopted. Although the capital cost differentials of EVs remain significant, in many instances they are more than compensated over time by lower maintenance and energy costs as well as reduced pollution externalities. Results are robust to further greening of the power grid or more pessimistic assumptions about declining battery costs. By and large, fiscal distortions are found to overly favor electric mobility given widespread taxation of gasoline and subsidization of electricity, meaning that accelerating electric mobility adoption is likely to reduce net fiscal revenues in the near term. The investment needs associated with such a transition are not insignificant. Carbon finance could make a substantial contribution to the financing of public investment needs, but private investments in more expensive EVs may pose affordability challenges in the context of low- and middle-income countries.

EVALUATING ELECTRIC MOBILITY AT THE COUNTRY SCALE

The economics of electric mobility at the country level can be evaluated by comparing the present value of all the lifetime capital and operating costs of the new vehicles entering the fleet as of 2030 under two scenarios. The first, referred to as the 30×30 scenario, incorporates an electric mobility policy target such that 30 percent of all new vehicles purchased should be electric by 2030. The baseline (BAU) scenario captures the situation in which no policy target is imposed for EVs and vehicle purchase decisions continue to reflect historical trends. This framework is represented by equation (2.1), where Δ denotes the difference between the 30×30 scenario and *BAU*, *NSC* denotes net social costs, *PV* denotes present value of costs, *CC* denotes vehicle capital costs, *OC* denotes vehicle operating costs, *CI* denotes charging infrastructure, *T* denotes taxes, *S* denotes subsidies, *EX* denotes environmental externality costs, *cap* denotes capital costs, and *ope* denotes operation costs.

$$\Delta NSC = PV_{30\times30}\,(Economic\ cost) - PV_{BAU}\,(Economic\ cost)$$

$$\Delta NSC = PV_{30\times30}\,(CC + OC + CI - T + S + EX) - PV_{BAU}\,(CC + OC + CI - T + S + EX)$$

Or, alternatively,

$$\Delta NSC = \underbrace{\Delta PV\,(CC - T_{cap} + S_{cap})}_{Capital} + \underbrace{\Delta PV\,(OC - T_{ope} + S_{ope})}_{Operations} + \underbrace{\Delta PV\,(CI)}_{\substack{Charging\\ infrastructure}} + \underbrace{\Delta PV\,(EX)}_{Environmental} \tag{2.1}$$

For exposition, it is useful to further decompose this overall difference in costs between the two scenarios into four components—see the alternative element in equation (2.1): the difference in vehicle fleet capital costs (adjusting for taxes and subsidies), the difference in vehicle fleet operating costs (including maintenance as well as running fuel or electricity and once again adjusting for relevant taxes and subsidies), the additional charging infrastructure required to support a higher penetration of EVs, and the reduction in vehicle fleet externalities. The decomposition makes it possible to understand which of these differences is primarily responsible for driving the results.

Because this is an economic analysis, taxes and duties must be subtracted from all capital and operating costs and subsidies must be added back in. Doing so makes it possible to understand the actual underlying relative costs of these two scenarios, as well as the extent to which fiscal policies may be responsible for distorting the choice between them, by comparing results with and without taxes and subsidies. Regarding the valuation of externalities, a value of US$40 per ton by 2020 is used for carbon, which is the lower bound of the World Bank's official guidance on the shadow value of carbon, and it gradually rises to US$50 per ton by 2030. In the case of local externalities, the damage coefficients are country specific and reflect local damages drawing from the World Bank's Carbon Pricing Assessment Tool. To calculate the present value of the cost differences, a discount rate of 6.6 percent is used. Again, the use of this value is in line with World Bank official guidance that the discount rate should be set at twice the projected growth in real per capita income in the developing world to reflect the social rate of time preference.

FIGURE 2.1 Prevalence of types of vehicles, 2020

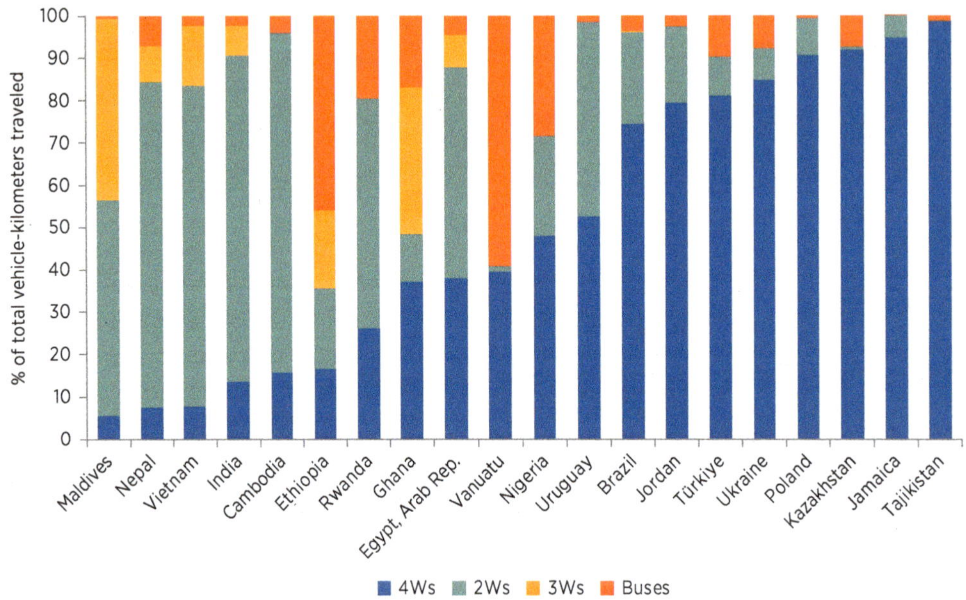

Source: World Bank.
Note: 2W = two-wheeler; 3W = three-wheeler; 4W = four-wheeler.

Comparing Vehicle Fleet Capital Costs

The composition of vehicle fleets varies widely across countries (figure 2.1). In particular, the prevalence of four-wheel cars ranges from under 10 percent of total passenger vehicle-kilometers traveled in Vietnam to almost 100 percent in Jamaica. The significance of four-wheel cars broadly increases with a country's national income but may also reflect a country's transportation culture. For instance, Tajikistan (a low-income country) depends almost entirely on four-wheel cars, whereas in Uruguay (a high-income country) only 50 percent of its vehicle-kilometers are traveled in four-wheelers. Where four-wheelers are not dominant, some countries—primarily low- and middle-income ones in Asia such as Cambodia, Maldives, Nepal, and Vietnam—depend primarily on two-wheel motorbikes and sometimes three-wheel rickshaws for 60 to 80 percent of their total passenger vehicle-kilometers. Conversely, several low- and middle-income African countries—such as Ethiopia, Nigeria, and Rwanda—rely on buses to provide 25 to 50 percent of their total passenger vehicle-kilometers. Given that the economics of electric mobility differ widely across vehicle types (see the following discussion), the nature of a country's fleet composition will significantly affect the economics of electric mobility adoption and is an important factor to consider.

Another relevant consideration is reliance on secondhand vehicle imports. Recent work by the United Nations Environment Programme has highlighted the extent to which low- and middle-income countries, particularly those in Africa, import a large share of their vehicles secondhand from high-income countries (UNEP 2020). Academic research confirms that, in a country like Uganda, the average age of imported vehicles exceeds 10 years and the average price is on the order of US$5,000 (Forster and Nakyambadde 2020a, 2020b). Of the 20 countries studied for this report, as many as 7 from across Africa and Asia import more than half of their cars secondhand (figure 2.2), which has implications for the adoption of relatively new EVs, suggesting a significant time lag before such vehicles become available in the global secondhand market on an affordable basis.

FIGURE 2.2 Reliance on secondhand vehicle imports, 2020

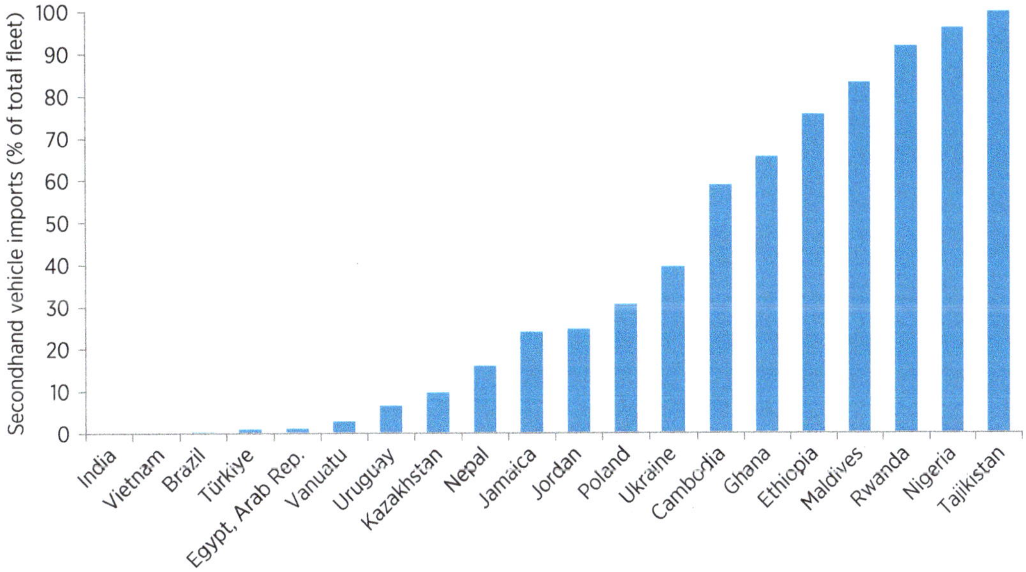

Source: World Bank.

FIGURE 2.3 Average cost of four-wheel vehicles, 2020

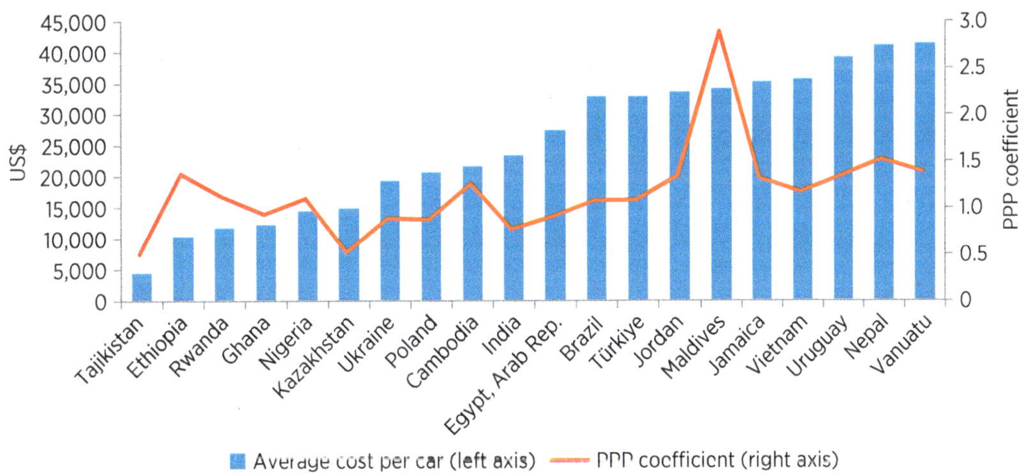

Source: World Bank.
Note: "Average cost per car" includes all taxes, subsidies, and duties. PPP = purchasing power parity.

All these factors contribute to the average cost of a "new" vehicle in a country, as do the specifications of the vehicles purchased, the extent to which vehicles are domestically manufactured, and country-specific factors such as vehicle shipment costs that may affect the relative cost of imports. Figure 2.3 illustrates how the weighted average cost of one standardized vehicle addition to the fleet ranges from under US$15,000 in the Sub-Saharan African countries to about US$40,000 in Nepal, Uruguay, and Vanuatu. These differences broadly follow the magnitude of the purchasing power parity (PPP) adjustment factor for vehicles as shown on the chart in orange. These differences are driven by the types of vehicles imported (whether

FIGURE 2.4 **Tax rate differential of ICEVs over BEVs, 2020**

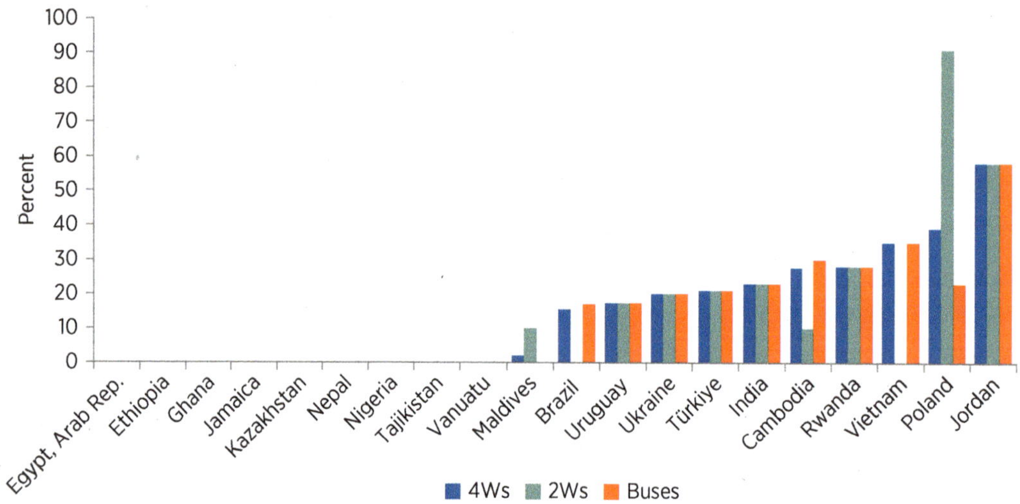

Source: World Bank.
Note: 2W = two-wheeler; 4W = four-wheeler; BEV = battery electric vehicle; ICEV = internal combustion engine vehicle.

two- or four-wheelers), whether the vehicles are secondhand, and whether the country faces some intrinsic cost disadvantage for the import of vehicles (remoteness and logistical complexity).

Purchased vehicles (whether new or secondhand) are often subject to significant taxes and import duties, whereas EV purchases are occasionally subsidized. Although these fiscal incentives are not considered in the *economic* analysis, they play an important role in the *financial* analysis. It is important to understand how high the vehicle tax burden is overall and to compare the extent to which the tax burden on EVs and ICEVs is even-handed or rather privileges one type of vehicle over another. In general, tax rates across vehicle types fall in the 15 to 25 percent range. Almost half the countries do not apply any differential taxation to gasoline ICEVs versus battery electric vehicles (BEVs) (figure 2.4). More widespread is the practice observed in various other countries—India, Jordan, Poland, Rwanda, Türkiye, Ukraine, Uruguay, and Vietnam—of taxing ICEVs at least 20 percentage higher than equivalent BEVs.

Finally, the relative capital cost of the 30×30 scenario relative to BAU is summarized in table 2.1. Throughout the chapter, the results of the economic analysis are expressed on a normalized per million passenger vehicle-kilometer basis, meaning that the total incremental costs of the transition to the 30×30 scenario are aggregated across the entire national fleet, and then divided by the total number of passenger vehicle-kilometers delivered by the incremental vehicles added to the fleet expressed in millions. As a point of reference, 1 million passenger vehicle-kilometers is a typical level of service provided by a private car across the entirety of its life cycle. Similarly, the results of the parallel financial analysis are normalized as the change in life-cycle costs per vehicle, allowing results to be disaggregated by vehicle category. The aggregate results of the financial analysis are also expressed in terms of differential cost per million passenger vehicle-kilometers to allow for a ready comparison with the results of the economic analysis.

In addition to presenting results for each of the 20 countries modeled, table 2.1 also includes results for various typologies of interest, which are based on the relevant subset of the

TABLE 2.1 Capital cost advantage of electric vehicles, 2030

	US$/Mpaxvkm			% of BAU values	
	Economic cost advantage (a)	Net taxes and subsidies (b)	Financial cost advantage (c = a + b)	Economic cost advantage	Financial cost advantage
Country					
Brazil	(21,880)	13,052	(8,828)	(8.3)	(2.4)
Cambodia	(12,724)	2,148	(10,576)	(16.4)	(8.1)
Egypt, Arab Rep.	(13,010)	254	(12,756)	(8.9)	(6.7)
Ethiopia	(4,692)	5,798	1,106	(16.8)	2.1
Ghana	(6,241)	(1,106)	(7,348)	(9.4)	(9.4)
India	(12,207)	10,051	(2,156)	(12.9)	(1.7)
Jamaica	(27,919)	(2,864)	(30,784)	(8.7)	(6.2)
Jordan	(41,124)	37,438	(3,685)	(15.2)	(0.8)
Kazakhstan	(8,347)	2,470	(5,877)	(5.6)	(3.2)
Maldives	(9,370)	8,399	(970)	(29.7)	(1.4)
Nepal	(39,111)	(27,515)	(66,626)	(52.2)	(30.3)
Nigeria	(6,511)	(976)	(7,488)	(10.3)	(9.8)
Poland	(26,712)	57,784	31,072	(5.4)	5.0
Rwanda	(5,112)	2,781	(2,331)	(12.2)	(3.9)
Tajikistan	1,351	1,290	2,641	2.4	3.8
Türkiye	(31,494)	3,930	(27,563)	(11.1)	(6.2)
Ukraine	(11,376)	10,595	(781)	(6.0)	(0.3)
Uruguay	(37,121)	37,615	493	(12.1)	(0.1)
Vanuatu	(3,915)	3,616	(299)	(2.1)	0.1
Vietnam	(22,595)	1,291	(21,305)	(27.6)	(15.8)
Typology					
Car dominant	(23,287)	16,361	(6,926)	(8.11)	(1.73)
Mixed fleet	(13,055)	7,907	(5,148)	(13.71)	(3.90)
Net oil exporter	(18,329)	9,905	(8,424)	(8.26)	(2.76)
Net oil importer	(14,465)	9,452	(5,013)	(12.35)	(3.07)
High-cost vehicles	(21,642)	6,582	(15,060)	(11.87)	(5.56)
Low-cost vehicles	(12,597)	10,577	(2,021)	(11.11)	(1.34)

Source: World Bank.

Note: Heading colors: blue = excluding taxes and subsidies, gray = fiscal wedge, green = including taxes and subsidies. Data in this table represent the "business as usual" (BAU) scenario minus the 30×30 scenario (averages for fleet additions). The BAU scenario assumes that no policy target will be imposed for electric vehicles and that vehicle purchase decisions will continue to reflect historical trends. The 30×30 scenario assumes that sales of electric cars and buses will reach 30 percent, and of two- and three-wheelers, 70 percent, by 2030. Red and parentheses indicate negative value. US$/Mpaxvkm = US dollars per million passenger vehicle-kilometers.

20 countries fulfilling those characteristics.[2] These results support wider inferences about countries not included in the sample by providing an understanding of three factors. First is how results are influenced by the composition of the vehicle fleet—whether car dominant or mixed, determined by whether car vehicle miles traveled (VMT) account for more than 80 percent of the total VMT. Second is the country's net oil exporting status (whether net importer or exporter). Third is the relative cost of vehicles, depending on whether the PPP index for vehicles, produced by the World Bank's International Comparison Program, is above or below one (ICP 2017).

The economic analysis indicates that, in just about every country, a capital cost premium is associated with purchasing EVs. Moreover, this premium is substantial—on the order of

US$10,000 to US$20,000 per million passenger vehicle-kilometers (the typical operating life of a family car). Turning to percentages, the 30×30 scenario presents a capital cost premium on the order of 10 percent over BAU, though this premium declines toward 5 percent when fiscal advantages are taken into account.

The only exception is Tajikistan, where a modest capital cost advantage is associated with EVs because the country relies heavily on imported secondhand vehicles. Because BEVs depreciate more rapidly than ICEVs, secondhand imports are cheaper, thereby reducing the capital cost of the transition. The capital cost premium is much larger for certain countries—notably Brazil, Jamaica, Jordan, Nepal, Poland, Türkiye, Uruguay, and Vietnam—where it ranges between US$20,000 and US$40,000 per million passenger vehicle-kilometers. In terms of the country typology, the capital cost premium is approximately twice as large for countries with car-dominated fleets, those that are net oil exporters, and those with high-cost vehicles. As noted in the case of Tajikistan, another factor driving the magnitude of the capital cost differential is the extent to which countries rely on the import of secondhand vehicles.

Reporting the fiscal wedge makes it possible to establish the extent to which the tax and subsidy regime supports EVs. Overall, more than half of the countries studied operate a fiscal regime for vehicles that favors the purchase of EVs; Maldives and Poland stand out for their explicit subsidy of US$2,000 and US$6,000 per car, and Uruguay for its sizable tax advantage. However, several countries—Ghana, Jamaica, Nepal, and Nigeria—stand out for applying a relatively punitive combination of taxes and duties on the purchase of EVs that amount to anywhere between US$1,000 and US$30,000 per million passenger vehicle-kilometers. In fact, Ethiopia, (especially) Poland, Tajikistan, and Uruguay are the only countries where the fiscal wedge is large enough to completely offset the capital cost premium associated with purchasing EVs, so that on average they appear to be cheaper financially to consumers. In terms of country typology, the largest fiscal wedge in favor of EVs is in countries with car-dominated fleets.

Finally, disaggregating the economic and financial analysis by vehicle category is illuminating. Table 2.2 shows that, in the case of four-wheel EVs, in only a handful of countries (India, Maldives, Nigeria, Poland, Rwanda, Tajikistan, Ukraine, and Uruguay) are these cheaper to purchase than their ICE counterparts. Poland is the only country that offers a significant financial advantage, on average US$1,096 per vehicle. Conversely, two-wheel EVs are more expensive than ICEVs except in Poland, albeit by a relatively modest sum amounting to no more than US$200 per vehicle in many cases. When it comes to electric buses, the financial premium is significant, on the order of US$10,000 per vehicle. However, Uruguay stands out for having electric buses US$10,000 cheaper than conventional ones in financial terms, thanks to a taxation policy that hugely favors electric buses with a 6 percent vehicle purchase tax versus 23 percent for diesel buses.

Comparing Vehicle Fleet Operating Costs

The two main components of vehicle fleet operation are fuel and maintenance costs. It is well known that maintenance costs of EVs are significantly lower than those associated with ICEVs because of the much simpler nature of the motors involved (see chapter 1).

As countries adopt more EVs, they will reduce their use of liquid transportation fuels, such as gasoline and diesel, and satisfy more of their transportation energy demand from electricity. How these changes affect the transportation sector's energy bill depends on the relative unit energy cost of transportation. This cost can usefully be broken down into two components: the cost per unit of energy delivered by electricity versus fossil fuels and the energy consumption per unit of transportation, reflecting the relative energy efficiency of EVs versus ICEVs.

TABLE 2.2 Capital cost advantage of electric vehicles, by vehicle category, 2030

US$/vehicle

	Electric buses		Two-wheel EVs		Four-wheel EVs	
	Economic cost advantage	Financial cost advantage	Economic cost advantage	Financial cost advantage	Economic cost advantage	Financial cost advantage
Country						
Brazil	(6,136)	2,055	(125)	(97)	(1,983)	(819)
Cambodia	(9,621)	(5,694)	(154)	(160)	(1,397)	(1,033)
Egypt, Arab Rep.	(12,107)	(15,412)	(202)	(237)	(1,100)	(783)
Ethiopia	(3,375)	1,952	(172)	(75)	(1,173)	(367)
Ghana	(7,738)	(9,212)	(71)	(82)	(290)	(331)
India	(14,027)	(10,400)	(199)	(44)	(1,412)	134
Jamaica	(5,219)	(7,393)	(305)	(435)	(2,010)	(2,203)
Jordan	(9,111)	(7,913)	(451)	(253)	(2,895)	(90)
Kazakhstan	(11,639)	(12,365)	(107)	(85)	(459)	(231)
Maldives	(5,501)	32	(231)	(63)	(2,011)	324
Nepal	(18,705)	(22,958)	(694)	(1,375)	(5,593)	(9,222)
Nigeria	(6,418)	(7,468)	(12)	(13)	308	383
Poland	(12,412)	(6,325)	(29)	73	(886)	1,096
Rwanda	(7,116)	(4,971)	(32)	(12)	18	406
Tajikistan	(6,226)	(6,130)	—	—	115	198
Türkiye	(12,982)	(10,699)	(368)	(355)	(2,172)	(1,917)
Ukraine	(10,558)	(7,804)	(128)	(65)	(712)	170
Uruguay	249	10,385	(404)	(304)	(2,866)	483
Vanuatu	996	1,318	(351)	(464)	(2,473)	(745)
Vietnam	(14,234)	(6,006)	(348)	(395)	(3,004)	(1,755)
Typology						
Car dominant	(10,383)	(6,088)	(161)	(128)	(1,591)	(394)
Mixed fleet	(11,162)	(8,647)	(225)	(123)	(1,426)	(62)
Net oil exporter	(6,736)	(4,966)	(114)	(89)	(1,731)	(711)
Net oil importer	(12,164)	(8,975)	(227)	(124)	(1,430)	(60)
High-cost vehicles	(8,325)	(5,005)	(314)	(372)	(2,056)	(1,104)
Low-cost vehicles	(13,255)	(10,738)	(198)	(58)	(1,232)	219

Source: World Bank.

Note: Heading colors: blue = excluding taxes and subsidies, green = including taxes and subsidies. Data in this table represent the "business as usual" (BAU) scenario minus the 30×30 scenario (averages for fleet additions). The BAU scenario assumes that no policy target will be imposed for electric vehicles and that vehicle purchase decisions will continue to reflect historical trends. The 30×30 scenario assumes that sales of electric cars and buses will reach 30 percent, and of two- and three-wheelers, 70 percent, by 2030. The "fiscal wedge" comprises net taxes and subsidies. Red and parentheses indicate negative value. EV = electric vehicle; — = not available.

See equation (2.2), where Δ denotes the difference between variables under the 30×30 scenario versus *BAU*, *CE* denotes the unit energy cost of transportation (US$ per vehicle-kilometer), *PE* denotes the unit energy price (US$ per joule), and *EFF* denotes the energy efficiency coefficient (joules per vehicle-kilometer).

$$\Delta CE = \Delta PE \times \Delta EFF \tag{2.2}$$

Variation in the price of both electricity and liquid fuels across countries is considerable. For example, in this sample, the price of electricity varies from US$0.02 per kilowatt-hour in Ethiopia to US$0.40 per kilowatt-hour in Vanuatu, and the price of liquid fuels varies from US$0.50 per liter in Kazakhstan to about US$1.40 per liter in Vanuatu.

One important reason for such variations in the price of energy across countries is a wide range of tax and subsidy policies that distort the relative cost of electricity and fossil fuels, and that need to be removed before economic analysis (figure 2.5). Most striking is that, across most countries, gasoline is taxed while electricity is subsidized. Taxes on gasoline are typically in the 40 to 140 percent range, whereas subsidies to the electricity sector are typically between 40 and 80 percent. This pattern of fiscal policy tends to favor BEVs over ICEVs *beyond what the underlying economic costs would suggest* by substantially altering the relative prices of these alternate energy sources. In effect, gasoline is *twice* as expensive relative to electricity than it would be in the absence of both the distortionary taxes and subsidies.

Once tax and subsidy distortions are removed, electricity and liquid fuel prices can be normalized into consistent units so that the underlying economic costs can be compared (figure 2.6a). Across countries, electricity is approximately twice as expensive as liquid fuels on a per unit of energy basis. This finding is not entirely unexpected given that liquid fuels are a raw form of energy, whereas electricity is a more extensively processed form of energy to which more economic value has been added through the production and delivery process.

Although electricity may typically be a more expensive form of energy per unit, the actual cost of using electricity for transportation may still be lower to the extent that EVs are more energy efficient than ICEVs powered by liquid fuels (see chapter 1). In fact, whereas BEVs consume only 0.70 to 1.00 megajoules per vehicle-kilometer, ICEVs powered by liquid fuels consume between 3.00 and 5.00 megajoules per vehicle-kilometer, depending on the vintage and fuel efficiency standards of the vehicle fleet. This difference in consumption makes BEVs several times more energy efficient than ICEVs (figure 2.7). In most low- and middle-income countries, gasoline vehicles consume four to five times more energy per vehicle-kilometer than electric vehicles, and diesel vehicles consume three to four times as much. Even in a country such as Türkiye, where ICEVs are relatively fuel efficient, they still consume two to three times more energy per vehicle-kilometer than BEVs.

FIGURE 2.5 Tax and subsidy rates for gasoline and electricity, 2020

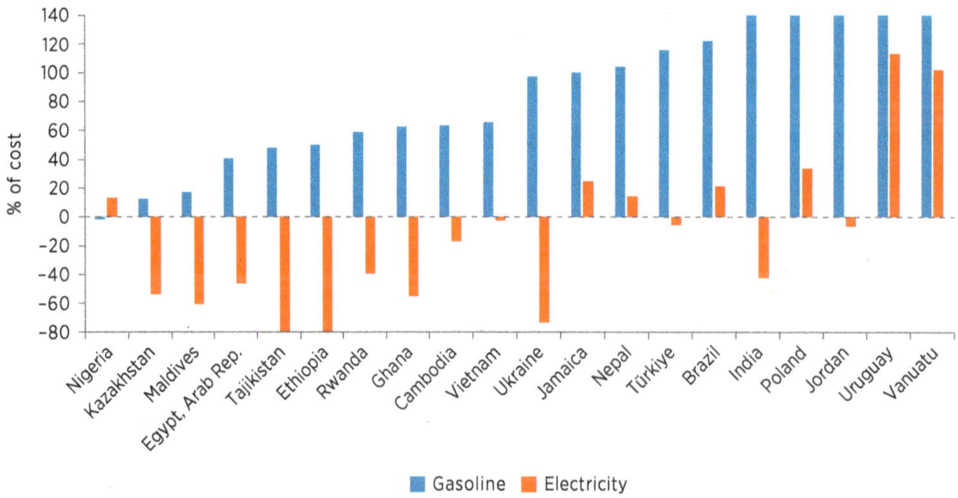

Source: World Bank.

FIGURE 2.6 Cost of electricity and gasoline per units of energy and travel, 2020

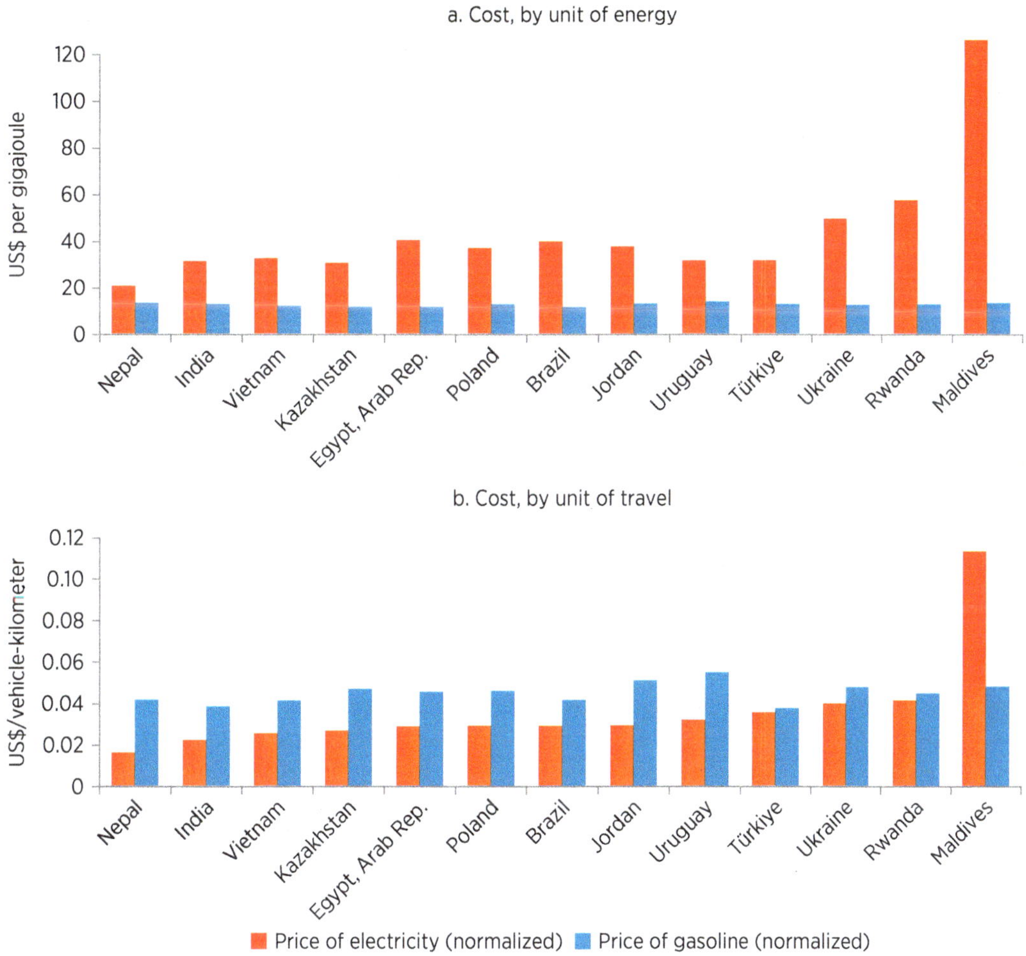

Source: World Bank.

FIGURE 2.7 Fuel consumption of ICEVs in excess over BEVs, 2020

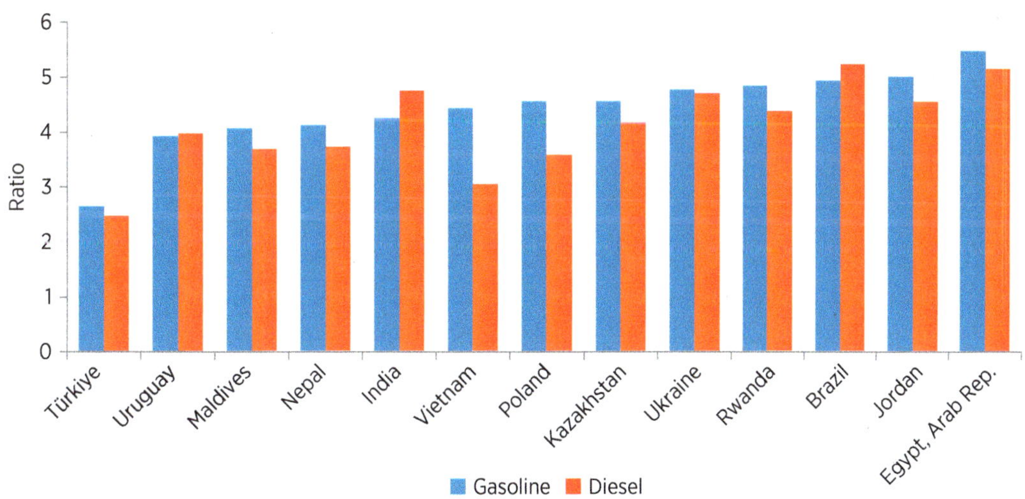

Source: World Bank.
Note: BEV = battery electric vehicle; ICEV = internal combustion engine vehicle.

Overall, therefore, the normalized cost of using electricity to power transportation is significantly lower than that for fossil fuels in terms of dollars per vehicle-kilometer (figure 2.6b). Even though electricity is twice as expensive as liquid fuels on a per unit of energy basis, only about a quarter of the energy is needed when vehicles are powered by electricity rather than fossil fuels. Thus the energy efficiency advantage of EVs more than offsets the apparent cost disadvantage of electricity (figure 2.6a and 2.6b).

The relative operating cost of the 30×30 scenario relative to BAU is summarized in tables 2.3 and 2.4. Clearly, vehicle maintenance costs are always reduced under the 30×30 scenario, reflecting the simpler nature of EVs and saving about US$5,000 to US$6,000 over a typical vehicle lifetime. Similarly, for almost every country, the net cost of fuels is lower under the 30×30 scenario by about US$5,000 to US$15,000 over a typical vehicle lifetime. Even though electricity is a more expensive form of energy, that cost is more than compensated by the greater energy efficiency of EVs, bringing overall fuel costs down. The only countries where energy becomes more expensive for EVs are small island developing countries (Vanuatu and particularly Maldives) because of the exceptionally high costs of electricity in those countries, which generate electricity primarily from imported oil in small, inefficient plants.

In almost every country, the fiscal regime for fuels and electricity works substantively in favor of electric mobility, reflecting the preponderance of gasoline and diesel taxes on the one hand and electricity subsidies on the other (see figure 2.5). This regime adds to a substantial fiscal advantage over the lifetime of a vehicle, between US$20,000 and US$30,000 per million passenger vehicle-kilometers in most cases. The most striking case is Maldives, where electricity is both very expensive and heavily subsidized, amounting to a fiscal advantage in favor of EV owners amounting to almost US$19,000 per million passenger vehicle-kilometers. Vanuatu is the only country with a sizable fiscal wedge that works against electric mobility, reflecting that electricity is relatively expensive and more heavily taxed than liquid fuels. Nigeria also stands out as the only country where the fiscal wedge is close to being neutral between the operation of EVs and ICEVs. Overall, the nature of the fiscal wedge means that the financial case for operating EVs is even stronger than the economic one, with the percentage operating cost advantage being 5 to 15 percent in economic terms and 10 to 30 percent in financial terms (table 2.3).

It is also of interest to consider how the financial savings in vehicle operating costs work out across categories of vehicles (table 2.4). The results are broadly as expected. The operational cost savings are larger for larger vehicles, reflecting their higher energy consumption. Over the life cycle of the vehicle, these financial operating cost savings typically amount to US$15,000 to US$30,000 for an electric bus, about US$2,000 for an electric four-wheeler, and usually well under US$1,000 for an electric two-wheeler.

Comparing Infrastructure Costs

An additional expense associated with EVs is the need to develop charging infrastructure of adequate density to allow EVs to circulate freely and recharge their batteries as needed. As noted in chapter 1, inadequate development of charging infrastructure can be a barrier to EV uptake; ensuring that investment in charging infrastructure keeps pace with the desired expansion of the EV fleet is necessary.

Multiple types of charging infrastructure would be needed to support the 30×30 scenario. Private individuals would need to invest in home charging infrastructure for their private vehicles, which would need to be complemented by a certain ratio of office charging facilities as well as public charging facilities allowing for rapid charging on the go. In addition, municipalities would need to invest in charging infrastructure for the electric bus fleet. All the relevant

TABLE 2.3 Operating cost advantage of electric vehicles, by economic and financial analyses, 2030

	US$/Mpaxvkm					% of BAU values	
	Economic cost advantage maintenance (a)	Economic cost advantage energy (b)	Economic cost advantage (c = a + b)	Net taxes and subsidies (d)	Financial cost advantage (e = c + d)	Economic cost advantage	Financial cost advantage
Country							
Brazil	5,567	5,287	10,855	22,491	33,346	6.7	12.8
Cambodia	5,178	14,077	19,254	14,561	33,815	12.0	17.0
Egypt, Arab Rep.	5,053	10,247	15,300	9,911	25,211	11.5	19.1
Ethiopia	1,838	5,082	6,920	5,561	12,480	3.4	6.0
Ghana	2,826	8,020	10,846	10,452	21,298	5.7	8.7
India	5,465	17,752	23,217	33,058	56,275	20.1	33.9
Jamaica	4,483	5,895	10,378	19,857	30,235	5.6	11.4
Jordan	5,356	7,187	12,543	21,794	34,337	6.2	12.3
Kazakhstan	5,448	2,834	8,283	10,303	18,586	4.8	10.1
Maldives	1,784	(13,074)	(11,290)	19,141	7,851	(11.9)	8.3
Nepal	7,174	25,545	32,720	13,587	46,307	21.6	24.8
Nigeria	2,888	7,962	10,850	(136)	10,714	5.5	5.2
Poland	10,379	4,460	14,838	22,621	37,459	5.2	9.1
Rwanda	2,523	3,833	6,356	22,329	28,686	3.2	9.5
Tajikistan	2,228	6,209	8,437	9,883	18,321	3.9	7.4
Türkiye	8,699	7,824	16,523	19,197	35,720	8.7	14.2
Ukraine	4,628	6,008	10,636	29,139	39,774	5.0	14.3
Uruguay	7,251	21,964	29,216	37,342	66,558	14.9	18.2
Vanuatu	7,386	(165)	7,221	(43,645)	(36,424)	3.2	(14.4)
Vietnam	9,186	21,892	31,078	25,160	56,238	22.6	32.2
Typology							
Car dominant	6,642	5,655	12,297	21,836	34,133	6.6	12.3
Mixed fleet	5,572	16,923	22,494	28,798	51,292	18.1	30.5
Net oil exporter	5,058	5,669	10,726	18,338	29,064	6.4	11.6
Net al importer	5,891	16,247	22,137	28,945	51,082	16.9	28.5
High-cost vehicles	6,431	10,715	17,145	19,670	36,815	10.3	16.1
Low-cost vehicles	5,538	16,251	21,789	30,299	52,088	17.4	29.9

Source: World Bank.
Note: Heading colors: blue = excluding taxes and subsidies, gray = fiscal wedge, green = including taxes and subsidies. Data in this table represent the "business as usual" (BAU) scenario minus the 30×30 scenario (averages for fleet additions). The BAU scenario assumes that no policy target will be imposed for electric vehicles and that vehicle purchase decisions will continue to reflect historical trends. The 30×30 scenario assumes that sales of electric cars and buses will reach 30 percent, and of two- and three-wheelers, 70 percent, by 2030. Red and parentheses indicate negative value. US$/Mpaxvkm = US dollars per million passenger vehicle-kilometers.

assumptions on the unit cost of charging stations, as well as the target density, are summarized in table 2.5.

The estimates for the cost of charging infrastructure associated with the 30×30 scenario are reported in table 2.6. The additional costs are typically about US$5,000 per million passenger vehicle-kilometers. About 60 percent of the cost of charging infrastructure is associated with providing public charging stations for four-wheelers and other privately owned vehicles. A further 20 percent is associated with investments in home-based charging that need to be made by EV owners. The remaining 20 percent is associated with charging electric buses.

TABLE 2.4 Operating cost advantage of electric vehicles, by vehicle type, 2030

US$/vehicle

	Electric buses		Two-wheel EVs		Four-wheel EVs	
	Economic cost advantage	Financial cost advantage	Economic cost advantage	Financial cost advantage	Economic cost advantage	Financial cost advantage
Country						
Brazil	15,207	35,389	361	1,033	650	2,174
Cambodia	20,299	30,141	334	631	613	1,102
Egypt, Arab Rep.	27,579	39,691	265	393	880	1,819
Ethiopia	6,809	12,269	129	255	376	664
Ghana	13,212	26,651	290	521	413	784
India	27,370	53,731	680	1,777	983	2,167
Jamaica	15,966	39,896	458	1,046	700	2,077
Jordan	14,088	21,975	434	1,469	633	1,774
Kazakhstan	6,043	15,721	413	702	572	1,239
Maldives	(29,435)	4,442	(234)	225	(948)	213
Nepal	29,789	34,723	449	786	1,276	1,842
Nigeria	5,222	5,335	254	229	1,043	996
Poland	11,529	20,452	82	244	470	1,212
Rwanda	5,825	28,203	148	553	246	1,127
Tajikistan	10,114	21,455	—	—	505	1,099
Türkiye	17,814	29,214	376	825	583	1,667
Ukraine	14,748	49,983	301	1,027	491	2,004
Uruguay	27,870	29,497	751	1,807	1,250	2,986
Vanuatu	7,367	(39,076)	283	866	227	(407)
Vietnam	34,576	40,132	605	1,158	942	1,565
Typology						
Car dominant	15,675	32,329	344	953	578	1,779
Mixed fleet	21,224	37,531	634	1,572	964	2,066
Net oil exporter	9,378	17,848	350	948	657	2,021
Net oil importer	22,990	41,529	631	1,566	835	1,916
High-cost vehicles	13,776	21,392	524	1,073	680	1,965
Low-cost vehicles	25,380	49,150	644	1,660	849	1,928

Source: World Bank.

Note: Heading colors: blue = excludes taxes and subsidies, green = includes taxes and subsidies. Data in this table represent the "business as usual" (BAU) scenario minus the 30×30 scenario (averages for fleet additions). The BAU scenario assumes that no policy target will be imposed for electric vehicles and that vehicle purchase decisions will continue to reflect historical trends. The 30×30 scenario assumes that sales of electric cars and buses will reach 30 percent, and of two- and three-wheelers, 70 percent, by 2030. Red and parentheses indicate negative value. EV = electric vehicle; — = not available.

TABLE 2.5 Model assumptions on electric vehicle charging infrastructure

Mode	Charger type	Unit cost (US$)	Density (chargers per 1,000 vehicles)
Car	Private chargers	875	1,000
	Workplace chargers	1,051	325
	Public slow chargers	9,713	100
	Public fast chargers	29,140	11
Bus	Workplace chargers	30,000	500
	Public fast chargers	50,000	250
3W	Public chargers	37	166
2W	Household outlets	0	n.a.

Source: World Bank.

Note: 2W = two-wheeler; 3W = three-wheeler; n.a. = not applicable.

TABLE 2.6 Charging infrastructure cost advantage, 2030

	US$/Mpaxvkm			
	4W private charging (a)	4W and 3W public charging (b)	Bus public charging (c)	Cost advantage (d = a + b + c)
Country				
Brazil	(1,367)	(4,051)	(693)	(6,111)
Cambodia	(316)	(911)	(1,482)	(2,709)
Egypt, Arab Rep.	(752)	(2,207)	(1,148)	(4,107)
Ethiopia	(36)	(108)	(1,368)	(1,512)
Ghana	(234)	(682)	(2,101)	(3,017)
India	(582)	(1,717)	(724)	(3,024)
Jamaica	(1,826)	(5,349)	(13)	(7,188)
Jordan	(1,436)	(4,242)	(480)	(6,158)
Kazakhstan	(1,587)	(4,705)	(900)	(7,192)
Maldives	(77)	(222)	(164)	(463)
Nepal	(182)	(529)	(3,541)	(4,252)
Nigeria	(311)	(885)	(3,134)	(4,330)
Poland	(3,338)	(9,871)	(563)	(13,772)
Rwanda	(185)	(524)	(2,054)	(2,762)
Tajikistan	(892)	(2,500)	(139)	(3,530)
Türkiye	(1,568)	(4,700)	(2,930)	(9,198)
Ukraine	(1,104)	(3,176)	(1,457)	(5,737)
Uruguay	(1,445)	(4,335)	(562)	(6,341)
Vanuatu	(274)	(789)	(5,566)	(6,629)
Vietnam	(265)	(784)	(705)	(1,754)
Typology				
Car dominant	(1,640)	(4,860)	(1,141)	(7,641)
Mixed fleet	(543)	(1,599)	(865)	(3,007)
Net oil exporter	(1,176)	(3,480)	(1,093)	(5,750)
Net oil importer	(683)	(2,016)	(889)	(3,589)
High-cost vehicles	(898)	(2,667)	(1,286)	(4,852)
Low-cost vehicles	(698)	(2,057)	(784)	(3,540)

Source: World Bank.
Note: Heading color: blue = excluding taxes and subsidies. Data in this table represent the "business as usual" (BAU) scenario minus the 30×30 scenario (averages for fleet additions). The BAU scenario assumes that no policy target will be imposed for electric vehicles and that vehicle purchase decisions will continue to reflect historical trends. The 30×30 scenario assumes that sales of electric cars and buses will reach 30 percent, and of two- and three-wheelers, 70 percent, by 2030. Red and parentheses indicate negative values. 3W = three-wheeler; 4W = four-wheeler; US$/Mpaxvkm = US dollars per million passenger vehicle-kilometers.

Finally, EV adoption also calls for significant investments in power infrastructure, in both the generation and the distribution tiers (as described in chapter 4). However, because the overall increment in electricity demand associated with the 30×30 scenario is marginal, well under 1 percent of total electricity consumption in the countries studied, it is assumed that these costs are fully captured through power purchases for EVs. These costs will be clarified in the discussion of investment needs.

Comparing Externality Costs

Transportation gives rise to carbon emissions as well as local air pollutants—including nitrogen oxides (NO_x), sulfur oxides (SO_x), and particulate matter (PM). In fact carbon emissions and local air pollutants are highly correlated whether transportation is powered by liquid fuels or electricity. Whether a switch to EVs presents an environmental advantage depends on two factors: the relative pollution intensity of the two sources of energy and the relative energy efficiency of the two types of vehicles (figure 2.8). A related factor is exposure, which depends on the proximity of the polluting source to vulnerable human subjects.

The pollution intensity of electricity generation varies widely across countries. In the case of local pollutants, such as PM, gasoline emits far more pollution per unit of energy produced (0.15 to 0.25 grams PM_{10} [PM less than 10 microns in diameter] per megajoule) than any of the electricity systems (no more than 0.05 grams PM_{10} per megajoule), even for power systems still heavily based on fossil fuels (figure 2.8a). Thus, electricity is unambiguously preferable to liquid fuels in terms of local pollution. When the energy efficiency advantage is additionally taken into account and the PM intensity expressed relative to units of travel, electricity becomes cleaner than gasoline by an order of magnitude (figure 2.8b). For details, see equation (2.3), where Δ

FIGURE 2.8 PM_{10} intensity of vehicle fuels in units of energy and travel, 2020

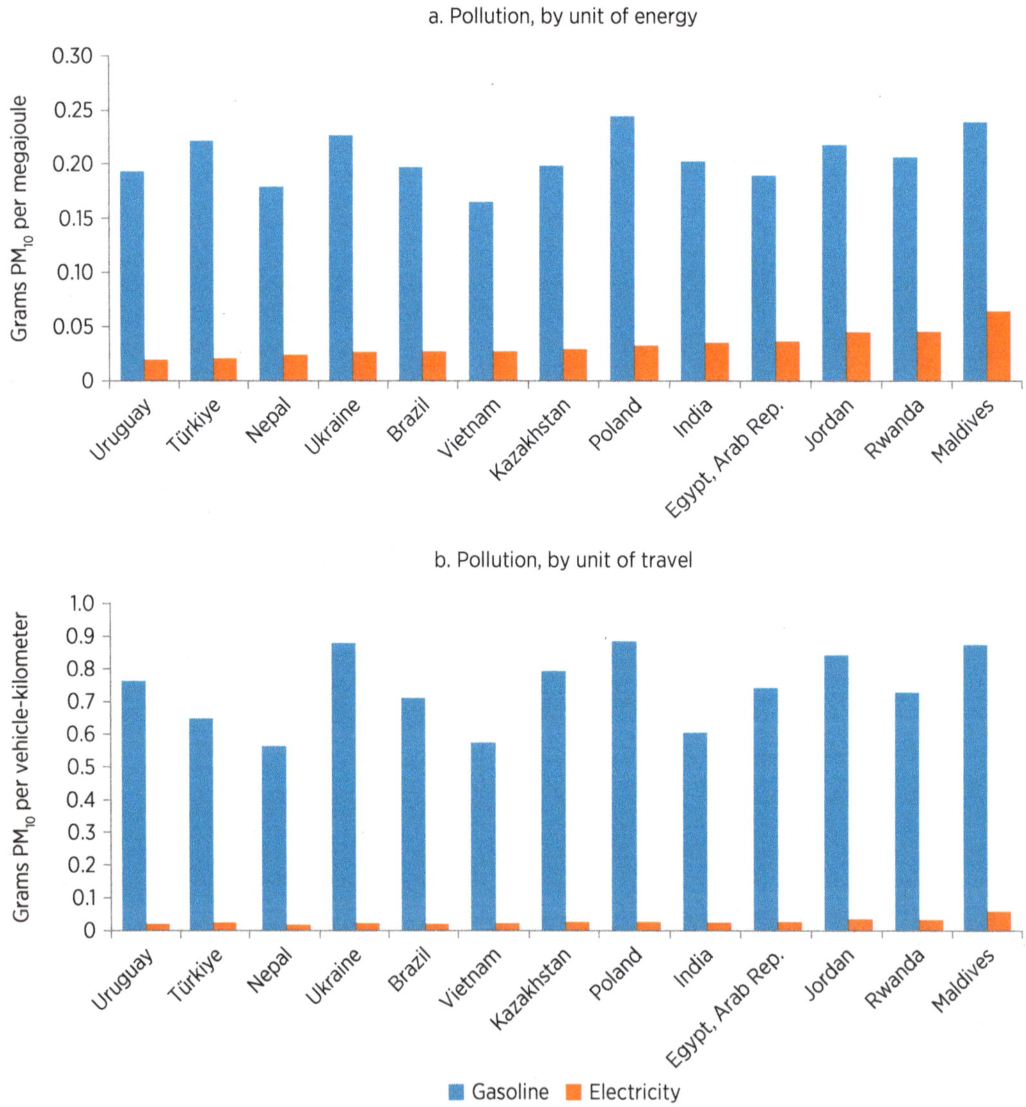

Source: World Bank.
Note: PM_{10} = particulate matter less than 10 microns in diameter.

denotes the difference between variables under the 30×30 scenario versus *BAU*, *CIT* denotes the carbon intensity of transportation (CO_2 [carbon dioxide] per vehicle-kilometer), *CIE* denotes the carbon intensity of energy (CO_2 per joule), and *EFF* denotes the energy efficiency coefficient (joules per vehicle-kilometer).

$$\Delta CIT = \Delta CIE \times \Delta EFF \tag{2.3}$$

In the case of carbon emissions, however, the relative carbon intensity of energy from gasoline versus electricity varies hugely depending on the composition of the generation mix (figure 2.9). At one end of the spectrum, hydro-reliant countries, such as Ethiopia, Nepal, and Uruguay, produce negligible externalities from power generation. At the other end, small

FIGURE 2.9 Carbon intensity of vehicle fuels in units of energy and travel, 2020

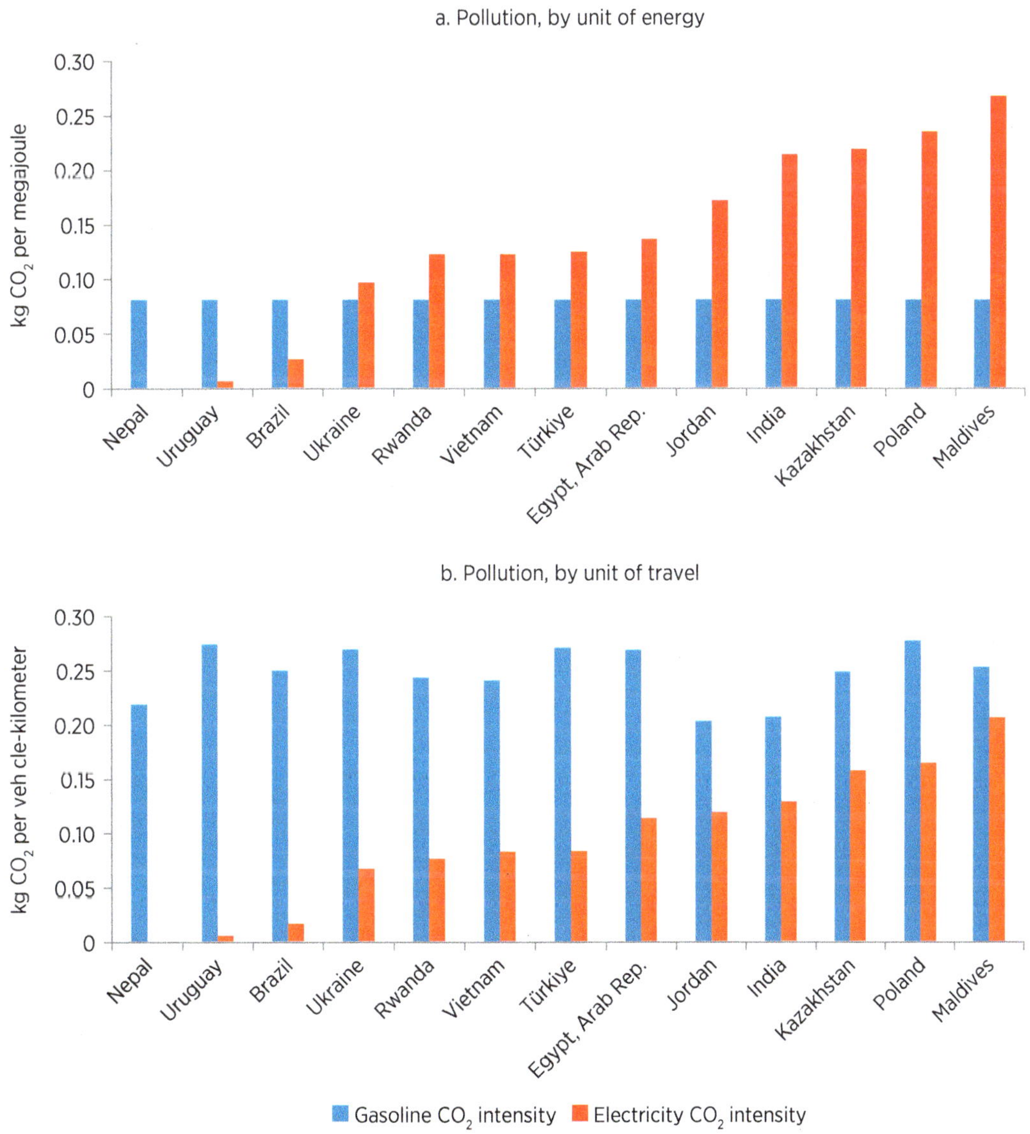

Source: World Bank.
Note: CO_2 = carbon dioxide; kg = kilogram.

islands that depend on oil (such as Maldives and Vanuatu) together with larger countries that depend on coal (such as India and Poland) produce substantial externalities from power generation. Thus, the carbon intensity of gasoline-based ICEs tends to lie at about 0.08 kilogram CO_2 per megajoule, whereas the carbon intensity of electricity varies from close to zero all the way up to about 0.25 kilogram CO_2 per megajoule (figure 2.9). One way of thinking about it is that the carbon intensity of liquid transportation fuels is broadly equivalent to the carbon intensity of a power grid that relies heavily on natural gas, such as those of Ghana or Nigeria.

However, as noted (see figure 2.7), BEVs are several times more energy efficient than ICEVs. When this additional energy efficiency is taken into account by normalizing carbon emissions against vehicle-kilometers of transportation services provided (figure 2.9b), electricity turns out to be a less carbon intensive fuel than gasoline for every country in the sample, *including those that continue to rely heavily on fossil fuels for power generation* (such as Kazakhstan, Maldives, and Poland). Moreover, this carbon footprint will fall over time as the electricity sector further decarbonizes.

The energy efficiency effect overwhelms the carbon intensity effect in the countries studied so that, even in the 30×30 scenario, *increasing electrification of the vehicle fleet brings both local and global environmental benefits irrespective of how carbon intensive a country's current power generation mix is* (table 2.7). In most countries, the value of externality costs saved as a result of the transition to electric mobility is on the order of US$5,000 per million passenger vehicle-kilometers. However, in a few cases, those savings can be much higher. Countries such as the Arab Republic of Egypt and Türkiye report higher externality cost savings, on the order of between US$10,000 and US$20,000, due to relatively high damage coefficients for pollutants and/or high bus mileage. In both countries, savings in local pollutant emissions are particularly high and account for the bulk of the externality benefits. Breaking down the externalities by vehicle type (table 2.8) illustrates how large the externality advantages associated with electric buses are for countries such as Egypt, Kazakhstan, and Maldives.

For many countries, the reduced externalities associated with local pollutants are significant, and in a handful—Egypt, Kazakhstan, Maldives, Poland, and Türkiye—they overwhelm the benefits from the reduced externalities associated with carbon emissions (figure 2.10). They do so because, in countries with severe urban air quality problems and high damage factors, electrifying the vehicle fleet brings substantial benefits in terms of local air pollution, resulting primarily from reductions in PM_{10}.

Aggregating across Cost Categories

The discussion has examined the relative costs of the 30×30 scenario for EV adoption by component. The results indicate that the 30×30 scenario entails a significant premium in vehicle capital costs and charging infrastructure, but that maintenance costs, energy costs, and environmental externalities are invariably lower. The remaining question is whether the substantial operating advantages of EVs outweigh the significant capital cost premium.

Table 2.9 considers this question at the national scale, allowing the economic cost differentials to accumulate step by step. When only capital cost differentials are considered, the 30×30 scenario is generally unattractive. Comparing the relative magnitude of the cost differentials for charging infrastructure and vehicle purchase suggests that the latter typically accounts for about 80 percent of the additional investment entailed by the electric mobility scenario. However, as soon as the lifetime advantage in operating costs is added to the capital costs (see the "Subtotal" column), the balance shifts to being at least slightly advantageous to EVs in 7 of the 20 countries considered—Cambodia, Ethiopia, Ghana, India, Nigeria, Tajikistan, and

TABLE 2.7 Environmental advantage of electric vehicles, 2030

	US$/Mpaxvkm			% of BAU values	Thousand tons of CO_2 equivalent		
	Local externalities (a)	Global externalities (b)	Economic cost advantage (c = a + b)	Economic cost advantage	Local externalities (a)	Global externalities (b)	Total externalities savings (c = a + b)
Country							
Brazil	1,143	3,553	4,697	24	72	20,179	20,251
Cambodia	189	2,415	2,604	18	0	27	28
Egypt, Arab Rep.	16,640	2,378	19,019	24	48	4,516	4,565
Ethiopia	7	1,323	1,330	7	0	134	135
Ghana	398	2,096	2;494	13	1	226	227
India	1,666	1,549	3,215	23	3	7,588	7,591
Jamaica	444	2,339	2,782	16	2	470	472
Jordan	1,193	813	2,006	9	2	97	100
Kazakhstan	6,459	1,017	7,476	12	1	398	399
Maldives	4,702	928	5,630	18	0	2	2
Nepal	456	4,253	4,709	31	0	158	158
Nigeria	240	1,695	1,935	12	5	972	977
Poland	2,408	652	3,060	8	0	1,233	1,233
Rwanda	225	1,535	1,760	9	0	15	15
Tajikistan	192	1,542	1,733	10	0	81	82
Türkiye	9,551	754	10,304	16	2	381	383
Ukraine	2,862	2,119	4,981	13	4	1,322	1,326
Uruguay	687	4,300	4,987	30	2	699	702
Vanuatu	210	2,036	2,247	11	0	1	1
Vietnam	4,195	3,916	8,110	34	4	1,037	1,041
Typology							
Car dominant	3,163	2,429	5,591	17	3,163	2,429	5,591
Mixed fleet	2,854	1,843	4,696	23	2,854	1,843	4,696
Net oil exporter	1,247	3,107	4,354	21	1,247	3,107	4,354
Net oil importer	3,180	1,769	4,949	22	3,180	1,769	4,949
High-cost vehicles	2,836	2,935	5,771	22	2,836	2,935	5,771
Low-cost vehicles	2,940	1,599	4,539	22	2,940	1,599	4,539

Source: World Bank.
Note: Heading color: blue = excluding taxes and subsidies. Data in this table represent the "business as usual" (BAU) scenario minus the 30×30 scenario (averages for fleet additions). The BAU scenario assumes that no policy target will be imposed for electric vehicles and that vehicle purchase decisions will continue to reflect historical trends. The 30×30 scenario assumes that sales of electric cars and buses will reach 30 percent, and of two- and three-wheelers, 70 percent, by 2030. "Local externalities" comprises local (NO_x, PM_{10}, SO_x) air pollution costs. "Global externalities" comprises global (CO_2) air pollution costs. CO_2 = carbon dioxide; NO_x = nitrogen oxides; PM_{10} = particulate matter less than 10 microns in diameter; SO_x = sulfur oxides.

Vietnam. In terms of the country typology, the balance becomes favorable for countries with mixed vehicle fleets, net oil importing status, or relatively low vehicle costs.

The balance only swings further in the direction of electric mobility when externality costs are further considered (see the column "Cost advantage (economic analysis)" in table 2.9), with 10 of the 20 countries now better off after adopting electric mobility. Thus, *the inclusion of externality costs changes the direction of the overall policy conclusion on electric mobility* in several cases—notably, Egypt, Kazakhstan, and Vanuatu.

Although the central focus of this report is on economic results, financial results, which portray the extent to which the switch to electric mobility is in the monetary interest of those

TABLE 2.8 Environmental advantage of electric vehicles, by vehicle type, 2030

US$/vehicle

	Electric buses			Two-wheel EVs			Four-wheel EVs		
	Local externalities (a)	Global externalities (b)	Total externalities (c = a + b)	Local externalities (a)	Global externalities (b)	Total externalities (c = a + b)	Local externalities (a)	Global externalities (b)	Total externalities (c = a + b)
Country									
Brazil	2,966	7,827	10,792	49	85	134	46	203	249
Cambodia	309	2,597	2,907	3	42	44	4	74	78
Egypt, Arab Rep.	33,680	4,470	38,150	170	33	203	1,255	161	1,416
Ethiopia	8	1,320	1,327	0	23	23	0	64	64
Ghana	568	2,681	3,249	7	49	56	8	72	80
India	3,094	1,310	4,405	54	53	108	17	33	50
Jamaica	998	3526	4,524	25	66	91	29	163	192
Jordan	1,836	1,177	3,013	41	39	80	55	33	89
Kazakhstan	14,662	1,458	16,120	152	46	198	230	55	284
Maldives	27,502	909	28,411	102	24	127	54	29	83
Nepal	637	3,848	4,486	3	59	61	1	170	171
Nigeria	126	764	890	5	42	47	20	178	198
Poland	5,156	500	5,656	34	9	43	63	20	84
Rwanda	259	1,531	1,790	3	30	33	4	55	59
Tajikistan	2,206	1,987	4,193	n.a.	n.a.	n.a.	3	92	95
Türkiye	10,536	1,090	11,625	132	26	158	360	11	370
Ukraine	8,363	2,882	11,245	25	56	80	11	100	111
Uruguay	859	5,096	5,954	30	88	118	6	214	220
Vanuatu	228	2,084	2,312	6	48	53	0	63	64
Vietnam	5,257	4,457	9,714	80	76	156	110	93	204
Typology									
Car dominant	7,661	3,429	11,090	87	48	136	104	108	213
Mixed fleet	4,562	1,784	6,347	47	47	94	142	54	196
Net oil exporter	1,717	3,228	4,945	26	56	82	55	189	244
Net oil importer	6,159	1,825	7,985	63	45	108	146	45	191
High-cost vehicles	3,167	2,521	5,688	43	44	88	115	147	263
Low-cost vehicles	6,927	1,793	8,720	65	50	115	131	45	175

Source: World Bank.

Note: Heading color: blue = excludes taxes and subsidies. Data in this table represent the "business as usual" (BAU) scenario minus the 30×30 scenario (averages for fleet additions). The BAU scenario assumes that no policy target will be imposed for electric vehicles and that vehicle purchase decisions will continue to reflect historical trends. The 30×30 scenario assumes that sales of electric cars and buses will reach 30 percent, and of two- and three-wheelers, 70 percent, by 2030. "Local externalities" comprises local (NO_x, PM_{10}, SO_x) air pollution costs. "Global externalities" comprises global (CO_2) air pollution costs. CO_2 = carbon dioxide; NO_x = nitrogen oxides; PM_{10} = particulate matter less than 10 microns in diameter; SO_x = sulfur oxides.

FIGURE 2.10 **Environmental benefits of switching to electric mobility**

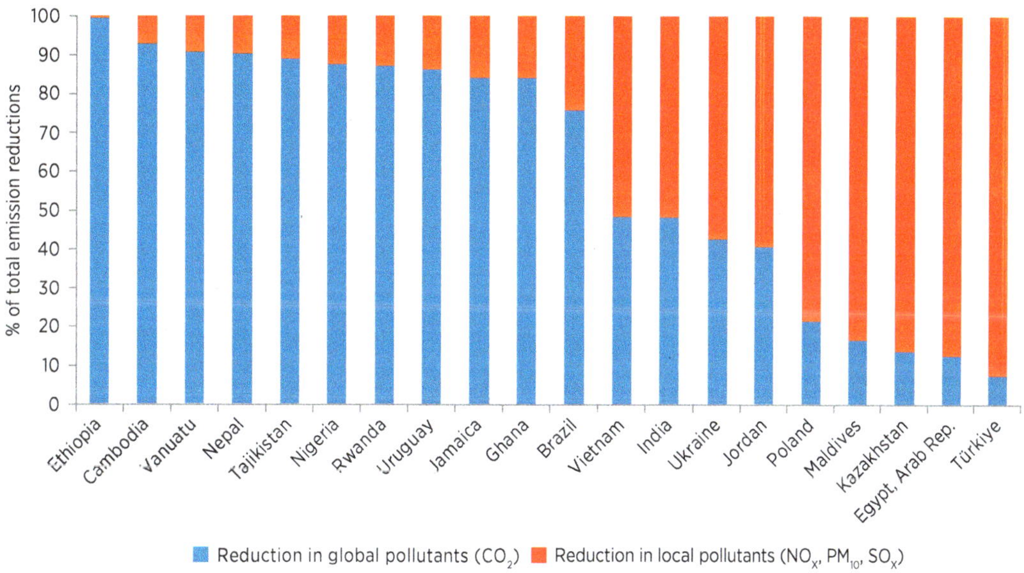

Source: World Bank.
Note: CO_2 = carbon dioxide; NO_x = nitrogen oxides; PM_{10} = particulate matter less than 10 microns in diameter; SO_x = sulfur oxides.

concerned, are also important. As noted, two factors drive the difference between the economic and financial results. The first is the exclusion of the externalities, which invariably makes electric mobility less desirable than when externalities are accounted for. The second is the reincorporation of taxes and subsidies, which more often than not makes electric mobility more attractive than in the economic analysis because of distortions in the fiscal regime in many countries that work in its favor.

In an ideal world, the fiscal policy toward transportation and energy would be aligned with the externality costs of transportation and energy decisions. In such a world, the magnitude of the fiscal wedge would be broadly consistent with the externality cost differential, obliging economic actors to pay financially for the environmental impacts of their actions. Overall, 17 of the 20 countries studied have fiscal wedges that favor the adoption of electric mobility, through favorable tax or subsidy differentials on vehicle purchase or energy purchase. In 16 of these cases, the fiscal advantage is larger than what is warranted by the externality costs, resulting in excessive incentives for adoption, as illustrated by the countries above the 45-degree line shown in figure 2.11.

The overall effect is that the number of countries for which the 30×30 scenario is financially advantageous as opposed to economically advantageous rises from 10 of 20 to 15 of 20. Relative to the results of the economic analysis, the fiscal wedge reverts the negative economic conclusion to a positive financial one in six countries—Brazil, Jordan, Maldives, Poland, Ukraine, and Uruguay. All have relatively large net subsidies in favor of adoption. However, in one country—Nigeria, where EVs are fiscally penalized—the fiscal wedge reverses a positive economic conclusion into a negative financial one.

Table 2.10 presents the same detailed set of results but disaggregated to display only the results for electric buses—a vehicle category of particular public policy interest. The results indicate that charging infrastructure investments for electric buses are about US$5,000 per vehicle.

TABLE 2.9 Aggregate cost advantage of electric vehicles, 2030

	US$/Mpaxvkm								% of BAU values	
	Charging infrastructure (a)	Vehicle capital cost (b)	Vehicle operating cost (c)	Subtotal (d = a + b + c)	Externality (e)	Economic cost advantage (f = d + e)	Net taxes and subsidies (g)	Financial cost advantage (h = d + g)	Economic cost advantage	Financial cost advantage
Country										
Brazil	(6,111)	(21,880)	10,855	(17,137)	4,697	(12,441)	35,543	18,406	(2.8)	2.9
Cambodia	(2,709)	(12,724)	19,254	3,822	2,604	6,426	16,708	20,530	2.5	6.2
Egypt, Arab Rep.	(4,107)	(13,010)	15,300	(1,817)	19,019	17,201	10,165	8,347	4.8	2.6
Ethiopia	(1,512)	(4,692)	6,920	715	1,330	2,045	11,359	12,074	0.8	4.6
Ghana	(3,017)	(6,241)	10,846	1,587	2,494	4,081	9,346	10,933	1.5	3.4
India	(3,024)	(12,207)	23,217	7,986	3,215	11,201	43,109	51,095	5.0	17.4
Jamaica	(7,188)	(27,919)	10,378	(24,729)	2,782	(21,947)	16,993	(7,736)	(4.2)	(1.0)
Jordan	(6,158)	(41,124)	12,543	(34,739)	2,006	(32,733)	59,233	24,494	(6.6)	3.3
Kazakhstan	(7,192)	(8,347)	8,283	(7,257)	7,476	219	12,773	5,516	0.1	1.5
Maldives	(463)	(9,370)	(11,290)	(21,123)	5,630	(15,492)	27,540	6,417	(9.8)	3.9
Nepal	(4,252)	(39,111)	32,720	(10,644)	4,709	(5,935)	(13,928)	(24,572)	(2.5)	(6.0)
Nigeria	(4,330)	(6,511)	10,850	9	1,935	1,944	(1,112)	(1,103)	0.7	(0.4)
Poland	(13,772)	(26,712)	14,838	(25,646)	3,060	(22,586)	80,405	54,759	(2.8)	5.3
Rwanda	(2,762)	(5,112)	6,356	(1,518)	1,760	243	25,110	23,592	0.1	6.5
Tajikistan	(3,530)	1,351	8,437	6,258	1,733	7,991	11,174	17,431	2.8	5.5
Türkiye	(9,198)	(31,494)	16,523	(24,169)	10,304	(13,865)	23,127	(1,042)	(2.6)	(0.1)
Ukraine	(5,737)	(11,376)	10,636	(6,478)	4,981	(1,497)	39,734	33,256	(0.3)	6.5
Uruguay	(6,341)	(37,121)	29,216	(14,247)	4,987	(9,260)	74,957	60,710	(1.8)	7.4
Vanuatu	(6,629)	(3,915)	7,221	(3,322)	2,247	(1,076)	(40,029)	(43,352)	(0.2)	(8.6)
Vietnam	(1,754)	(22,595)	31,078	6,728	8,110	14,839	26,451	33,179	6.1	10.7
Typology										
Car dominant	(7,641)	(23,287)	12,297	(18,632)	5,591	(13,040)	38,198	19,566	(2.6)	2.9
Mixed fleet	(3,007)	(13,055)	22,494	6,433	4,696	11,129	36,705	43,138	4.6	14.4
Net oil exporter	(5,750)	(18,329)	10,726	(13,352)	4,354	(8,998)	28,242	14,891	(2.2)	2.7
Net oil importer	(3,589)	(14,465)	22,137	4,083	4,949	9,032	38,397	42,480	3.3	12.4
High-cost vehicles	(4,852)	(21,642)	17,145	(9,348)	5,771	(3,577)	26,252	16,904	(1.0)	3.4
Low-cost vehicles	(3,540)	(12,597)	21,789	5,652	4,539	10,191	40,875	46,527	3.9	14.3

Source: World Bank.

Note: Heading colors: blue = excluding taxes and subsidies, gray = fiscal wedge, green = including taxes and subsidies. Data in this table represent the "business as usual" (BAU) scenario minus the 30×30 scenario (averages for fleet additions). The BAU scenario assumes that no policy target will be imposed for electric vehicles and that vehicle purchase decisions will continue to reflect historical trends. The 30×30 scenario assumes that sales of electric cars and buses will reach 30 percent, and of two- and three-wheelers, 70 percent, by 2030. "Externality" comprises the combination of global (CO_2) and local (NO_x, PM_{10}, SO_x) air pollution costs. Red and parentheses indicate negative values. CO_2 = carbon dioxide; NO_x = nitrogen oxides; PM_{10} = particulate matter less than 10 microns in diameter; SO_x = sulfur oxides; US$/Mpaxvkm = US dollars per million passenger vehicle-kilometers.

FIGURE 2.11 Relative value of the fiscal wedge and the externality cost advantage of the 30×30 scenario

Thousand US$ per Mpaxvkm

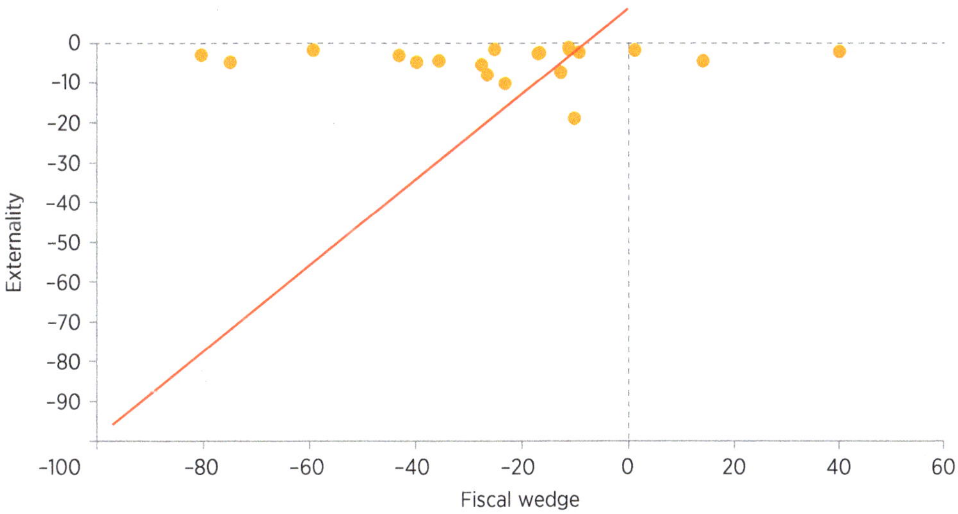

Source: World Bank.

Note: Data in this figure represent the "business as usual" (BAU) scenario minus the 30×30 scenario (averages for fleet additions). The BAU scenario assumes that no policy target will be imposed for electric vehicles and that vehicle purchase decisions will continue to reflect historical trends. The 30×30 scenario assumes that sales of electric cars and buses will reach 30 percent, and of two- and three-wheelers, 70 percent, by 2030. "Externality" comprises the combination of global (CO_2) and local (NO_x, PM_{10}, SO_x) air pollution costs. "Fiscal wedge" comprises taxes and subsidies. CO_2 = carbon dioxide; Mpaxvkm = million passenger vehicle-kilometers; NO_x = nitrogen oxides; PM_{10} = particulate matter less than 10 microns in diameter; SO_x = sulfur oxides.

The incremental capital costs associated with their purchase are somewhat higher than the cost of charging infrastructure and much more variable, typically between US$6,000 and US$18,000. Only in Uruguay and Vanuatu is there a modest capital cost advantage from purchasing an electric bus. In Vanuatu, this advantage is explained by the exceptionally high cost of diesel buses.

Nevertheless, the associated operating cost savings are substantial given these buses' relatively long mileage, amounting to almost US$10,000 on average per bus over its entire life cycle. Operating cost savings are particularly high in some countries—such as Nepal and Uruguay—where they exceed US$20,000 per vehicle and are attributable to relatively large operating cost savings driven by low-cost electricity.

Considering the overall balance of these economic costs and benefits before taking externalities into account reveals that electric buses are already economically desirable in 13 of the 20 countries studied: Brazil, Cambodia, Egypt, Ethiopia, Ghana, India, Jamaica, Jordan, Nepal, Tajikistan, Uruguay, Vanuatu, and Vietnam. However, their externality benefits are large given their high mileage and major contribution to local air pollution, amounting to over US$10,000 over their life cycle. After accounting for these externalities, the number of countries where electric buses are economically desirable rises from 13 to 16 of the 20 studied. Specifically, the inclusion of externalities tips the balance in their favor in Kazakhstan, Türkiye, and Ukraine. Nevertheless, the cost advantage is no more than 10 percent of the BAU.

Finally, as noted, many countries operate a fiscal regime that further favors electric mobility in financial terms. When it comes to electric buses, switching from an economic to a financial lens, Maldives, Poland, and Rwanda also become favorable. However, the composition of the country list has changed somewhat. In the case of Kazakhstan and Vanuatu, the fiscal regime

TABLE 2.10 Aggregate cost advantage for electric buses, 2030

	US$/vehicle								% of BAU values	
	Charging infrastructure (a)	Vehicle capital cost (b)	Vehicle operating cost (c)	Subtotal (d = a + b + c)	Externality (e)	Economic cost advantage (f = d + e)	Net taxes and subsidies (g)	Financial cost advantage (h = d + g)	Economic cost advantage	Financial cost advantage
Country										
Brazil	(6,102)	(6,136)	15,207	2,969	10,792	13,762	28,373	31,342	3.5	6.1
Cambodia	(5,180)	(9,621)	20,299	5,497	2,907	8,404	13,770	19,267	2.6	5.0
Egypt, Arab Rep.	(6,036)	(12,107)	27,579	9,437	38,150	47,587	8,806	18,243	10.0	5.5
Ethiopia	(1,545)	(3,375)	6,809	1,890	1,327	3,217	10,787	12,676	1.3	5.0
Ghana	(3,675)	(7,738)	13,212	1,800	3,249	5,048	11,965	13,765	1.8	4.1
India	(6,104)	(14,027)	27,370	7,239	4,405	11,644	29,988	37,227	3.6	9.7
Jamaica	(5,759)	(5,219)	15,966	4,989	4,524	9,513	21,756	26,745	2.8	6.0
Jordan	(3,653)	(9,111)	14,088	1,324	3,013	4,336	9,086	10,409	1.5	3.2
Kazakhstan	(3,516)	(11,639)	6,043	(9,112)	16,120	7,008	8,952	(160)	2.2	(0.1)
Maldives	(2,871)	(5,501)	(29,435)	(37,807)	28,411	(9,397)	39,411	1,604	(1.8)	0.5
Nepal	(6,102)	(18,705)	29,789	4,981	4,486	9,467	681	5,663	3.6	1.4
Nigeria	(2,668)	(6,418)	5,222	(3,863)	890	(2,973)	(938)	(4,801)	(2.2)	(3.5)
Poland	(5,911)	(12,412)	11,529	(6,794)	5,656	(1,138)	15,011	8,217	(0.5)	3.3
Rwanda	(3,054)	(7,116)	5,825	(4,346)	1,790	(2,556)	24,523	20,178	(1.0)	5.5
Tajikistan	(2,098)	(6,226)	10,114	1,790	4,193	5,983	11,437	13,227	2.2	5.1
Türkiye	(6,088)	(12,982)	17,814	(1,256)	11,625	10,370	13,684	12,428	3.9	4.1
Ukraine	(4,525)	(10,558)	14,748	(334)	11,245	10,911	37,988	37,653	3.1	10.4
Uruguay	(6,013)	249	27,870	22,106	5,954	28,060	11,764	33,869	7.7	6.8
Vanuatu	(6,082)	996	7,367	2,281	2,312	4,594	(46,122)	(43,840)	1.2	(10.4)
Vietnam	(6,102)	(14,234)	34,576	14,239	9,714	23,953	13,784	28,023	5.7	6.2
Typology										
Car dominant	(5,759)	(10,383)	15,675	(467)	11,090	10,623	20,949	20,482	3.4	5.6
Mixed fleet	(4,876)	(11,162)	21,224	5,186	6,347	11,533	18,822	24,008	3.8	7.3
Net oil exporter	(3,898)	(6,736)	9,378	(1,256)	4,945	3,688	10,240	8,983	1.5	3.2
Net oil importer	(5,377)	(12,164)	22,990	5,449	7,985	13,434	21,728	27,178	4.2	7.7
High-cost vehicles	(4,121)	(8,325)	13,776	1,329	5,688	7,017	10,936	12,266	2.7	4.1
Low-cost vehicles	(5,852)	(13,255)	25,380	6,273	8,720	14,992	26,288	32,561	4.4	8.9

Source: World Bank.

Note: Heading colors: blue = excluding taxes and subsidies, gray = fiscal wedge, green = including taxes and subsidies. Data in this table represent the "business as usual" (BAU) scenario minus the 30×30 scenario (averages for fleet additions). The BAU scenario assumes that no policy target will be imposed for electric vehicles and that vehicle purchase decisions will continue to reflect historical trends. The 30×30 scenario assumes that sales of electric cars and buses will reach 30 percent, and of two- and three-wheelers, 70 percent, by 2030. "Externality" comprises the combination of global (CO_2) and local (NO_x, PM_{10}, SO_x) air pollution costs. Red and parentheses indicate negative values. CO_2 = carbon dioxide; NO_x = nitrogen oxides; PM_{10} = particulate matter less than 10 microns in diameter; SO_x = sulfur oxides.

is stacked against electric buses, flipping a positive economic evaluation to a negative financial one. Overall, the financial results for electric buses tend to be more favorable in countries with lower dominance of private cars, those that import oil, and those that have access to relatively low-cost vehicles.

Table 2.11 repeats these detailed results for two-wheel EVs only. The economic conclusions are particularly favorable for this vehicle category. Even without considering externalities, two-wheel EVs are economically attractive in 14 of the 19 countries for which data are available. Considering externalities increases the number of countries with favorable results to 15 out of 19. Moreover, once the fiscal wedge is included, electric two-wheelers turn out to be financially advantageous in 18 of the 19 countries. Moreover, the percentage of cost advantages for electric two-wheelers is especially large. In economic terms, electric two-wheelers have a 10 to 15 percent cost advantage over their conventional counterparts; in financial terms, this advantage further rises to 20 to 30 percent.

Finally, table 2.12 presents detailed results for electric four-wheelers only, the most challenging economic case for electric mobility. Excluding externalities, only three countries (Nigeria, Rwanda, and Tajikistan) have operating cost savings that outweigh the higher capital costs. When externalities are considered, an additional country—Egypt—achieves a favorable economic balance. However, fiscal advantages of owning an electric four-wheeler are large enough to tip the financial balance in their favor in as many as 14 of the 20 countries. Countries where fiscal incentives make all the difference include Brazil, Ethiopia, Ghana, India, Jordan, Kazakhstan, Maldives, Poland, Ukraine, and Uruguay. Nevertheless, even in financial terms, the advantage of owning a four-wheeler is typically no more than 2 to 3 percent of life-cycle costs.

EXPLORING SENSITIVITY OF RESULTS

Although the results of the cost-benefit analysis presented provide an illustrative reference scenario for the acceleration of electric mobility, they are based on numerous assumptions that may not materialize. It is therefore important to undertake sensitivity analyses to examine the robustness of the results and to explore plausible alternative scenarios. This section presents sensitivity analyses against five important dimensions: the greening of the power grid, the evolving price of batteries, the management of bus fleets, targeted adoption for taxi fleets, and pursuit of greater fuel efficiency in conventional ICEVs. In what follows, the results of the corresponding green grid scenario, scarce minerals scenario, efficient bus scenario, taxi fleet scenario, and fuel efficiency scenario are compared, in turn, against the 30×30 scenario.

Green Grid Scenario

The 30×30 scenario explores the accelerated adoption of electric mobility while holding constant a country's power generation mix. In many countries, power generation remains carbon intensive, holding longer-range plans to decarbonize the system only gradually. The greener a country's power generation mix, the larger the externality benefits associated with electric mobility. This sensitivity analysis compares the 30×30 scenario results with those of a green grid scenario, in which countries achieve by 2030 certain region-specific targets for acceleration of renewable energy, based on authoritative simulations by the International Renewable Energy Agency (IRENA). Specifically, IRENA sets target renewable energy shares by 2030 of 60 percent for East Asia, 55 percent for the European Union, 85 percent for Latin America

TABLE 2.11 Aggregate cost advantage for two-wheelers, 2030

	US$/vehicle								% of BAU values	
	Charging infrastructure (a)	Vehicle capital cost (b)	Vehicle operating cost (c)	Subtotal (d = a + b + c)	Externality (e)	Economic cost advantage (f = d + e)	Net taxes and subsidies (g)	Financial cost advantage (h = d + g)	Economic cost advantage	Financial cost advantage
Country										
Brazil	0	(125)	361	236	134	370	700	936	13.9	25.6
Cambodia	0	(154)	334	180	44	224	291	471	10.5	17.3
Egypt, Arab Rep.	0	(202)	265	63	203	266	93	156	12.9	8.9
Ethiopia	0	(172)	129	(43)	23	(20)	223	180	(1.2)	9.2
Ghana	0	(71)	290	219	56	275	220	439	13.9	18.7
India	0	(199)	680	481	108	589	1,252	1,733	21.4	43.8
Jamaica	0	(305)	458	153	91	243	458	611	9.2	16.6
Jordan	0	(451)	434	(17)	80	63	1,233	1,216	2.6	28.3
Kazakhstan	0	(107)	413	306	198	504	311	618	22.6	29.6
Maldives	0	(231)	(234)	(465)	127	(338)	627	162	(14.5)	7.3
Nepal	0	(694)	449	(245)	61	(183)	(344)	(589)	(10.3)	(19.3)
Nigeria	0	(12)	254	243	47	290	(27)	216	15.0	12.3
Poland	0	(29)	82	53	43	96	263	316	3.7	11.8
Rwanda	0	(32)	148	115	33	149	425	540	8.5	20.4
Tajikistan	—	—	—	—	—	—	—	—	—	—
Türkiye	0	(368)	376	8	158	166	461	469	7.2	16.6
Ukraine	0	(128)	301	173	80	253	789	961	11.9	33.1
Uruguay	0	(404)	751	347	118	466	1,156	1,503	16.7	30.7
Vanuatu	0	(351)	283	(68)	53	(15)	469	401	(0.5)	8.3
Vietnam	0	(348)	605	258	156	413	506	764	13.3	19.7
Typology										
Car dominant	0	(161)	344	183	110	293	642	825	11.3	23.9
Mixed fleet	0	(225)	634	409	117	526	1,040	1,449	19.2	38.4
Net oil exporter	0	(114)	350	236	132	368	623	859	14.2	24.9
Net oil importer	0	(227)	631	404	108	513	1,038	1,442	18.8	38.2
High-cost vehicles	0	(314)	524	209	134	343	492	702	12.0	19.1
Low-cost vehicles	0	(198)	644	446	104	550	1,156	1,602	20.4	42.4

Source: World Bank.

Note: Heading colors: blue = excluding taxes and subsidies, gray = fiscal wedge, green = including taxes and subsidies. Data in this table represent the "business as usual" (BAU) scenario minus the 30×30 scenario (averages for fleet additions). The BAU scenario assumes that no policy target will be imposed for electric vehicles and that vehicle purchase decisions will continue to reflect historical trends. The 30×30 scenario assumes that sales of electric cars and buses will reach 30 percent, and of two- and three-wheelers, 70 percent, by 2030. "Externality" comprises the combination of global (CO_2) and local (NO_x, PM_{10}, SO_x) air pollution costs. Red and parentheses indicate negative value. CO_2 = carbon dioxide; NO_x = nitrogen oxides; PM_{10} = particulate matter less than 10 microns in diameter; SO_x = sulfur oxides; — = not available.

TABLE 2.12 Aggregate cost advantage for four-wheelers, 2030

	US$/vehicle								% of BAU values	
	Charging infrastructure (a)	Vehicle capital cost (b)	Vehicle operating cost (c)	Subtotal (d = a + b + c)	Externality (e)	Economic cost advantage (f = d + e)	Net taxes and subsidies (g)	Financial cost advantage (h = d + g)	Economic cost advantage	Financial cost advantage
Country										
Brazil	(529)	(1,983)	650	(1,862)	249	(1,612)	2,688	827	(4.3)	1.5
Cambodia	(363)	(1,397)	613	(1,147)	78	(1,069)	852	(295)	(4.1)	(0.8)
Egypt, Arab Rep.	(567)	(1,100)	880	(787)	1,416	629	1,256	469	1.5	1.1
Ethiopia	(142)	(1,173)	376	(939)	64	(875)	1,093	154	(4.3)	0.6
Ghana	(232)	(290)	413	(110)	80	(30)	332	222	(0.1)	0.8
India	(568)	(1,412)	983	(997)	50	(947)	2,731	1,733	(3.2)	4.5
Jamaica	(527)	(2,010)	700	(1,837)	192	(1,645)	1,184	(652)	(4.3)	(1.2)
Jordan	(441)	(2,895)	633	(2,703)	89	(2,615)	3,946	1,243	(7.6)	2.4
Kazakhstan	(540)	(459)	572	(427)	284	(142)	895	468	(0.5)	1.7
Maldives	(211)	(2,011)	(948)	(3,170)	83	(3,087)	3,496	326	(10.4)	0.7
Nepal	(504)	(5,593)	1,276	(4,820)	171	(4,649)	(3,063)	(7,884)	(18.5)	(13.8)
Nigeria	(342)	308	1,043	1,009	198	1,206	29	1,038	3.9	3.2
Poland	(460)	(886)	470	(876)	84	(793)	2,725	1,848	(2.9)	5.3
Rwanda	(249)	18	246	15	59	74	1,268	1,283	0.3	4.3
Tajikistan	(221)	115	505	399	95	494	677	1,077	2.8	5.5
Türkiye	(574)	(2,172)	583	(2,163)	370	(1,792)	1,338	(825)	(4.9)	(1.7)
Ukraine	(393)	(712)	491	(615)	111	(503)	2,396	1,781	(1.7)	4.9
Uruguay	(555)	(2,866)	1,250	(2,171)	220	(1,951)	5,085	2,914	(4.7)	4.4
Vanuatu	(550)	(2,473)	227	(2,796)	64	(2,733)	1,094	(1,702)	(6.1)	(2.8)
Vietnam	(569)	(3,004)	942	(2,631)	204	(2,427)	1,872	(759)	(6.7)	(1.4)
Typology										
Car dominant	(507)	(1,591)	578	(1,520)	213	(1,308)	2,397	877	(3.9)	1.9
Mixed fleet	(556)	(1,426)	964	(1,017)	196	(821)	2,466	1,448	(2.6)	3.7
Net oil exporter	(512)	(1,731)	657	(1,587)	244	(1,342)	2,384	797	(3.7)	1.6
Net oil importer	(541)	(1,430)	835	(1,136)	191	(944)	2,451	1,315	(3.0)	3.3
High-cost vehicles	(528)	(2,056)	680	(1,904)	263	(1,642)	2,238	333	(4.5)	0.6
Low-cost vehicles	(537)	(1,232)	849	(920)	175	(745)	2,530	1,610	(2.5)	4.3

Source: World Bank.

Note: Heading colors: blue = excluding taxes and subsidies, gray = fiscal wedge, green = including taxes and subsidies. Data in this table represent the "business as usual" (BAU) scenario minus the 30×30 scenario (averages for fleet additions). The BAU scenario assumes that no policy target will be imposed for electric vehicles and that vehicle purchase decisions will continue to reflect historical trends. The 30×30 scenario assumes that sales of electric cars and buses will reach 30 percent, and of two- and three-wheelers, 70 percent, by 2030. "Externalities" comprise the combination of global (CO_2) and local (NO_x, PM_{10}, SO_x) air pollution costs. Red and parentheses indicate negative value. CO_2 = carbon dioxide; NO_x = nitrogen oxides; PM_{10} = particulate matter less than 10 microns in diameter; SO_x = sulfur oxides.

and the Caribbean, 27 percent for the Middle East and North Africa, 66 percent for Oceania, 52 percent for the rest of Asia, 42 percent for the rest of Europe, 53 percent for Southeast Asia, and 67 percent for Sub-Saharan Africa—using IRENA's regional classifications (IRENA 2020).

As anticipated, the results show that the savings in externality costs are noticeably larger under the green grid scenario than under the 30×30 scenario (table 2.13). This is true both for local and global externalities. What is most striking, however, is that the incorporation of the larger externality benefits does not fundamentally alter the overall conclusion regarding the desirability of electric mobility adoption at the country level. In general, the increase of externality benefits either reduces the magnitude of the net costs of electric mobility or increases the magnitude of the net benefits without changing the sign from net costs to net benefits. This result illustrates that many of the externality benefits of vehicle electrification were already captured by the energy efficiency savings in the 30×30 scenario, such that a relatively modest increase in renewables penetration contemplated in the green grid scenario was not enough to change the conclusions of the analysis.

It is interesting to examine how the percentage reduction in externality costs under the green grid scenario varies across countries and types of externalities (figure 2.12). Evidently, those countries whose grids are already almost entirely renewable—notably hydro-dependent Cambodia, Ethiopia, Nepal, Tajikistan, and Uruguay—offer no scope for further greening of the grid, and the

TABLE 2.13 Comparison of the 30×30 and green grid scenarios, 2030

US$/Mpaxvkm

	Local externalities		Global externalities		Total externalities		Aggregate results	
	30×30	Green grid	30×30	Green grid	30×30	Green grid	30×30	Green grid
Country								
Brazil	1,143	1,302	3,553	3,601	4,697	4,903	(12,441)	(12,234)
Cambodia	189	189	2,415	2,415	2,604	2,604	6,426	6,426
Egypt, Arab Rep.	16,640	23,228	2,378	2,593	19,019	25,821	17,201	24,004
Ethiopia	7	7	1,323	1,323	1,330	1,330	2,045	2,045
Ghana	398	445	2,096	2,302	2,494	2,746	4,081	4,334
India	1,666	2,141	1,549	2,356	3,215	4,497	11,201	12,483
Jamaica	444	605	2,339	2,801	2,782	3,406	(21,947)	(21,323)
Jordan	1,193	2,148	813	1,133	2,006	3,281	(32,733)	(31,458)
Kazakhstan	6,459	11,620	1,017	1,568	7,476	13,189	219	5,932
Maldives	4,702	5,722	928	1,253	5,630	6,975	(15,492)	(14,148)
Nepal	456	456	4,253	4,253	4,709	4,709	(5,935)	(5,935)
Nigeria	240	261	1,695	1,874	1,935	2,136	1,944	2,145
Poland	2,408	5,832	652	1,024	3,060	6,856	(22,586)	(18,790)
Rwanda	225	411	1,535	1,886	1,760	2,297	243	779
Tajikistan	192	192	1,542	1,542	1,733	1,733	7,991	7,991
Türkiye	9,551	14,662	754	1,041	10,304	15,704	(13,865)	(8,465)
Ukraine	2,862	3,033	2,119	2,318	4,981	5,351	(1,497)	(1,127)
Uruguay	687	687	4,300	4,300	4,987	4,987	(9,260)	(9,260)
Vanuatu	210	236	2,036	3,274	2,247	3,510	(1,076)	187
Vietnam	4,195	5,602	3,916	4,604	8,110	10,206	14,839	16,935

Source: World Bank.

Note: Data in this table represent the "business as usual" (BAU) scenario minus the 30×30 and green grid scenarios (averages for fleet additions). The 30×30 scenario assumes that sales of electric cars and buses will reach 30 percent, and of two- and three-wheelers, 70 percent, by 2030. The green grid scenario assumes that countries achieve certain region-specific targets for acceleration of renewable energy, as defined by the International Renewable Energy Agency (IRENA 2020). "Local externalities" comprises local (NO_x, PM_{10}, SO_x) air pollution costs. "Global externalities" comprises global (CO_2) air pollution costs. Red and parentheses indicate negative values. CO_2 = carbon dioxide; NO_x = nitrogen oxides; PM_{10} = particulate matter less than 10 microns in diameter; SO_x = sulfur oxides; US$/Mpaxvkm = US dollars per million passenger vehicle-kilometers.

FIGURE 2.12 **Change in externality cost advantage under the green grid scenario**

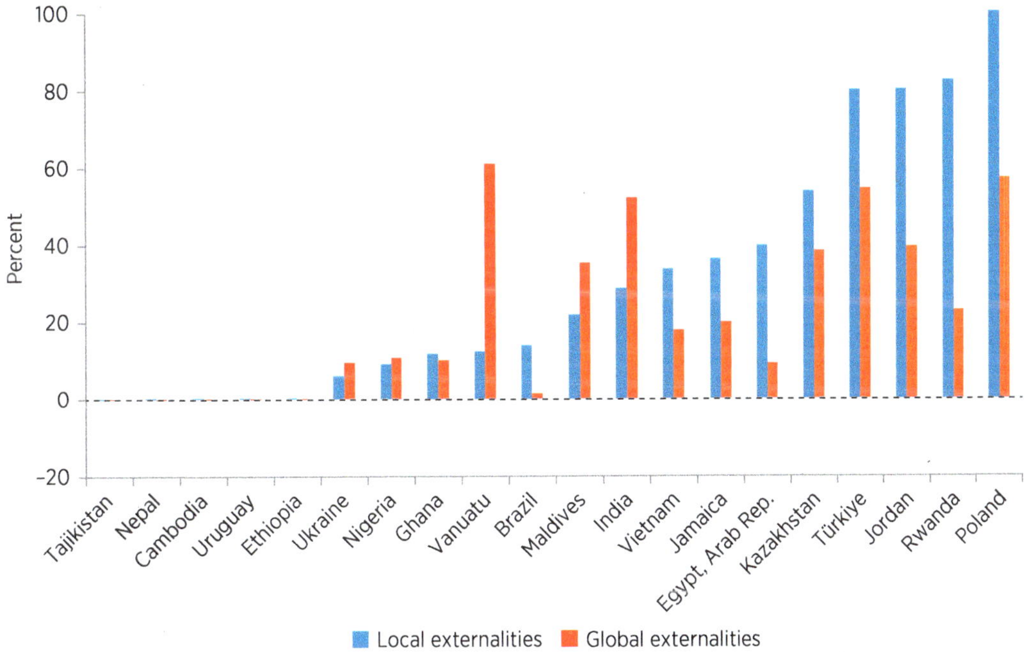

Source: World Bank.
Note: Data in this figure compare the green grid scenario with the 30×30 scenario. The 30×30 scenario assumes that sales of electric cars and buses will reach 30 percent, and of two- and three-wheelers, 70 percent, by 2030. The green grid scenario assumes that countries furthermore achieve certain region-specific targets for acceleration of renewable energy, as defined by the International Renewable Energy Agency (IRENA 2020). "Local externalities" comprises local (NO_x, PM_{10}, SO_x) air pollution costs. "Global externalities" comprises global (CO_2) air pollution costs. CO_2 = carbon dioxide; NO_x = nitrogen oxides; PM_{10} = particulate matter less than 10 microns in diameter; SO_x = sulfur oxides.

value of externalities is thus unchanged. Among countries with more carbon-intensive grids, the percentage reduction in externalities can be quite large, averaging about 30 percent overall. In the vast majority of cases, the percentage reduction in local externality costs as a result of greening the grid is substantially higher than for global externalities. Indeed, the reduction in local externalities is about 2 to 5 times as large as that for global externalities in Jordan, Maldives, and Poland, and about 8 to 10 times as large for Egypt, Türkiye, and Kazakhstan.

Scarce Minerals Scenario

An important assumption driving the results of the 30×30 scenario is the projected reduction in the cost of batteries for EVs. As a result of technological change, these costs have been falling sharply in recent years. Extrapolating on historical trends, the model predicts a comparable further reduction by 2030. About half of the cost of an EV is accounted for by the battery, the remainder by the vehicle body. Whereas the cost of vehicle bodies has remained relatively stable, the cost of batteries has been falling in response to rapid technological change. In the scenarios presented, a log-linear function was fitted to the historical cost of batteries and used to extrapolate battery cost over time. The resulting decline of approximately 7 percent annually was found to be consistent with estimates elsewhere in the literature.

However, according to Bloomberg New Energy Finance's *Battery Price Survey* 2021, it may not be possible to sustain historical cost reduction trends going forward (Frith 2021). The reason is not related so much to the pace of technological change as to the limited availability and steeply rising prices of minerals (such as lithium and cobalt) that are the critical ingredients of battery manufacture. In view of this situation, the scarce minerals scenario explores how the results of the analysis might change were battery costs to fall at only half the historically observed rate through 2030.

Evidently, slowing the pace of reduction of battery costs leads to substantially higher capital cost differentials for EVs (table 2.14). Overall, the percentage increase in vehicle capital costs associated with the more pessimistic assumptions regarding the evolution of battery costs is typically about 40 percent (figure 2.13). In Vanuatu, however, the differential becomes more than 100 percent.

Because vehicle capital costs are an important component of the overall case for EVs the overall results deteriorate under the scarce minerals scenario (table 2.14). Nevertheless, in the vast majority of cases, the higher capital costs either make an existing total cost premium larger or reduce an existing cost advantage, without reversing the overall balance of costs and benefits. Only in Kazakhstan, Nigeria, and Rwanda is the additional battery cost effect large enough to convert a positive evaluation of EVs into a negative one.

Efficient Bus Scenario

The economic analysis of electric buses is highly sensitive to good management practices in the procurement of vehicles and their subsequent operation. The 30×30 scenario draws on

TABLE 2.14 Comparison of the 30×30 and scarce minerals scenarios, 2030
US$/Mpaxvkm

	30×30	Scarce minerals	30×30	Scarce minerals
	Vehicle capital costs		Aggregate results	
Country				
Brazil	(21,880)	(31,234)	(12,441)	(22,047)
Cambodia	(12,724)	(16,860)	6,426	1,696
Egypt, Arab Rep.	(13,010)	(19,252)	17,201	10,536
Ethiopia	(4,692)	(6,170)	2,045	70
Ghana	(6,241)	(8,741)	4,081	528
India	(12,207)	(16,662)	11,201	6,483
Jamaica	(27,919)	(39,989)	(21,947)	(34,021)
Jordan	(41,124)	(51,711)	(32,733)	(43,562)
Kazakhstan	(8,347)	(13,378)	219	(5,278)
Maldives	(9,370)	(11,104)	(15,492)	(17,325)
Nepal	(39,111)	(46,449)	(5,935)	(14,560)
Nigeria	(6,511)	(8,612)	1,944	(2,139)
Poland	(26,712)	(41,506)	(22,586)	(37,589)
Rwanda	(5,112)	(6,701)	243	(2,522)
Tajikistan	1,351	818	7,991	7,366
Türkiye	(31,494)	(43,733)	(13,865)	(27,171)
Ukraine	(11,376)	(17,040)	(1,497)	(7,796)
Uruguay	(37,121)	(50,012)	(9,260)	(22,356)
Vanuatu	(3,915)	(10,604)	(1,076)	(9,792)
Vietnam	(22,595)	(28,694)	14,839	8,484

Source: World Bank.
Note: Data in this table represent the "business as usual" (BAU) scenario minus the 30×30 and scarce minerals scenarios (averages for fleet additions). The 30×30 scenario assumes that sales of electric cars and buses will reach 30 percent, and of two- and three-wheelers, 70 percent, by 2030. The scarce minerals scenario assumes that battery cost will decline by approximately 7 percent annually. Red and parentheses indicate negative value. US$/Mpaxvkm = US dollars per million passenger vehicle-kilometers.

FIGURE 2.13 Change in vehicle capital costs under the scarce minerals scenario

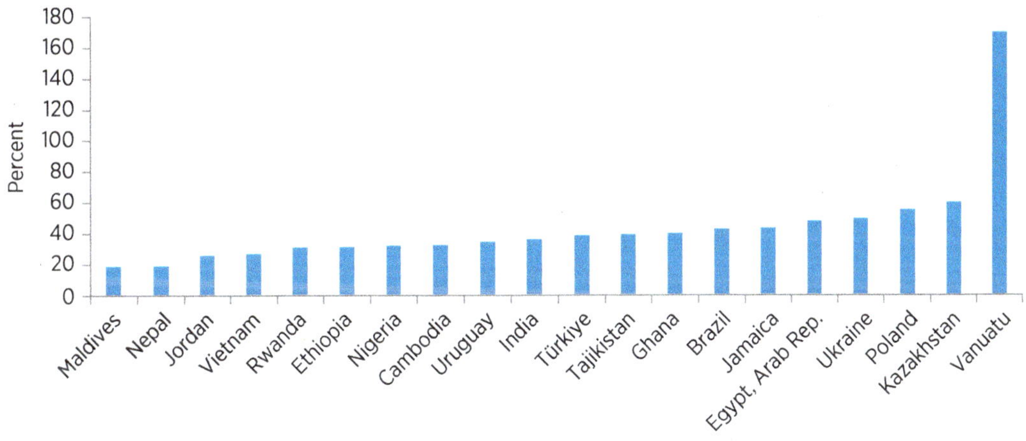

Source: World Bank.
Note: Data in this figure compare the scarce minerals scenario with the 30×30 scenario. The 30×30 scenario assumes that sales of electric cars and buses will reach 30 percent, and of two- and three-wheelers, 70 percent, by 2030. The scarce minerals scenario assumes that battery cost will decline by approximately 7 percent annually.

historical procurement data to establish the baseline capital cost of vehicles and uses historical mileage data to estimate the operating cost savings associated with electric buses. Nevertheless, some pioneering countries, notably China and India, are showing that the economics of electric buses can be significantly improved by adopting more efficient practices.

In the efficient bus scenario, municipalities collaborate at a national or regional scale to permit much larger procurement packages, realizing capital cost reductions of 35 percent in the procurement of buses, such as those recently observed in India. Further, municipalities optimize the design and operation of bus routes to allow EVs to extend their lifetime mileage to 75,000 kilometers for countries with large conurbations, 60,000 kilometers for those with midsize conurbations, and 35,000 for those with relatively small ones. Given that EVs present higher capital costs than ICEVs yet provide operational savings that accumulate with use, the case for electric mobility is clearly stronger the more passenger vehicle-kilometers a vehicle accumulates throughout its life. This is particularly true of buses; because of their public service nature and nearly continuous operation, they can achieve higher lifetime mileage than private vehicles.

The combined effect of these measures is to reduce both the capital cost and operating cost associated with electric buses (table 2.15). The magnitude of the overall savings obtained ranges from about US$4,000 over the life cycle of a vehicle in Maldives to almost US$30,000 in Nepal, but more typically amounts to about US$15,000 per vehicle (figure 2.14). The value of the capital cost savings (blue bars) is largest in countries where buses are currently more expensive, such as Türkiye or Ukraine, whereas the value of operating cost savings (red bars) is largest in countries where buses currently accumulate relatively low mileage, such as Nepal or Poland.

What is most striking is that such cost savings, achievable through better management of costs along the life cycle of buses, are large enough to revert the economic balance in favor of electric buses in many countries (table 2.15). Specifically, for Nigeria, Poland, and Rwanda, they become economically viable under the efficient bus scenario. In other countries, where they were already viable even before the adoption of such efficient practices, the economic case only becomes stronger. In fact, under the efficient bus scenario, in only one country—Maldives—are electric buses still not economical.

TABLE 2.15 Comparison of the 30×30 and efficient bus scenarios, electric buses only, 2030
US$/vehicle

	30×30	Efficient bus	30×30	Efficient bus	30×30	Efficient bus
	Vehicle capital costs		Operating costs		Aggregate results	
Country						
Brazil	(6,136)	7,599	15,207	15,506	13,762	27,796
Cambodia	(9,621)	1,316	20,299	24,250	8,404	24,025
Egypt, Arab Rep.	(12,107)	1,318	27,579	31,042	47,587	70,395
Ethiopia	(3,375)	101	6,809	8,120	3,217	8,337
Ghana	(7,738)	(1,367)	13,212	16,076	5,048	15,093
India	(14,027)	(288)	27,370	28,817	11,644	27,071
Jamaica	(5,219)	7,124	15,966	16,293	9,513	22,182
Jordan	(9,111)	(2,806)	14,088	17,178	4,336	14,486
Kazakhstan	(11,639)	(5,749)	6,043	6,655	7,008	14,615
Maldives	(5,501)	(1,570)	(29,435)	(29,006)	(9,397)	(5,035)
Nepal	(18,705)	(4,970)	29,789	46,179	9,467	42,835
Nigeria	(6,418)	(3,102)	5,222	11,091	(2,973)	7,558
Poland	(12,412)	742	11,529	26,750	(1,138)	45,854
Rwanda	(7,116)	(2,628)	5,825	7,134	(2,556)	3,688
Tajikistan	(6,226)	(3,860)	10,114	12,707	5,983	11,980
Türkiye	(12,982)	710	17,814	28,499	10,370	46,394
Ukraine	(10,558)	(1,606)	14,748	20,770	10,911	32,198
Uruguay	249	13,729	27,870	33,285	28,060	48,444
Vanuatu	996	14,670	7,367	7,668	4,594	18,568
Vietnam	(14,234)	(499)	34,576	34,876	23,953	37,988

Source: World Bank.
Note: Data in this table represent the "business as usual" (BAU) scenario minus the 30×30 and efficient bus scenarios (averages for fleet additions). The 30×30 scenario assumes that sales of electric cars and buses will reach 30 percent, and of two- and three-wheelers, 70 percent, by 2030. The efficient bus scenario assumes a capital cost reduction of 35 percent in the procurement of buses as well as optimized bus routes to increase the annual mileage of electric buses. Red and parentheses indicate negative values.

FIGURE 2.14 Overall cost savings of the efficient bus scenario, electric buses only, 2030

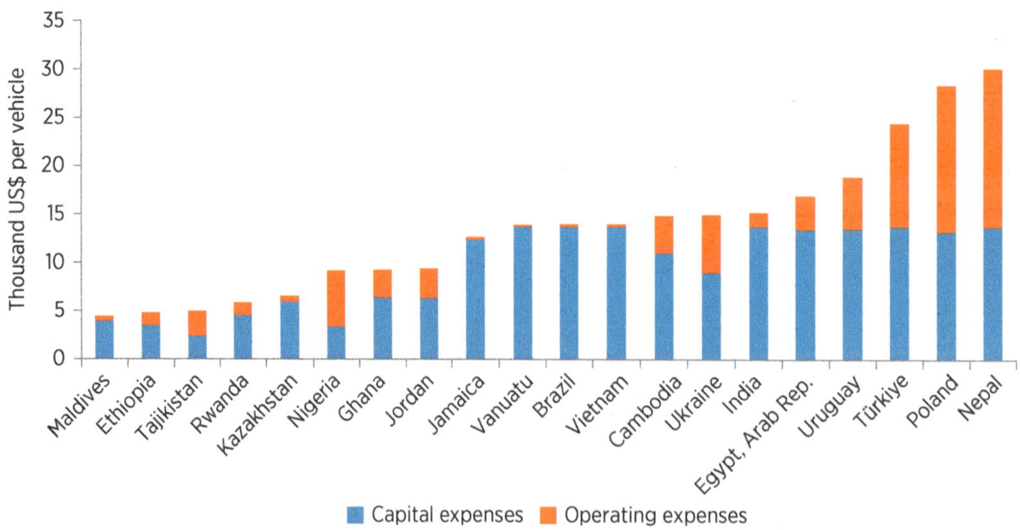

Source: World Bank.
Note: Data in this figure compare the efficient bus scenario with the 30×30 scenario. The 30×30 scenario assumes that sales of electric cars and buses will reach 30 percent, and of two- and three-wheelers, 70 percent, by 2030. The efficient bus scenario further assumes a capital cost reduction of 35 percent in the procurement of buses as well as optimized bus routes to increase the annual mileage of electric buses.

Taxi Fleet Scenario

Although the economics of electric mobility for four-wheel vehicles were not especially favorable in many countries, the efficient bus scenario illustrates that the case improves for more intensively used vehicles. In that sense, it is possible that electrifying intensively used four-wheel vehicle fleets—such as taxis, shared ride vehicles, or corporate cars—may yield a more attractive balance of economic costs and benefits than electrification of lightly used private family cars.

To investigate this issue, the taxi fleet scenario examines the case of intensively used commercial vehicles, primarily taxis, and compares them with normally used four-wheel EVs. To represent the scenario, two important changes in assumptions are in order. The first is the lifetime vehicle mileage, which increases four times in each country to reflect greater usage and leading to a larger saving in operating costs. The second is to increase the investment in public charging infrastructure by doubling the fast charger density for cars in recognition that it would be necessary to support a larger electric taxi fleet. As for maintenance, the maintenance cost for cars is doubled; it assumes two battery replacements during lifetime for EVs, at years 5 and 10. Because these changes affect the results in opposite directions, the outcome cannot be readily predicted.

The results in table 2.16 indicate that the increase in operating cost savings largely exceeds the higher investment needed in charging infrastructure. Nevertheless, the positive impact is

TABLE 2.16 Comparison of the 30×30 and taxi fleet scenarios, four-wheelers only, 2030

US$/vehicle

	Charging infrastructure costs		Operating costs		Aggregate results	
Country	30×30	Taxi fleet	30×30	Taxi fleet	30×30	Taxi fleet
Brazil	(529)	(583)	650	348	(1,612)	(1,182)
Cambodia	(363)	(401)	613	883	(1,069)	(591)
Egypt, Arab Rep.	(567)	(626)	880	1,077	629	5,573
Ethiopia	(142)	(157)	376	884	(875)	(182)
Ghana	(232)	(256)	413	643	(30)	427
India	(568)	(627)	983	1,438	(947)	(349)
Jamaica	(527)	(582)	700	722	(1,645)	(1,078)
Jordan	(441)	(486)	633	587	(2,615)	(2,377)
Kazakhstan	(540)	(595)	572	(68)	(142)	212
Maldives	(211)	(233)	(948)	(4,602)	(3,087)	(6,494)
Nepal	(504)	(557)	1,276	2,932	(4,649)	(2,509)
Nigeria	(342)	(378)	1,043	2,718	1,206	3,439
Poland	(460)	(508)	470	(116)	(793)	(1,059)
Rwanda	(249)	(276)	246	(59)	74	(79)
Tajikistan	(221)	(244)	505	1,108	494	1,358
Türkiye	(574)	(633)	583	(174)	(1,792)	(1,033)
Ukraine	(393)	(435)	491	285	(503)	(395)
Uruguay	(555)	(612)	1,250	2,599	(1,951)	30
Vanuatu	(550)	(608)	227	(1,552)	(2,733)	(4,351)
Vietnam	(569)	(628)	942	1,029	(2,427)	(1,681)

Source: World Bank.

Note: Data in this table represent the "business as usual" (BAU) scenario minus the 30×30 and taxi fleet scenarios (averages for fleet additions). The 30×30 scenario assumes that sales of electric cars and buses will reach 30 percent, and of two- and three-wheelers, 70 percent, by 2030. The taxi fleet scenario assumes that the lifetime mileage of intensively used commercial vehicles will increase by four times in each country, that public investment in charging infrastructure will double the fast charger density for cars, and that the maintenance cost for cars will be doubled (assuming two battery replacements in their lifetime). Red and parentheses indicate negative value.

seldom large enough to reverse the prior conclusions regarding the economic case for electrifying four-wheelers. In fact, in only three countries do the conclusions switch from unfavorable to favorable for electric mobility: Ghana, Kazakhstan, and Uruguay.

Fuel Efficiency Scenario

As noted, ICEVs in developing countries are characterized by low fuel efficiency (see figure 2.7), which makes energy-efficient EVs look particularly attractive in operating cost terms. However, this situation raises the question of whether increasing the fuel efficiency of conventional vehicles might not be a more cost-effective decarbonization strategy. The fuel efficiency scenario explores this possibility by doubling the annual rate of improvement of fuel efficiency assumed for the ICEV fleet from 15 to 30 percent.

This increased fuel efficiency has the effect of reducing the operating cost advantage of EVs by 20 to 40 percent in most cases. However, it does not generally affect the overall case for electric mobility. In fact, only three countries—Ethiopia, Kazakhstan, and Rwanda—actually experience a reversal with the overall balance of economic benefits tilting away from electric mobility (table 2.17).

TABLE 2.17 Comparison of the 30×30 and fuel efficiency scenarios, 2030

US$/Mpaxvkm

	30×30	Fuel efficiency	30×30	Fuel efficiency
	Operating costs		Aggregate results	
Country				
Brazil	10,855	6,163	(12,441)	(18,037)
Cambodia	19,254	16,156	6,426	2,959
Egypt, Arab Rep.	15,300	11,082	17,201	9,479
Ethiopia	6,920	5,077	2,045	(6)
Ghana	10,846	8,415	4,081	1,344
India	23,217	20,101	11,201	7,634
Jamaica	10,378	4,856	(21,947)	(28,194)
Jordan	12,543	8,896	(32,733)	(37,041)
Kazakhstan	8,283	4,956	219	(4,504)
Maldives	(11,290)	(11,826)	(15,492)	(16,134)
Nepal	32,720	28,186	(5,935)	(10,987)
Nigeria	10,850	9,619	1,944	558
Poland	14,838	11,015	(22,586)	(27,415)
Rwanda	6,356	4,813	243	(1,484)
Tajikistan	8,437	7,768	7,991	7,240
Türkiye	16,523	11,850	(13,865)	(20,860)
Ukraine	10,636	6,741	(1,497)	(5,887)
Uruguay	29,216	23,088	(9,260)	(16,112)
Vanuatu	7,221	(582)	(1,076)	(9,758)
Vietnam	31,078	27,062	14,839	9,914

Source: World Bank.

Note: Data in this table represent the "business as usual" (BAU) scenario minus the 30×30 and fuel efficiency scenarios (averages for fleet additions). The 30×30 scenario assumes that sales of electric cars and buses will reach 30 percent, and of two- and three-wheelers, 70 percent, by 2030. The fuel efficiency scenario assumes that the rate of improvement of fuel efficiency for the internal combustion engine fleet will double from 15 percent to 30 percent. Red and parentheses indicate negative values. US\$/Mpaxvkm = US dollars per million passenger vehicle-kilometers.

CONSIDERING FINANCIAL IMPLICATIONS

As noted, the transition to electric mobility has major financial implications. The associated aggregate investment requirements are substantial and dispersed across sectors and actors. For private individuals, issues of affordability and the potential need for financing arise. When it comes to the public sector, the transition to electric mobility may reduce fiscal revenues, given the nature of existing distortions in energy pricing. This situation makes it much less likely that the shift could be partially self-financing through government revenue flows. A final possibility is that of tapping carbon finance, which depends on the implicit carbon price associated with EV adoption, as well as the share of investment potentially coverable through carbon credits. Each of these aspects is explored in the following section by repurposing data and drawing on calculations undertaken for the cost-benefit analysis.

Assessing Investment Needs

Behind the economic results are a significant volume of investments that different actors need to make. To begin with, both private and public vehicle owners will face incremental capital costs associated with vehicle purchase. In addition, significant expansions of public infrastructure are needed to support the expanded EV fleet, notably charging stations. Although there are also implications for investments in the power sector, given that the 30×30 scenario simulated entails only a tiny growth in electricity demand of well under 1 percentage point, they are not considered here, and would in any case be fully funded through the payment of the electricity tariff.

The additional total investments associated with the 30×30 scenario are expressed in terms of the absolute value of the additional capital expenditure needed in 2030, which functions as a representative year (table 2.18). The investment needs are broken down between additional capital costs of vehicles and construction of charging infrastructure facilities. The relative importance of these different types of investments varies hugely across countries (figure 2.15).

In relatively developed countries—such as Brazil, Jamaica, Poland, Türkiye, Ukraine, and Uruguay—that rely heavily on cars, the bulk of the investment needs is associated with the higher capital cost of electric four-wheelers incurred by private actors. In lower-middle-income Asian countries, a large share comes from private actors purchasing more expensive electric two-wheelers—such as in Cambodia, Maldives, Nepal, and Vietnam. In African countries, the additional cost of electric buses accounts for the largest share of investment—such as in Ethiopia, Ghana, Nigeria, and Rwanda. In another group of countries—Kazakhstan, Tajikistan, and Vanuatu—the largest share of investment is associated with public charging infrastructure, both for private cars and municipal buses.

These investment components fall to different economic actors. Private households and enterprises will face higher vehicle costs as well as the need to install in-house vehicle charging infrastructure. Public authorities will incur the additional cost of electric buses and once again the associated charging infrastructure. In figure 2.15, countries are ranked according to public versus private investment needs. Those with the highest share of investment needs falling on the private sector appear to the right side of the graphic. Examples include Jordan, Maldives, and Uruguay, where 80 to 90 percent of investment needs can be expected to fall on the private sector. At the other end of the spectrum, in countries such as Ghana, Nigeria, and Rwanda, more than 80 percent of investment needs fall on the public sector.

Because the absolute investment needs vary hugely with the size of the country, it is helpful to normalize them for the purposes of comparison (figure 2.16). Total investment needs can usefully be expressed as a percentage of gross domestic product, which ranges from less than

TABLE 2.18 Additional investment needs of pursuing the 30×30 scenario

US$, millions

	Vehicle capital investment					Charging infrastructure				Total		
Country	4Ws	2Ws	3Ws	Buses	Total	4W private	3W and 4W public	Bus public	Total	Private	Public	Aggregate
Brazil	5,088	213	3	174	5,479	342	1,014	174	1,530	5,646	1,362	7,009
Cambodia	13	15	n.a.	8	36	1	3	4	8	29	15	44
Egypt, Arab Rep.	799	548	143	320	1,810	105	307	160	571	1,594	787	2,381
Ethiopia	64	21	6	160	252	2	6	73	81	93	240	333
Ghana	24	4	10	92	129	5	14	43	62	42	149	192
India	8,410	6,375	722	2,449	17,956	857	2,525	1,065	4,447	16,364	6,039	22,403
Jamaica	150	3	n.a.	0	153	10	29	0	39	163	30	193
Jordan	219	16	n.a.	7	242	8	25	3	36	243	35	278
Kazakhstan	87	0	n.a	48	135	26	76	15	116	113	139	251
Maldives	3	6	1	0	10	0	0	0	0	9	1	10
Nepal	134	338	9	185	666	3	9	60	72	485	254	739
Nigeria	(43)	2	n.a	305	263	13	36	127	175	(29)	467	438
Poland	1,399	5	n.a.	65	1,469	184	543	31	757	1,587	639	2,226
Rwanda	(0)	1	0	12	13	0	1	5	7	1	19	20
Tajikistan	(3)	n.a.	n.a.	1	(2)	1	4	0	5	(1)	5	3
Türkiye	1,981	130	n.a.	522	2,633	131	393	245	769	2,242	1,160	3,402
Ukraine	243	7	n.a.	107	357	35	100	46	180	285	252	537
Uruguay	242	59	n.a.	0	301	12	35	5	51	313	39	352
Vanuatu	1	0	n.a.	0	1	0	0	1	2	1	1	2
Vietnam	863	2,047	374	258	3,542	41	123	111	275	3,325	491	3,817

Source: World Bank.

Note: Data in this table compare the 30×30 scenario with the "business as usual" (BAU) scenario (averages for fleet additions). The BAU scenario assumes that no policy target will be imposed for electric vehicles and that vehicle purchase decisions will continue to reflect historical trends. The 30×30 scenario assumes that sales of electric cars and buses will reach 30 percent, and of two- and three-wheelers, 70 percent, by 2030. Red and parentheses indicate negative value. 2W = two-wheeler; 3W = three-wheeler; 4W = four-wheeler; n.a. = not applicable.

FIGURE 2.15 Additional investment needs, by public and private shares, under the 30×30 scenario, 2030

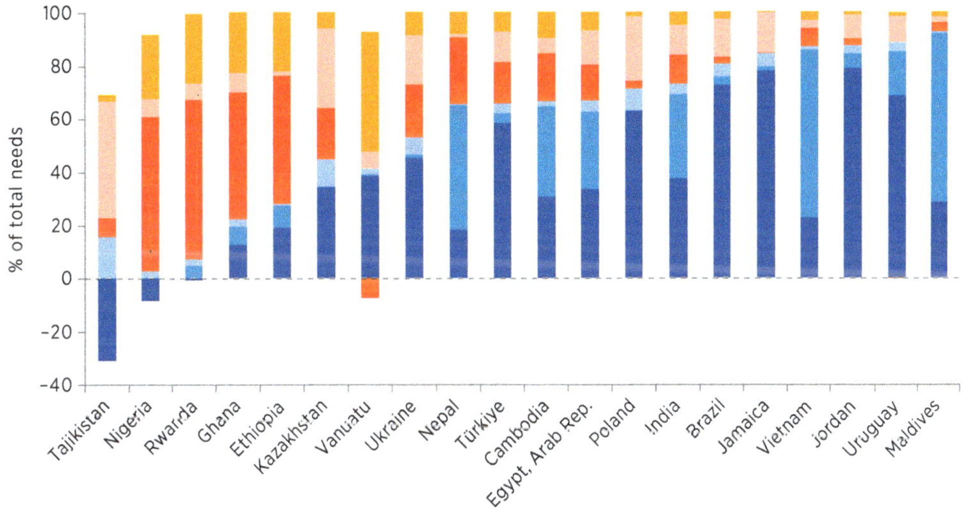

Source: World Bank.
Note: Data in this figure compare the 30×30 scenario with the "business as usual" (BAU) scenario (averages for fleet additions). The BAU scenario assumes that no policy target will be imposed for electric vehicles and that vehicle purchase decisions will continue to reflect historical trends. The 30×30 scenario assumes that sales of electric cars and buses will reach 30 percent, and of two- and three-wheelers, 70 percent, by 2030. 2W = two-wheeler; 3W = three-wheeler; 4W = four-wheeler.

FIGURE 2.16 Additional investment needs, normalized, under the 30×30 scenario, 2030

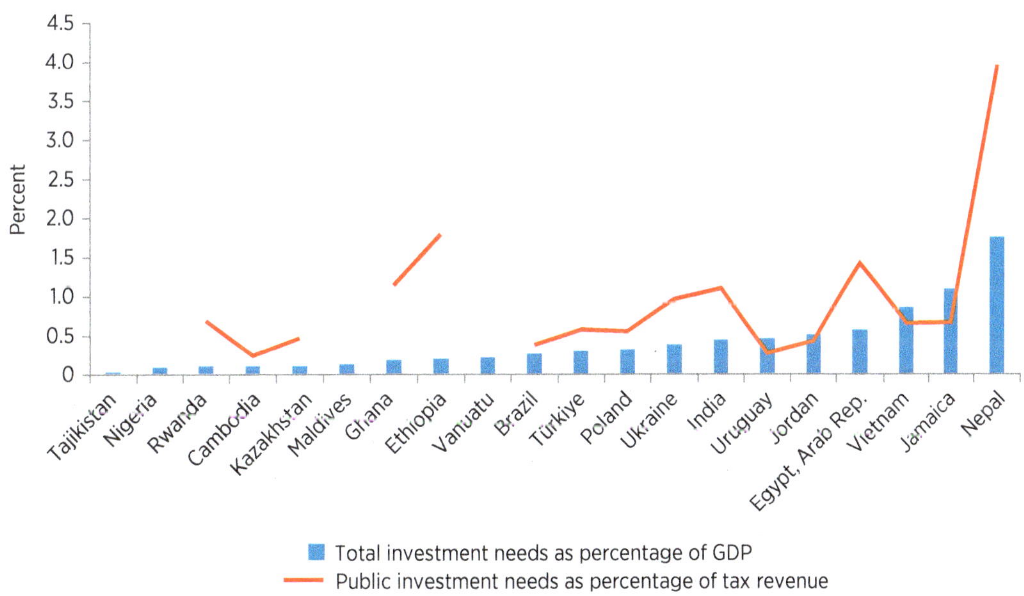

Source: World Bank.
Note: Data in this figure compare the 30×30 scenario with the "business as usual" (BAU) scenario (averages for fleet additions). The BAU scenario assumes that no policy target will be imposed for electric vehicles and that vehicle purchase decisions will continue to reflect historical trends. The 30×30 scenario assumes that sales of electric cars and buses will reach 30 percent, and of two- and three-wheelers, 70 percent, by 2030. GDP = gross domestic product.

0.1 percent in Cambodia, Kazakhstan, Maldives, Nigeria, and Tajikistan to more than 1 percent in Jamaica and Nepal. Another useful normalization is to look at the public component of the investment needs against the tax revenues of the country. Where possible, this normalization ranges from 0.4 percent of tax revenues in Jordan to 4 percent in Nepal.

These findings illustrate the diverse financing challenges that countries face in embarking on the transition to electric mobility and underscore the importance of bringing together a range of financing mechanisms to support electric mobility, specifically tailored to the needs of various actors. Given the significance of household investment, consumer finance clearly has a place to support the up-front investments involved in transitioning to electric mobility. With regard to charging infrastructure, the world offers a variety of business models. It is clearly possible for such infrastructure to be fully financed by the private sector, as long as a policy commitment to stimulate demand for electric mobility is sufficiently clear. Nevertheless, the segment of the investment that would fall to the public budget is significant, notably all of that associated with electrification of buses.

Assessing Fiscal Implications

Given the significant demands that electric mobility can make on public investment, it is relevant to consider the fiscal implications of adoption. One question is whether increased penetration of electric mobility will lead to better or worse public finances, and whether this will help or hinder financing the associated costs.

In view of the extensive web of taxes and subsidies covering liquid transportation fuels and electricity, the acceleration of electric mobility will likely have fiscal implications. Specifically, this study finds that, overall, countries are more likely to tax petroleum and diesel and to subsidize electricity. In those cases, a shift toward electric mobility could have adverse effects on the government's net fiscal position by reducing tax revenues from liquid transportation fuels while drawing additional subsidies into the power sector. Further, the extent to which the vehicle taxation regime favors EVs correlates with the reduction in fiscal revenues as the uptake of EVs accelerates.

The simulations indicate that, in the vast majority of countries, the 30×30 scenario leads to a deterioration in government finances (figure 2.17). The fiscal impact is measured as the net present value of the change in the cumulative stream of net tax revenues received over time from the EVs purchased in 2030 under the 30×30 scenario relative to BAU. The absolute value of the fiscal impact is reported in table 2.19, broken down both by revenue stream and by vehicle category. The impact on fiscal revenues is overwhelmingly negative in most countries.

For comparison and interpretation, normalizing the fiscal impact is helpful to understanding the sign and key drivers of changes on the government's projected tax revenue stream for 2030. Across countries, by far the largest negative effect on public finances is a significant reduction in revenues collected from gasoline and diesel taxes. In addition, several countries' public finances are adversely affected by a significant increase in subsidies to the electricity sector—in particular Egypt, Ethiopia, Kazakhstan, Maldives, Tajikistan, and Ukraine.

The impact via vehicle taxes, subsidies, and duties is more ambiguous, bringing a significant increase in fiscal revenues for some countries (Jamaica, Nepal, and Nigeria) and a significant reduction in others (Ethiopia, Jordan, Poland, Ukraine, and Uruguay).

The overall conclusion is that, in the absence of significant fiscal reform in the energy sector, the adoption of EVs—far from generating the fiscal revenues needed to finance the associated public investments—is more likely to lead to a deterioration in public finances.

FIGURE 2.17 **Relative fiscal impact of electric mobility, by tax stream, under the 30×30 scenario, by 2030**

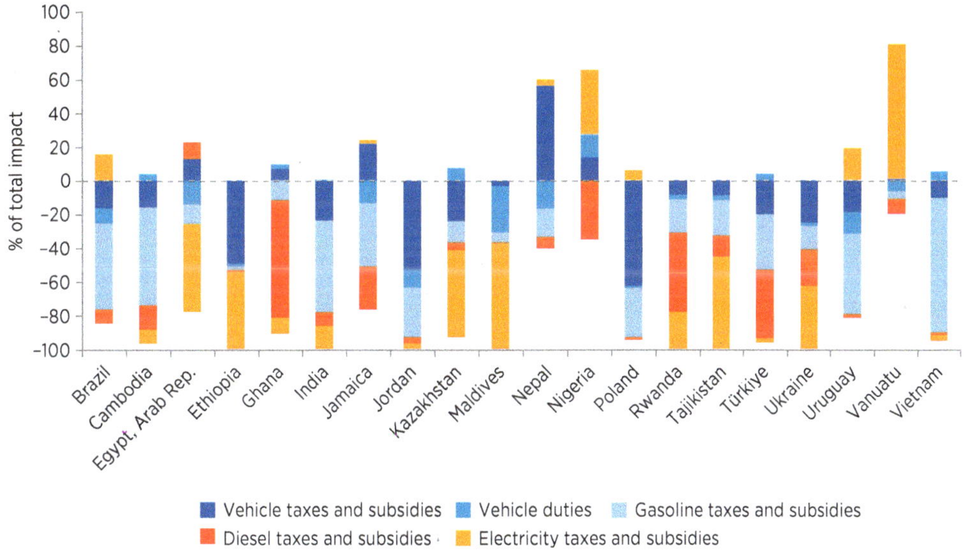

Source: World Bank.
Note: Data in this figure compare the 30×30 scenario with the "business as usual" (BAU) scenario (averages for fleet additions). The BAU scenario assumes that no policy target will be imposed for electric vehicles and that vehicle purchase decisions will continue to reflect historical trends. The 30×30 scenario assumes that sales of electric cars and buses will reach 30 percent, and of two- and three-wheelers, 70 percent, by 2030.

Assessing Affordability

When it comes to incremental vehicle capital costs that private households assume, it becomes pertinent to ask whether these costs are likely to be affordable, given relatively modest budgets in low- and middle-income countries. Whereas four-wheelers are likely to be purchased primarily by the wealthiest households, two-wheelers tend to be in the purview of poorer families as well as small and midsize enterprises running transportation businesses.

To evaluate this issue, the incremental capital cost associated with EVs is expressed as a percentage of gross national income (GNI) per capita in the 20 countries studied (figure 2.18). The results indicate that two-wheel EVs are relatively affordable, carrying a capital cost increment typically no higher than 10 percent of GNI per capita, with the notable exception of Nepal, where the premium rises to a prohibitive 80 percent. When it comes to four-wheel EVs, the capital cost premium exceeds 20 percent of GNI per capita in a significant minority of countries (Cambodia, Ethiopia, Jamaica, and Vietnam)—and is in excess of 100 percent in Nepal. Given that four-wheel EVs tend to be luxury goods, assessing the extent to which these cost differentials may be binding is more difficult.

Assessing Prospects for Carbon Finance

Given the significant investments associated with electric mobility, as well as the associated reduction in carbon emissions, it is interesting to explore whether part of these capital costs could be met through carbon finance. To evaluate this possibility, it is necessary to calculate the implicit carbon price associated with electric mobility to see how it aligns with market rates, and to explore what percentage of the associated investments could potentially be covered by carbon credits.

TABLE 2.19 Net fiscal impact of the 30×30 scenario compared with the BAU scenario, 2030

US$, millions

	Fiscal revenue stream						Vehicle category				
	Vehicle taxes and subsidies	Vehicle duties	Gasoline taxes and subsidies	Diesel taxes and subsidies	Electricity taxes and subsidies	Total	4Ws	2Ws	3Ws	Buses	Total
Country											
Brazil	(2,120)	(1,148)	(6,619)	(1,064)	2,051	(8,900)	(6,897)	(1,192)	(4)	(807)	(8,900)
Cambodia	(8)	2	(30)	(8)	(4)	(48)	(8)	(28)	0	(11)	(48)
Egypt, Arab Rep.	335	(370)	(296)	254	(1,336)	(1,414)	(912)	(252)	(17)	(233)	(1,414)
Ethiopia	(301)	(10)	(11)	(9)	(279)	(609)	(59)	(28)	(10)	(512)	(609)
Ghana	17	6	(28)	(166)	(23)	(193)	(27)	(11)	(14)	(142)	(193)
India	(14,881)	98	(34,687)	(5,178)	(8,761)	(63,410)	(16,258)	(40,137)	(1,780)	(5,235)	(63,410)
Jamaica	39	(23)	(68)	(45)	4	(93)	(89)	(4)	0	(0)	(93)
Jordan	(183)	(37)	(102)	(13)	(14)	(348)	(299)	(42)	0	(7)	(348)
Kazakhstan	(58)	18	(31)	(11)	(125)	(207)	(169)	(1)	0	(37)	(207)
Maldives	(1)	(8)	(2)	(0)	(18)	(28)	(5)	(16)	(5)	(2)	(28)
Nepal	666	(198)	(195)	(80)	44	237	74	168	3	(7)	237
Nigeria	20	20	1	(50)	55	45	(4)	5	0	45	45
Poland	(3,117)	(61)	(1,457)	(79)	292	(4,422)	(4,301)	(42)	0	(79)	(4,422)
Rwanda	(5)	(2)	(13)	(30)	(14)	(64)	(9)	(13)	(0)	(42)	(64)
Tajikistan	(1)	(0)	(3)	(2)	(9)	(17)	(16)	0	0	(1)	(17)
Türkiye	(414)	85	(704)	(844)	(58)	(1,934)	(1,221)	(162)	0	(551)	(1,934)
Ukraine	(310)	(22)	(176)	(268)	(470)	(1,247)	(818)	(45)	0	(384)	(1,247)
Uruguay	(182)	(123)	(466)	(21)	185	(607)	(429)	(170)	0	(9)	(607)
Vanuatu	0	(1)	(1)	(1)	12	9	(0)	(0)	0	10	9
Vietnam	(463)	261	(3,716)	(89)	(138)	(4,146)	(537)	(2,981)	(378)	(250)	(4,146)

Source: World Bank.

Note: Heading color: gray = fiscal wedge. Data in this figure compare the 30×30 scenario with the "business as usual" (BAU) scenario (averages for fleet additions). The 30×30 scenario assumes that sales of electric cars and buses will reach 30 percent, and of two- and three-wheelers, 70 percent, by 2030. The "business as usual" (BAU) scenario assumes that no policy target will be imposed for electric vehicles and that vehicle purchase decisions will continue to reflect historical trends. Red and parentheses indicate negative value. 2W = two-wheeler; 3W = three-wheeler; 4W = four-wheeler.

FIGURE 2.18 **Capital cost of an electric vehicle**

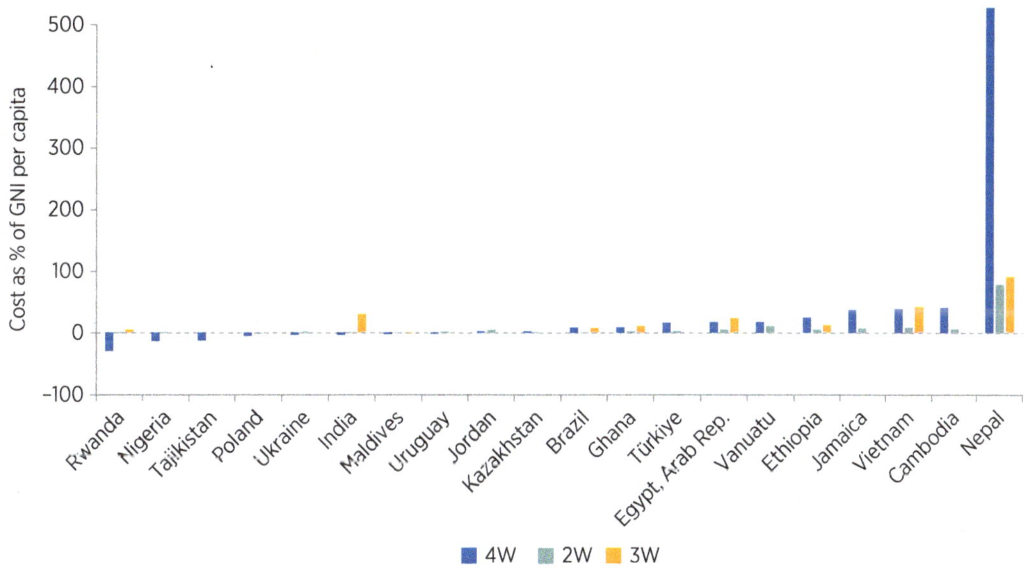

Source: World Bank.
Note: 2W = two-wheeler; 3W = three-wheeler; 4W = four-wheeler; GNI = gross national income.

The implicit carbon price is calculated as the economic cost differential between the 30×30 scenario and BAU in 2030 divided by the lifetime carbon savings of the additional EVs entering the fleet during that year (table 2.20). It is important to note that the economic cost differential incorporates the local externality benefits of electric mobility adoption, although excluding them does not make much difference to the results in most cases. As previously noted, in 8 out of the 20 countries, electric mobility adoption is already advantageous economically, resulting in negative implicit carbon prices, meaning that the carbon abatement essentially comes "for free," as in Cambodia, Egypt, Ethiopia, Ghana, India, Nigeria, Tajikistan, and Vietnam. Among countries with an overall positive implicit carbon price, three—Kazakhstan, Rwanda, and Vanuatu—have relatively low implicit carbon prices, ranging between US$20 and US$40, suggesting that acceleration of electric mobility is a relatively cost-effective means of carbon abatement (figure 2.19). The implicit carbon price for the remaining countries—Brazil, Jamaica, Jordan, Maldives, Nepal, Poland, Türkiye, Ukraine, and Uruguay—is much higher, between US$45 and US$1,000, suggesting that acceleration of electric mobility is a relatively costly carbon abatement strategy.

Although the overall country-level implicit carbon prices are informative, in many ways it is more relevant to examine implicit carbon prices by vehicle category (table 2.20). In particular, in as many as about three-quarters of the studied countries, the implicit carbon price associated with the adoption of electric two-wheelers and buses is negative, suggesting that carbon abatement is a by-product of other economically attractive benefits. Even in countries with relatively high implicit carbon prices at the national level, two-wheelers and/or buses remain attractive forms of decarbonization. This is true for Maldives, Nigeria, Poland, and Rwanda. In fact, because small islands face extreme energy prices, only in Maldives is electric mobility still unattractive as a form of carbon abatement, even disaggregating by vehicle category. Clearly, four-wheel EVs are the most expensive form of carbon abatement, with implicit carbon prices in the range of US$200 to US$700 in the vast majority of countries. Only in a handful of cases

TABLE 2.20 Implicit carbon price of the 30×30 scenario compared with the BAU scenario, by vehicle category, 2030

	Implicit carbon price (US$/ton)					Potential carbon financing as share of investment (%)				
	4Ws	2Ws	3Ws	Buses	Total	4Ws	2Ws	3Ws	Buses	Charging[a]
Country										
Brazil	230.9	(86.9)	0.2	(19.6)	116.4	8	68	25	64	51
Cambodia	401.1	(112.9)	n.a.	(57.8)	(43.0)	4	27	n.a.	18	27
Egypt, Arab Rep.	(75.2)	(180.9)	221.9	(249.5)	(161.2)	10	16	4	25	38
Ethiopia	380.1	48.6	(65.4)	(37.2)	(14.1)	5	13	31	27	60
Ghana	36.7	(119.3)	(77.5)	(22.8)	(24.5)	14	69	32	23	42
India	769.2	(258.9)	(197.8)	(203.9)	(161.1)	2	27	19	7	8
Jamaica	287.6	(69.4)	n.a.	(43.9)	268.5	6	22	n.a.	32	41
Jordan	2057.9	(15.4)	n.a.	(69.4)	1066.5	1	9	n.a.	9	10
Kazakhstan	93.4	(258.7)	n.a.	(98.4)	20.3	5	43	n.a.	10	14
Maldives	2773.8	386.8	273.8	293.3	457.6	1	11	45	11	19
Nepal	733.6	106.7	(59.9)	(37.8)	61.9	3	8	19	16	45
Nigeria	(149.6)	(152.6)	n.a.	126.5	(3.8)	516	364	n.a.	8	70
Poland	1040.7	(262.8)	n.a.	84.7	921.2	2	30	n.a.	3	6
Rwanda	(8.8)	(103.8)	(90.6)	69.0	21.8	24	92	73	15	30
Tajikistan	(113.4)	n.a.	n.a.	(52.0)	(108.2)	87	n.a.	n.a.	24	56
Türkiye	4318.8	(136.5)	n.a.	(220.3)	501.5	0	7	n.a.	6	3
Ukraine	155.8	(92.0)	n.a.	(72.1)	44.1	9	43	n.a.	19	34
Uruguay	261.2	(111.1)	n.a.	(116.5)	81.5	6	22	n.a.	88	51
Vanuatu	1141.9	33.7	n.a.	(31.1)	39.5	2	14	n.a.	41	16
Vietnam	697.8	(114.7)	(42.4)	(113.1)	(72.1)	3	21	16	22	22

Source: World Bank.

Note: The 30×30 scenario assumes that sales of electric cars and buses will reach 30 percent, and of two- and three-wheelers, 70 percent, by 2030. The "business as usual" (BAU) scenario assumes that no policy target will be imposed for electric vehicles and that vehicle purchase decisions will continue to reflect historical trends. Red and parentheses indicate negative value. 2W = two-wheeler; 3W = three-wheeler; 4W = four-wheeler; n.a. = not applicable.

a. This calculation is based on the assumption that all of the carbon savings associated with 4Ws are allocated to the associated public charging infrastructure and that the government accesses carbon financing to develop it.

FIGURE 2.19 **Implicit carbon prices associated with the 30×30 scenario**

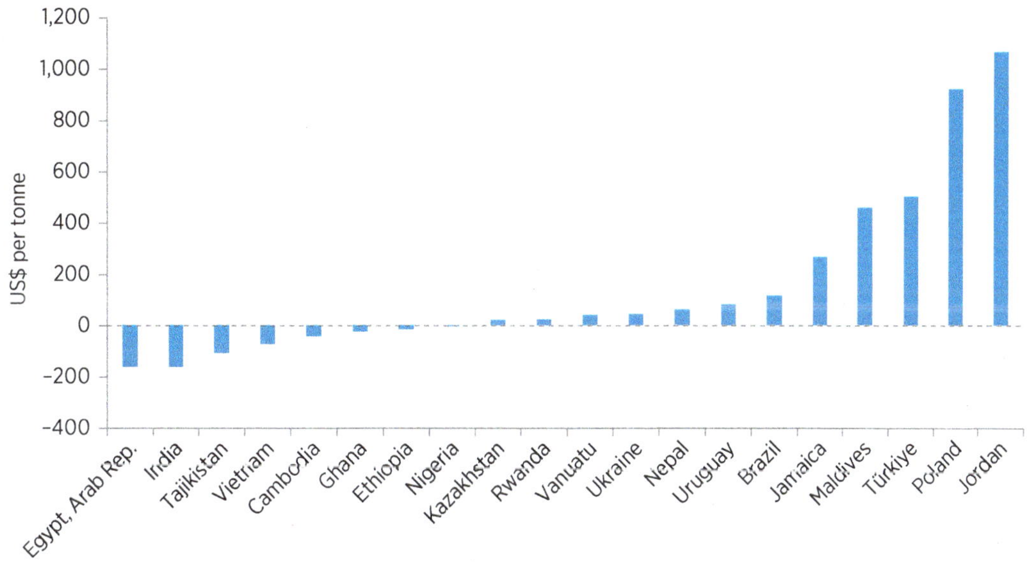

Source: World Bank.
Note: The 30×30 scenario assumes that sales of electric cars and buses will reach 30 percent, and of two- and three-wheelers, 70 percent, by 2030.

does four-wheel electric transportation provide negative implicit carbon prices: Egypt, Nigeria, Rwanda, and Tajikistan.

The projects best suited to carbon finance are those that can cover a significant percentage of their incremental capital costs with the carbon credits created. To evaluate this issue, the carbon savings associated with the 30×30 scenario are valued at the World Bank's reference price of carbon for 2030, at US$50 per ton, and this value is divided by the total incremental investment associated with the transition (figure 2.20). The results are encouraging. In the case of electric buses, carbon financing could potentially cover 20 to 75 percent of the incremental capital costs in the majority of cases. Similarly, when it comes to two-wheel EVs, carbon finance could cover about 50 percent of the incremental capital costs. The situation is not as promising for four-wheel EVs: carbon finance is unlikely to cover more than 20 percent in all but a handful of cases. Nevertheless, if the carbon savings associated with four-wheelers are allocated entirely to the associated public charging infrastructure, it would be enough to cover more than half of the investments associated with public charging infrastructure in most countries.

These estimates of the potential contribution of carbon finance to cover incremental costs associated with electric mobility are purely illustrative simulations. For this source of finance to be realized, suitable contractual and institutional mechanisms would need to be identified to secure the related carbon transactions.

GENERALIZING THE TYPOLOGY

Throughout this chapter, results are presented in a typology that distinguishes between countries with and without car-dominated vehicle fleets, countries that import rather than export oil, and countries that face high rather than low vehicle purchase costs. These three factors

FIGURE 2.20 Value of carbon savings from the 30×30 scenario as a share of incremental capital costs

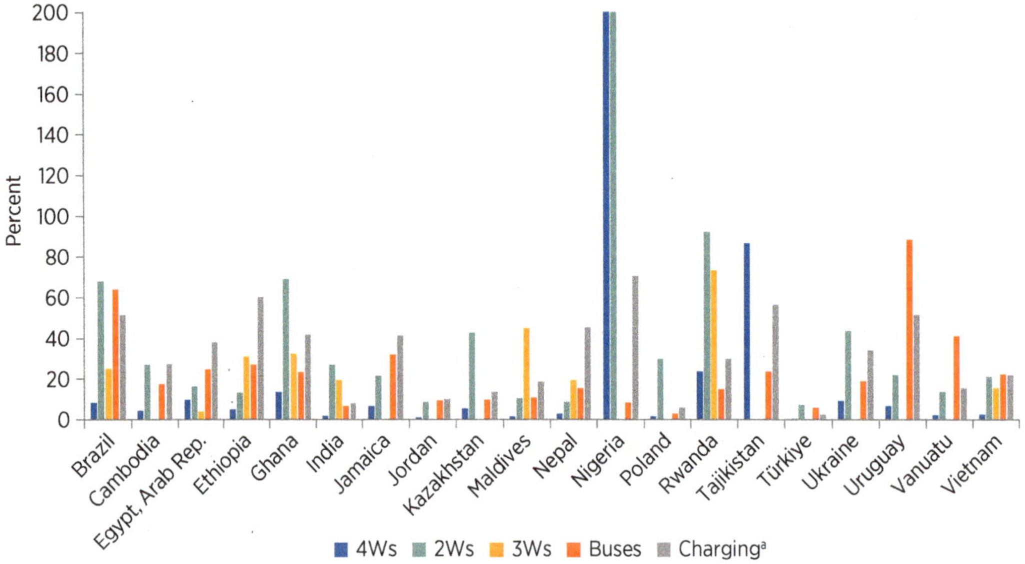

Source: World Bank.

Note: Data in this figure compare the "business as usual" (BAU) scenario with the 30×30 scenario (averages for fleet additions). The BAU scenario assumes that no policy target will be imposed for electric vehicles and that vehicle purchase decisions will continue to reflect historical trends. The 30×30 scenario assumes that sales of electric cars and buses will reach 30 percent, and of two- and three-wheelers, 70 percent, by 2030.

a. This calculation is based on the assumption that all of the carbon savings associated with four-wheelers are allocated to the associated public charging infrastructure and that the government accesses carbon financing to develop it.

systematically affect results in the sample, with the most favorable conditions for electric mobility appearing in countries that have relatively few four-wheel vehicles, import oil, and can purchase vehicles at relatively low cost (and vice versa).

Given that this study was able to examine the economics of electric mobility for a diverse cross-section of only 20 low- and middle-income countries, the typology provides an approximative way of gauging how promising electric mobility might be in countries outside the sample.

IMPLICATIONS AND CONCLUSIONS

In summary, the main findings of this analysis are that, first, EVs across all vehicle categories present significant capital cost differentials. Although these cost differentials are falling over time, they nonetheless present a significant affordability challenge and may prompt some consideration of consumer financing policies. The differentials are still quite prohibitive for cars, but less so for two-wheelers.

Second, in about one-third of the countries studied, the lower operating costs of EVs over the lifetime of the vehicles more than justify the additional capital costs, in economic terms. EVs not only are cheaper to maintain but also consume a fraction of the energy of ICEVs, thanks to greater energy efficiency. This energy efficiency effect overwhelms the fact that electricity is a significantly more expensive source of energy in economic terms on a normalized per unit of energy basis.

Third, because of highly distortionary taxes and subsidies, the financial case for EVs is stronger than the economic case, making two-wheelers and electric buses attractive across the majority of countries studied—although to a far lesser extent for four-wheelers. With some notable exceptions, the tax treatment of electric and conventional vehicles is not all that different. However, across countries, the tendency is to tax gasoline and subsidize electricity, which accentuates the energy cost advantage of electric mobility beyond what is economically justifiable.

Fourth, the reduced local (PM) and global (CO_2) environmental externalities associated with EVs amplify the case for their adoption. Even in countries with carbon-intensive electricity generation, electric mobility is found to bring environmental benefits, given that (once again) the energy efficiency benefit of EVs overwhelms any disadvantage they might have in terms of carbon intensity. However, the analysis did not find any cases in which the electrification of transportation was justified solely on the basis of externality benefits. Instead, externality benefits strengthened the case in countries where a pecuniary advantage already existed. In countries with poor urban air quality, the local externality benefits were found in some cases to be even larger than the global ones.

Fifth, national-scale adoption of electric mobility is economically advantageous in half of the countries studied but becomes financially advantageous in three-quarters of them. Specifically, the case for electric two-wheelers is strong across the majority of countries studied, but the same cannot be said for four-wheelers. The economic case for electric buses is both economically and financially favorable in three-quarters of the countries studied.

Sixth, sensitivity analysis demonstrates that the case for electric mobility improves under the green grid scenario (in which the expansion of renewable electricity is accelerated) and deteriorates under the scarce minerals scenario (in which the decline in battery costs slows down to half its former level). The fuel efficiency scenario (which makes ICEVs increasingly efficient) slightly weakens the case for electric mobility but typically does not reverse it. Nevertheless, the former results remain robust because these sensitivities rarely change the overall direction of the conclusion, either for or against electric mobility.

Seventh, the economic case for electric buses can be greatly strengthened through the efficient bus scenario, in which capital costs are lowered in large-scale performance efforts, and lifetime savings are optimized by greater bus mileage. Such efficient practices could make electric buses economically advantageous in all but the most challenging environments. However, the same cannot be said for four-wheel EV fleets: despite more intensive use, they do not materially improve the economic case for the adoption of electric mobility.

Eighth, the investment needs associated with the electric mobility transition are substantial (up to 1 percent of gross domestic product) and fall differentially on public and private actors across countries. Public financing of electric mobility is not helped by the fact that distortions in energy taxation mean that electric mobility has an adverse fiscal impact. However, carbon finance offers some potential for covering public investments, given implicit carbon prices that are relatively favorable in many cases.

Last, although the results reported in this chapter are based on a sample of only 20 countries, some degree of further generalization is possible based on the presentation of different country typologies. Overall, the case for the electrification of transportation is expected to be stronger in countries that have vehicle fleets not dominated by cars, a net oil importing status, and relatively low-cost vehicles.

NOTES

1. Based on IRENA analysis, the target renewable energy share for 2030 by region is defined as 60 percent for East Asia, 55 percent for the European Union, 85 percent for Latin America and the Caribbean, 27 percent for the Middle East and North Africa, 60 percent for North America,

66 percent for Oceania, 52 percent for the rest of Asia, 42 percent for the rest of Europe, 53 percent for Southeast Asia, and 67 percent for Sub-Saharan Africa.

2. For the most part, the variables defining these typologies are not highly correlated with one another. However, the degree of correlation (correlation coefficient −0.2 to −0.4) between being a net oil exporter and having a carbon-intensive power grid is moderately negative, as it is between having a car-dominated fleet and relatively expensive vehicle purchase costs.

REFERENCES

Forster, Felix, and Dorothy Nakyambadde. 2020a. "Indirect Network Effects and Vehicle Choice in LICs." Working paper, University of Warwick, UK.

Forster, Felix, and Dorothy Nakyambadde. 2020b. "Managing Trade in Clunkers: Evidence from Uganda." Working paper, University of Warwick, UK.

Frith, James. 2021. "Battery Price Declines Slow Down in Latest Pricing Survey." Bloomberg.com, November 30, 2021. https://www.bloomberg.com/news/articles/2021-11-30/battery-price-declines-slow-down-in-latest-pricing-survey#xj4y7vzkg.

ICP (International Comparison Program). 2017. "PPP-Based GDP, GDP Per Capita and GCP Price Level Index, 2017." World Bank, Washington, DC. https://www.worldbank.org/en/programs/icp.

IRENA (International Renewable Energy Agency). 2020. *Global Renewables Outlook: Energy Transformation 2050*. Abu Dhabi: IRENA. https://www.irena.org/publications/2020/Apr/Global-Renewables-Outlook-2020.

UNEP (United Nations Environment Programme). 2020. *Used Vehicles and the Environment: A Global Overview of Used Light Duty Vehicles: Flow, Scale and Regulation*. New York: United Nations. https://wedocs.unep.org/20.500.11822/34175.

3

Transportation Policies to Promote the Adoption of Electric Passenger Vehicles

INTRODUCTION

With rising adoption of electric vehicles (EVs) in major markets, their prices have been falling and their quality has been improving, but not always to a point where market forces alone can bring about the transition to electric mobility. As highlighted in chapter 2, governments may often find themselves in a situation where electric mobility is both economically and financially attractive on a life-cycle basis, but the significant need for additional up-front investments in charging infrastructure and more expensive vehicles continues to present an important barrier to adoption, particularly in view of the limited sources of finance. Public policies are therefore necessary to overcome such barriers. Persistent market failures justify active policies, most of all the environmental externalities from the burning of fossil fuels, leading to significant local and global externalities that are not priced and therefore provide an unfair advantage to conventional vehicles. Likely underinvestment in environmental technologies (including EVs), incomplete information among producers and consumers, and the interdependence of EV adoption and charging infrastructure strengthen the case for proactive support to the electric mobility transition.

Low- and middle-income countries (LMICs) can learn from mounting experience among earlier adopters in China, Europe, and North America. Governments have used a range of policy instruments, including supply-side incentives such as research support or zero-emission vehicle mandates; demand incentives such as purchase subsidies or high-occupancy vehicle (HOV) privileges; investments in public charging infrastructure; and switching public vehicle fleets to electric to provide demonstration effects.

LMICs can also learn from one another, because a variety of innovative policies have been set in place to unlock EV adoption across vehicle categories, making EVs more affordable, inclusive, and favorable to local economies.

Experience from wealthier countries and early LMIC adopters is useful as a starting point, but policy priorities and instruments need to be adapted to local circumstances and constraints, and also scaled up and replicated across countries more systematically. Approaches with low and predictable cost as well as those that yield benefits beyond EV adoption are preferable. Those approaches include the development of financial structures and business models that reduce the financing risk and burden of up-front capital costs and improve the bankability of charging infrastructure and EV rollout projects. Governments can also prioritize public transit and fleet operations, as well as electric two- and three-wheelers that are within reach of less affluent residents. Scaling up successful demand aggregation exercises—using cross-country mechanisms, if necessary—can increase the bargaining power of purchasers in small markets. Most important, despite the understandable current excitement about electric mobility, policy makers should not lose sight of the broader goal of achieving a sustainable transportation system—regardless of the technologies that power it.

THE CASE FOR EV POLICIES

The case for initial public policy support to promote the electric mobility transition is strong. Ideally, adoption of EVs would occur spontaneously, driven by rapidly changing consumer preferences and market forces. Given the large investments by automobile companies in EV production, one might assume that markets are indeed driving the transition to electric mobility. In just about all countries, however, policies have induced and sustained this process through mandates and incentives. Without them, car companies would have had little incentive to switch from vehicles fueled by gasoline or diesel. Policy makers are justified in using such policies because the persistence of internal combustion engine vehicles (ICEVs) is attributable to several market failures (Rapson and Muehlegger 2021). The most important is their contribution to climate change, but other market failures hinder the electric mobility transition more directly. Such problems are common in the adoption of new technologies, including those that reduce environmental harm, such as EVs (Jaffe, Newell, and Stavins 2005). Reviewing some of the market failures related to transportation technology provides a context for the policies discussed in this chapter.

The electric mobility rapid adoption cannot rely on market forces alone for at least six reasons. First, conventional ICEVs produce local and climate pollution, which creates costs that are borne by everyone and that ICEV drivers are not paying for—a classic case of an environmental externality. ICEV drivers therefore have little incentive to purchase more expensive EVs that would reduce or eliminate pollution. Taxing vehicle emissions, increasing gas taxes, or imposing strict fuel efficiency and emission standards are all ways to address the problem. Implementation of such measures, though, has been limited in many countries because the measures are politically unpopular.

Innovation market failures are a second factor affecting countries with the potential to manufacture EVs (Bryan and Williams 2021). Companies are reluctant to invest in environmental technology while uncertainty about the returns to a high fixed investment in research and development (R&D) is high. For many technologies, the expected benefits for society are also larger than the private returns for inventors. For these reasons, development of environmental technology tends to be lower than it might be. These problems justify public support for R&D at initial stages of technology development until product and process innovation become self-sustaining. Renewable energy technologies are examples of publicly funded research and initial support for deployment leading to rapidly falling prices to the point that they are now market competitive with conventional alternatives.

Information failures are a third barrier to fast adoption of EVs. Producers, distributors, and service providers are uncertain about the size of required investments and future profitability. Consumers are uncertain about the long-term cost and performance of a new technology. Both supply and demand of EVs are therefore lower than they would be if everyone had full information. Governments signaling a strong commitment to the electric mobility transition help overcome these information problems.

The need for a new EV fueling infrastructure is a fourth barrier to widespread adoption. This need presents a classic chicken-and-egg problem: for EVs to become attractive to consumers requires a dense and convenient charging infrastructure; yet, to make major investments in charging networks, investors need to be sure of a sufficiently large market. EV purchases or charging networks may therefore require initial support until a critical mass has been achieved. More generally, EV buyers will be better off the more others adopt EVs, creating a process of dynamic increasing returns similar to network effects in many digital services.

A fifth failure comes from the mismatch between the tenor of available financing instruments in local markets and the EV technology payback period. In a life-cycle analysis, EV adoption is becoming economically and financially advantageous in a significant number of countries (see chapter 2). Yet the high capital cost remains a barrier because the operating and maintenance benefits occur over a longer period that exceeds most available commercial market tenors, in the case of private EVs, and concession contract duration, in the case of buses and charging infrastructure. In this case, it might be necessary to establish a financial bridge to make it through the initial period from capital investment in the electric technology, such as subsidies or guarantees, until benefits turn positive over time in the form of public sector undertaking. Special considerations for a financial bridge will not be necessary once capital cost parity is reached between EVs and ICEVs.

The fragmentation of demand into small markets is a sixth failure that reduces the bargaining power of buyers and hampers economies of scale of emerging EV producers. In many LMICs, projects and procurement batches are small in size, causing municipalities and even countries to pay huge capital costs. At worst, the projects are not attractive enough for commercial financiers to step in. Through a combination of economies of scale in procurement, consolidation of demand, and contractual improvements, governments can reduce the unit cost of vehicles and mobilize commercial financiers (Acharya, Gadepalli, and Ollivier 2022; World Bank 2022a).

Government failures also hold back EV adoption. Many policies favor harmful incumbent technologies. In many oil-exporting countries, fossil fuel subsidies make ICEVs cheaper than they would be if drivers had to pay full market prices, including the full cost of environmental damages if emissions are priced. Instead, fuel prices are more often determined by a country's politics, revenue needs, and resource endowments—in mid-2020 a liter of gasoline cost US$0.02 in República Bolivariana de Venezuela and US$2.24 in Hong Kong SAR, China (Mahdavi, Martinez-Alvarez, and Ross 2020). Likewise, governments must be careful not to introduce new distortions when addressing perceived market failures (box 3.1) or to be overly generous with subsidies that may reward choices consumers would have made in any case. An interesting observation from chapter 2 is that such government failures can also run in favor

BOX. 3.1

Government support for EVs can be motivated by industrial policy

Electric mobility promotion is motivated by environmental goals, but electric vehicles (EVs) also disrupt an important industrial sector and present a massive market opportunity. Thus, in a few cases, government support for EVs is an industrial rather than just a climate policy. Strong economic interests seek to influence where EVs and associated technologies, such as batteries, will be produced. Many governments justify EV policies by citing job creation, international competitiveness, or technology leadership, in addition to global warming and air quality. Policies in the European Union and the United States have been motivated by climate change, but also seek to protect jobs and ensure the competitiveness of their domestic vehicle industries (van der Steen et al. 2015). Similarly, Japan and the Republic of Korea seek to support their vehicle sectors, which emerged from industrial policies in the last century (Åhman 2006; Lane et al. 2013; Lee and Mah 2020). China and India, whose urban areas are severely affected by air pollution, also intend to take advantage of the shift to EVs to build globally competitive vehicle sectors (Liu et al. 2020). In Africa, governments are increasingly encouraging domestic production or assembly of EVs by granting favorable tax regimes and affordable leases on state-owned land.

of EV adoption, as in countries where gasoline is taxed while electricity is subsidized. Such a fiscal differential can be an appropriate way of reflecting the externality benefits of electricity. However, in some countries, the financial incentive may even go beyond what would be warranted by the externality.

ASSESSING EV POLICIES

The objective of policies that promote electric mobility is to make EVs better, more affordable, and more convenient than conventional vehicles. *Better*, in that the technology should provide superior performance in issues such as range, speed, noise, and environmental footprint. Support for R&D is one type of policy that can help improve EV technology. *More affordable*, so that EVs are more accessible to own than ICEVs. Until technology drives down the up-front cost below parity, as is widely expected to happen in due course, targeted incentives or special financing structures can reduce the burden to the consumer and help attract commercial finance. *More convenient*, so that no more effort is required to operate an EV, especially in terms of fueling. Ensuring a dense and easy-to-use charging infrastructure is critical.

This section reviews policy instruments aimed at promoting EVs and grouped into the broad categories listed in table 3.1. Most of the policy experience has been in high- and upper-middle-income countries where the transition to EVs started earlier. The following section discusses the relevance of these policy instruments for countries with fewer resources, where the electric mobility transition is still at an early stage, and where some degree of adaptation would be needed.

TABLE 3.1 Policies that promote the electric mobility transition

Policy type or area	Main barrier or market failure	Objective
Supply incentives	Innovation market failure; need to jump-start supply	Promote technology development; encourage manufacturers to bring more EVs to market
Direct demand incentives	• Unpriced environmental externalities; need to jump-start demand • Consumers and municipalities credit-constrained and possibly unable to access necessary finance	• Reduce cost of EVs to consumers to make EVs price competitive with ICEVs • Provide credit lines or leasing mechanisms to facilitate purchase of EVs; unlock access to carbon finance for charging infrastructure
Indirect demand incentives	Information market failures	Provide nonmonetary inducements such as informing potential EV owners or making EV operation more convenient
Charging and power infrastructure	Network dependencies ("chicken-egg" problem)	Reduce EV owners' anxiety about reliable operation of vehicles
Public, shared, and fleet operations	Unpriced environmental externalities	Jump-start demand; encourage bus operators, taxis, or ride-sharing firms to shift to EVs as an efficient way to mainstream the technology
Procurement and consolidation mechanisms	Small and fragmented demand	Increase bargaining power of consumers and attract commercial financing through demand aggregation vehicles
Vehicle disposal regulations	Environmental externalities	Ensure that the full environmental cost of EVs is reflected in prices, even after their useful life span
Energy pricing	Fiscal distortions in taxes and subsidies affecting electricity and liquid transportation fuels	Provide accurate price signals on the relative costs of different types of energy for transportation, capturing externality effects

Source: World Bank.
Note: EV = electric vehicle; ICEV = internal combustion engine vehicle.

Supply Incentives

Policies targeting the supply of EVs in a market aim to reduce the risk to producers and importers unsure whether the market in a relatively new and locally unproven technology will be profitable. Such actors may put less effort into developing, producing, and marketing EVs if they think consumers will find ICEVs to be preferable. R&D support through tax incentives or direct public investments reduce innovation-related risks. Almost all Organisation for Economic Co-operation and Development countries provide R&D tax breaks or subsidies, ranging—across all sectors of the economy—from about 0.01 percent of gross domestic product in Latvia or Mexico to about 0.40 percent in France (Bryan and Williams 2021). Information on how much of this type of incentive goes to EV-related firms is not available. Although most EV R&D will be funded by industry, direct public support is needed for fundamental research of uncertain profitability or neglected areas such as development of lower-cost technologies that most benefit lower-income countries.

Another strategy to increase the supply of EVs to national markets is to impose increasingly stringent vehicle emission regulations such as the US CAFE (corporate average fuel economy) standard or China's CAFC (corporate average fuel consumption) rules that cover fuel consumption evaluation methods and targets for passenger cars. Such regulations make ICEVs cleaner but also more expensive, and they strengthen the role of EVs, especially where automobile firms face fleetwide emission standards. The International Energy Agency estimates that more than 85 percent of global car sales now face carbon dioxide (CO_2)or other tailpipe emission standards (IEA 2021). Going a step further, California and China, for instance, mandate sales targets that force producers and importers to sell a certain share of EVs. Most often, these mandates require a new zero-emission vehicle market share of about 15 percent by 2025; some jurisdictions recently announced longer-term mandates of up to 100 percent (Axsen, Plötz, and Wolinetz 2020). Early mandates—California's date to the early 1990s—have sent a strong transformative signal to the car industry, triggering R&D investments that have helped bring EV prices down significantly.

Where such policies are linked to an emission trading system, companies that produce a large share of EVs benefit by selling emission allowances (or regulatory credits) to laggards that still rely on ICEV sales. For such policies to be effective, a clear commitment to such regulations is needed. Uncertainty over the stringency of CO_2 emission standards in the next decade caused many legacy automakers to rely on non-EV-related compliance options to meet the standard in recent years (Mathieu and Poliscanova 2020). Such uncertainty could hold back the supply of electric cars throughout the 2020s even as the technology matures and consumer demand rises in the European Union (EU)(Mock 2021). The strictest regulation finally is to phase out ICEVs completely. An increasing number of cities, regions, and countries have announced target dates for prohibiting the sale or operation of ICEVs (Wappelhorst 2020). In 2022, California, the largest auto market in the United States, introduced a ban on the sale of new gasoline cars by 2035. The most aggressive goal is in Norway, however, where all new passenger vehicles and light vans need to be electric by 2025.

Many types of incentives used by governments aim to achieve not only environmental goals but also economic objectives. Targeted aid to domestic EV-related industries is expected to boost labor markets and help firms stay competitive in the face of a massive technology shift. Some countries see it as an opportunity to create a new industry or leapfrog to a globally leading position. EV support then becomes an element of green industrial policies. EVs are technologically simpler than ICEVs and have more standardized components.

Significant barriers remain, however, to creating competitive firms in a fiercely contested global market, or even just to become a location for component production or vehicle assembly. Factors that make success more likely include a large domestic or easily accessible regional market, comparative advantages like a skilled labor force and access to low-cost and clean energy, and a sound investment and business climate. Where these conditions are absent, attempts at creating local champions or attracting investors have low chances of success.

Whether policies promoting EVs and other green technologies are motivated by environmental concerns or industrial policy objectives does not matter greatly as long as the policies are well designed and implemented. In fact, because climate change policies tend not only to incur local costs but also to bring global gains, they are often a hard sell. Highlighting the domestic economic benefits makes approval more likely. But it is still important to be aware of potential pitfalls given the mixed track record of industrial policy (Oqubay et al. 2020). The main concern is that governments tend to have limited information about which firms or industries to help and how to best provide support—they should let markets allocate resources rather than try to "pick winners." Examples of poor targeting resulting in wasted money and white elephants are in fact numerous. Also, the risk of rent-seeking and collusion where support goes to the well-connected rather than the best prepared is real.

A guiding principle for green industrial policy should be to consider whether support is likely to be economically efficient. Industrial policy is what economists call a second-best policy to combat climate change. It will be less efficient than a simple price instrument such as a carbon or energy tax that enables markets to allocate resources and provide incentives. Instruments used in industrial policies, however, also differ in terms of efficiency, largely depending on how narrowly they target.

- Most restrictive are *tariffs*, a form of protectionism that will make green technology more expensive for local consumers and hurt domestic industries that depend on imports. US tariffs on solar panels introduced in 2018 raised prices, reduced investment, and cost many jobs (SEIA 2019). By sheltering local firms, tariffs will inhibit domestic innovation.
- *Support for specific domestic firms* is a pure form of picking winners and is perhaps most subject to rent-seeking and collusion. Nevertheless, it can sometimes be successful. In 2009, the US government bailed out Tesla with a US$465 million loan guarantee. The firm's later success created useful competitive pressure that accelerated the shift to EVs.
- *Support for domestic sectors* often involves rules restricting beneficiaries of subsidies. Especially in public procurement, governments tend to limit subsidies to domestic suppliers. If multiple domestic firms compete, incentives to offer lower prices and better products will remain. India's recent round of electric bus procurement, for instance, saw five domestic firms or consortia compete to supply 5,450 urban buses (World Bank 2021). The terms of the winning bids were considerably lower than for previous purchases. Local content requirements are another approach that also aims to promote technology transfer. EV producers in the Republic of Korea had to set up battery production in China so that their cars sold in the country would qualify for subsidies (Lutsey et al. 2018).
- The least restrictive approach is *technology-specific support* without rules of origin. Green incentives for EVs or solar panels in the EU or United States tend to be open to foreign-made products. In fact, subsidies for solar panels in several EU countries and US states helped pay for panels made by firms in East Asia, mostly China. Incidentally, those firms also received significant initial support such as cheap land and finance in their home countries. In the interest of industrial policy objectives, the Chinese government, in effect, subsidized consumers in California and Spain.

Although green industrial policies may often be justified, governments still need to minimize the risks inherent in interventionist approaches. Rodrik (2014) proposes three simple rules. First, industrial policy should not be seen as a fixed set of instruments but as a process of learning and adapting. Governments do not have full information and will not get everything right. The failure of individual projects or measures matters less when the overall portfolio of support succeeds over time. Responding quickly to problems will depend on close interaction between bureaucrats administering policies and beneficiaries, which requires safeguards to prevent capture.

Second, governments need to be clear about their objectives. Policies will not always efficiently serve multiple objectives. Not all climate change mitigation measures also create jobs, but they may still be necessary. Clarity also helps determine measures of success that facilitate program evaluation. For environmental objectives, the cost reductions of green technology such as EVs will often be the best measure.

Finally, accountability is essential and should be clear. Governments need to explain to the public what they are doing and why they are doing it. Transparent disclosure of budgets, beneficiaries, and outcomes will reduce the risk of rent-seeking and capture. Appointing a high-level official as the public face of green industrial policies can make communication more effective.

EV supply chain bottlenecks, above all in the production and availability of batteries, call for government interventions. The skyrocketing production of EVs reveals that the battery-manufacturing industry will soon be challenged. First, China accounts for 80 percent of global battery production, which increases the risks to global EV manufacturers regarding supply chain disruptions. Second, despite ambitious plans by leading battery makers (BYD, CATL, LG, Samsung, and SK) and many newcomers to develop a total global capacity of close to 6,000 gigawatt-hours, the lead time for establishing a battery-manufacturing plant is between three and five years. Finally, uncertainty in the availability of the key rare earth minerals needed for battery production is already affecting the price of nickel, cobalt, and more prominently lithium, which increased for the first time in 2022 (Economist 2022; Frith 2021). Despite possibly ample mineral reserves, developing mines takes time and in a few cases involves tapping into artisanal and informal mining under questionable labor conditions. This situation is making the battery industry innovate by looking for new battery chemistries that reduce the dependance on these minerals. More important, governments are fostering battery recycling more systematically as well as the adoption of smaller EVs and smaller batteries (IEA 2021).

In incipient EV markets, pilot projects structured as a cooperation between private sector, government, and international organizations can provide a good jump start. East Africa exemplifies an active arena for piloting projects. In Rwanda, electrification of mototaxis (collaboration of Ampersand and Fonerma), installation of charging points accessible via app for taxi services (Siemens, Volkswagen, and Radisson Blu), e-motorbikes (SafiRide and Rwanda Electric Mobility), and e-bike sharing services (Gura Ride) are just a few examples of pilots with private and public collaboration. Similar examples can be found in Kenya, where there are several start-ups for deployment of electric and solar powered vehicles (Solar-E-Cycles) and innovative manufacturing schemes to lower EV capital costs by replacing the internal combustion engines (ICEs) of trucks and buses with electric power trains and producing low-cost e-mopeds (Sguazzin 2022). Similar projects—such as the Global Environmental Facility, in Burundi, Sierra Leone, Togo, and Uganda—have been launched with the support of the United Nations Environment Programme (Arroyo Arroyo and Vesin 2021; World Bank 2022a).

Direct Demand Incentives

Direct incentives to encourage consumers to purchase EVs are the most visible types of policies. As noted in chapter 2, the additional capital costs associated with EVs represent one of the single most important barriers to adoption. Rebates are essentially subsidies by which a portion of the purchase price is covered by the government. Tax reductions or credits similarly shift some of the cost to the public. *Feebates* are a combination of a reward (bonus) for buyers of vehicles that are, for example, cleaner than some benchmark, and a penalty (malus) on vehicles that are more polluting. If well designed, they can be revenue neutral. Countries have used varying bonus-malus schedules (figure 3.1). Scrappage programs have been popular during financial crises as a way to increase demand for new cars. By offering a seller of an ICEV a higher price than could be realized in the market, such programs reduce the cost of a new EV similar to a rebate or subsidy. Finally, a more coercive approach is to restrict the import of polluting cars outright in markets that have no domestic car industry.

Subsidies are an effective policy tool that may be initially necessary to create EV demand and bring down prices. But subsidies are expensive. A study of global EV adoption between 2013 and 2020 estimated that it took about US$10,000 in consumer purchase subsidies to induce one additional EV adoption (Li, Wang, et al. 2021). In

FIGURE 3.1 Passenger car subsidies and taxes based on tailpipe CO_2 emissions, select countries, 2018

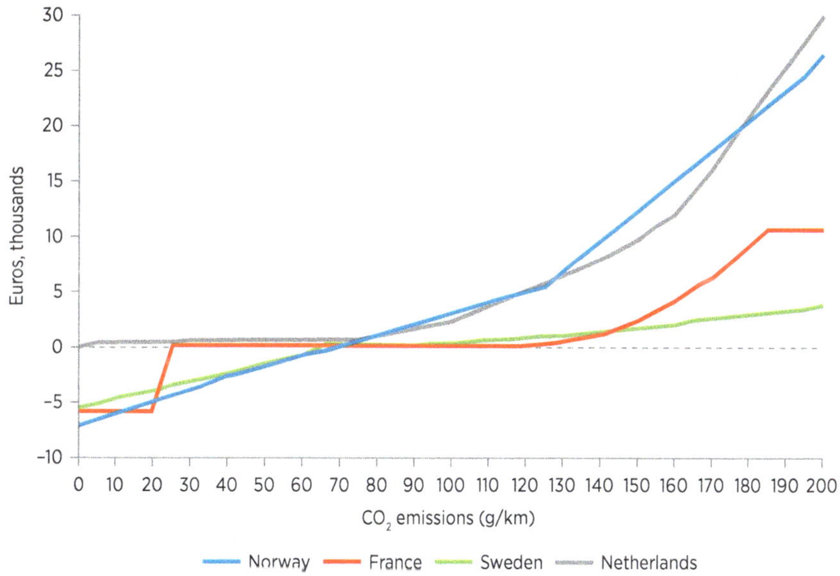

Source: IEA 2021.
Note: The figure shows the total subsidy or tax that the owner of a new gasoline vehicle would incur over the first three years of ownership; owners of diesel vehicles would pay an extra fee. CO_2 = carbon dioxide; g/km = grams per kilometer.

contrast, it took only a US$1,600 investment in charging infrastructure. In leading markets there are indications that—as EV technology is becoming cheaper—direct subsidies are becoming relatively less important compared to consumers' own spending. In 2020, governments across the world spent US$14 billion on direct purchase incentives and tax deductions for electric cars, a 25 percent rise year-on-year. In 2021, government subsidies doubled to nearly US$30 billion, even as consumer spending doubled to nearly US$250 billion (figure 3.2). In contrast, the share of government incentives in total spending on EVs has been declining from roughly 20 percent in 2017 to 10 percent in 2021 (IEA 2021).

As the cost of EV ownership falls further, governments will be able to reduce or phase out direct purchase incentives. China had intended to phase out related subsidies and tax break policies in 2020, but extended them to 2022 in response to the economic impact of COVID-19. Subsidies are also becoming unnecessary where EVs are already cost competitive, for instance, for some types of intensely used commercial or smaller vehicles.

The total cost of ownership of ride-hailing cars in European cities is already estimated to be lower for EVs (Le Petit and Mathieu 2020). The same goes for the overall cost of electric light-duty commercial vehicles in urban duty cycles, which was lower in 2020 in Germany than for equivalent diesel vehicles (McKerracher et al. 2021). For short-distance travel, the total cost of ownership of low-speed electric scooters is lower than for conventional gasoline scooters in Delhi (Rokadiya and Bandivadekar 2016). In some regions with high taxation on ICEVs, the tipping point for cost parity has been reached for electric cars; in Norway, for example, the market share of EVs was 54 percent by 2021 (Reuters 2021). In many LMICs, electric vehicles and their components are exempt from import duties and excise duties (Poland, Rwanda, Ukraine, Uruguay, and Vanuatu); in some favorable fiscal regimes, subsidies are given for EVs (Maldives and Poland).

FIGURE 3.2 Consumer spending on electric cars relative to government spending, 2017–21

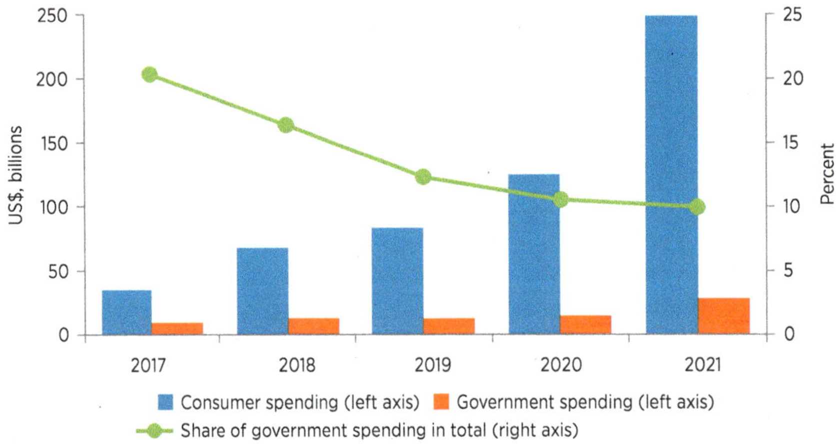

Source: IEA 2021.

Although subsidies may be helpul, at least initially and in places that have adequate fiscal resources, policies need to be designed carefully. Generous direct incentives can have unintended consequences, one of which is *border leakage*. At first, Sweden's subsidy for EV buyers was a straightforward incentive but eventually converted to a feebate system. Although the feebate system appeared more efficient, many Swedes were selling their new EVs to Norwegians who were claiming an EV rebate on the other side of the border. This practice led to oversubsidization: most of the EVs subsidized in Sweden ended up within a year in another country where they received additional incentives (Riedl 2020). Germany has faced a similar problem. EV buyers received up to €9,000 and could then, after six months, sell these cars in countries that do not offer comparable subsidies (Seyerlein 2022). An estimated 30,000 recently purchased EVs disappeared from the German market between January and September 2021. One way to reduce this subsidy leakage is to require a longer minimum ownership period. Another problem has been encountered where subsidies did not distinguish by type of EV. In the Netherlands and some other countries, plug-in hybrid electric vehicles received the same subsidies as pure battery electric vehicles. But many owners of plug-in hybrid electric vehicles rarely drove in electric mode, and recent research suggests that these vehicles are more polluting in nonelectric mode than previously thought (Poliscanova 2020).

The capital cost premium associated with EVs remains a barrier to adoption, but it need not necessarily give rise to purchase subsidies, which tend to be costly and likely regressive in distributional impact, given that EVs remain something of a luxury good. Another potential policy approach is to focus on spreading the cost of EV purchase rather than reducing it, particularly when lifetime costs may already be advantageous, as is the case for two-wheelers. This approach points to the potential use of financial structures and (possibly subsidized) consumer credit lines for EV purchase and risk mitigation financing structures, particularly in the market for two- and three-wheelers as well as electric buses.

In terms of financial instruments that would bring in commercial financiers, some countries have considered interest-free loans. Others have introduced sophisticated schemes based on market incentives to bring in the private sector. For example, India's 2021 Faster Adoption and Manufacturing of Hybrid and Electric Vehicles (FAME) initially increased subsidies and benefits to two-wheelers, aiming to reach price parity with their ICE counterparts. However, a key barrier for the uptake turned out to be the limited financing flows from commercial lenders. Even when credit lines are available, interest rates may be prohibitively high given technological risks, risk of default in a market characterized by high informality, the absence of credit scores, and restricted access to finance.

To reduce the cost of funds to users, the government of India introduced the Electric Vehicles Risk Sharing Program as part of FAME II to offer a first-loss partial credit guarantee to financial institutions. The partial guarantee is intended to reduce the risk premium for EVs, unlock commercial financing availability at concessional rates for EV financing, and bring down the cost of finance for the purchase of electric two- and three-wheelers. The scheme targets the two- and three-wheeler markets; two-wheelers are the largest segment in the Indian automobile industry with domestic sales of 15.1 million units in fiscal year 2021 and contributing to about 81 percent of total automobile sales volume, making the support of EV adoption a progressive scheme within an inclusive and development mobility agenda (World Bank 2021). The World Bank will finance the capital base of the partial credit guarantee.

Alternatively, leasing models, which allow consumers to pay the capital cost of the vehicle gradually over time, are already widespread in Organisation for Economic Co-operation and Development countries and could be particularly suitable for EVs in LMICs. Leasing EVs can be effective in mitigating the ownership risks of EVs by consumers and transferring them to leasing companies that may be better equipped to deal with the key risks. For example, the concept of "battery as a service" (BaaS) introduces a business model in which the cost of the battery is decoupled from the vehicle and allows for leasing as well as mitigation of technology (obsolescence) risks. For the lithium-ion battery of EVs, the major degradation occurs early on in the life cycle, easily leading to a cumulative depreciation rate of 90 percent of value in the first two years of use (World Bank 2021). Moreover, the cost of batteries is the primary reason EVs cost more to buy than ICE equivalents. To address this issue, the deployment of e-motorbikes in Rwanda has been combined with a battery-swapping business model and leasing schemes, significantly lowering the cost per passenger vehicle-kilometer (World Bank 2022b). Similarly, leasing schemes have been introduced to make the adoption of electric buses more palatable.

In Chile, the business model used for the implementation of electric buses in Santiago consists of a public-private partnership between the state (Ministry of Transportation and Telecommunications) and private companies (energy companies Enel and Engie, which are bus operators and investors), with the financing coming from traditional sources and bringing in—with adequate policies—incentivizing companies (such as utilities) to invest and bear the technology risk, minimizing the fiscal burden. For Santiago's electric buses, fleet provision and depot ownership are separated from the operation of buses in the street, introducing two types of contracts: one for operations and another for the enabling infrastructure and assets. Financing of charging infrastructure and electric buses was developed as part of a scheme in the core business of Enel and Engie, which developed leasing contracts with private bus operator companies to include monthly payments to cover fleet provision, charging infrastructure, and energy supply (World Bank 2020).

Rwanda is also introducing a model for electric buses in Kigali, separating the sourcing of finance and procurement of assets while retaining asset ownership under a publicly owned company and leasing the buses to operators. By ultimately bearing the credit risk, the public sector lowers user costs and offsets the risks of a technology whose financial benefits extend beyond the concession tenor (IFC 2021). In a similar vein, increased reliance on shared mobility and "mobility as a service" models is a way of shifting the burden of higher capital costs to firms with potentially easier access to credit and having consumers pay gradually per trip or via monthly subscriptions.

Indirect Demand Incentives

Consumers can be nudged more indirectly to switch to EVs in many ways (Li, Zhu et al. 2021). Many EV drivers not only wish to reduce their pollution and carbon footprint but also want to be seen doing so. Special license plates, for instance, which allow drivers to make a statement, appear to be an effective (and inexpensive) instrument to promote EVs. Adding to the attraction of a new and somewhat futuristic new technology, this kind of virtue signaling benefits the driver and helps advertise that EVs are becoming mainstream. Other types of regulations make EVs relatively more convenient by allowing them privileged use of HOV or toll lanes, parking spots, or restricted traffic zones (Hardman 2019). In Norway, EV uptake was highest on the Finnøy archipelago, where EV drivers were exempt from high toll charges to use an undersea tunnel (IEA 2018). In Oslo, early benefits for EV drivers such as cordon toll exemptions, free parking, free charging, and access to bus lanes also led to high adoption rates.

Enforcing such privileges is made easier by special license plates that make it easy to identify eligible vehicles.

Charging and Power Infrastructure

Limited access to convenient chargers is one of the biggest barriers to EV adoption because many consumers do not have the option of home charging, and range anxiety persists for longer trips (Colle et al. 2021; Lee and Clark 2018). For urban charging, the challenge is greater in countries with dense settlement patterns, such as China, Korea, or the Netherlands. The Nordic countries, Canada, and the United States have lower population densities and more single-family housing, facilitating access to home charging (Hall and Lutsey 2017; Hardman 2019). Governments have a range of options for facilitating a dense charging infrastructure. They can directly invest in charging facilities or adapt regulations to make it easier for private providers to build and operate chargers. Another important role for the public sector is to ensure the availability of an affordable and clean electricity supply for charging.

Public support helps create a critical mass of charging stations that encourages initial EV adoption, which will then motivate private providers to invest. Generally, charging infrastructure appears to rise in line with EV adoption (figure 3.3). Subsidies can support chargers at the workplace, in public locations, and at home. A variety of charging options not only increases convenience but can also distribute the load on the energy system, for instance, by encouraging charging at work during the day when solar power is most abundant. As noted earlier, subsidies for expanding charging infrastructure are about six times more cost effective than purchase subsidies (Li, Wang et al. 2021).

Private investments in chargers need to be recouped by selling electricity. In some cases, governments have subsidized electricity rates for charging, but doing so involves an uncertain financial commitment and can lead to overconsumption. Furthermore, as chapter 2 shows, many countries already subsidize electricity for all uses, often to the tune of 20 to 40 percent. Electricity should instead be priced to reflect its social marginal cost for all uses,

FIGURE 3.3 Ratio of public chargers per EV stock, 2020

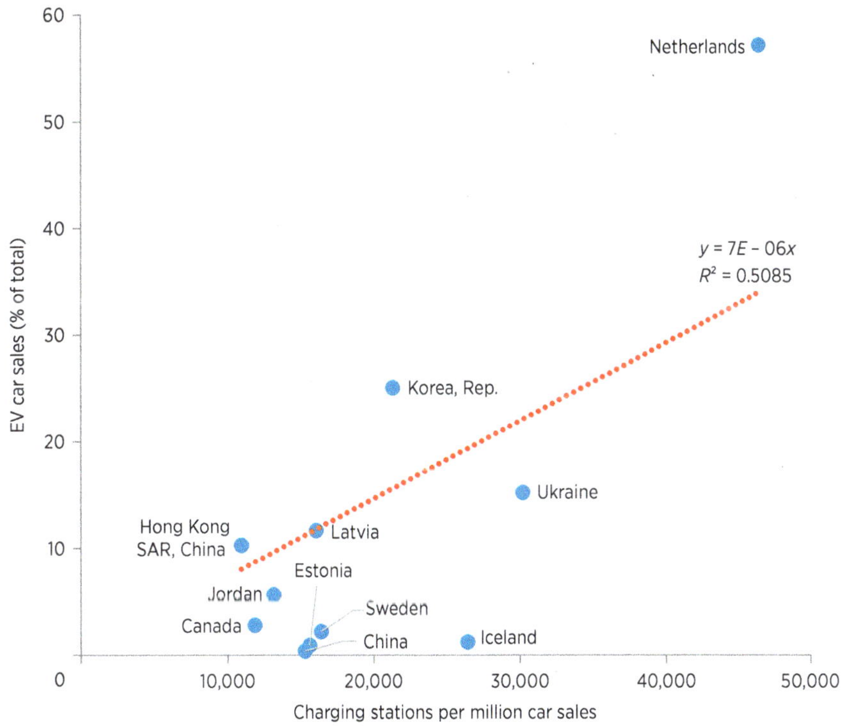

Source: Alam and Lee 2021.
Note: EV = electric vehicle.

addressing affordability concerns with targeted measures (Laderchi, Olivier, and Trimble 2013; Rapson and Muehlegger 2021). More important is to use regulatory approaches to ensure an open and competitive charging ecosystem that keeps rates affordable. Ideally, charging facilities should be developed as easily as gas stations. However, in practice, hurdles are numerous. They range from charging stations being restricted to service certain vehicle brands or payment systems, to lack of standardization of charging adapters.

Governments can also facilitate the development of a charging infrastructure by ensuring that building codes and land use regulations allow or even mandate charger construction. Creative solutions for public charge points include equipping lamp posts with chargers. By switching streetlights to LED, some places have freed up line capacity to allow vehicle charging. Chapter 4 discusses policies related to power systems in more detail. In Sahelian countries, electric mobility is challenged by the scarcity of electricity, but its piloting adoption can start when underpinning social and economic initiatives in selected niches (box 3.2).

The lack of charging infrastructure has been a key concern among consumers. In LMICs, the absence of formal charging stations has been circumvented by the development of simpler, lower-cost approaches, such as battery-swapping arrangements. Some manufacturers have already set up battery-swapping stations on a pilot basis, where delivery personnel of e-commerce companies using EVs can replace their batteries (World Bank 2022a, 2022b). The main constraints preventing a more rapid scale-up of this promising approach are product standardization and proprietary issues around battery technology that can impede ready swapping

BOX 3.2

Electric mobility uptake and broader initiatives in the Sahel

Estimates are that, under the existing meager supply conditions, changing 5 percent of current two- and three-wheelers to electric models would consume 1.3 percent (in Bamako, Mali) and 6.9 percent (in Ouagadougou, Burkina Faso) of the respective countries' electricity production. Changing 70 percent of current two- and three-wheelers to electric models would consume 19.5 percent (in Bamako) and 82 percent (in Ouagadougou) of the countries' electricity production. This situation calls for conscious sequencing in relation to power sector development and a phased and targeted deployment of electric vehicles via piloting exercises. More important, it calls for investment and interventions that would help with the adoption of electric mobility while targeting key development objectives such as creating jobs and mobility-enhancing investment propositions. Sahelian countries have identified several—soon to be implemented—pilot exercises that could provide win-win alternatives to electric vehicle entry points:

- *Electric mototaxis in Bamako* would be introduced in close collaboration with one or more official mototaxi companies already operational in Bamako, allowing pilot projects for a battery-swapping system. This investment concept should be carried out according to the same franchise formula currently in place for internal combustion engine mototaxis. To ensure that the periodic amount paid by the riders to the mototaxi company is not higher than at present, it will be important to select low-cost electric motorcycles that have already (or nearly) achieved price parity with the gasoline-powered ones.
- *Electric bicycles for students and employees in Ouagadougou* would be a pilot project targeting students in higher education (secondary and/or university level), public sector employees, and university administrative staff. Because schools are expected to have a more reliable electricity supply than private homes, charging bicycle batteries would be done during school hours. Participants in the pilot should be identified on a voluntary basis and receive the vehicle free of charge from the sponsoring institutions. In universities, electric bicycles could be used in shared hailing schemes.
- *Electric scooters for mail or newspaper delivery services in Bamako and Ouagadougou* would introduce, in the short term, a few electric scooters to be used for mail or newspaper delivery services. This concept will necessarily have to be realized in close cooperation with the company (public or private) in charge of the delivery. During the pilot phase, the deployment could be limited to 20 electric scooters assigned to a single mail carrier for a fixed period of time (such as six months) in order to collect enough information on driving habits and driving patterns, testing the use of light electric vehicles on targeted and fixed routes with battery recharging during nonworking hours. Recharging would take place at the headquarters of the companies involved, which are assumed to have a reliable electricity supply. Operational costs (charging, maintenance, and so on) should be fully covered by the delivery company.
- *Electric scooters for public sector employees in Bamako and Ouagadougou* for their daily home-to-work commute targets some trips already made by internal combustion engine vehicles. Given the limited accessibility to electricity at home and unstable electricity supply, recharging would need to take place in the offices.

Source: Arroyo Arroyo and Vesin 2021; World Bank 2022a.

of batteries among different brands of EVs. Partnership across manufacturers seems to be a prerequisite for these swapping schemes to succeed. Nonetheless, battery swapping has been seen in China, India, and Thailand and increasingly in Africa. BaaS might be a key enabler for electrification of micromobility and truck fleets (Madalin 2022).

Public, Shared, and Fleet Operations

Transitioning public and shared transportation to EVs poses similar challenges as promoting the adoption of private EVs. This sector includes city buses, minibuses, taxis, ride-shares and—in many lower-income countries—the use of two-wheelers for specific niches and public service provision. First, the role of two- and three-wheelers in the provision of the last mile as a complement to public transportation in rural and remote areas increases the interest in the rollout of e-mototaxis and e-bikes. The use of online payment, booking, and information applications is an opportunity for enhanced services. Thus, shifting two- and three-wheelers to electric can be a good opportunity to tap into the formalization and training of informal mobility providers (Arroyo Arroyo and Vesin 2021). Second, the supply chain for parts is currently concentrated in China and other parts of Asia, while the opportunity to develop greater manufacturing capacity and associated skilled jobs in Africa is being pursued by countries such as Rwanda.

Chinese cities are furthest along in electrifying public transportation and provide useful policy experience. In Shenzhen, a city of about 12 million in southern China, all city buses and taxis are now electric (Berlin, Zhang, and Chen 2020). Effective since 2020, ride-sharing vehicles must also be electric. The city started in the early 2010s with initial pilots and by 2018 had replaced its entire bus fleet. It limited purchases to only a few bus models to reach favorable procurement terms and created a financial leasing arrangement to spread out the total costs. The city still had to rely on national and local subsidies to manufacturers, the bus operating agency, and the provider of charging infrastructure (which it outsourced). Without the subsidy, the total cost of ownership of electric buses in 2020 would have been about 20 percent higher than for diesel buses. As electric bus production becomes more efficient, the authorities are beginning to reduce subsidies, aiming to phase them out completely in time.

Shenzhen's electric buses have sufficient range to run all day, especially given that most bus routes are now shorter feeder lines serving metro stations. As a result, all buses can be charged nightly at central charging depots. Electric buses have cut public transportation CO_2 emissions per 100 kilometers traveled to about half. (Vehicle and electricity production still cause emissions.) Electricity and battery production remain large emitters because of the heavy reliance on fossil fuels in the power sector. Most local air pollution from public transit has been eliminated, which had been the main policy motivation for switching to EVs. The success of Shenzhen's transformation of the public and shared transit sector shows the importance of detailed planning, clear objectives, and a comprehensive road map that reflects transportation, environmental, and industrial policy priorities. Implementation benefited from close partnership among bus operators, bus manufacturers, financial organizations, and charging companies, which has reduced technology uncertainty and costs.

The bus system in Santiago, Chile, is another example of electrification of public transportation in a country that does not have local electric bus manufacturing (World Bank 2020). The system is organized as a public-private partnership under which the government acts as the regulator that collects and distributes revenues; six private operators run the bus lines with a shared electronic payment system; and the main energy companies financed the initial purchases of Chinese-made electric buses, set up the charging system, and provided electricity.

The initial pilots—which demonstrated the suitability of electric buses in the transportation system, showing improvements in quality and convenience for passengers, including noise reductions—will reduce emissions of carbon and other pollutants and pave the way for further conversion of the public vehicle fleet.

As noted in chapter 2, the capital cost premium associated with electric buses can be substantial, particularly given that the number of manufacturers globally is currently quite limited. This premium makes the overall economic and financial case for such vehicles particularly sensitive to the anticipated vehicle mileage and suggests that targeting public transportation systems and routes with particularly high vehicle mileage may be helpful during the transition. Furthermore, packaging bus procurements at the national or even regional level to achieve larger scale could help achieve significant capital cost savings.

Phase II of India's FAME II has been in effect since 2013 and prioritizes the electrification of public transportation. The approach includes earmarked funds for targeted subsidies and a heavy-handed procurement in support of electric bus provision across cities in various provinces. FAME II simultaneously strengthens the bargaining power of states to reduce prices for electric buses and supports the Indian automaking sector. This procurement process, which resulted in prices less than in the gross-cost contracting model, is also known as the Grand Challenge process and has represented an inflection point in India's efforts to scale up electric buses.

Procurement Practices and Demand Consolidation Mechanisms

Governments are trying to overcome the combination of two key obstacles that are keeping the price of EVs relatively high. On the supply side, it is well known that production of EVs is highly concentrated; conversely, the demand side is characterized by small and fragmented markets with little bargaining power and limited access to financing schemes. To overcome these challenges, in phase II of FAME II, India adopted an aggregated procurement approach with concentrated large-scale deployment and standardized procurement specifications to achieve economies of scale. Demand was aggregated across nine major cities having a population of over 4 million (Mumbai, Delhi, Bengaluru, Hyderabad, Ahmedabad, Chennai, Kolkata, Surat, and Pune), buying a total of 5,450 buses with tendered prices on average 37 percent (but up to 52 percent in the Kolkata electric bus batch) lower than previous procurement under phase I, which had the same subsidy (Acharya, Gadepalli, and Ollivier 2022).

The same economic rationale of aggregating demand to increase economies of scale and mitigate risks can be applied at a multicountry scale. Multilateral organizations such as the World Bank Group can play a role in setting in place regional, multicountry facilities that would consolidate and aggregate demand across countries with small markets to attract major commercial financiers. Such facilities could offer blended financing, putting together commercial finance and concessional resources, providing technical assistance, and bringing in the experience and creditworthiness of multilateral development banks to compensate for the lack of a track record of many governments, to mobilize long-term financing to support and accelerate development in a low-carbon transportation sector. A regional financing facility to support clean mobility could bring scale to compensate for the low competition on the supply side of EV production, diversify risks of still-new technologies, reduce transaction costs (many of which are linked to information asymmetries), and address financing needs more flexibly at the country or asset level.

Vehicle Disposal Regulations

Although recycling and reuse of most parts of an EV are no different from standard cars, the expected volume of used batteries will pose new challenges for reuse and recycling. These batteries contain raw materials such as lithium and cobalt that are expensive to mine but can be recovered and reused for manufacturing new batteries. The EU expects annual lithium recycling volumes to eventually reach 33,000 tons (NOW-GmbH 2020).

China expects that, by 2029, 3 million used EV battery packs will be available annually, equivalent to about 108 gigawatts of storage capacity. The EU battery directive regulates requirements for collection, recycling, and disposal techniques. In China, all batteries since 2018 are registered on a platform that tracks each battery through the supply chain. A government directive mandates the establishment of collection plants that will manage batteries' second life (recycling).

Recycling is made complicated by varying battery chemistries and often complex installations, making standardized procedures difficult. So far, demand is low for used batteries for a second life in stationary applications, although new business models are likely to emerge as EVs age and used battery volumes grow. Governments need to use the time until the first cohorts of EVs are retired to put the regulations and infrastructure in place for sustainable reuse and recycling. This problem also has an international dimension. For smaller countries, volumes may be too small for a domestic battery recycling facility. Establishing cross-country networks can create the economies of scale necessary. Given experience from past exports of electronic waste to less affluent countries with inadequate disposal capacity, international regulations should be established to manage the export of EV-related waste (see box 3.3).

BOX 3.3

EV battery recycling: A quick snapshot

The life span of electric vehicle (EV) batteries is generally labeled as eight years or 100,000 miles, which is consistent with battery warranties provided by various EV manufacturers (Kelleher Environmental 2020). Battery failure (manufacturing defects, overheating, faulty charging, and so on) or vehicle collisions could result in an end-of-life sooner than eight years. The life span of an electric bus can vary more dramatically. BYD, a publicly listed Chinese manufacturing company, claimed that its lithium iron phosphate batteries can last up to 7,200 charge-discharge cycles. If assuming one charging cycle per day, the electric bus life span is in the range of 20 years (California Air Resources Board 2020).

Recycling Rate

Battery recycling is one method to reclaim the expensive minerals from the batteries. Reported recycling rates vary dramatically across processes and minerals, but the lithium-ion battery collection recycling rate is about 15 to 25 percent (Larouche et al. 2020). This number could increase to 90 percent by 2030 (Slowik, Lutsey, and Hsu 2020). Motivated by economic policy objectives, China and European countries are the most advanced in recycling capacity, representing about 50 and 33 percent of

(continued)

BOX 3.3 *(continued)*

global capacity, respectively (Steward, Mayyas, and Mann 2019). In 2016, the global battery recycling capacity was 94,000 kilotonnes per year. By 2022, it had increased to about 200 kilotonnes per year, with China accounting for about half (IEA 2021).

Cost of Recycling

The US Department of Energy's National Renewable Energy Laboratory developed a tool in 2016 for calculating the cost of repurposing EV batteries: "PHEV [plug-in hybrid electric vehicle] batteries can be repurposed for as little as US$20/kWh [kilowatt-hour] or US$500 per battery."[a] Adding other aspects of reusing a battery into the equation, the total battery recycling costs would be about US$50 per 100 kWh. "The dynamics of the EV battery recycling market would change when the cost of new EV batteries fell to US$100/kWh" (Kelleher Environmental 2020).

a. See the National Renewable Energy Laboratory's B2U Repurposing Cost Calculator, https://www.nrel.gov/transportation/battery-second-use.html.

Although many countries have invested in developing battery recycling methods and adopted policies pertaining to the handling of hazardous materials, few countries have introduced policies for mandating or incentivizing reuse or recovery of lithium-ion batteries with combined economic and environmental focus. A notable exception is Asia, particularly China and Japan. Europe is only recently considering the inception of a comprehensive regulatory framework for storage management, with the United States and India lagging well behind.

So far, the most promising approach to promote battery recycling lies in extended producer responsibility regulation to make battery recycling effective and economical: "assigning responsibility for recycling while allowing flexibility in its execution would facilitate adaptation to technological developments while ensuring the throughput necessary for recycling facilities" (Bird et al. 2022). Where implemented, this approach is starting to induce joint ventures among manufacturers, with a notable example being Korea's SK Group and Kia Motors initiatives in battery recycling.

Energy Pricing

The decision to purchase an EV is driven not only by the relative capital costs but also by the relative costs of operating the vehicle. The most significant difference in operating costs between ICEVs and EVs is the switch from liquid fuels, such as gasoline and diesel, to electricity. As shown in chapter 2, and discussed in further detail in chapter 4, most countries maintain significant taxes and subsidies affecting the absolute and relative prices of electricity and liquid fuels. Other incentives assign favorable electric tariffs to charging stations and to recharging during off-peak hours.

Although in many cases gasoline and diesel are quite heavily taxed and electricity is subsidized, the opposite can also be true. Moreover, the taxes and subsidies levied on energy products do not necessarily capture the associated environmental externalities. As a result, the choice between ICEVs and EVs can be significantly distorted, and the true relative cost advantages even reversed. In that sense, the reform of energy taxes and subsidies is a critical part of creating the enabling policy environment for EVs—one that neither penalizes EV adoption nor favors it beyond what is warranted economically. Energy subsidies are addressed in further detail in chapter 4.

POLICY PRIORITIES FOR LOW- AND MIDDLE-INCOME COUNTRIES

EV policy experience around the world provides useful insights for countries still in the early stages of the electric mobility transition. These countries can build not only on policies in industrialized countries but also on the rich experience of LMICs. One reason is that the opportunity cost of using scarce resources to fund costly incentives is higher. Most countries face more urgent needs in the transportation sector and beyond. Lower-income countries also have different travel patterns and vehicle fleets. Public transit and smaller vehicles remain more important than in places where car ownership is near saturation levels. Countries should therefore rely less on expensive subsidies and other incentives and instead focus on investments in transportation and energy infrastructure that are needed independently of electric mobility. Additionally, rather than supporting electric car purchases by individuals who are likely more well-off, they should focus on electrifying public transit where feasible and promote electrification of lower-cost two- and three-wheelers, which will benefit lower-income groups.

Most important, countries should concentrate less on specific technologies and instead pursue the broader policy goal of sustainable and affordable transportation. All of these insights suggest five simple principles for electric mobility in low- and middle-income countries.

Avoid Vehicle Subsidization Policies with High Fiscal Costs

EV policies can be costly. EV purchase incentives in leading markets have been effective because they are generous. One study estimated that 13 surveyed countries spent about US$43 billion on demand-side incentives between 2013 and 2020 (Li, Yang et al. 2021). Few low- or middle-income countries can afford to subsidize each EV purchase with US$7,500 as in the United States or €9,000 as in Germany in 2021 (ACEA 2021). Other forms of incentives can also have high fiscal costs. Colombia eliminated the 19 percent sales tax and 35 percent import tariff for fully electric vehicles and reduced both to 5 percent for hybrids (Callejas, Linn, and Steinbuks 2021). These purchase incentives had an average fiscal cost of between US$350 and US$515 per ton of CO_2 avoided. Although reasons might be good to reduce distortionary sales taxes or import tariffs, the revenue loss needs to be made up elsewhere. Moreover, the fact that EVs are already economically or financially attractive on a life-cycle basis in many countries (chapter 2) further weakens the case for subsidizing ownership.

Should LMICs emulate direct purchase incentive programs? For most, the fiscal cost would be too high and the feasible volume of subsidies too small to achieve significant domestic EV adoption. In fact, analysis shows that subsidies to the purchase of EVs are not a very cost-effective way of promoting uptake (Lee, Zhu et al. 2021). Furthermore, EV buyers receiving these subsidies would likely be more well-off residents, so this policy would be regressive because the cost is borne by all taxpayers. For most lower-income countries, a better strategy would be to let richer economies drive down EV costs, then benefit from lower prices and better performance as later adopters—similar to past experience with solar panels or mobile phones.

Target Industrial Policy Measures toward Low-Cost Vehicles

Industrial policy is a different motivation for generous subsidies. Many countries want to support their legacy automakers as they transition to manufacturing a rising share of EVs; alternatively, they may aim to attract new entrants in the market for manufacturing of EVs and components such as batteries. China's central government started an EV subsidy program in 2009 with some local governments providing additional incentives (Li, Zhu et al. 2021), eventually helping China to become a large manufacturer of electric cars and electric buses.

In middle-income countries with significant vehicle manufacturing, direct incentives may sometimes be justified to promote a local industry. Subsidies could be targeted to support domestic production of smaller, more affordable electric cars or electric two- or three-wheelers that are closer to cost parity with ICEVs and are within reach of a broader segment of the population.

Use Public and Shared Transportation as an Entry Point

Public and shared transit is more important in lower-income countries, where a larger share of the population cannot afford a car or motorbike. This segment of the transportation sector includes buses, minibuses like the matatus of Kenya, and taxis and ride-sharing vehicles. Many of these services are informally organized and are essential for providing mobility to the poor. Electrifying some of these fleets would have a useful demonstration effect and address specific transportation problems. Several factors also make public and shared transportation easier to electrify. Charging buses or fleets could be centralized in depots, reducing investment costs. Battery swapping is therefore also easier, though not yet widespread. Vehicles run up high mileage quickly, so higher capital costs amortize faster. Also, lower maintenance needs of EVs keep them on the road more dependably.

The main barrier to broader adoption of electric public and shared transit is, as with private adoption, the higher purchase cost (Alves et al. 2019; BNEF 2018). The purchase cost of electric buses remains somewhat higher than that of diesel buses, in part because the number of manufacturers has so far been limited. However, as shown in chapter 2, given lower maintenance and fuel operating costs, life-cycle costs are already lower in a significant number of cases, particularly when bus mileage is relatively high, and when externality costs are fully accounted for. The "efficient bus" scenario discussed in chapter 2 illustrates how smart procurement and intensive usage of electric buses can significantly improve the economic case.

For public transit, procurement is by governments, so administratively complex subsidy schemes or regulations are not needed. The extra spending also benefits the broader public rather than individual, often well-off, drivers. Also, where diesel vehicles and fuel are expensive, the cost difference shrinks. Countries could explore green financing options to cover the remaining incremental costs. Finally, the benefits of locally pollution-free transportation could be high in areas of a city characterized by severe air pollution. Prioritizing electric buses in such locations can bring targeted relief. Even if electric buses are still expensive, countries should explore opportunities for building local electric bus manufacturing capacity. Electric buses will eventually displace diesel buses, and having more producers will help bring costs down more quickly.

Promote Two- and Three-Wheel Transportation

Whether privately owned or used commercially, two- and three-wheelers provide mobility for lower-income groups in urban and rural areas of many countries. In India, two- and three-wheelers together account for 83 percent of all vehicles (Das, Chandana, and Ray 2020). Globally, as many as 900 million two- and three-wheelers may be on the road today (BNEF 2020). In contrast to electric cars, electric two- and three-wheelers already offer lower life-cycle costs in the vast majority of countries (see chapter 2). Their potential to reduce emissions and noise pollution is considerable, especially in rapidly growing cities in developing countries.

For example, Rwanda has announced ambitious plans to phase out nonelectric two-wheelers (Peters 2020). Currently 20,000 to 30,000 mototaxis operate in Kigali, and a local company has begun producing electric two-wheelers whose batteries can be easily swapped. Or, again, India's main program for electrifying vehicles set aside 23 percent of its funds to support two-wheel rickshaw electrification and 29 percent for three-wheelers (Das, Chandana, and Ray 2020). Initial pilots have begun to replace some of the 51,000 mototaxis in Bangkok with electric two-wheelers (Praiwan 2021).

Yet two- and three-wheelers are often excluded from discussions about electrifying transportation. Instead, they should be seen as an effective and affordable step in the electric mobility transition that complements rather than competes with public and nonmotorized transportation (Berlin, Goetsch, and Alam 2022). Relative to electric cars, electric two- and three-wheelers are more amenable to being manufactured in many LMICs, are easier to maintain, take up less road space, are easier to charge, and are more affordable to a larger share of the population. In addition to electric motorbikes, e-bikes (bicycles) and e-scooters can fill niches in local transportation systems given how short most urban trips are. In cities, local governments can provide the legal basis for such vehicles such as treating them like regular bicycles that do not require licensing or insurance, setting and enforcing standards such as speed limits or helmet requirements, and creating safe infrastructure such as protected bike lanes (ITDP 2019). Even where smaller EVs are cost competitive, additional public support is arguably more justified than for electric cars, because these smaller vehicles tend to promote access to jobs and opportunity for poorer population groups, advancing both equity and environmental objectives.

Focus on Sustainable Mobility Rather Than Specific Technologies

Much of the current attention in the transportation sector is on EVs. They are an important tool for reducing the sector's climate change impacts, but far from the only one. It is important to distinguish between outcomes and ultimate impacts. The proximate outcome of EV policies is increased adoption of such vehicles. But the impact that countries are really after is a reduction in air pollution and greenhouse gases. That means that EV policies "compete" with other policies that achieve the same goals and that may be cheaper, more effective, or better at also addressing other transportation sector objectives such as equitable and affordable access. Examples are policies that reduce the need for travel, make nonmotorized transportation safer, or make public transit use cheaper and more convenient. EV policies should therefore be embedded in broader sustainable transportation strategies such as the Avoid-Shift-Improve paradigm discussed in chapter 1.

EV policies then become one element in an integrated policy mix that addresses all factors contributing to the transportation sector's environmental impacts: the carbon or pollution intensity of vehicle fuels, the vehicles' efficiency in using those fuels, and the amount of vehicle travel (table 3.2). All these factors need to be considered in designing a comprehensive sustainable transportation road map, because they often interact.

For instance, fuel efficiency improvements reduce vehicle operating costs, which could induce more travel and thus potentially cause an offsetting increase in energy consumption and pollution—the well-documented rebound effect, or Jevon's paradox. Easier remote work could encourage sprawl and increased nonwork travel as people move out of dense cities. Measures that address individualized motorized travel demand, such as active (nonmotorized) travel, public transportation, land use changes, or reducing the need for travel through remote work, all contribute to pollution mitigation in transportation. Available evidence,

TABLE 3.2 Pathways to greater road transportation sustainability

Policies	Pollution intensity	Energy consumption	Travel demand
Regulations	• Low-carbon fuel standards • Vehicle emission standards • EV mandates and privileges (HOV lanes, parking)	• Fuel-efficiency standards • Speed limits	n.a.
Prices (taxes, fees, tariffs)	• Carbon taxes • Pollution-based import tariffs	Fuel taxes	Road or mobility charges
Investments (incentives)	• R&D subsidies • Information programs • EV purchase subsidies or tax and tariff reductions	• R&D subsidies • Information programs • Support for nonmotorized (active) travel • Convenient and affordable public transit • Transit-oriented development	• Information programs • Compact development • Support for remote work (such as digital connectivity)

Source: Axsen, Plötz, and Wolinetz 2020.
Note: EV = electric vehicle; HOV = high-occupancy vehicle; n.a. = not applicable; R&D = research and development.

though, shows that their individual impact is often modest or can be realized only in the long term. Countries with continued high population growth and urbanization still have options for avoiding lock-in to unsustainable land-use and transportation systems. The evidence over recent decades has not been encouraging, however. More policy experimentation will be necessary in developing countries to determine the optimal policy mix of regulations favoring low- and zero-emission vehicles, pricing instruments, and measures to reduce travel demand.

Prioritize Policies with General Purpose Benefits

Avoiding expensive subsidy programs does not mean that lower-income countries should ignore the global shift to EVs. Rather than spend on direct demand incentives, they could prepare for the electric mobility transition in ways that have little downside risk. Such no-regrets policies have general purpose benefits, or they involve incentives with low fiscal costs:

- Put institutions and regulations in place that govern imports, sales, maintenance, recycling, and disposal of EVs and components such as batteries.
- Remove existing distortions in the domestic vehicle market caused by protective regulations or high import tariffs (Barwick, Cao, and Li 2021). Such distortions can change the welfare effects of environmental policies, including those promoting EVs.
- Consider fuel-neutral regulatory instruments that encourage the switch to cleaner transportation independent of vehicle type or drivetrain such as tighter emission standards, limits on imports of polluting used cars, or general carbon taxes. In Colombia, a carbon tax would have been more effective at reducing vehicle CO_2 emissions than the government's costly reduction of EV sales taxes and import tariffs, because it encourages substitution within and across fuel types to lower-emitting vehicles (Callejas, Linn, and Steinbuks 2021).

- Prepare for a quick rollout of charging infrastructure once EV adoption becomes widespread. This preparation includes putting aside space for future charging points or adapting building regulations to require charging facilities.
- Develop EV-oriented training programs that will benefit future EV production and maintenance but that also teach portable skills that are useful as economies become increasingly electrified.
- Use inexpensive incentives to encourage early EV adopters such as information programs, special license plates, and incentives that make it more convenient to use EVs, like parking or HOV preferences.
- Improve the power infrastructure, as discussed in chapter 4. Any measures to strengthen national power infrastructure and accelerate its decarbonization will greatly enhance a country's readiness to adopt electric mobility.

REFERENCES

ACEA (European Automobile Manufacturers' Association). 2021. "Electric Vehicles: Tax Benefits and Purchase Incentives." ACEA, Brussels. https://www.acea.auto/files/Electric_vehicles-Tax_benefits_purchase_incentives_European_Union_2021.pdf.

Acharya, Mahua, Ravi Gadepalli, and Gerald Ollivier. 2022. "Grand Challenge for Electric Bus Deployment: Outcomes and Lessons for the Future." Unpublished, World Bank, Washington, DC.

Åhman, M. 2006. "Government Policy and the Development of Electric Vehicles in Japan." *Energy Policy* 34 (4): 433–43. https://doi.org/10.1016/j.enpol.2004.06.011.

Alam, Muneeza Mehmood, and Yoomin Lee. 2021. *Cleaner Vehicles and Charging Infrastructure: Greening Passenger Fleets for Sustainable Mobility.* Transport Decarbonization Investment Series. Washington, DC: World Bank. https://openknowledge.worldbank.org/handle/10986/36516.

Alves, Bianca B., Kavita Sethi, Abel Lopez Dodero, Alejandro Hoyos Guerrero, Diego Puga, Eugenia Yeghyaian, Fiamma Perez Prada, et al. 2019. *Green Your Bus Ride: Clean Buses in Latin America; Summary Report.* Washington, DC: World Bank. https://documents.worldbank.org/en/publication/documents-reports/documentdetail/410331548180859451/green-your-bus-ride-clean-buses-in-latin-america-summary-report.

Arroyo Arroyo, Fatima, and Vincent Vesin. 2021. *Pathways to Electric Mobility in the Sahel: Two and Three-Wheelers in Bamako and Ouagadougou.* Washington, DC: World Bank. https://openknowledge.worldbank.org/handle/10986/37046.

Axsen, Jonn, Patrick Plötz, and Michael Wolinetz. 2020. "Crafting Strong, Integrated Policy Mixes for Deep CO_2 Mitigation in Road Transport." *Nature Climate Change* 10 (9): 809–18. https://www.nature.com/articles/s41558-020-0877-y.

Barwick, Panle Jia, Shengmao Cao, and Shanjun Li. 2021. "Local Protectionism, Market Structure, and Social Welfare: China's Automobile Market." *American Economic Journal: Economic Policy* 13 (4): 112–51. https://doi.org/10.1257/pol.20180513.

Berlin, Annika, Helena Goetsch, and Muneeza Alam. 2022. "Two- and Three-Wheeler Electrification in the Urban Context for Middle- and Low-Income Countries." Background paper prepared for this report, World Bank, Washington, DC.

Berlin, Annika, X. Zhang, and Y. Chen. 2020. "Case Study: Electric Buses in Shenzhen, China." Unpublished, International Energy Agency, Paris. https://iea.blob.core.windows.net/assets/db408b53-276c-47d6-8b05-52e53b1208e1/e-bus-case-study-Shenzhen.pdf.

Bird, Robert, Zachary J. Baum, Xiang Yu, and Jia Ma. 2022. "The Regulatory Environment for Lithium-Ion Battery Recycling." *ACS Energy Letters* 7 (2): 736–40. https://doi.org/10.1021/acsenergylett.1c02724.

BNEF (Bloomberg New Energy Finance). 2018. *Electric Buses in Cities: Driving towards Cleaner Air and Lower CO_2.* New York: BNEF.

BNEF (Bloomberg New Energy Finance). 2020. *Electric Vehicle Outlook 2020.* New York: BNEF.

Bryan, Kevin A., and Heidi L. Williams. 2021. "Innovation: Market Failures and Public Policies." In *Handbook of Industrial Organization*, vol. 5, edited by Kate Ho, Ali Hortaçsu, and Alessandro Lizzeri, 281–388. New York: Elsevier.

California Air Resources Board. 2020. "Appendix E: Battery Cost for Heavy-Duty Electric Vehicles." https://ww2.arb.ca.gov/sites/default/files/2020-06/Appendix%20E%20Battery%20Cost%20for%20Heavy-Duty%20Electric%20Vehicles.pdf.

Callejas, J., Joshua Linn, and Jevgenijs Steinbuks. 2021. "Welfare and Environmental Benefits of Electric Vehicle Tax Policies in Developing Countries: Evidence from Colombia." Policy Research Working Paper 10001, World Bank, Washington, DC. https://openknowledge.worldbank.org/handle/10986/37286.

Colle, Serge, Randy Miller, Theirry Mortier, Marc Coltelli, Andrew Horstead, Kristian Ruby, and Petar Geogiev. 2021. *Accelerating Fleet Electrification in Europe: When Does Reinventing the Wheel Make Perfect Sense?* Brussels: EY Global Power and Eurelectric. https://assets.ey.com/content/dam/ey-sites/ey-com/en_gl/topics/energy/ey-accelerating-fleet-electrification-in-europe-28012021-v2.pdf.

Das, Shyamasis, Chandana Sasidharan, and Anirudh Ray. 2020. *Charging India's Two- and Three-Wheeler Transport: A Guide for Planning Charging Infrastructure for Two- and Three-Wheeler Fleets in Indian Cities.* New Delhi: Alliance for an Energy Efficient Economy. https://aeee.in/our-publications/charging-indias-two-and-three-wheeler-transport/.

Economist. 2022. "Could the EV Boom Run Out of Juice Before It Really Gets Going?" *Economist*, August 14, 2022. https://www.economist.com/business/2022/08/14/could-the-ev-boom-run-out-of-juice-before-it-really-gets-going.

Frith, James. 2021. "Battery Price Declines Slow Down in Latest Pricing Survey." Bloomberg, November 30, 2021. https://www.bloomberg.com/news/articles/2021-11-30/battery-price-declines-slow-down-in-latest-pricing-survey.

Hall, Dale, and Nic Lutsey. 2017. "Emerging Best Practices for Electric Vehicle Charging Infrastructure." White Paper, International Council on Clean Transportation, Washington, DC. https://theicct.org/publication/emerging-best-practices-for-electric-vehicle-charging-infrastructure/.

Hardman, Scott. 2019. "Understanding the Impact of Reoccurring and Non-financial Incentives on Plug-In Electric Vehicle Adoption—A Review." *Transportation Research Part A: Policy and Practice* 119: 1–14. https://doi.org/10.1016/j.tra.2018.11.002.

IEA (International Energy Agency). 2018. *Nordic EV Outlook 2018: Insights from Leaders in Electric Mobility.* Organisation for Economic Co-operation and Development/IEA. https://www.nordicenergy.org/wp-content/uploads/2018/05/NordicEVOutlook2018.pdf.

IEA (International Energy Agency). 2021. *Global EV Outlook 2021.* Paris: IEA. https://www.iea.org/reports/global-ev-outlook-2021.

IFC (International Finance Corporation). 2021. "Electric Bus Concept Validation in Kigali, Rwanda." Unpublished, IFC, Washington, DC.

ITDP (Institute for Transportation and Development Policy). 2019. "E-bikes and E-scooters: Drivers of Climate Action." *Transport Matters* (blog), September 24, 2019. https://www.itdp.org/2019/09/24/e-bikes-e-scooters-drivers-of-climate-action.

Jaffe, Adam B., Richard G. Newell, and Robert N. Stavins. 2005. "A Tale of Two Market Failures: Technology and Environmental Policy." *Ecological Economics* 54 (2–3): 164–74. https://doi.org/10.1016/j.ecolecon.2004.12.027.

Kelleher Environmental. 2020. *Research Study on Reuse and Recycling of Batteries Employed in Electric Vehicles: The Technical, Environmental, Economic, Energy, and Cost Implications of Reusing and Recycling EV Batteries; Summary Report.* Washington, DC: Energy API (American Petroleum Institute). https://www.api.org/-/media/files/oil-and-natural-gas/fuels/ev battery reuse recyc api summary report 24Nov2020.pdf.

Laderchi, Caterina Ruggeri, Anne Olivier, and Chris Trimble. 2013. *Balancing Act: Cutting Energy Subsidies while Protecting Affordability.* Eastern Europe and Central Asia Reports. Washington, DC: World Bank. https://openknowledge.worldbank.org/handle/10986/12296/.

Lane, Bradley W., Natalie Messer-Betts, Devin Hartmann, Sanya Carley, Rachel M. Krause, and John D. Graham. 2013. "Government Promotion of the Electric Car: Risk Management or Industrial Policy?" *European Journal of Risk Regulation* 4 (2): 227–45. https://www.jstor.org/stable/24323358.

Larouche, François, Farouk Tedjar, Kamyab Amouzegard, Georges Houlachi, Patrick Bouchard, George P. Demopoulos, and Karim Zaghib. 2020. "Progress and Status of Hydrometallurgical and Direct Recycling of Li-Ion Batteries and Beyond." *Materials* 13 (3): 801. https://doi.org/10.3390/ma13030801.

Le Petit, Yoann, and Lucien Mathieu. 2020. *Why Uber Should Go Electric.* Brussels: European Federation for Transport and Environment AISBL. https://www.transportenvironment.org/discover/why-uber-should-go-electric.

Lee, Euna, and Jai S. Mah. 2020. "Industrial Policy and the Development of the Electric Vehicles Industry: The Case of Korea." *Journal of Technology Management & Innovation* 15 (4): 71–80. http://dx.doi.org/10.4067/S0718-27242020000400071.

Lee, Henry, and Alex Clark. 2018. "Charging the Future: Challenges and Opportunities for Electric Vehicle Adoption." HKS Working Paper RWP18-026, Kennedy School of Government, Harvard University, Cambridge, MA. https://www.hks.harvard.edu/publications/charging-future-challenges-and-opportunities-electric-vehicle-adoption.

Li, Shanjun, Binglin Wang, Muxi Yang, and Fan Zhang. 2021. "The Global Diffusion of Electric Vehicles: Lessons from the First Decade." Policy Research Working Paper 9882, World Bank, Washington, DC. https://openknowledge.worldbank.org/handle/10986/36740.

Li, Shanjun, Xianglei Zhu, Yiding Ma, Fan Zhang, and Hui Zhou. 2021. "The Role of Government in the Market for Electric Vehicles: Evidence from China." *Journal of Policy Analysis and Management* 41 (2): 450–85. https://doi.org/10.1002/pam.22362.

Liu, Lanjian, Tian Zhang, Anne-Perinne Avrin, and Xianwen Wang. 2020. "Is China's Industrial Policy Effective? An Empirical Study of the New Energy Vehicles Industry." *Technology in Society* 63: 101356. https://doi.org/10.1016/j.techsoc.2020.101356.

Lutsey, Nic, Mikhail Grant, Sandra Wappelhorst, and Huan Zhou. 2018. "Power Play: How Governments Are Spurring the Electric Vehicle Industry." White Paper, International Council on Clean Transportation, Washington, DC. https://theicct.org/sites/default/files/publications/EV_Government_WhitePaper_20180514.pdf.

Madalin. 2022. "Battery Swapping for Electric Vehicles 2022–2032." *Hafenstrom* (blog), July 7, 2022. https://hafenstrom.com/battery-swapping-for-electric-vehicles-2022-2032.

Mahdavi, Paasha, Cesar B. Martinez-Alvarez, and Michael Ross. 2020. "Why Do Governments Tax or Subsidize Fossil Fuels?" Working Paper 541, Center for Global Development, Washington, DC.

Mathieu, Lucien, and Julia Poliscanova. 2020. *Mission (Almost) Accomplished: Carmakers' Race to Meet the 2020/21 CO_2 Targets and the EU Electric Cars Market.* Brussels: European Federation for Transport and Environment AISBL. https://www.transportenvironment.org/wp-content/uploads/2021/05/2020_10_TE_Car_CO2_report_final-1.pdf.

McKerracher, Colin, Aleksandra O'Donovan, Nikolas Soulopoulos, Andrew Grant, Siyi Mi, David Doherty, Ryan Fisher, et al. 2021. *Electric Vehicle Outlook 2021.* New York: Bloomberg New Energy Finance. https://about.newenergyfinance.com/electric-vehicle-outlook.

Mock, Peter. 2021. "Europe's Lost Decade: About the Importance of Interim Targets." *International Council on Clean Transportation* (blog), May 9, 2021. https://theicct.org/blog/staff/interim-targets-europe-may2021.

NOW-GmbH. 2020. "Factsheet: Electric Mobility and Recycling: What Happens to Lithium-Ion Batteries from E-vehicles?" NOW-GmbH, Berlin. https://www.now-gmbh.de/wp-content/uploads/2020/10/EN_Factsheet_RecyclingSecondLife_2020.pdf.

Oqubay, Arkebe, Christopher Cramer, Ha-Joon Chang, and Richard Kozul-Wright, eds. 2020. *The Oxford Handbook of Industrial Policy.* Oxford: Oxford University Press. https://doi.org/10.1093/oxfordhb/9780198862420.001.0001.

Peters, Adele. 2020. "This Electric Motorcycle Startup Is Transforming the Rwandan Taxi Industry." *Fast Company,* February 6, 2020. https://www.fastcompany.com/90460273/this-electric-motorcycle-startup-is-transforming-the-rwandan-taxi-industry.

Poliscanova, Julia. 2020. "Plug-In Hybrids in New Emissions Scandal as Tests Show Higher Pollution than Claimed." European Federation for Transport and Environment AISBL, Brussels. https://www.transportenvironment.org/discover/plug-hybrids-new-emissions-scandal-tests-show-higher-pollution-claimed.

Praiwan, Yuthana. 2021. "Test Run of Electric Motorcycle Taxis." *Bangkok Post,* December 27, 2021. https://www.bangkokpost.com/thailand/general/2238543/test-run-of-electric-motorcycle-taxi.

Rapson, David S., and Erich Muehlegger. 2021. "The Economics of Electric Vehicles." NBER Working Paper W29093, National Bureau of Economic Research, Cambridge, MA. https://www.nber.org/papers/w29093.

Reuters. 2021. "Electric Cars Rise to Record 54% Market Share in Norway." *Guardian*, January 5, 2021. https://www.theguardian.com/environment/2021/jan/05/electric-cars-record-market-share-norway.

Rodrik, Dani. 2014. "Green Industrial Policy." *Oxford Review of Economic Policy* 30 (3): 469–91. https://www.jstor.org/stable/43664659.

Rokadiya, Shikha, and Anup Bandivadekar. 2016. "Hybrid and Electric Vehicles in India: Current Scenario and Market Incentives." Working Paper 2016-26, International Council on Clean Transportation, Washington, DC.

SEIA (Solar Energy Industries Association). 2019. "The Adverse Impact of Section 201 Tariffs: Lost Jobs, Lost Deployment and Lost Investments." SEIA, Washington, DC. https://seia.org/sites/default/files/2019-12/SEIA-Tariff-Analysis-Report-2019-12-3-Digital.pdf.

Seyerlein, Christoph. 2022. "Habeck Wants to Put a Stop to Mass Exports of Subsized E-cars." *Next Mobility*, February 17, 2022. https://www.next-mobility.de/habeck-will-massenhaften-exporten-subventionierter-e-autos-den-riegel-vorschieben-a-1096432.

Sguazzin, Anthony. 2022. "Opibus of Kenya Launches Its First Africa-Designed Electric Bus." Bloomberg, January 19, 2022. https://www.bloomberg.com/news/articles/2022-01-19/opibus-of-kenya-launches-its-first-africa-designed-electric-bus#xj4y7vzkg.

Slowik, Peter, Nic Lutsey, and Chih-Wei Hsu. 2020. "How Technology, Recycling, and Policy Can Mitigate Supply Risks to the Long-Term Transition to Zero-Emission Vehicles." White Paper, International Council on Clean Transportation, Washington, DC. https://theicct.org/publication/how-technology-recycling-and-policy-can-mitigate-supply-risks-to-the-long-term-transition-to-zero-emission-vehicles/.

Steward, Darlene, Ahmad Mayyas, and Margaret Mann. 2019. "Economics and Challenges of Li-Ion Battery Recycling from End-of-Life Vehicles." *Procedia Manufacturing* 33: 272–79. https://doi.org/10.1016/j.promfg.2019.04.033.

van der Steen, Martjin, R. M. Van Schelven, R. Kotter, M. J. W. van Twist, and Peter van Deventer. 2015. "EV Policy Compared: An International Comparison of Governments' Policy Strategy towards E-Mobility." In *E-mobility in Europe*, edited by Walter Leal Filho and Richard Kotter, 27–53. Cham, Switzerland: Springer. https://doi.org/10.1007/978-3-319-13194-8_2.

Wappelhorst, Sandra. 2020. "The End of the Road? An Overview of Combustion-Engine Car Phase-Out Announcements across Europe." Briefing, International Council on Clean Transportation, Washington, DC. https://theicct.org/publications/combustion-engine-car-phase-out-EU.

World Bank. 2020. *Lessons from Chile's Experience with E-mobility: The Integration of E-Buses in Santiago.* Report AUS0001853. Washington, DC: World Bank. https://openknowledge.worldbank.org/handle/10986/34435.

World Bank. 2021. "Design and Implementation of the Proposed Electric Vehicles Risk Sharing Program (EV-RSP) for India." Unpublished, World Bank, Washington, DC.

World Bank. 2022a. "Pathways to Electric Mobility in the Sahel: Two and Three-Wheelers in Bamako and Ouagadougou." World Bank, Washington, DC.

World Bank. 2022b. "Rwanda: Inclusive and Electric Last Mile Connectivity Study; Component E: Final Summary Report." Unpublished, World Bank, Washington, DC.

4

Energy Policies to Support the Transition to Electric Mobility

INTRODUCTION

As electric vehicles (EVs) gradually replace gas- and diesel-fueled vehicles, the absolute increase in power demand will likely be less a concern to governments and utilities than the distribution of this new demand over time and space (Engel et al. 2018). Managing the necessary upgrades to transmission and distribution infrastructure will be challenging for any power system, but particularly so in low- and middle-income countries, where utilities struggle to provide basic services. An equally important challenge will be to adapt the energy pricing and fiscal regime to ensure that consumers have the incentive to behave efficiently in regard to vehicle charging, and that the financial equilibrium of power utilities is not further stressed. Without early and comprehensive preparation, countries risk further degrading power supply systems that are essential to growth and welfare.

A review of early evidence and academic studies suggests three policy priorities. First, countries should conduct detailed power system planning based on modeling and simulations to assess the impact of electric mobility on their power system, including not only generation but also, and crucially, the transmission and distribution grid. Such analyses will inform concrete investment plans and regulatory reforms that get the power system in shape for widespread EV adoption. Second, a critical element of EV-oriented power sector strategies is demand management that shaves off peak loads and ultimately makes EVs an integral part of the power system by tight grid integration. An important element of demand management will be correcting numerous distortions in electricity and fuel pricing. Third, to secure the greatest possible climate and pollution reduction benefits from EVs, policy makers and utilities need to continue

This chapter was made possible thanks to funding from the World Bank's Energy Sector Management Assistance Program (ESMAP) under the Zero Carbon Public Sector.

to advance with improvements in energy efficiency along the electricity supply chain, as well as in the greening of power generation, in all policy decisions.

The International Energy Agency (IEA) expects EV demand for electricity globally to rise from 55 terawatt-hours (TWh) in 2020 to 1,150 TWh by 2030 if stated policies are implemented. That demand is roughly equivalent to twice today's total electricity use in Brazil (IEA 2022). For most countries, IEA expects that the EV share of power consumption will not exceed 6 percent by 2030 and 10 percent by 2040, relative to about 1 percent today. Moreover, its power consumption needs to be considered in the context of wider electrification of many other uses of energy (such as heating and cooling), shifting patterns of sectoral demand due to economic restructuring, and the general trend toward greater energy efficiency. A greater concern is that this demand will likely be concentrated when many EV owners charge at once or where adoption is high. Uncoordinated charging—which carries the attendant risk that vehicle recharging could be highly concentrated in certain locations or at certain times of day—may overwhelm existing distribution networks or require expensive upgrades to match short-duration peak demand. Such concerns could either be addressed by further investment in grid upgrades or be more cost-effectively resolved by demand management measures, which redistribute charging activity across locations and time periods. Options range from relatively simple information and incentive programs to more complex technical solutions. Time-of-use electricity pricing creates incentives for EV users to charge when overall demand is lowest. Closer integration of EVs with the grid through smart charging allows system operators to guide charging schedules and may in the future make EV batteries an integral part of the grid. However, such integration may require additional investments in smart charging infrastructure. The payoff is a more stable power system and savings from avoided grid reinforcements.

EVs will be just one new use of electricity that will strain power supply systems, already struggling to keep pace with the demands of economic development while on a decarbonization trajectory. Upgrading generation and transmission requires considerable investment but is relatively concentrated in a few "lumpy" projects. Much more challenging will be to upgrade local distribution and feeder systems, which can number in the hundreds of thousands and may be overstretched in areas of rapid urbanization. As noted in chapter 2, making the required investments will be harder if persistent price distortions in many countries' energy sectors are not removed.

Ensuring security of supply requires integrated power planning to assess the impact of EV adoption scenarios, both at the systems level and for local distribution systems. Planning and analysis will identify the most efficient technical options, gauge the required level of investment, and suggest regulatory and market reforms that help pay for the investments and ensure security of supply.

As discussed in chapter 2, because EVs are considerably more efficient in their energy use, they already contribute to the global goal of avoiding dangerous climate change even in countries where fossil fuels dominate electricity generation. Nevertheless, carbon benefits can be further enhanced as power systems decarbonize. Throughout the process of preparing for electric mobility, policy makers and utilities need to search for opportunities to improve the efficiency of the power system and to shift to zero carbon energy sources. Wind and solar energy are already cost competitive, but reliable power supply also requires large-scale electricity storage, the cost of which is expected to fall over the coming years. Table 4.1 presents an overview of the main concerns discussed in this chapter in the context of developing countries.

TABLE 4.1 EV power system impacts in the context of developing countries

Category	Impacts	Developing country context
Impact on power demand	• Increase in total energy consumption • Reshaping daily load curve • Changing the magnitude, the duration, and potentially the timing of the peak load • Changing the variability of the load profile and increasing the uncertainty of load	• Geographical location, extreme weather, demography, and driving patterns also affect uptake, EV power consumption, and charging behavior • E2Ws and E3Ws might be a dominant mode in many economies • Economic, regulatory, and geographical barriers in establishing public charging infrastructure
Impact on distribution system	• Overloading of feeders and transformers • Additional power losses • Voltage deviations • Power quality issues (harmonic distortion)	• Inadequately designed and weak distribution systems • High level of distribution system losses • High rate of transformer failures • Lack of appropriate management, standards, and regulations • Already high reinforcement requirements due to growing demand
Impact on transmission system	• Risk of congestion because of insufficient transmission capacity • Increased need for flexible reactive power	• Low level of interconnectivity and cross-border capacity • Lack of appropriate regulations holding back Investments • High investment requirements to provide adequate level of interconnections with growing demand
Impact on generation	• Need for new generation capacity investments • Increased power system emissions • High ramping requirements due to sharp increase in power demand • Increased need for ancillary services • Increased need for storage	• Insufficient capacity and reliability to satisfy even current needs • High generation investment requirements due to rapidly growing demand • Carbon-intensive generation fleet, often based on poor-quality fossil-fuel-powered units • Poor electricity market regulation and difficulties in providing reserves
Impact on utilities	• Electricity tariff structures not designed with EV charging in mind • Where electricity is subsidized, financial position of utilities may be weakened by EV adoption	• Increasing block tariffs commonplace and may penalize EV charging • Time-of-use charging and associated smart meters relatively rare • Electricity prices tend to embody significant subsidies and cross-subsidies

Source: World Bank.
Note: E2W = electric two-wheeler; E3W = electric three-wheeler; EV = electric vehicle.

ELECTRIC MOBILITY POSES CHALLENGES FOR POWER SYSTEMS

EV adoption poses a range of challenges for power systems. Perhaps the most obvious challenge, the boost to electricity demand, turns out to be the least problematic to handle. Of greater concern is the significant redistribution of load and resulting potential for localized grid overload. Less often discussed, but equally important, electric mobility throws into relief numerous inadequacies in the pricing framework and fiscal regime for the electricity sector.

EV Adoption Will Boost Demand for Electricity

Switching a rising share of the vehicle fleet to electric motors will reduce the demand for oil and increase demand for electricity. In many developing countries, new EV demand could worsen existing shortcomings in the power supply sector, among them aging and inefficient generation units, underinvestment, and poor market design.

EV demand will coincide with new demand from other uses, such as space cooling, as well as growing demand from population and income growth. Large and growing countries such as Brazil, Nigeria, and Pakistan expect large increases in electricity consumption and consequently a vast need for additional generation capacity. In such contexts, EV demand will be just one among many factors driving investment needs.

IEA's "stated policies" scenario predicts an increase of the global stock of EVs (excluding two- and three-wheelers) from 18 million in 2020 to almost 100 million, or 10 percent of the road vehicle fleet, by 2030 (IEA 2022). In 2020, EVs used about 55 TWh of electricity globally, of which 5 TWh were consumed by electric two- and three-wheelers in China and equate roughly to current total electricity demand in the Czech Republic. Under IEA's stated policies scenario, electricity demand from EVs reaches 780 TWh by 2030 (IEA 2021b). In the "announced pledge" scenario that includes all recent major national announcements of 2030 targets and longer-term net zero and other pledges, demand would increase to 1,100 TWh by the end of the decade, with the largest demand in China (330 TWh), Europe (187 TWh), and the United States (153 TWh).

Even in optimistic scenarios, additional power demand from EVs is significant but not overwhelming, with very few salient exceptions. A case in point is Sahelian countries (see chapter 3). Electricity generation will need to rise in any case. Decarbonization will shift additional energy uses such as industrial processes or heating from fossil fuels to electricity (IEA 2021a). Rising temperatures and growing wealth will increase electricity use for air conditioning. In lower-income countries, expanding electricity access to underserved and growing populations remains an urgent task. Improved energy efficiency and economic shifts to less-energy-intensive sectors may dampen some expected demand growth. Against this backdrop, EV demand will not dramatically change the power sector outlook in most countries, especially because it will unfold gradually, with relatively slow uptake expected in lower-income countries. In most scenarios, the EV share of power consumption does not exceed 6 percent by 2030 and 10 percent by 2040 (IEA 2022; Taljegard et al. 2019), and much less in emerging markets at the initial stages of the electric mobility transition (Kapustin and Grushevenko 2020).

More detailed studies have looked at the impacts in specific places. A scenario for Colombia estimates that a 10 percent share of electric or hybrid cars by 2030 would trigger an annual electricity demand of 2.9 TWh, which corresponds to about 3 percent of total national consumption (Unidad de Planeación Minero-Energética 2020).

If all passenger car sales in India were electric by 2030, the additional demand would reach 82 TWh per year, some 3.3 percent of total demand (Abhyankar et al. 2017). In Türkiye, 2.5 million EVs in 2030 (10 percent of the stock and 55 percent of sales) translates into an additional 4.1 TWh annually and a 12.5 percent increase in peak demand (Saygin et al. 2019). In Vietnam, a 20 percent EV penetration for cars and motorcycles would raise power demand to 9 TWh per year, some 3.3 percent of total demand (IES and MKE 2016). Another interesting scenario undertaken for Chile assumes a level of 150,000 electric cars, 28,000 taxis and 360 buses (Manríquez et al. 2020). The study estimates this level will lead to an increase in generation investments of about 3 percent (US$18 million) and increased operational costs of 1 percent (US$18 million). A study for Chongqing, China, assumes 2 million electric cars and unmanaged charging (Li et al. 2020). It finds that evening peaks would increase by about 7 percent, requiring an increase in operating costs of almost 8 percent (US$6.5 billion). For India, finally, a national-level study assumes a stock of electric two-wheelers of 367 million in addition to 89 million electric cars by 2030 (Abhyankar et al. 2017). The findings suggest that the peak charging load will exceed 30 gigawatts, which will be 6 percent of the total peak load by 2030, and that this additional demand can be fully met with planned capacity expansion.

EVs Will Significantly Redistribute Power Load

The specific profile of electricity demand from EVs could pose a greater challenge to national and local power grids than the overall associated increase in electricity usage. Before EVs, most power systems experience an evening peak for residential use and a morning or evening peak for commercial use. EV charging will not be distributed uniformly over time and space, so peaking demand could stress power systems even if capacity is adequate overall. The pattern of EV charging will depend on a number of variables that shape the so-called load curve. One factor is the vehicle mode, because different types of EVs will be charged at different times of the day (IEA 2020). Charging demand will tend to peak in the evening after private car owners return from work and public buses return to the depot for overnight charging. These times coincide with existing high domestic demand periods, such as in the predicted load patterns for Malé in Maldives in figure 4.1. Electric two- and three-wheelers have small batteries, and their charging is more likely to be distributed over the course of the day (Weiss, Cloos, and Helmers 2020). Light commercial vehicles such as delivery vans and shared transportation such as taxis are also more likely to require additional charging during the day. Overall, a concentration of charging demand during the evening across a range of EV types seems likely.

FIGURE 4.1 Predicted power loads in Malé, Maldives, on a typical working day in 2030, with and without EVs

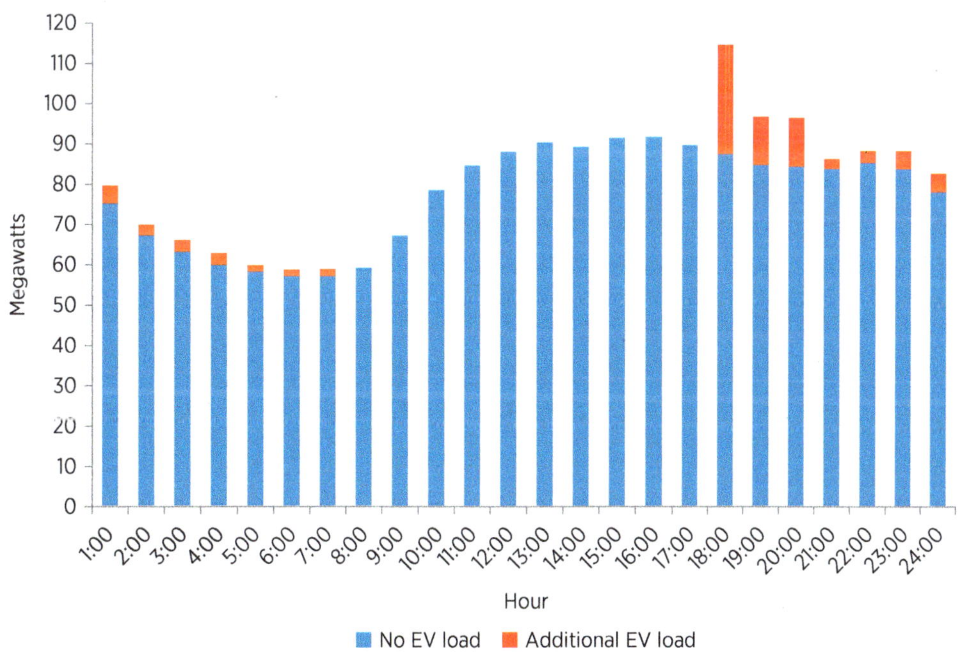

Source: Suski et al. 2021.
Note: EV = electric vehicle.

Although the broad demand patterns are similar, the vehicle mix in a given location shapes the aggregate charging pattern. In higher-income countries, personal cars will likely make up the largest share of the EV fleet. As shown in chapter 2, in many developing countries, buses, two- and three-wheelers, or taxis dominate the vehicle fleet and thus the emerging EV market. Differences between workdays or weekends, or increased demand at certain times of the year such as the beginning or end of major public holidays, further complicate demand patterns. For example, during the month of the 2018 Spring Festival holiday in China, demand at highway charge points doubled compared to the prior month (Hove and Sandalow 2019).

Geographic concentration of EVs, particularly those with large charging demand, could cause spikes in the load curve even if overall EV penetration remains small. For instance, a larger number of electric cars in a high-income neighborhood could stress the local distribution system if charging is uncoordinated. Sudden loads from buses at fast charging stations can cause high variability and load spikes locally (Rogge, Wollny, and Sauer 2015). Geography also influences absolute demand. Congestion, very high or very low temperatures, and hilly terrain all cause efficiency losses in EVs and increase demand for electricity (Florio, Absi, and Feillet 2021). Use of heating and air conditioning, for instance, can reduce an EV's range by up to 50 percent in hot and humid conditions, and steep hills by more than 20 percent (IEA 2019; Liu, Yamamoto, and Morikawa 2017).

Other factors affecting the magnitude and timing of local demand include the type of EV: plug-in hybrids have smaller batteries and might be more appropriate initially in developing countries with fewer charging points and geographic characteristics that reduce the range of pure EVs. Demography can also play a role (Zhang et al. 2020). For instance, rural residents tend to drive longer distances than urban ones. Or again, younger and wealthier drivers tend to cause later charging peaks. Understanding these patterns and trends helps utilities and policy makers anticipate where and when transportation demand for electricity will be concentrated, supporting proactive rather than reactive power system planning.

Discussions about the electric mobility transition often overlook the importance of local distribution systems. This part of the electric power system will need perhaps the largest improvements. EV charging will require some new access points, often along highway corridors and at higher voltages for fast charging. However, much of the requisite vehicle charging will be conducted at traditional end-use locations such as homes or businesses, placing additional strain on systems not designed to sustain such loads. In many developing countries, the distribution system is the weakest link in the power supply system. Without sufficient upgrades, extensive EV charging could cause overloading of feeders and transformers, voltage deviations, power losses, and power quality problems (Crozier, Morstyn, and McCulloch 2020). Given the inadequacies of existing distribution infrastructure, such upgrades will likely be required in any case, and electrification of transportation will help increase the economic benefit and financial return associated with these necessary investments.

Even at moderate EV penetration, vehicle charging could stress local power systems, creating hotspots in higher-income neighborhoods with higher EV adoption, or at higher-use charging locations such as parking lots. Although most EVs are likely to be recharged slowly using conventional power connections at homes and offices, to the extent that fast-charging systems are adopted, the load requirements may be multiple times higher (Hensley, Knupfer, and Pinner 2018). In many places, buses and fleet vehicles like taxis are likely the first to be electrified at larger scale. Those types of vehicles rely on centralized charging facilities, which will greatly increase power demand at specific locations. For instance, almost 300,000 taxi minibuses in South Africa that could be electrified provide three-quarters of all work and school trips (ESMAP, forthcoming).

A depot for 75 buses in Chile needed 6 megawatts of power, requiring upgrades of local distribution infrastructure. And, in India, a bus depot charger may require US$150,000 in distribution system upgrades (Acharya, Gadepalli, and Ollivier 2022).

The biggest concern in distribution grids is overloading transformers and feeders. One study estimates that 312,000 low-voltage feeders in the United Kingdom—one-third of all such feeders in the country—will need to be upgraded by 2050 to manage EV charging that is often clustered locally (EA Technology 2016). A large share of the distribution system is aging even in higher-income countries, and overloading will reduce the lifetime further. The costs will add up (Sahoo, Mistry, and Baker 2019). In a Danish region with 127 EVs, the local distribution grid would require a €52,000 investment to upgrade transformers and cables (ESMAP, forthcoming). Electrification of 500 vehicles in 25 postal hubs in Madrid would require more than €120,000 in upgrades in the distribution network to enable fast charging. In New Zealand, a 10 percent EV penetration would require US$22 million in upgrades, rising to US$154 million with a 40 percent adoption rate.

Higher levels of EV charging can also cause voltage instability, power quality problems, and power losses. System voltage should normally remain within 10 percent of optimal levels for safe operations, which can be exceeded during charging peaks. When EV chargers draw a great deal of power, they cause highly variable loads, which can lead to so-called harmonic distortions, which are the main cause of power quality issues. A large proportion of solar photovoltaic energy in the local power supply could worsen these problems, requiring upgrades of distribution systems (Angelim and Affonso 2019). Low power quality and power losses during transmission and distribution are already a major problem in many developing regions. India has been losing 26 percent of power annually and up to 60 percent in some regions; Latin America and the Caribbean and Sub-Saharan Africa have losses of about 17 percent (ESMAP, forthcoming). Poor planning and regulation, limited resources often related to large electricity subsidies, and hasty deployment have made power systems prone to failures, especially in rural areas, where feeders need to cover large distances. In many contexts, meshed distribution networks rather than the more common radial or tree architecture could be better suited for many developing country contexts, including small island developing states (IRENA 2019a).

Large-scale EV deployment will also affect transmission lines. Estimates of how much upgrading will be necessary vary widely. One study for the Nordic countries expects a 60 percent capacity increase with full EV penetration and uncoordinated charging by 2050 (ESMAP, forthcoming). In contrast, another study for Chile found no major upgrades were required even at high levels of EV adoption. For the US market, a 15 percent EV penetration requires a US$420 transmission investment per EV through 2030. Even without major EV adoption, large investments will be required in lower-income regions because of investment backlog and rising demand. Africa will need to spend between US$3.2 billion and US$4.3 billion annually between 2015 and 2040 (African Development Bank 2019). India expects that US$24 billion will be needed by 2025 (Economic Times 2020; Zhang 2019). More broadly, IEA estimates that universal access to electricity by 2030 will require additional investments of US$391 billion, of which US$115 billion will be for distribution and transmission upgrades (IEA 2019).

Electric Mobility May Also Exacerbate Financial Stress on Power Utilities

In addition to any physical stresses that EV adoption may place on power systems is the potential for significant financial stresses. These stresses arise from the electricity sector's price distortions. Two issues are of particular relevance—the level of prices and the structure of tariffs.

Subsidization of electricity supply is widespread in low- and middle-income countries (Parry, Black, and Vernon 2021). Even if individual consumers and firms benefit from lower prices, electricity subsidies typically represent a net cost to society. They cause fiscal deficits and weaken power utility finances, starving them of necessary funds for preventive maintenance and new investment, and gradually leading to a deterioration in service quality. Subsidies also encourage waste from overuse of electricity, potentially leading to shortages and excessive environmental impacts. In the context of electric mobility, subsidization of electricity supply poses two distinct risks.

First, subsidization of electricity may lead to overadoption of EVs. As noted in chapter 2, a key advantage of EVs from a consumer standpoint is lower energy bills. Although electricity has a natural cost advantage over liquid fuels in transportation, given the higher energy efficiency of electric motors, this advantage will be exaggerated if electricity is subsidized or at least taxed less heavily than gasoline and diesel. Some fiscal differentiation may be warranted by the fact that electricity typically has lower associated externality costs than liquid fuels. However, for most countries studied, the fiscal advantage of electricity over liquid fuels significantly exceeds the associated difference in externality costs. The result may be to accelerate the transition to electric mobility beyond what would be warranted on economic grounds. This concern underscores the importance of looking at electricity pricing policy not only in isolation but also in relation to substitute sources of energy for the transportation sector. The relative price of electricity needs to be considered alongside its absolute price.

Second, electricity subsidization may exacerbate the precarious finances of many power utilities across the developing world. When subsidy policies lead power utilities to charge tariffs below cost recovery levels, the utilities lose money on every unit of electricity sold. Thus an important new source of power demand—electric mobility—will only widen the power sector's financial deficit. In the short term, this will create many operational and financial challenges for the utility, likely to result in undermaintenance of the system and an accumulation of debts on the balance sheet. Further, the rationale for subsidizing electricity for household use may not necessarily carry over to subsidizing electricity for transportation, particularly if private EVs are regarded as something of a luxury good. Electricity subsidies are already widely known for being regressive in distributional impact (Komives et al. 2005), which the adoption of electric mobility could aggravate.

Another important issue is that electricity tariff structures are often designed in ways not especially compatible with EV adoption. Across low- and middle-income countries, rising block tariff structures remain widespread (Foster and Witte 2020), the implication being that home charging of EVs is likely to take households into more highly priced consumption blocks. To some extent, this situation might be viewed as a counterweight to concerns about distributional incidence. However, depending on the specificities of the tariff structure design, it could mean that vehicle charging attracts punitive rates that dissuade adoption. Additionally, time-of-day pricing, which is essential to managing demand for charging EVs and directing it toward off-peak periods, is comparatively rare in low- and middle-income countries, in part because of the prerequisite investment in smart meters to make it technically possible.

POWER SYSTEM IMPACTS OF ELECTRIC MOBILITY NEED TO BE CAREFULLY MANAGED

The physical and financial stresses that chaotic adoption of electric mobility may place on the power system can be managed in a variety of ways. The classic response of investing in infrastructure upgrades to accommodate new system demands may be inevitable in some instances. However, the extent of necessary investment can be significantly curtailed through proactive adoption of a range of demand management measures, encompassing both technical fixes and financial incentives, as illustrated by a recent evaluation of EV adoption undertaken in New Delhi (box 4.1).

Some Degree of Power System Reinforcement May Be Needed

Satisfying increased peak demand requires flexible and more expensive generation units that can be ramped up quickly, such as gas turbines. Pumped or battery storage can also fulfill this role but is not yet always a feasible or cost-effective option. Maintaining capacity will therefore be a challenge. Already, supply-demand balances are tight in many places, as indicated by frequent load shedding in countries such as Kenya, Nepal, and South Africa. Also, smaller island nations or countries with complex topography, such as Indonesia, have limited options for balancing out demand and supply across wider geographic areas or international borders.

Adding to these challenges is the need to decarbonize electricity generation. Although EVs do not emit greenhouse gases during operation, they still have a carbon footprint if the electricity stored in their batteries and used in their manufacturing is generated using fossil fuels. Overall, the emission intensity depends on the generation mix and how different types of generation units are deployed. Baseload is often provided by coal,

BOX 4.1

Detailed analysis of distribution systems aids large-scale EV integration

India will likely become one of the largest electric vehicle (EV) markets in the world, but its power distribution system already struggles to keep up with rising demand. Identifying its shortcomings is a crucial first step in supporting large-scale EV adoption. An example is a study of 10 distribution feeders in New Delhi that collected load and voltage profiles and information on distribution transformers, consumer mixes, and energy consumption (GIZ 2019). It allowed careful modeling of the impact of charging stations on load flow, load volumes, voltage, and harmonics. For three of these feeders, the study then conducted detailed simulations in five areas: travel patterns, energy consumption, power consumption, EV penetration levels, and EV charging strategies. The simulations investigated various scenarios that varied EV penetration levels, installation of public chargers, the addition of electricity storage facilities, or the integration of solar photovoltaic energy.

This study found that, with the appropriate balance of network improvements and time-of-use tariffs, the distribution systems operator can manage a high level of EV deployment, provided the distribution systems operator as well as commercial charging operators follow grid connection standards and practices to avoid equipment failures. The study showed that comprehensive network analysis provides full quantification of the potential impact of EV integration, enables assessment of various scenarios and system designs, and yields valuable information about required network upgrades and charging locations.

hydro, or nuclear power along with varying levels of wind and solar power depending on conditions, whereas management of peak loads or periods of low wind and solar generation relies on gas, diesel generators, or stored energy. The impact of additional EV demand on the emission intensity of the electricity supply is therefore highly country specific (Pavarini and Mattion 2019), and such national averages hide considerable within-country, as well as seasonal and even daily, variability in the generation mix. As illustrated by the widely varying estimations of investment needs in chapter 2, each country faces a unique set of conditions in terms of the status and reliability of the existing grid, fuel sources, the vehicle fleet, the likely EV adoption path, and so on. That is, even though no simple prescriptions for readying the power sector for the electric mobility transition are possible, several useful general observations are.

First, given the long lead time for energy sector investments, preparing for the EV transition needs to start early. Integrated power sector models help assess the implications of a rising share of EVs on the electricity supply infrastructure along the electricity supply chain, from generation to transmission and distribution. They provide a basis for scenario analysis and comprehensive planning, especially when used in conjunction with EV-specific analyses.

An example for a comprehensive analysis of the impact of EV adoption on the power sector is a study undertaken for Maldives by Suski et al. (2021). The study began with forecasts of electricity demand for each type of EV over the period between 2021 and 2030. Defining the likely charging profile under different charging strategies yields EV load curves for typical days. This information fed into the World Bank's Electricity Planning Model to suggest least-cost generation and expansion plans accounting for detailed technological, economic, and environmental parameters of the country's electricity system. Outputs included parameters such as dispatch schedules of the generation units, power system emissions, and operational costs. Comparing results with and without EVs, and under different assumptions of charging behavior, generated policy-relevant information such as the incremental investments in additional generation or emission intensities under different scenarios. In addition to aggregating capacity expansion requirements, detailed modeling also helped identify transmission and distribution bottlenecks. Accompanying these systemwide analyses, separate simulation studies for distribution networks subsequently identified the impacts of EV charging on local feeder networks (see box 4.1).

Second, greening the power sector must be a key consideration in any power sector planning exercise. Mobility cannot be fully green as long as vehicle manufacturing and electricity generation rely on fossil fuels. As illustrated by the "green grid" scenario discussed in chapter 2, the net benefits of electric mobility are significantly amplified as countries progress further with the decarbonization of their power generation mix.

Returning to the Maldives example, emissions could actually increase in the scenario with coordinated charging because more charging would happen off-peak, when generation uses diesel-based units. Replacing those generators with renewable energy from the country's ample solar resources would require battery storage that chargers can draw on during the night. So far, large-capacity batteries are expensive but so are diesel imports, and electricity storage technology will likely benefit from massive current investments to drive costs down.

Third, universal access remains an important consideration and an unfinished agenda. Globally, 733 million people still live without electricity at home (IEA 2022). Many low- and middle-income countries continue to work toward universal electrification. As more and more activities—and notably transportation—become electrified during the decarbonization process, it becomes increasingly important to ensure that all citizens can use this cleaner form of energy.

Managing Charging Behavior Will Reduce Investment Needs

Another important insight is that demand management is often the most effective way to mitigate the potential negative impacts of EV adoption on the grid, given the bunching of charging load at certain times in certain places. The ability to manage EV charging demand is an additional source of flexibility for the power system as a whole—comparable to dispatchable resources such as gas turbines. Such demand management measures should be prioritized, given that they are likely to cost far less than investing in additional peak demand capacity that will be used only infrequently.

Returning to the Maldives example, that study assumed a 30 percent share of EVs by 2030, including the country's large number of two-wheelers. The scenario with uncoordinated charging predicted a relatively modest increase in energy demand of 3.1 percent. But, because much of that demand was predicted to occur at peak times, it would require a 26.1 percent increase in generation capacity, entailing 16 percent more investment than in the base case without EVs. Introducing demand management, in the form of an optimized charging regime, would reduce generation capacity additions to just 1.8 percent and would also reduce stress on distribution systems.

Although demand management is complex, managing loads can be substantially more cost effective than capacity additions and grid enforcement, especially in systems that already require very large improvements because of investment backlog and rising demand from all sources. Moreover, a wide array of technical fixes for demand management are available—from the simple to the sophisticated.

The most straightforward approach to demand management is to use information programs to encourage EV owners to charge during off-peak periods, either in general or through real-time push notifications. Such programs have been successful in reducing energy consumption for heating (Gillingham, Keyes, and Palmer 2018), though they may be most effective when combined with time-differentiated charging.

Another strategy for managing demand is to increase the density of public charging infrastructure. If charging points are more widely available and spread out geographically, EV owners will also be more likely to spread out vehicle charging over time, allowing for smaller but more frequent "top-ups"—at work, at store parking lots, or along city streets—as opposed to concentrating charging at home during the evening peak.

Electricity storage is another approach to better adapt electric power demand to supply. It involves equipping charging stations with battery storage systems that can balance supply from the grid. If charged, for example, by locally produced solar photovoltaic energy, this storage also yields additional revenue for station owners (Feng et al. 2020). Adding storage can also be attractive to fleet operators. In the case of adding storage to a fast-charging station for electric buses, costs were 23 percent lower than without storage (Ding, Hu, and Song 2015).

Rather than using intermediate storage in regular charging systems, some operators replace discharged vehicle batteries with fully charged ones. For electric cars, battery swapping is not yet widely used. A lack of standard design limits interoperability, so swapping works only in specific cases such as taxi fleets. Battery swapping is more suitable for smaller EVs, especially two- or three-wheelers. Several battery swapping services have emerged in India, including subscription services for station networks where electric two- and three-wheelers can swap in fully charged battery packs (Das and Tyagi 2020). Moreover, India expects the market for battery swapping to grow by more than 30 percent annually during this decade (Kumar, Bhat, and Srivastava 2021). China and Indonesia, among other countries, also promote battery swapping mostly for electric two-wheelers.

Beyond these relatively simple solutions, smart charging provides the ultimate technical fix for managing power demand for EV charging, allowing the power system operator some control over the timing and duration of vehicle charging. Such smart charging infrastructure allows electric utilities to manage the process, whether in one direction (sending power to the vehicle) or both directions (additionally taking power from the vehicle).

In unidirectional vehicle-to-grid integration (V1G), the operator can manage EV charging to reduce grid congestion, regulate frequency, and avoid peak period overloading. In various studies and pilot applications, V1G provided considerable savings. One modeling study in an urban setting estimated a reduction of 34 percent of the local marginal cost (Heinisch et al. 2021). In a study of a low-voltage Danish distribution network with a 50 percent EV share, charging costs decreased by 17 percent in addition to other benefits, such as more balanced voltage (García-Villalobos et al. 2016).

Bidirectional controlled vehicle-to-grid integration (V2G) allows EVs to become electricity storage systems, returning power to the grid, for instance, when demand from other uses is strong and tariffs are high. In more local versions, a vehicle could similarly be integrated with just a single home or building. The potential benefits are large in that V2G could, in principle, provide almost 600 gigawatts of flexible capacity across China, India, the European Union, and the United States by 2030, saving 470 TWh and avoiding 330 million tons of carbon dioxide emissions (IEA 2020). Importantly, V2G can make grid integration of renewables easier by providing flexible power at times when wind or solar production is low (Richardson 2013). Several studies have estimated the prospective financial benefits of V2G, mostly in high-income countries. Although estimates vary widely, all studies find significant cost savings for system operators in addition to reductions in carbon emissions (see, for example, Oldfield et al. 2021 and Park, Yoon, and Hwang 2016).

A study in Chile found that smart charging enables a larger proportion of solar electricity in the system, which reduces operational and environmental costs and offsets investment costs (Manríquez et al. 2020). V2G technology connecting 2,500 EVs in Mexico could improve the power supply's technical performance, leading to a 69 percent decline in power losses (Khan et al. 2017). A particularly interesting example of an electric mobility program built around advocacy and smart charging is South Africa's uYilo program, which is one of the few field applications of V1G and V2G in the developing world (box 4.2).

Implementation of EV power demand management has been slow. In high-income countries, it could be because of a lack of urgency while EV penetration is low and because such approaches are complex to implement. They require additional software, communications, and control equipment in electrical systems and cars, as well as regulatory frameworks that guide the technology and economics. In developing countries, applications have been mostly pilot projects and proof-of-concept studies.

Scaling up requires a gradual build-out of smart charging infrastructure and regulatory reforms in electricity markets that signal to EV buyers, manufacturers, and charging companies that investments will yield adequate returns. The benefits of a smoothly operating charging ecosystem in lower-income countries could be large: lower charging costs, reduced power generation investments, more stable electricity supply, and lower operation and maintenance costs for power operators. These potential benefits underscore the strategic importance of establishing such systems at an early stage to avoid the burgeoning power system costs that might otherwise ensue.

BOX 4.2

South Africa's uYilo electric mobility program

South Africa's national electric mobility program, known as uYilo (Xhosa for "to create"), developed successful pilot projects in smart charging and electric mobility advocacy. Addressing more than just electric vehicles (EVs), uYilo focuses on developing the entire ecosystem for successful electric mobility implementation—from sustainable energy generation through skills development to circular economy. In 2013, uYilo established the Smart Grid EcoSystem facility to analyze EV-grid interoperability and to determine the future challenges regarding the control of the entire electric mobility system. The facility includes integrated photovoltaic panels, storage through second-life EV batteries, vehicle-to-grid services, energy management systems, and various types of chargers. With that infrastructure in place, uYilo tests energy optimization techniques to provide reliable and undisturbed service to the connected loads under various available grid capacities (including blackouts or brownouts) or availability of renewable energy and level of integrated energy storage. The system's primary goal is resilience, shifting to alternative and available sources of energy when needed and making sure that the EV is always charged. The facility is also used to test smart grid remote communications standards between various players in the system and the grid operator. uYilo uses the outcomes of the ongoing field experiments to campaign for electric mobility benefits in the region. Furthermore, the experience and insights gained inform conversations with decision-makers, regulators, and utilities to promote smart charging strategy implementation alongside transportation electrification.

Source: Based on information provided by Hiten Parmar (Director, uYilo e-Mobility Programme) in a phone conversation, June, 2021.

Pricing Reform Is a Critical Aspect of Demand Management

Given the prevalence of distortions in energy pricing, and the importance of harnessing demand management approaches, electricity tariff reform will need to play an important role in the transition to electric mobility.

Getting electricity prices right is not only helpful in its own right but also a valuable complement to some of the technical solutions presented earlier, which can further incentivize their uptake and amplify their respective impacts. The two critical aspects of electricity pricing reform are ensuring that prices attain cost recovery levels and redesigning electricity tariff structures to align with and influence electric mobility demand patterns (IRENA 2019b).

Making the transition to electric mobility sustainable will require comprehensive electricity (as well as fossil fuel) subsidy reform where prices do not currently reflect the full cost of production—let alone their full social cost. Such reforms have proved difficult. Often introduced as well-intentioned efforts to stabilize prices or reduce price volatility, subsidies become entrenched and widely popular. Yet many countries have successfully carried out electricity subsidy reform, among them Armenia, Brazil, China, the Arab Republic of Egypt, Kenya, Morocco, the Philippines, Türkiye, Uganda, and the United Arab Emirates (Sovacool 2017).

A main lesson from successful cases is that subsidy reform is largely a political economy problem rather than a purely fiscal issue (Flochel and Gooptu 2017; Inchauste and Victor 2017). It will require strong administrative capacity to design and implement an effective reform strategy consisting of best practice subsidy measurement, subsidy impact analysis, a reform schedule, and a plan for distributional concerns. Reform is generally easier when beneficiaries are concentrated—such as when most of the support goes to a few large firms—rather than diffused. Reform efforts are also easier to defend politically when robust social protection systems are in place that buffer the effect of price reforms on poor households and small firms.

Besides freeing up scarce fiscal resources that can be recycled into service expansion and improvement, reform also pays immediate environmental dividends. Energy subsidy reform in Indonesia led to lower demand and a change in energy mix that will reduce greenhouse gas emissions by between 5 percent and 9 percent by 2030 (Sovacool 2017).

When it comes to the reform of energy tariff structures, a first step is to move away from increasing block tariff structures toward linear pricing, to ensure that vehicle charging demand is not unduly penalized. Beyond this, the key issue is to influence the timing of vehicle charging in such a way as to avoid accentuating demand peaks. To this end, time-of-use (TOU) tariff schedules that charge higher prices during peak hours are the most suitable pricing instrument—once the necessary smart meter infrastructure is in place to permit their implementation. Under TOU pricing schemes, electricity tariffs could be predetermined based on historical load patterns (static pricing), or they could adjust continuously based on prevailing wholesale market signals (dynamic pricing). In both cases, users save money from lower rates and utilities from avoided investments. For example, the Jamaican utility JPS designed a TOU tariff scheme that will be implemented alongside infrastructure investments (Jamaica, Office of Utilities Regulation 2020).

Experience has shown that TOU schemes work quite well. A significant proportion of EV owners adjust charging time in response to price signals, in one case reducing spikes in power demand by 64 percent (Gao et al. 2012). In another case, among 8,000 urban EVs in China, peak-valley differences dropped by 16 percent and charging costs by 4 percent (Chen et al. 2018). Reducing the variability of electricity demand also benefits the grid infrastructure by reducing power losses, voltage deviations, and overloading, thus extending the life span of transformers and other equipment (Klettke and Mose 2018). Implementation of TOU pricing schemes requires careful design to avoid unintended side effects, such as peak shifting (creating new demand peaks in formerly off-peak hours). The regulatory tariff-setting process can be complex and requires lengthy preparation (European Commission 2015).

CONCLUSION

As long as electric mobility scales up gradually, the impact on overall electricity demand will be relatively modest, except perhaps in the most fragile power systems. What is more relevant is how the timing of uncoordinated EV charging may accentuate system peaks and how potential geographical concentration of charging could create overload on local distribution networks. Despite a small aggregate impact, such concentrated impacts could be much larger and more significant. Moreover, they could be exacerbated by the subsidization of electricity, which in turn could incentivize overuse, as well as the prevalence of antiquated electricity tariff structures, which are not necessarily helpful in shaping demand.

The key implication is that the transition to electric mobility needs to be anticipated and proactively managed by power systems. An important starting point is to integrate transportation demand into generation, transmission, and distribution master plans. A certain amount of additional investment may be inevitable to reinforce the weakest links in the grid, but a great deal of investment can be avoided by proactive demand management measures, aimed particularly at shifting vehicle charging outside peak periods. This can already be done through relatively straightforward measures, such as information campaigns and battery swapping arrangements. Ultimately, full grid integration of EV batteries would allow more sophisticated centralized management of charging and even allow EVs to become grid storage assets. In any case, pricing reform will be a critical component of any demand management effort, and—in particular—a shift toward TOU pricing promises to be an effective approach to influencing behavior.

REFERENCES

Abhyankar, Nikit, Anand R. Gopal, Colin Sheppard, Won Young Park, and Amol A. Phadke. 2017. "All Electric Passenger Vehicle Sales in India by 2030: Value Proposition to Electric Utilities, Government, and Vehicle Owners." LBNL Report 1007121, US Department of Energy, Ernest Orlando Lawrence Berkeley National Laboratory. https://escholarship.org/uc/item/5xh282r8#main%0A.

Acharya, Mahua, Ravi Gadepalli, and Gerald Ollivier. 2022. "Grand Challenge for Electric Bus Deployment: Outcomes and Lessons for the Future." Unpublished, World Bank, Washington, DC.

African Development Bank. 2019. "Africa Needs Bolder Private Financing Models for Power Transmission Lines—Energy Experts." News Release, July 4, 2019. https://www.afdb.org/en/news-and-events/press-releases/africa-needs-bolder-private-financing-models-power-transmission-lines-energy-experts-24422.

Angelim, Jorge H., and Carolina de M. Affonso. 2019. "Probabilistic Impact Assessment of Electric Vehicles Charging on Low Voltage Distribution Systems." In *2019 IEEE PES Conference on Innovative Smart Grid Technologies Conference—Latin America (ISGT Latin America)*, 1–6. New York: Institute of Electrical and Electronics Engineers. https://doi.org/10.1109/ISGT-LA.2019.8895494.

Chen, Jiejun, Jun Yang, Jie Zhu, Xianglong Li, Shuang Zeng, Yixin Li, Xinpu Wang, and Yufei Tang. 2018. "An Optimal Regional Time-of-Use Charging Price Model for Electric Vehicles." In *IEEE Power & Energy Society General Meeting*, 1–5. New York: Institute of Electrical and Electronics Engineers. https://doi.org/10.1109/PESGM.2017.8273797.

Crozier, Constance, Thomas Morstyn, and Malcolm McCulloch. 2020. "The Opportunity for Smart Charging to Mitigate the Impact of Electric Vehicles on Transmission and Distribution Systems." *Applied Energy* 268: 114973. https://doi.org/10.1016/j.apenergy.2020.114973.

Das, Shyamasis, and Bhawna Tyagi. 2020. *EV—A New Entrant to India's Electricity Consumer-Basket; Impact on Utility Cost of Supply and the Need for a New Approach for Tariff-Setting.* New Delhi: Alliance for an Energy Efficient Economy. https://aeee.in/our-publications/ev-a-new-entrant-to-indias-electricity-consumer-basket/.

Ding, Huajie, Zechun Hu, and Yonghua Song. 2015. "Value of the Energy Storage System in an Electric Bus Fast Charging Station." *Applied Energy* 157: 630–39. https://doi.org/10.1016/j.apenergy.2015.01.058.

EA Technology. 2015. "Intelligent Management of Electric Vehicles Charging." Working Paper, EA Technologies, Cheshire. https://studylib.net/doc/18046398/intelligent-management-of-electric-vehicle-charging-a-whi.

Economic Times. 2020. "India's Power Transmission Segment May Attract Rs 1.8 Lakh Cr Investment by FY25: Report." *Economic Times*, August 7, 2020. https://economictimes.indiatimes.com/industry/energy/power/indias-power-transmission-segment-may-attract-rs-1-8-lakh-cr-investment-by-fy25-report/articleshow/77417138.cms.

Engel, Hauke, Russell Hensley, Stefan Knupfer, and Shivika Sahdev. 2018. "The Potential Impact of Electric Vehicles on Global Energy Systems." McKinsey & Company, August 8, 2018. https://www.mckinsey.com/industries/automotive-and-assembly/our-insights/the-potential-impact-of-electric-vehicles-on-global-energy-systems.

ESMAP (Energy Sector Management Assistance Program). Forthcoming. "E-Mobility and Power Systems." Background paper, World Bank, Washington, DC.

European Commission. 2015. "Study on Tariff Design for Distribution Systems—Final Report." European Commission, Brussels. https://ppp.worldbank.org/public-private-partnership/sites/ppp.worldbank.org/files/2022-04/20150313%20Tariff%20report%20fina_revREF-E.PDF.

Feng, Jiawei, Shengya Hou, Lijun Yu, Nikolay Dimov, Pei Zheng, and Chunping Wang. 2020. "Optimization of Photovoltaic Battery Swapping Station Based on Weather/Traffic Forecasts and Speed Variable Charging." *Applied Energy* 264: 114708. https://doi.org/10.1016/j.apenergy.2020.114708.

Flochel, Thomas, and Sundarshan Gooptu. 2017. "The Energy Subsidy Reform Assessment Framework (ESRAF): Good Practice Notes: Toward Evidence-Based Energy Subsidy Reforms." Overview Note, World Bank, Washington, DC. https://openknowledge.worldbank.org/handle/10986/28863.

Florio, Alexandre M., Nabil Absi, and Dominique Feillet. 2021. "Routing Electric Vehicles on Congested Street Networks." *Transportation Science* 55 (1): 238–56. https://doi.org/10.1287/TRSC.2020.1004.

Foster, Vivien, and Samantha Witte. 2020. "Falling Short: A Global Survey of Electricity Tariff Design." Policy Research Working Paper 9174, World Bank, Washington, DC. https://openknowledge.worldbank.org/handle/10986/33417.

Gao, Yajing, Chen Wang, Zhi Wang, and Haifeng Liang. 2012. "Research on Time-of-Use Price Applying to Electric Vehicles Charging." In *IEEE PES Innovative Smart Grid Technologies*, 1–6. New York: Institute of Electrical and Electronics Engineers. https://doi.org/10.1109/ISGT-Asia.2012.6303297.

García-Villalobos, Javier, Immaculada Zamora, Katarina Knezović, and Mattia Marinelli. 2016. "Multi-objective Optimization Control of Plug-In Electric Vehicles in Low Voltage Distribution Networks." *Applied Energy* 180: 155–68. https://doi.org/10.1016/j.apenergy.2016.07.110.

Gillingham, Kenneth, Amelia Keyes, and Karen Palmer. 2018. "Advances in Evaluating Energy Efficiency Policies and Programs." *Annual Review of Resource Economics* 10: 511–32. https://doi.org/10.1146/annurev-resource-100517-023028.

GIZ (Deutsche Gesellschaft für Internationale Zusammenarbeit). 2019. "Impact Assessment of Large Scale Integration of Electric Vehicle Charging Infrastructure on Distribution Systems." *Changing Transport*, August 2019. https://changing-transport.org/publication/ev-charging-and-electricity-grid/.

Heinisch, Verena, Lisa Göransson, Rasmus Erlandsson, Henrik Hodel, Filip Johnsson, and Mikael Odenberger. 2021. "Smart Electric Vehicle Charging Strategies for Sectoral Coupling in a City Energy System." *Applied Energy* 288 (April 15, 2021): 116640. https://doi.org/10.1016/j.apenergy.2021.116640.

Hensley, Russell, Stefan Knupfer, and Dickon Pinner. 2018. "Three Surprising Resource Implications from the Rise of Electric Vehicles." *McKinsey Quarterly*, May 23, 2018. https://www.mckinsey.com/industries/automotive-and-assembly/our-insights/three-surprising-resource-implications-from-the-rise-of-electric-vehicles.

Hove, Anders, and David Sandalow. 2019. "Electric Vehicle Charging in China and the United States." Center on Global Energy Policy, Columbia University, New York. https://www.energypolicy.columbia.edu/wp-content/uploads/2019/02/EV_ChargingChina-CGEP_Report_Final.pdf.

IEA (International Energy Agency). 2019. *Cooling on the Move: The Future of Air Conditioning in Vehicles*. Paris: IEA. https://doi.org/10.1787/fa9c12d3-en.

IEA (International Energy Agency). 2020. *Global EV Outlook 2020: Entering the Decade of Electric Drive?* Paris: OECD Publishing. https://doi.org/10.1787/d394399e-en.

IEA (International Energy Agency). 2021a. *Global EV Outlook 2021: Accelerating Ambitions despite the Pandemic*. Paris: OECD Publishing. https://www.iea.org/reports/global-ev-outlook-2021.

IEA (International Energy Agency). 2021b. *Net Zero by 2050: A Roadmap for the Global Energy Sector*. Paris: IEA. https://iea.blob.core.windows.net/assets/deebef5d-0c34-4539-9d0c-10b13d840027/NetZeroby2050-ARoadmapfortheGlobalEnergySector_CORR.pdf.

IEA (International Energy Agency). 2022. *Global EV Outlook 2022: Securing Supplies for an Electric Future*. Paris: OECD Publishing. https://www.oecd-ilibrary.org/energy/global-ev-outlook-2022_c83f815c-en.

IES (Intelligent Energy Systems) and MKE (Mekong Economics). 2016. *Alternatives for Power Generation in the Greater Mekong Sub-region—Volume 1: Power Sector Vision for the Greater Mekong Region*. Crows Nest, Australia: IES.

Inchauste, Gabriela, and David G. Victor. 2017. *The Political Economy of Energy Subsidy Reform*. Directions in Development—Public Sector Governance. Washington, DC: World Bank. http://hdl.handle.net/10986/26216.

IRENA (International Renewable Energy Agency). 2019a. "Innovation Landscape Brief: Flexibility in Conventional Power Plants." IRENA, Abu Dhabi, United Arab Emirates. https://www.irena.org/-/media/Files/IRENA/Agency/Publication/2019/Sep/IRENA_Flexibility_in_CPPs_2019.pdf.

IRENA (International Renewable Energy Agency). 2019b. "Innovation Landscape Brief: Time-of-Use Tariffs." IRENA, Abu Dhabi, United Arab Emirates. https://www.irena.org/-/media/Files/IRENA/Agency/Publication/2019/Feb/IRENA_Innovation_ToU_tariffs_2019.pdf.

Jamaica, Office of Utilities Regulation. 2020. "JPS 2019–2024 Tariff Review Process Application Summary." Media statement, May 21, 2020, Office of Utilities Regulation, Kingston, Jamaica. https://our.org.jm/document/summary-2019-24-jps-tariff-application-electricity-sector/.

Kapustin, Nikita O., and Dmitry A Grushevenko. 2020. "Long-Term Electric Vehicles Outlook and Their Potential Impact on Electric Grid." *Energy Policy* 137 (February 2020): 111103. https://doi.org/10.1016/j.enpol.2019.111103.

Khan, Sohail, Ulises Cano Castillo, Alfredo Espinosa Reza, Javier dela Cruz Soto, and Hector Aguilar Valenzuela. 2017. "V2G Study for Electric Grid Reinforcement in a Commercial Feeder in Mexico City." In *2017 IEEE International Autumn Meeting on Power, Electronics and Computing (ROPEC)*, 1–6. https://doi.org/10.1109/ROPEC.2017.8261596.

Klettke, Annika, and Albert Mose. 2018. "Effect of Electric Mobility on the Power System and the Integration of RES." Study S13, Publications Office of the European Union. https://op.europa.eu/en/publication-detail/-/publication/0d44e933-6d4d-11e9-9f05-01aa75ed71a1/language-en/format-PDF/source-96288622.

Komives, Kristin, Vivien Foster, Jonathan Halpern, and Quentin Wodon. 2005. *Water, Electricity and the Poor: Who Benefits from Utility Subsidies?* Directions in Development. Washington, DC: World Bank. https://openknowledge.worldbank.org/handle/10986/6361.

Kumar, Parveen, Arya Bhat, and Vishal Srivastava. 2021. "Battery Swapping: An Alternative Fast Re-fueling Option for E-2Ws and E-3Ws in India." *WRI India* (blog), March 24, 2021. https://wri-india.org/blog/battery-swapping-alternative-fast-re-fueling-option-e-2ws-and-e-3ws-india.

Li, Bo, Minyou Chen, Qiang Li, Tingli Cheng, Ziming Ma, Shujun Zhang, and Xiao Qian. 2020. "Integration of Battery Electric Vehicles in a Regional Hydro–Wind–Thermal Power System." *Energy Reports* 6 (S9): 1199–205. https://doi.org/10.1016/j.egyr.2020.11.054.

Liu, Kai, Toshiyuki Yamamoto, and Takayuki Morikawa. 2017. "Impact of Road Gradient on Energy Consumption of Electric Vehicles." *Transportation Research Part D: Transport and Environment* 54: 74–81. https://doi.org/10.1016/j.trd.2017.05.005.

Manríquez, Francisco, Enzo Sauma, José Aguado, Sebastián de la Torre, and Javier Contreras. 2020. "The Impact of Electric Vehicle Charging Schemes in Power System Expansion Planning." *Applied Energy* 262 (March 15): 114527. https://doi.org/10.1016/j.apenergy.2020.114527.

Oldfield, Frank, Krunal Kumpavat, Rebecca Corbett, Andrew Price, Marko Aunedi, Goran Strbac, Cormac O'Malley, Darren Gardner, Dominik Pfeiffer, and Jan-Torben Kamphus. 2021. "The Drive towards a Low-Carbon Grid: Unlocking the Value of Vehicle-to-Grid Fleets in Great Britain." NISSAN Motor Corporation, e-on Drive, and Imperial College, London. https://www.eonenergy.com/content/dam/eon-energy-com/Files/vehicle-to-grid/The%20Drive%20Towards%20A%20Low-Carbon%20Grid%20Whitepaper.pdf.

Park, Daehan, Seungwook Yoon, and Euiseok Hwang. 2016. "Cost Benefit Analysis of Public Service Electric Vehicles with Vehicle-to-Grid (V2G) Capability." In *2016 IEEE Transportation Electrification Conference and Expo, Asia-Pacific (ITEC Asia-Pacific)*, 234–39. New York: Institute of Electrical and Electronics Engineers. https://ieeexplore.ieee.org/document/7512954.

Parry, Ian W. H., Simon Black, and Nate Vernon. 2021. "Still Not Getting Energy Prices Right: A Global and Country Update of Fossil Fuel Subsidies." IMF Working Paper 21/236, International Monetary Fund, Washington, DC. https://www.imf.org/en/Publications/WP/Issues/2021/09/23/Still-Not-Getting-Energy-Prices-Right-A-Global-and-Country-Update-of-Fossil-Fuel-Subsidies-466004.

Pavarini, Claudia, and Francesco Mattion. 2019. "Commentary: Tracking the Decoupling of Electricity Demand and Associated CO2 Emissions." International Energy Agency, Paris, March 8, 2019. https://www.iea.org/commentaries/tracking-the-decoupling-of-electricity-demand-and-associated-co2-emissions.

Richardson, David B. 2013. "Electric Vehicles and the Electric Grid: A Review of Modeling Approaches, Impacts, and Renewable Energy Integration." *Renewable and Sustainable Energy Reviews* 19: 247–54. https://doi.org/10.1016/j.rser.2012.11.042.

Rogge, Matthias, Sebastian Wollny, and Dirk Uwe Sauer. 2015. "Fast Charging Battery Buses for the Electrification of Urban Public Transport—A Feasibility Study Focusing on Charging Infrastructure and Energy Storage Requirements." *Energies* 8 (5): 4587–606. https://doi.org/10.3390/en8054587.

Sahoo, Anshuman, Karan Mistry, and Thomas Baker. 2019. "The Costs of Revving Up the Grid for Electric Vehicles." Boston Consulting Group, December 20, 2019. https://www.bcg.com/pl-pl/publications/2019/costs-revving-up-the-grid-for-electric-vehicles.

Saygin, Değer, Osman Bülent Tör, Saeed Teimourzadeh, Mehmet Koç, Julia Hildermeier, and Christos Kolokathis. 2019. *Transport Sector Transformation: Integrating Electric Vehicles into Turkey's Distribution Grids.* Istanbul: SHURA Energy Transition Center.

Sovacool, Benjamin K. 2017. "Reviewing, Reforming, and Rethinking Global Energy Subsidies: Towards a Political Economy Research Agenda." *Ecological Economics* 135: 150–63.

Suski, Adam, Tom Remy, Debabrata Chattopadhyay, Chong Suk Song, Ivan Jaques, Tarek Keskes, and Yanchao Li. 2021. "Analyzing Electric Vehicle Load Impact on Power Systems: Modeling Analysis and a Case Study for Maldives." *IEEE Access* 9: 125640–57. https://ieeexplore.ieee.org/stamp/stamp.jsp?arnumber=9530709.

Taljegard, Maria, Lisa Göransson, Mikael Odenberger, and Filip Johnsson. 2019. "Impacts of Electric Vehicles on the Electricity Generation Portfolio—A Scandinavian-German Case Study." *Applied Energy* 235 (1): 1637–50. https://doi.org/10.1016/j.apenergy.2018.10.133.

Unidad de Planeación Minero-Energética. 2020. *Plan Energético Nacional 2020–2050: La Transformación Energética que Habilita el Desarrolla Sostenible.* Bogatá: Unidad de Planeación Minero-Energética, República de Columbia. https://www1.upme.gov.co/DemandayEficiencia/Documents/PEN_2020_2050/Plan_Energetico_Nacional_2020_2050.pdf.

Weiss, Martin, Kira Christina Cloos, and Eckard Helmers. 2020. "Energy Efficiency Trade-Offs in Small to Large Electric Vehicles." *Environmental Sciences Europe* 32: Article 46. https://doi.org/10.1186/s12302-020-00307-8.

Zhang, Fan. 2019. *In the Dark: How Much Do Power Sector Distortions Cost South Asia?* South Asia Development Forum. Washington, DC: World Bank. https://openknowledge.worldbank.org/handle/10986/30923.

Zhang, Jing, Jie Yan, Yongqian Liu, Haoran Zhang, and Guoliang Lv. 2020. "Daily Electric Vehicle Charging Load Profiles Considering Demographics of Vehicle Users." *Applied Energy* 274 (September 15): 115063. https://doi.org/10.1016/j.apenergy.2020.115063.

Appendix: Countries at a Glance

A.1 PASSENGER ELECTRIC MOBILITY IN BRAZIL

Country Typology

Vehicle fleet composition: Car dominant
Net oil trading status: Exporter
Relative cost of vehicles: High

Country Background

The dominant vehicle type in Brazil is cars (84.3 percent), followed by two-wheelers (14.5 percent), buses (1.0 percent) and three-wheelers (0.2 percent) (ANFAVEA 2020). In 2021, electricity was generated primarily from renewable sources (85 percent)—notably, hydro (65.2 percent), wind (8.8 percent), solar (0.6 percent), and biomass and waste (9.1 percent). Gas (8.3 percent) is the largest fossil source for electricity generation, followed by oil (2.1 percent) and coal (2.7 percent).[1] Brazil is one of the largest vehicle manufacturers in the world, with its own large domestic market. The expansion of electric vehicles in the country has been slow (Marchán and Viscidi 2015) partly because of the country's prioritization of ethanol to mitigate carbon dioxide emissions from the transportation sector. In 2019, more than 92 percent (Costa 2020) of the Brazilian cars sold were powered by flex-fuel.[2] More recently, e-mobility implementation in Brazil has been ramping up, on both the policy side and infrastructure supply. Electric buses are tax-exempt in seven Brazilian states, with a reduced tax rate in three further states. From 2022, national electric bus manufacturers are fully tax-exempt for bus chassis assembly machines and lithium-ion batteries, but import duties to electric vehicles remain in place. These incentives are sponsored by the National Development Bank (UNEP and European Union 2016). However, the Brazilian manufacturing industry produces diesel buses at very low cost, which makes for a tough competitive market despite said incentives.

Overall Messages

Brazil faces many conditions that are less favorable toward electric mobility, including a car-dominated fleet, relatively high-cost vehicles, and energy-exporting status (figure A.1.1a). Although electrification of transportation does not yet look economically favorable as a national strategy, this is largely driven by the fact that the electrification of four-wheel vehicles is not attractive under current conditions, given large capital cost differentials (table A.1.1). By contrast, there is a strong case for adoption of two-wheel electric motorbikes (figure A.1.1b), which present a life-cycle cost advantage of almost 14 percent (almost 26 percent in financial terms). In addition, the 8 percent capital cost differential associated with electric two-wheelers looks relatively affordable, representing no more than 1 percent of gross national income per capita. Furthermore, electric buses are beginning to offer modest economic advantages to the order of 3.5 percent of life-cycle cost.

The externality benefits of electric mobility in Brazil are relatively small (figure A.1.1c), perhaps because of the existing prevalence of biofuel. An important exception is provided by two-wheel electric vehicles, which present much lower externalities than their conventional counterparts (figure A.1.1d). Otherwise, fuel cost savings are the main advantage associated with electric mobility in Brazil. Given a fiscal regime that taxes gasoline and diesel two to three times as heavily as electricity, these fuel cost savings are accentuated in financial terms, which is why the overall case for electric mobility in Brazil looks better in financial than in economic terms (figure A.1.1a).

The total investment needs associated with the 30×30 scenario amount to US$7 billion per year by 2030 (or 0.27 percent of Brazilian gross domestic product). About three-quarters of the required outlay is associated with the incremental capital cost of electric vehicles (figure A.1.2a). In terms of public investment, the most significant item is the provision of public charging infrastructure for private vehicles (figure A.1.2a). Given that implicit carbon prices associated with electric two-wheelers and buses in Brazil are negative (see table A.1.3), there is significant scope to cover 50–70 percent of public investment costs through carbon financing arrangements (figure A.1.2b). However, for four-wheel electric vehicles, the implicit carbon price exceeds US$200 per ton.

The overall economic case for electric mobility in Brazil certainly does not improve under more conservative assumptions about the cost of batteries ("scarce minerals" scenario) and the fuel efficiency of internal combustion engines ("fuel efficiency" scenario), nor is there much scope for further decarbonization of the power sector ("green grid" scenario) table A.1.2. On a positive note, the emerging advantage associated with electrification of buses can be as much as doubled through the more efficient procurement and operation of vehicles ("efficient bus" scenario). However, there is no real case for electrification of four-wheelers even when it comes to taxi fleets and other intensively used vehicles ("taxi fleet" scenario). If the appropriate road safety measures are in place, the two-wheel segment of the fleet is an enormous opportunity and should be prioritized for Brazil, given the many strong advantages.

Figures and tables start on the next page.

Figures and Tables

FIGURE A.1.1 Advantage of EV adoption in Brazil, by type of vehicle

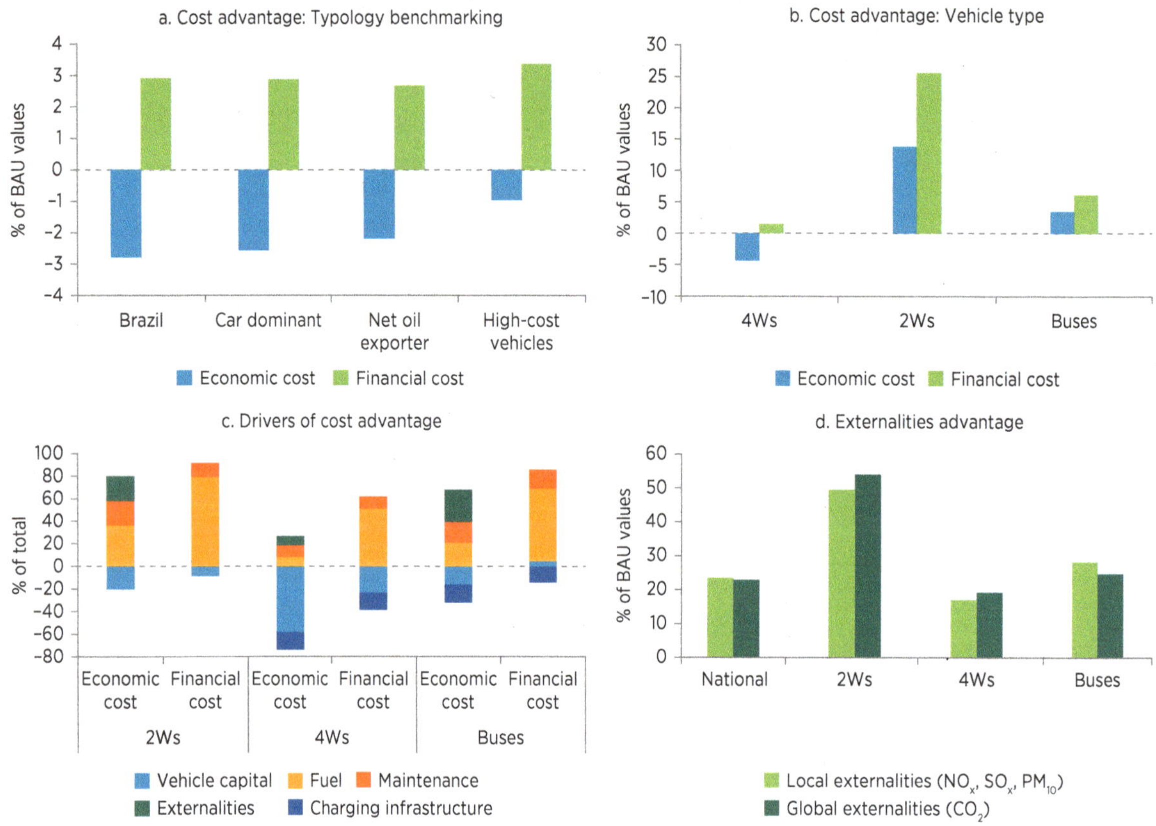

Source: World Bank.

Note: Data in this figure represent the "business as usual" (BAU) scenario minus the 30×30 scenario (averages over fleet additions). The BAU scenario assumes that no policy target will be imposed for electric vehicles and that vehicle purchase decisions will continue to reflect historical trends. The 30×30 scenario assumes that sales of electric cars and buses will reach 30 percent, and of two- and three-wheelers, 70 percent, by 2030. 2W = two-wheeler; 4W = four-wheeler; CO_2 = carbon dioxide; EV = electric vehicle; NO_x = nitrogen oxides; PM_{10} = particulate matter less than 10 microns in diameter; SO_x = sulfur oxides.

TABLE A.1.1 Cost advantage of accelerated EV adoption in Brazil, 2030

	US$/vehicle									% of BAU values	
	Charging infrastructure	Vehicle capital cost	Vehicle operating cost	Subtotal	Local externalities	Global externalities	Economic cost advantage	Net taxes and subsidies	Financial cost advantage	Cost advantage	Financial cost advantage including fiscal wedge
	(a)	(b)	(c)	(d) = (a + b + c)	(e)		(f) = (d + e)	(g)	(h) = (d + g)		
Mode											
2Ws	0	(125)	361	236	49	85	370	700	936	13.9	25.6
4Ws	(529)	(1,983)	650	(1,862)	46	203	(1,612)	2,688	827	(4.3)	1.5
Buses	(6,102)	(6,136)	15,207	2,969	2,966	7,827	13,762	28,373	31,342	3.5	6.1

Source: World Bank.

Note: Heading colors: blue = excluding taxes and subsidies, gray = fiscal wedge, green = including taxes and subsidies. 2W = two-wheeler; 4W = four-wheeler; "Local externalities" comprises local (NO_x, PM_{10}, SO_x) air pollution costs. "Global externalities" comprises global (CO_2) air pollution costs. CO_2 = carbon dioxide; NO_x = nitrogen oxides; PM_{10} = particulate matter less than 10 microns in diameter; SO_x = sulfur oxides. Red and parentheses indicate negative value.

FIGURE A.1.2 Investment and financing needs for EV adoption in Brazil, 2030

a. Breakdown of investment needs (US$7,009 million or 0.27% of GDP)

b. Investment needs potentially covered by carbon financing

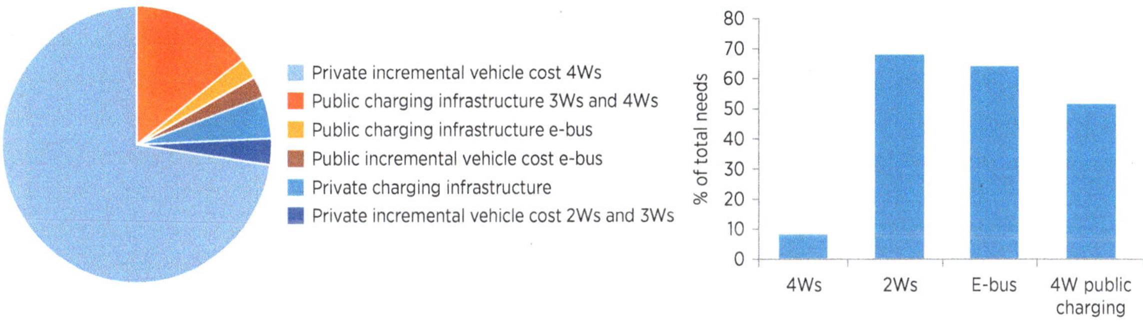

Source: World Bank.
Note: Data in this figure represent the "business as usual" (BAU) scenario minus the 30×30 scenario (averages over fleet additions). The BAU scenario assumes that no policy target will be imposed for electric vehicles and that vehicle purchase decisions will continue to reflect historical trends. The 30×30 scenario assumes that sales of electric cars and buses will reach 30 percent, and of two- and three-wheelers, 70 percent, by 2030. 2W = two-wheeler; 3W = three-wheeler; 4W = four-wheeler; EV = electric vehicle; GDP = gross domestic product.

TABLE A.1.2 Cost advantage of EV adoption in Brazil, by scenario, 2030

	National results				Bus only		4W only	
	30×30 scenario	Green grid scenario	Scarce minerals scenario	Fuel efficiency scenario	30×30 scenario	Efficient bus scenario	30×30 scenario	Taxi fleet scenario
	US$/Mpaxvkm				US$/vehicle			
Type of cost								
Vehicle capital cost	(21,880)	(21,880)	(31,234)	(21,880)	(6,136)	7,599	(1,983)	(1,983)
Vehicle maintenance cost	5,567	5,567	5,315	5,567	7,199	7,499	373	(760)
Vehicle fuel cost	5,287	5,287	5,287	596	8,007	8,007	277	1,107
Private charging infrastructure	(1,367)	(1,367)	(1,367)	(1,367)	n.a.	n.a.	(133)	(133)
Public charging infrastructure	(4,744)	(4,744)	(4,744)	(4,744)	(6,102)	(6,102)	(395)	(450)
Subtotal	(17,137)	(17,137)	(26,743)	(21,829)	2,969	17,003	(1,862)	(2,219)
Local externalities (NO_x, SO_x, PM_{10})	1,143	1,302	1,143	996	2,966	2,966	46	196
Global externalities (CO_2)	3,553	3,601	3,553	2,796	7,827	7,827	203	842
Economic cost advantage	(12,441)	(12,234)	(22,047)	(18,037)	13,762	27,796	(1,612)	(1,182)
Fiscal wedge	35,543	35,543	34,055	29,829	28,373	28,373	2,688	7,260
Financial cost advantage	18,406	18,406	7,312	8,001	31,342	45,376	827	5,041
Economic cost advantage, by type of vehicle	US$/vehicle							
4Ws	(1,612)	(1,598)	(2,413)	(2,016)	n.a.	n.a.	n.a.	n.a.
2Ws	370	372	284	327	n.a.	n.a.	n.a.	n.a.
E-buses	13,762	14,131	6,528	3,464	n.a.	n.a.	n.a.	n.a.

Source: World Bank.
Note: Data in this table represent the "business as usual" (BAU) scenario minus the named scenario (averages over fleet additions). The BAU scenario assumes that no policy target will be imposed for electric vehicles and that vehicle purchase decisions will continue to reflect historical trends. The 30×30 scenario assumes that sales of electric cars and buses will reach 30 percent, and of two- and three-wheelers, 70 percent, by 2030. The green grid scenario assumes that countries achieve certain region-specific targets for acceleration of renewable energy, as defined by the International Renewable Energy Agency (IRENA 2020). The scarce minerals scenario assumes that battery cost will decline by approximately 7 percent annually. The fuel efficiency scenario assumes that the rate of improvement of fuel efficiency for the internal combustion engine fleet will double from 15 percent to 30 percent. The efficient bus scenario assumes a capital cost reduction of 35 percent in the procurement of buses as well as optimized bus routes to increase the annual mileage of electric buses. The taxi fleet scenario assumes that the lifetime mileage of intensively used commercial vehicles will increase by four times in each country, that public investment in charging infrastructure will double the fast charger density for cars, and that the maintenance cost for cars will be doubled (assuming two lifetime battery replacements). Results have been normalized by new vehicles entering the market in 2030. The "fiscal wedge" comprises net taxes and subsidies. Red and parentheses indicate negative value. 2W = two-wheeler; 4W = four-wheeler; CO_2 = carbon dioxide; EV = electric vehicle; NO_x = nitrogen oxides; PM_{10} = particulate matter less than 10 microns in diameter; SO_x = sulfur oxides; US$/Mpaxvkm = US dollars per million passenger vehicle-kilometers; n.a.= not applicable.

TABLE A.1.3 Supporting information on parameters and results for EV adoption in Brazil

Price (US$/vehicle)

Parameter	Value
Price of ICE 4W	31,534
Price of EV 4W	35,267
Price of ICE 2W	1,101
Price of EV 2W	1,278
Price of ICE bus	136,359
Price of e-bus	135,324

Other parameters

Parameter	Value
Net tax difference on EV 4W (%)	15
Net tax difference on EV 2W (%)	0
Net tax difference on e-bus (%)	17
Price of gasoline (US$/liter)	0.46
Net gasoline tax (US$/liter)	0.62
Price of diesel (US$/liter)	0.50
Net diesel tax (US$/liter)	0.36
Price of electricity (US$/kWh)	0.13
Net electricity tax (US$/kWh)	0.05
Electricity carbon intensity (g/kWh)	93
Discount rate (%)	6.6

Key characteristics

Parameter	Value
4W mileage (km)	17,459
2W mileage (km)	7,627
Bus mileage (km)	78,699
4W lifetime (years)	22
2W lifetime (years)	17
Bus lifetime (years)	20
4W secondhand (%)	0.2
2W secondhand (%)	0.2
Bus secondhand (%)	0.05
4W share (% paxvkm)	72
2W share (% paxvkm)	10
Bus share (% paxvkm)	18

Efficiency (MJ/km)

Parameter	Value
Efficiency ICE 4W	2.18
Efficiency EV 4W	0.67
Efficiency ICE 2W	0.85
Efficiency EV 2W	0.20
Efficiency ICE bus	15.61
Efficiency EV bus	5.17

Other results for 30×30 scenario

Other results for 30×30 scenario	Value
Overall investment needs (US$, millions)	7,009
—of which 4W purchase	5,088
—of which 2W purchase	213
—of which e-bus purchase	174
Fiscal impact (US$, millions)	(8,900)
—of which vehicle duties	(1,148)
—of which vehicle taxes/subsidies	(2,120)
—of which gasoline taxes/subsidies	(6,619)
—of which diesel taxes/subsidies	(1,064)
—of which electricity taxes/subsidies	2,051
Implicit carbon price (US$/ton)	116
—of which for 4W	231
—of which for 2W	(87)
—of which for buses	(20)
Pollution reduction (tons)	35
—of which local (SO_x, NO_x, PM_{10})	0.19
—of which global (CO_2)	34.40
Affordability of EV 2W (Δ cost % GNI pc)	0.9
Affordability of EV 4W (Δ cost % GNI pc)	8.0

Source: World Bank.
Note: Red and parentheses indicates negative value. 2W = two-wheeler; 4W = four-wheeler; CO_2 = carbon dioxide; EV = electric vehicle; g = gram; GNI pc = gross national income per capita; ICE = internal combustion engine; kWh = kilowatt-hour; km = kilometer; MJ = megajoule; NO_x = nitrogen oxides; paxvkm = passenger vehicle-kilometer; PM_{10} = particulate matter less than 10 microns in diameter; SO_x = sulfur oxides.

Notes

1. Data from IEA (2020), US Energy Information Administration international database, and World Bank.
2. Flex-fuel means that the cars run on ethanol and gasoline at the same time.

References

ANFAVEA (Associação Nacional dos Fabricantes de Veículos Automotores [Brazilian Automative Industry Association]). 2020. *Anuário da Indústria Automobilística Brasileira* [Brazilian Automotive Industry Yearbook] 2020. São Paulo: ANFAVEA.

Costa, Evaldo. 2020. "The Future of Electric Vehicles in Brazil." *Behavioural & Social Sciences,* October 12, 2020. https://socialsciences.nature.com/posts/the-future-of-electric-vehicles-in-brazil.

IEA (International Energy Agency). 2020. World Energy Balances: Energy Balances for 150 Countries and 35 Regional Aggregates. Online database. IEA, Paris. https://www.iea.org/data-and-statistics/data-product/world-energy-balances.

IRENA (International Renewable Energy Agency). 2020. *Global Renewables Outlook: Energy Transformation 2050.* Masdar City: IRENA.

Marchán, Estefania, and Lisa Viscidi. 2015. "Green Transportation: The Outlook for Electric Vehicles in Latin America." Energy Working Paper, October 2015, The Dialogue: Leadership for the Americas, Washington, DC.

UNEP (United Nations Environment Programme) and European Union. 2016. *Movilidad Eléctrica: Oportunidades para Latinoamérica.* Panama City: UNEP Regional Office for Latin America and the Caribbean.

A.2 PASSENGER ELECTRIC MOBILITY IN CAMBODIA

Country Typology

Vehicle fleet composition: Mixed fleet
Net oil trading status: Importer
Relative cost of vehicles: High

Country Background

The dominant vehicle type in Cambodia is two-wheelers (78 percent), followed by cars (15 percent) and buses (6 percent)(Global Green Growth Institute 2021). In 2018, electricity was primarily generated from renewable sources (60 percent) and less from fossil fuels (40 percent). Coal (36 percent) is the largest fossil fuel source for electricity generation, followed by oil (4 percent). Hydro (59 percent) and solar and biomass (together barely 1 percent) form part of the renewable sources of electricity generation, with most of the balance coming from coal (36 percent). The Cambodian government has stepped up to explore the increase in the adoption of low-carbon vehicles in the transportation eco-system. In 2019, the Global Green Growth Institute became a delivery partner of the National Council for Sustainable Development to deliver its Green Climate Fund for promoting green mobility through electric vehicles. The several pilot schemes launched in the country include the electric motorbike-sharing system called Go2, making electric vehicles more accessible to consumers (Niuseiy 2021). The country has introduced electric buses fitted with solar panels. The supporting charging infrastructure placed along the bus routes is also solar powered (de Carteret 2014). In 2021, the National Council for Sustainable Development prepared a strategy for promoting electric two-wheelers in the country (Global Green Growth Institute).[1] In addition, the national energy policy sets important objectives for increasing renewable energy with greater reliance on private investment.

Overall Messages

Despite facing relatively expensive vehicle costs, the case for electric mobility in Cambodia benefits from the dominance of two-wheel vehicles in the fleet, as well as the country's status as an oil importer (figure A.2.1a). As a result, the overall case for electric mobility in the country is good (table A.2.1). There is a strong case for adoption of two-wheel electric motorbikes (figure A.2.1b), which present a life-cycle cost advantage of over 10 percent (almost 20 percent in financial terms). Nevertheless, the capital cost premium for electric two-wheel vehicles in Cambodia is particularly high at about 29 percent and represents as much as 6 percent of gross national income per capita, suggesting that provision of credit lines may be important to support adoption. At the same time, electric buses are beginning to offer modest economic advantages on the order of 3 percent of life-cycle cost. By contrast, the economics of electric four-wheel vehicles is quite marginal, and the associated capital cost premium prohibitive at 40 percent of gross national income per capita.

The externality benefits of electric mobility in Cambodia are relatively small (figure A.2.1c), perhaps because of the existing prevalence of hydro energy and limited urban air quality issues. An important exception is provided by two-wheel electric vehicles, which present much lower externalities than their conventional counterparts (figure A.2.1d). Otherwise, fuel cost savings are the main advantage associated with electric mobility in Cambodia.

The fiscal regime neither incentivizes nor disincentivizes the purchase of electric vehicles. However, fiscal policies do accentuate the fuel cost advantage of owning them, given that gasoline and diesel are taxed at 20–50 percent, whereas electricity is slightly subsidized. Consequently, the overall case for electric mobility in Cambodia looks better in financial than in economic terms (figure A.2.1a).

The total investment needs associated with the 30×30 scenario amount to US$44 million per year by 2030 (or 0.1 percent of Cambodian gross domestic product). About two-thirds of the required outlay is associated with the incremental capital cost of electric vehicles (figure A.2.2a). In terms of public investment, the most significant item is the provision of public charging infrastructure for private vehicles and buses (figure A.2.2a). Given that implicit carbon prices associated with electric two-wheelers and buses in Cambodia are negative (see table A.2.3), there is significant scope to cover 17–27 percent of public investment costs through carbon financing arrangements (figure A.2.2b.). However, for four-wheel electric vehicles, the implicit carbon price exceeds US$400 per ton.

The overall economic case for electric mobility in Cambodia is robust to more conservative assumptions about the cost of batteries ("scarce minerals" scenario) and the fuel efficiency of internal combustion engines ("fuel efficiency" scenario), and there is not much scope for further decarbonization of the power sector ("green grid" scenario) (table A.2.2). On a positive note, the emerging advantage associated with electrification of buses can be as much as tripled through the more efficient procurement and operation of vehicles ("efficient bus" scenario). However, the case for electrification of four-wheelers is only marginally improved in the case of taxi fleets and other intensively used vehicles ("taxi fleet" scenario). It's clear that electric mobility in Cambodia needs to prioritize the two-wheel segment of the fleet, which offers so many strong advantages.

Figures and tables start on the next page.

Figures and Tables

FIGURE A.2.1 Advantage of EV adoption in Cambodia, by type of vehicle

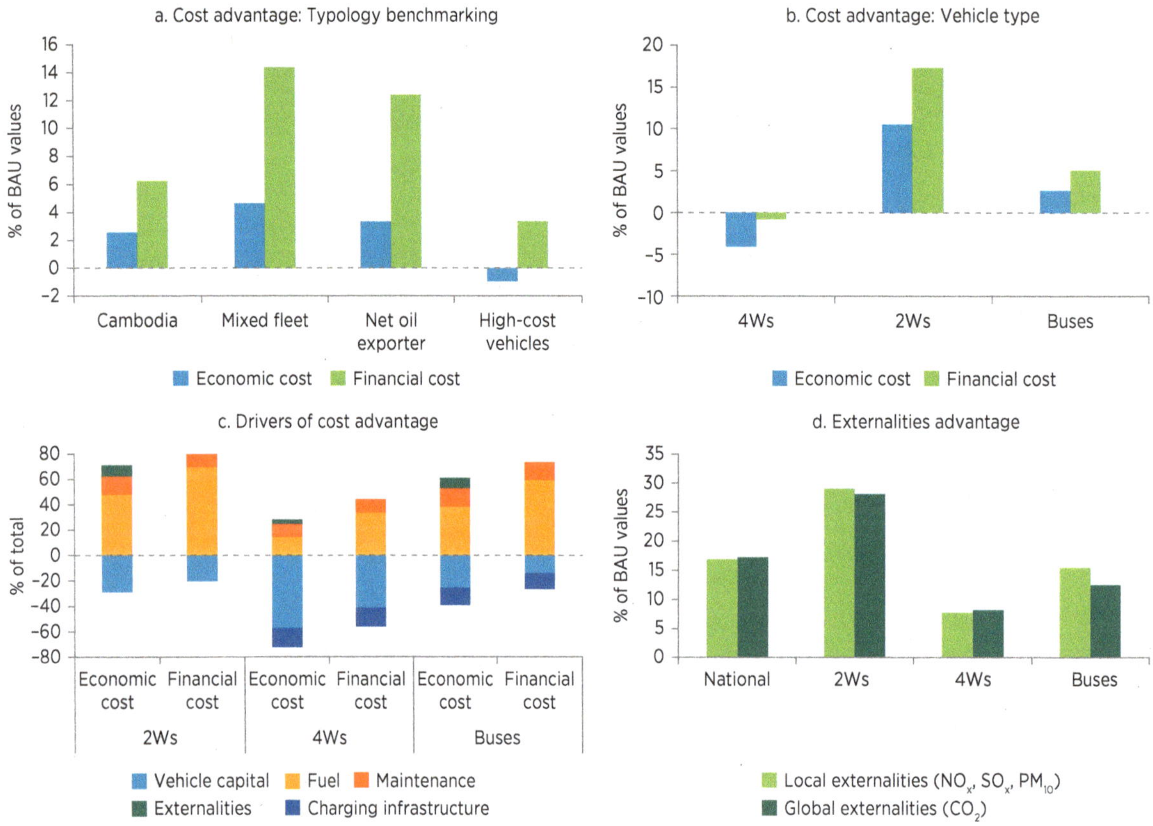

Source: World Bank.

Note: Data in this figure represent the "business as usual" (BAU) scenario minus the 30×30 scenario (averages over fleet additions). The BAU scenario assumes that no policy target will be imposed for electric vehicles and that vehicle purchase decisions will continue to reflect historical trends. The 30×30 scenario assumes that sales of electric cars and buses will reach 30 percent, and of two- and three-wheelers, 70 percent, by 2030. 2W = two-wheeler; 4W = four-wheeler; CO_2 = carbon dioxide; EV = electric vehicle; NO_x = nitrogen oxides; PM_{10} = particulate matter less than 10 microns in diameter; SO_x = sulfur oxides.

TABLE A.2.1 Cost advantage of accelerated EV adoption in Cambodia, 2030

	US$/vehicle									% of BAU values	
	Charging infrastructure	Vehicle capital cost	Vehicle operating cost	Subtotal	Local externalities	Global externalities	Economic cost advantage	Net taxes and subsidies	Financial cost advantage	Cost advantage	Financial cost advantage including fiscal wedge
	(a)	(b)	(c)	(d) = (a + b + c)	(e)		(f) = (d + e)	(g)	(h) = (d + g)		
Mode											
2Ws	0	(154)	334	180	3	42	224	291	471	10.5	17.3
4Ws	(363)	(1,397)	613	(1,147)	4	74	(1,069)	852	(295)	(4.1)	(0.8)
Buses	(5,180)	(9,621)	20,299	5,497	309	2,597	8,404	13,770	19,267	2.6	5.0

Source: World Bank.

Note: Heading colors: blue = excluding taxes and subsidies, gray = fiscal wedge, green = including taxes and subsidies. 2W = two-wheeler; 4W = four-wheeler; "Local externalities" comprises local (NO_x, PM_{10}, SO_x) air pollution costs. "Global externalities" comprises global (CO_2) air pollution costs. CO_2 = carbon dioxide; NO_x = nitrogen oxides; PM_{10} = particulate matter less than 10 microns in diameter; SO_x = sulfur oxides. Red and parentheses indicate negative value.

FIGURE A.2.2 Investment and financing needs for EV adoption in Cambodia, 2030

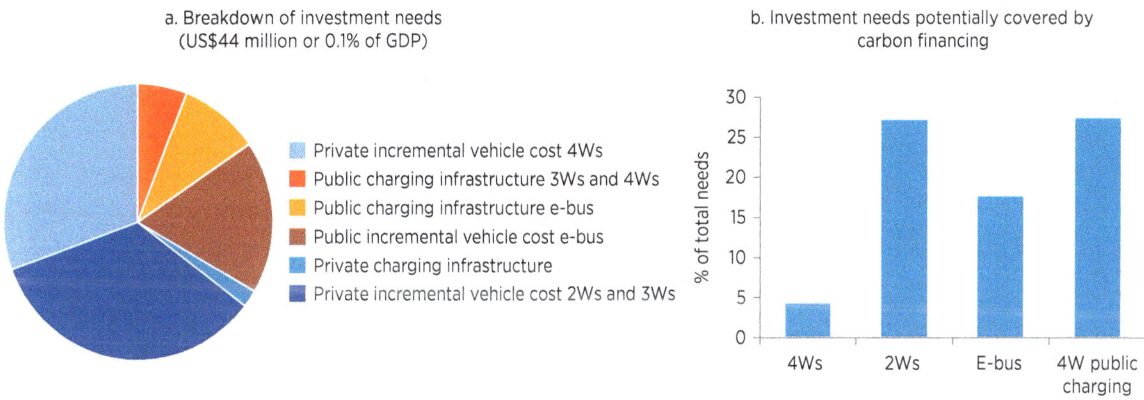

Source: World Bank.
Note: Data in this figure represent the "business as usual" (BAU) scenario minus the 30×30 scenario (averages over fleet additions). The BAU scenario assumes that no policy target will be imposed for electric vehicles and that vehicle purchase decisions will continue to reflect historical trends. The 30×30 scenario assumes that sales of electric cars and buses will reach 30 percent, and of two- and three-wheelers, 70 percent, by 2030. 2W = two-wheeler; 3W = three-wheeler; 4W = four-wheeler; EV = electric vehicle; GDP = gross domestic product.

TABLE A.2.2 Cost advantage of EV adoption in Cambodia, by scenario, 2030

	National results				Bus only		4W only	
	30×30 scenario	Green grid scenario	Scarce minerals scenario	Fuel efficiency scenario	30×30 scenario	Efficient bus scenario	30×30 scenario	Taxi fleet scenario
	US$/Mpaxvkm				*US$/vehicle*			
Type of cost								
Vehicle capital cost	(12,724)	(12,724)	(16,860)	(12,724)	(9,621)	1,316	(1,397)	(1,397)
Vehicle maintenance cost	5,178	5,178	4,584	5,178	5,700	6,036	258	(537)
Vehicle fuel cost	14,077	14,077	14,077	10,979	14,599	18,214	355	1,420
Private charging infrastructure	(316)	(316)	(316)	(316)	n.a.	n.a.	(94)	(94)
Public charging infrastructure	(2,392)	(2,392)	(2,392)	(2,392)	(5,180)	(5,180)	(270)	(308)
Subtotal	3,822	3,822	(908)	724	5,497	20,386	(1,147)	(915)
Local externalities (NO_x, SO_x, PM_{10})	189	189	189	178	309	386	4	17
Global externalities (CO_2)	2,415	2,415	2,415	2,057	2,597	3,253	74	307
Economic cost advantage	6,426	6,426	1,696	2,959	8,404	24,025	(1,069)	(591)
Fiscal wedge	16,708	16,708	15,423	15,772	13,770	19,869	852	2,319
Financial cost advantage	20,530	20,530	14,515	16,496	19,267	40,255	(295)	1,404
Economic cost advantage, by type of vehicle	*US$/vehicle*							
4Ws	(1,069)	(1,069)	(1,532)	(1,268)	n.a.	n.a.	n.a.	n.a.
2Ws	224	224	182	200	n.a.	n.a.	n.a.	n.a.
E-buses	8,404	8,404	2,334	1,557	n.a.	n.a.	n.a.	n.a.

Source: World Bank.
Note: Data in this table represent the "business as usual" (BAU) scenario minus the named scenario (averages over fleet additions). The BAU scenario assumes that no policy target will be imposed for electric vehicles and that vehicle purchase decisions will continue to reflect historical trends. The 30×30 scenario assumes that sales of electric cars and buses will reach 30 percent, and of two- and three-wheelers, 70 percent, by 2030. The green grid scenario assumes that countries achieve certain region-specific targets for acceleration of renewable energy, as defined by the International Renewable Energy Agency (IRENA 2020). The scarce minerals scenario assumes that battery cost will decline by approximately 7 percent annually. The fuel efficiency scenario assumes that the rate of improvement of fuel efficiency for the internal combustion engine fleet will double from 15 percent to 30 percent. The efficient bus scenario assumes a capital cost reduction of 35 percent in the procurement of buses as well as optimized bus routes to increase the annual mileage of electric buses. The taxi fleet scenario assumes that the lifetime mileage of intensively used commercial vehicles will increase by four times in each country, that public investment in charging infrastructure will double the fast charger density for cars, and that the maintenance cost for cars will be doubled (assuming two lifetime battery replacements). Results have been normalized by new vehicles entering the market in 2030. The "fiscal wedge" comprises net taxes and subsidies. Red and parentheses indicate negative value. 2W = two-wheeler; 4W = four-wheeler; CO_2 = carbon dioxide; EV = electric vehicle; NO_x = nitrogen oxides; PM_{10} = particulate matter less than 10 microns in diameter; SO_x = sulfur oxides; US$/Mpaxvkm = US dollars per million passenger vehicle-kilometers; n.a.= not applicable.

TABLE A.2.3 Supporting information on parameters and results for EV adoption in Cambodia

Price (US$/vehicle)

Parameter	Value
Price of ICE 4W	32,349
Price of EV 4W	41,899
Price of ICE 2W	1,193
Price of EV 2W	1,683
Price of ICE bus	151,773
Price of e-bus	162,388

Other parameters

Parameter	Value
Net tax difference on EV 4W (%)	28
Net tax difference on EV 2W (%)	10
Net tax difference on e-bus (%)	30
Price of gasoline (US$/liter)	0.60
Net gasoline tax (US$/liter)	0.32
Price of diesel (US$/liter)	0.74
Net diesel tax (US$/liter)	0.14
Price of electricity (US$/kWh)	0.14
Net electricity tax (US$/kWh)	(0.01)
Electricity carbon intensity (g/kWh)	398
Discount rate (%)	6.6

Key characteristics

Parameter	Value
4W mileage (km)	15,224
2W mileage (km)	7,627
Bus mileage (km)	48,092
4W lifetime (years)	22
2W lifetime (years)	17
Bus lifetime (years)	20
4W secondhand (%)	73.3
2W secondhand (%)	73.3
Bus secondhand (%)	31.5
4W share (% paxvkm)	21
2W share (% paxvkm)	52
Bus share (% paxvkm)	28

Efficiency (MJ/km)

Parameter	Value
Efficiency ICE 4W	2.31
Efficiency EV 4W	0.45
Efficiency ICE 2W	0.87
Efficiency EV 2W	0.20
Efficiency ICE bus	16.58
Efficiency EV bus	5.69

Other results for 30×30 scenario

Other results for 30×30 scenario	Value
Overall investment needs (US$, millions)	44
—of which 4W purchase	13.4
—of which 2W purchase	15
—of which e-bus purchase	7.8
Fiscal impact (US$, millions)	(48)
—of which vehicle duties	2.0
—of which vehicle taxes/subsidies	(8.2)
—of which gasoline taxes/subsidies	(30)
—of which diesel taxes/subsidies	(7.5)
—of which electricity taxes/subsidies	(4.1)
Implicit carbon price (US$/ton)	(43)
—of which for 4W	401
—of which for 2W	(113)
—of which for buses	(58)
Pollution reduction (tons)	0.3
—of which local (SO_x, NO_x, PM_{10})	0.003
—of which global (CO_2)	0.27
Affordability of EV 2W (Δ cost % GNI pc)	6.2
Affordability of EV 4W (Δ cost % GNI pc)	39.9

Source: World Bank.
Note: Red and parentheses indicates negative value. 2W = two-wheeler; 4W = four-wheeler; CO_2 = carbon dioxide; EV = electric vehicle; g = gram; GNI pc = gross national income per capita; ICE = internal combustion engine; kWh = kilowatt-hour; km = kilometer; MJ = megajoule; NO_x = nitrogen oxides; paxvkm = passenger vehicle-kilometer; PM_{10} = particulate matter less than 10 microns in diameter; SO_x = sulfur oxides.

Note

1. Data from US Energy Information Administration international database and World Bank.

References

de Carteret, Daniel. 2014. "Solar Buses at the Temples of Angkor" *Phnom Penh Post,* September 6, 2014. http://www.phnompenhpost.com/post-weekend/solar-buses-temples-angkor.

Global Green Growth Institute. 2021. *Promoting Green Mobility through Electric Motorbikes in Cambodia.* Seoul, Korea: Global Green Growth Institute.

IRENA (International Renewable Energy Agency). 2020. *Global Renewables Outlook: Energy Transformation 2050.* Masdar City: IRENA.

Niuseiy, Sao Phal. 2021. "A Campaign to Promote the Use of Electric Vehicles Is Held This Month in Phnom Penh." *Cambodianess,* February 7, 2021. https://cambodianess.com/article/a-campaign-to-promote-the-use-of-electric-vehicles-is-held-this-month-in-phnom-penh.

A.3 PASSENGER ELECTRIC MOBILITY IN THE ARAB REPUBLIC OF EGYPT

Country Typology

Vehicle fleet composition: Mixed fleet
Net oil trading status: Importer
Relative cost of vehicles: Low

Country Background

The dominant vehicle type in the Arab Republic of Egypt is the car (57.5 percent) (OICA 2020; Statista 2019), and electricity is primarily generated from fossil fuels (90.8 percent).[1] Electric vehicle (EV) adoption has been slow, but the government is redoubling efforts to mainstream electric vehicles (El-Dorghamy 2019) by considering the inception of (1) an integrated framework for sustainable transportation and green urban development that would include EV adoption as one of its pillars; (2) policies to prioritize electrification of shared services and public transportation; (3) motorization management practices to address vehicle registration and licensing, scrapping, and fleet renewal; and (4) policies to improve fuel standards and use of cleaner nonelectricity fuels to address air quality while in transition. In the power sector, the current energy plans and policies aim at increasing the country's renewable share to 25 percent by 2030 (IRENA 2018); doing so will have a compound effect on the benefits of EV adoption. Further, investments have been set in place to install 300 EV charging points by 2023, of which 150 charging points at 40 stations have already been built (Hardhat 2020). Finally, Egypt is pursuing a joint venture between a state-owned automotive industry and a Chinese company for setting in place a domestic EV assembly line deployment of EV charging facilities (Enterprise 2021).

Overall Messages

Electric mobility in Egypt looks to be a promising strategy (table A.3.1). Egypt shares many characteristics with other countries that are favorable toward the economics of electric mobility, including the relatively low cost of vehicles, a diversified mixed fleet, and being an oil importer (figure A.3.1a). The economic case for electric two-wheelers and buses is particularly strong, providing a lifetime cost advantage on the order of 10–15 percent (figure A.3.1b). When it comes to four-wheel vehicles, however, the case for electric mobility is much more marginal (figure A.3.1b).

From an affordability standpoint, two-wheel electric motorbikes also look to be more within reach. Although the associated capital cost premium exceeds 25 percent, it is under 5 percent of gross national income per capita, suggesting that the extra cost might potentially be affordable with some kind of consumer finance (see table A.3.3). By contrast, the 3 percent capital cost premium associated with four-wheel EVs exceeds 17 percent of gross national income per capita and therefore requires some financial support to be affordable (table A.3.3).

One of the main factors driving the case for electric mobility in Egypt is the very high externality costs associated with internal combustion engine vehicles (figure A.3.1c). Poor urban air quality, and resulting health impacts, is a very serious issue for the country—particularly in the Greater Cairo area—leading to local externality benefits of electric mobility that are even larger than global externality savings associated with reduced carbon emissions (figure A.3.1d).

Egypt has a fiscal regime neutral to the actual purchase of EVs, but gasoline is taxed at over 20 percent and electricity subsidized by over 50 percent, which substantially reduces the operating cost of EVs and leads to fuel savings when expressed in financial terms (figure A.3.1c). Nevertheless, the sizable fiscal wedge in favor of electric mobility does not come close to matching the social costs associated with internal combustion engines. As a result, electric mobility in Egypt is more attractive in economic terms than in financial terms, even though it remains financially advantageous (table A.3.1).

The overall investment needs associated with the 30×30 scenario amount to US$2.3 billion per year by 2030 (or 0.56 percent of Egyptian gross domestic product). About two-thirds of the required outlays fall on the private sector because of the incremental capital cost associated with EVs and private charging infrastructure (figure A.3.2a). Nevertheless, the public sector would need to find financing for about one-third of this total to cover the higher cost of electric buses and the provision of public charging infrastructure for the overall fleet. The good news is that, given the negative implicit carbon prices associated (table A.3.3), there is significant scope to cover 25–35 percent of public investment costs of electric mobility through carbon financing arrangements (figure A.3.2b).

The economic case for electric mobility remains robust (table A.3.2), even under more conservative assumptions about the cost of batteries ("scarce minerals" scenario) and the fuel efficiency of internal combustion engines ("fuel efficiency" scenario), while benefits are significantly amplified as Egypt further decarbonizes its electricity sector ("green grid" scenario). Furthermore, the advantage associated with electrification of buses can be further increased through more efficient procurement and operation of the vehicles ("efficient bus" scenario), and the electrification of four-wheelers also becomes more advantageous when confined to taxi fleets and other intensively used vehicles ("taxi fleet" scenario).

Figures and tables start on the next page.

Figures and Tables

FIGURE A.3.1 Advantage of EV adoption in the Arab Republic of Egypt, by type of vehicle

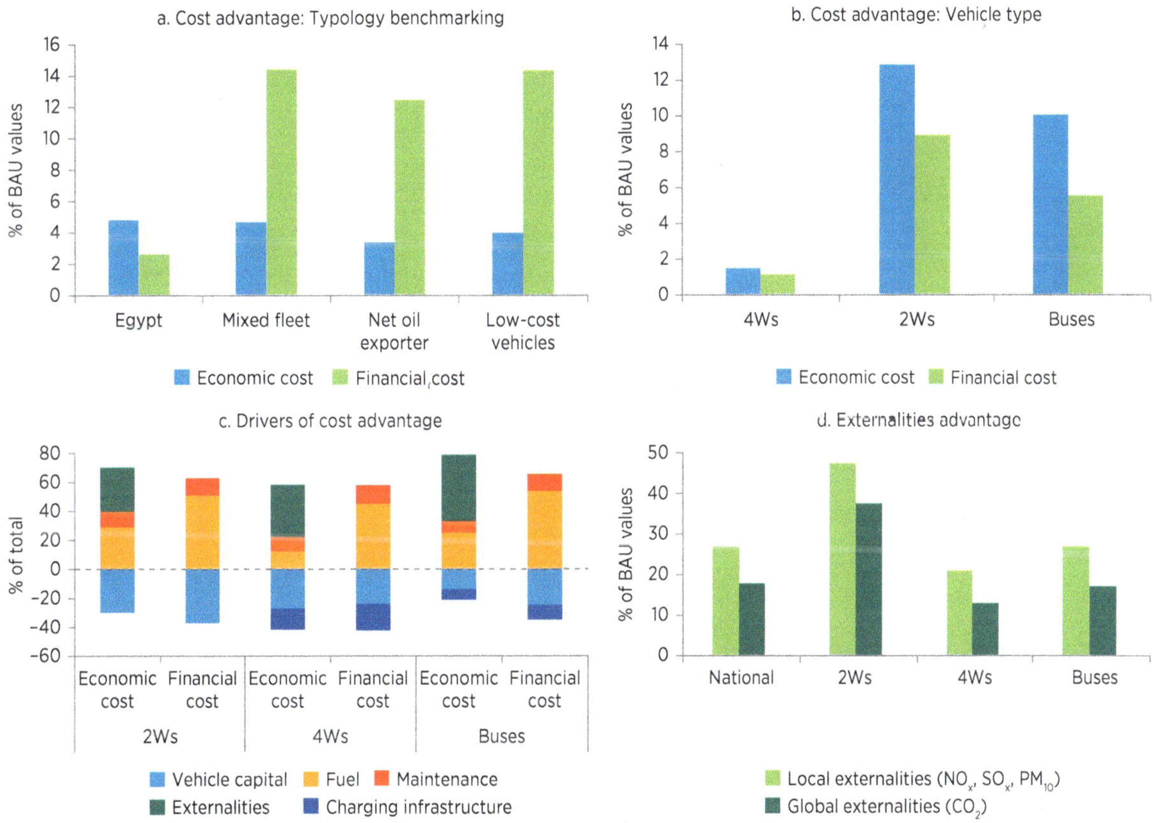

Source: World Bank.
Note: Data in this figure represent the "business as usual" (BAU) scenario minus the 30×30 scenario (averages over fleet additions). The BAU scenario assumes that no policy target will be imposed for electric vehicles and that vehicle purchase decisions will continue to reflect historical trends. The 30×30 scenario assumes that sales of electric cars and buses will reach 30 percent, and of two- and three-wheelers, 70 percent, by 2030. 2W = two-wheeler; 4W = four-wheeler; CO_2 = carbon dioxide; EV = electric vehicle; NO_x = nitrogen oxides; PM_{10} = particulate matter less than 10 microns in diameter; SO_x = sulfur oxides.

TABLE A.3.1 Cost advantage of accelerated EV adoption in the Arab Republic of Egypt, 2030

	US$/vehicle									% of BAU values	
	Charging infrastructure	Vehicle capital cost	Vehicle operating cost	Subtotal	Local externalities	Global externalities	Economic cost advantage	Net taxes and subsidies	Financial cost advantage	Cost advantage	Financial cost advantage including fiscal wedge
	(a)	(b)	(c)	(d) = (a + b + c)	(e)		(f) = (d + e)	(g)	(h) = (d + g)		
Mode											
2Ws	0	(202)	265	63	170	33	266	93	156	12.9	8.9
4Ws	(567)	(1,100)	880	(787)	1,255	161	629	1,256	469	1.5	1.1
Buses	(6,036)	(12,107)	27,579	9,437	33,680	4,470	47,587	8,806	18,243	10.0	5.5

Source: World Bank.
Note: Heading colors: blue = excluding taxes and subsidies, gray = fiscal wedge, green = including taxes and subsidies. 2W = two-wheeler; 4W = four-wheeler; "Local externalities" comprises local (NO_x, PM_{10}, SO_x) air pollution costs. "Global externalities" comprises global (CO_2) air pollution costs. CO_2 = carbon dioxide; NO_x = nitrogen oxides; PM_{10} = particulate matter less than 10 microns in diameter; SO_x = sulfur oxides. Red and parentheses indicate negative value.

FIGURE A.3.2 Investment and financing needs for EV adoption in the Arab Republic of Egypt, 2030

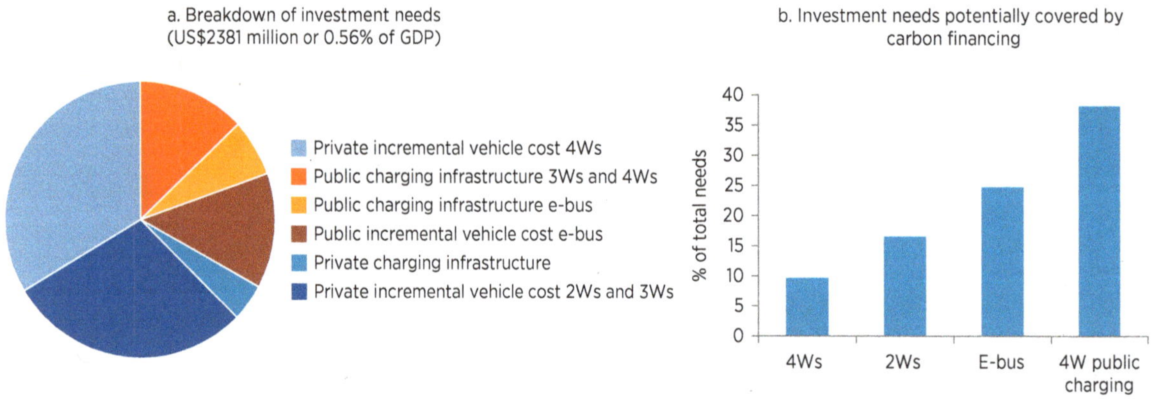

Source: World Bank.
Note: Data in this figure represent the "business as usual" (BAU) scenario minus the 30×30 scenario (averages over fleet additions). The BAU scenario assumes that no policy target will be imposed for electric vehicles and that vehicle purchase decisions will continue to reflect historical trends. The 30×30 scenario assumes that sales of electric cars and buses will reach 30 percent, and of two- and three-wheelers, 70 percent, by 2030. 2W = two-wheeler; 3W = three-wheeler; 4W = four-wheeler; EV = electric vehicle; GDP = gross domestic product.

TABLE A.3.2 Cost advantage of EV adoption in the Arab Republic of Egypt, by scenario, 2030

	National results				Bus only		4W only	
	30×30 scenario	Green grid scenario	Scarce minerals scenario	Fuel efficiency scenario	30×30 scenario	Efficient bus scenario	30×30 scenario	Taxi fleet scenario
	US$/Mpaxvkm				*US$/vehicle*			
Type of cost								
Vehicle capital cost	(13,010)	(13,010)	(19,252)	(13,010)	(12,107)	1,318	(1,100)	(1,100)
Vehicle maintenance cost	5,053	5,053	4,630	5,053	7,065	7,371	406	(818)
Vehicle fuel cost	10,247	10,247	10,247	6,029	20,514	23,670	474	1,895
Private charging infrastructure	(752)	(752)	(752)	(752)	n.a.	n.a.	(144)	(144)
Public charging infrastructure	(3,355)	(3,355)	(3,355)	(3,355)	(6,036)	(6,036)	(423)	(481)
Subtotal	(1,817)	(1,817)	(8,483)	(6,035)	9,437	26,324	(787)	(649)
Local externalities (NO_x, SO_x, PM_{10})	16,640	23,228	16,640	13,733	33,680	38,905	1,255	5,550
Global externalities (CO_2)	2,378	2,593	2,378	1,781	4,470	5,167	161	672
Economic cost advantage	17,201	24,004	10,536	9,479	47,587	70,395	629	5,573
Fiscal wedge	10,165	10,165	8,885	10,178	8,806	14,152	1,256	4,072
Financial cost advantage	8,347	8,347	402	4,143	18,243	40,476	469	3,422
Economic cost advantage, by type of vehicle	*US$/vehicle*							
4Ws	629	629	(96)	(168)	n.a.	n.a.	n.a.	n.a.
2Ws	266	266	195	230	n.a.	n.a.	n.a.	n.a.
E-buses	47,587	47,587	40,459	32,698	n.a.	n.a.	n.a.	n.a.

Source: World Bank.
Note: Data in this table represent the "business as usual" (BAU) scenario minus the named scenario (averages over fleet additions). The BAU scenario assumes that no policy target will be imposed for electric vehicles and that vehicle purchase decisions will continue to reflect historical trends. The 30×30 scenario assumes that sales of electric cars and buses will reach 30 percent, and of two- and three-wheelers, 70 percent, by 2030. The green grid scenario assumes that countries achieve certain region-specific targets for acceleration of renewable energy, as defined by the International Renewable Energy Agency (IRENA 2020). The scarce minerals scenario assumes that battery cost will decline by approximately 7 percent annually. The fuel efficiency scenario assumes that the rate of improvement of fuel efficiency for the internal combustion engine fleet will double from 15 percent to 30 percent. The efficient bus scenario assumes a capital cost reduction of 35 percent in the procurement of buses as well as optimized bus routes to increase the annual mileage of electric buses. The taxi fleet scenario assumes that the lifetime mileage of intensively used commercial vehicles will increase by four times in each country, that public investment in charging infrastructure will double the fast charger density for cars, and that the maintenance cost for cars will be doubled (assuming two lifetime battery replacements). Results have been normalized by new vehicles entering the market in 2030. The "fiscal wedge" comprises net taxes and subsidies. Red and parentheses indicate negative value. 2W = two-wheeler; 4W = four-wheeler; CO_2 = carbon dioxide; EV = electric vehicle; NO_x = nitrogen oxides; PM_{10} = particulate matter less than 10 microns in diameter; SO_x = sulfur oxides; US$/Mpaxvkm = US dollars per million passenger vehicle-kilometers; n.a.= not applicable.

TABLE A.3.3 Supporting information on parameters and results for EV adoption in the Arab Republic of Egypt

Price (US$/vehicle)

Parameter	Value
Price of ICE 4W	25,777
Price of EV 4W	29,790
Price of ICE 2W	913
Price of EV 2W	1,249
Price of ICE bus	114,338
Price of e-bus	160,359

Other parameters

Parameter	Value
Net tax difference on EV 4W (%)	0
Net tax difference on EV 2W (%)	0
Net tax difference on e-bus (%)	0
Price of gasoline (US$/liter)	0.48
Net gasoline tax (US$/liter)	0.09
Price of diesel (US$/liter)	0.61
Net diesel tax (US$/liter)	(0.07)
Price of electricity (US$/kWh)	0.15
Net electricity tax (US$/kWh)	(0.08)
Electricity carbon intensity (g/kWh)	464
Discount rate (%)	6.6

Key characteristics

Parameter	Value
4W mileage (km)	20,000
2W mileage (km)	7,000
Bus mileage (km)	65,000
4W lifetime (years)	20
2W lifetime (years)	7
Bus lifetime (years)	20
4W secondhand (%)	5.6
2W secondhand (%)	5.6
Bus secondhand (%)	30.8
4W share (% paxvkm)	42
2W share (% paxvkm)	27
Bus share (% paxvkm)	25

Efficiency (MJ/km)

Parameter	Value
Efficiency ICE 4W	2.36
Efficiency EV 4W	0.66
Efficiency ICE 2W	0.85
Efficiency EV 2W	0.11
Efficiency ICE bus	15.58
Efficiency EV bus	3.78

Other results for 30×30 scenario

Other results for 30×30 scenario	Value
Overall investment needs (US$, millions)	2,381
—of which 4W purchase	799
—of which 2W purchase	548
—of which e-bus purchase	320
Fiscal impact (US$, millions)	(1,414)
—of which vehicle duties	(370)
—of which vehicle taxes/subsidies	335
—of which gasoline taxes/subsidies	(296)
—of which diesel taxes/subsidies	254
—of which electricity taxes/subsidies	(1,336)
Implicit carbon price (US$/ton)	(161)
—of which for 4W	(75)
—of which for 2W	(181)
—of which for buses	(249)
Pollution reduction (tons)	13
—of which local (SO_x, NO_x, PM_{10})	0
—of which global (CO_2)	13
Affordability of EV 2W (Δ cost % GNI pc)	5
Affordability of EV 4W (Δ cost % GNI pc)	17

Source: World Bank.

Note: Red and parentheses indicates negative value. 2W = two-wheeler; 4W = four-wheeler; CO_2 = carbon dioxide; EV = electric vehicle; g = gram; GNI pc = gross national income per capita; ICE = internal combustion engine; kWh = kilowatt-hour; km = kilometer; MJ = megajoule; NO_x = nitrogen oxides; paxvkm = passenger vehicle-kilometer; PM_{10} = particulate matter less than 10 microns in diameter; SO_x = sulfur oxides.

Note

1. Data from US Energy Information Administration international database and World Bank.

References

El-Dorghamy, Ahmed. 2019. *Mainstreaming Electric Mobility in Egypt.* Policy Brief, Friedrich-Ebert-Stiftung, Arab Republic of Egypt—Ministry of Environment, and Center for Environment and Development for the Arab Region and Europe [updated 2019]. Cairo: Friedrich-Ebert-Stiftung. https://egypt.fes.de/fileadmin/user_upload/images/Policy_Brief_FINAL___Updates_-_Nov_2019_compressed.pdf.

Enterprise. 2021. "One Step Forward for Our EV Future." Enterprise: The State of the Nation, January 19, 2021. https://enterprise.press/stories/2021/01/19/one-step-forward-for-our-ev-future-29775/.

Hardhat. 2020. "Is Egypt Ready for Electric Vehicles?" *Hardhat,* June 10, 2020. https://enterprise.press/hardhats/egypt-ready-electric-vehicles/.

IRENA (International Renewable Energy Agency). 2018. *Renewable Energy Outlook: Egypt.* Abu Dhabi, United Arab Emirates: IRENA.

IRENA (International Renewable Energy Agency). 2020. *Global Renewables Outlook: Energy Transformation 2050.* Masdar City: IRENA.

OICA (Organisation Internationale des Constructeurs d'Automobiles [International Organization of Motor Vehicle Manufacturers]). 2021. "Global Sales Statistics, 2019–2021." OICA, Paris. https://www.oica.net/global-sales-statistics-2019-2021/.

Statista. 2019. "Number of Licensed Buses in Egypt from 2012 to 2017." Statista, Hamburg, Germany. https://www.statista.com/statistics/988687/egypt-number-licensed-buses/.

A.4 PASSENGER ELECTRIC MOBILITY IN ETHIOPIA

Country Typology

Vehicle fleet composition: Mixed fleet
Net oil trading status: Importer
Relative cost of vehicles: High

Country Background

The vehicle fleet in Ethiopia is quite diverse: about half of the fleet is buses (49.7 percent), followed by cars (22.8 percent), three-wheelers (16.5 percent), and two-wheelers (11.0 percent).[1] Close to 100 percent of the electricity comes from renewable sources: hydro (95.64 percent) and wind (3.96 percent).[2] Adoption of electric mobility has been very limited in Ethiopia and is particularly difficult because of the country's high reliance on imported secondhand vehicles, almost all of them more than 11 years old (Aventa 2021). Other challenges include the lack of electric vehicle charging facilities and skill shortages in the local labor market for production and maintenance of electric vehicles (Ethiopian Monitor 2020). The Ethiopian government developed a Climate Resilient Green Economy strategy, which promotes a shift toward more sustainable urban transportation, including investment in the light-rail transit and bus rapid transit systems, and also emphasizes the use of hybrid and plug-in electric vehicles (Federal Democratic Republic of Ethiopia 2011). Moreover, the Ethiopian Federal Environmental Protection Authority, together with a private organization and supported by the United Nations Development Programme, launched an electric vehicles pilot project in Ethiopia in 2013; a private Ethiopian transit and cargo company has announced its plan to establish an electric bicycle assembly plant in Ethiopia (2Merkato 2013).

Overall Messages

Despite the country's relatively expensive vehicle costs, the case for electric mobility in Ethiopia benefits from the dominance of buses in the vehicle fleet, as well as the country's status as an oil importer (figure A.4.1a). That the overall case for electric mobility in the country is good (table A.4.1.,) is entirely attributable to the favorable balance of economic benefits for the electrification of buses (figure A.4.1b), which leads to a modest life-cycle cost advantage of a few percentage points. Unlike in many other countries, the case for two-wheel electric vehicles in Ethiopia is very marginal, given a capital cost premium of more than 25 percent, which represents a share of about 5 percent of gross national income per capita (table A.4.3). The capital cost premium for four-wheel electric vehicles also exceeds 3 percent and is equivalent to over 23 percent of gross national income per capita (table A.4.3).

The externality benefits of electric mobility in Ethiopia are relatively small (figure A.4.1c), perhaps because of the existing prevalence of hydro energy and limited urban air quality issues. Across all vehicle types, two-wheel electric vehicles present the greatest advantage on externalities relative to their conventional counterparts (figure A.4.1d). Otherwise, fuel cost savings are the main advantage associated with electric mobility in Ethiopia, particularly for two-wheelers and buses. The fiscal regime neither incentivizes nor disincentivizes the purchase of electric vehicles. However, fiscal policies do accentuate the fuel cost advantage of owning them, given that gasoline is taxed at about 25 percent, whereas electricity is heavily subsidized.

Consequently, the overall case for electric mobility in Ethiopia looks better in financial than in economic terms (figure A.4.1a).

The total investment needs associated with the 30×30 scenario amount to US$333 million per year by 2030 (or 0.2 percent of Ethiopian gross domestic product). About half of the required outlay is associated with the incremental capital cost of private electric vehicles, and the remaining half is mainly public investment associated with charging infrastructure for electric buses (figure A.4.2a). Given that implicit carbon prices associated with electric buses in Ethiopia are negative (table A.4.3), there is significant scope to cover 25–60 percent of associated public investment costs through carbon financing arrangements (figure A.4.2b). However, for four-wheel electric vehicles, the implicit carbon price exceeds US$300 per ton.

The overall economic case for electric mobility in Ethiopia is robust to more conservative assumptions about the cost of batteries ("scarce minerals" scenario) and the fuel efficiency of internal combustion engines ("fuel efficiency" scenario), but there is not much scope for further decarbonization of the power sector ("green grid" scenario) (table A.4.2). On a positive note, the emerging advantage associated with electrification of buses can be as much as doubled through the more efficient procurement and operation of vehicles ("efficient bus" scenario). However, the case for electrification of four-wheelers remains negative even for taxi fleets and other intensively used vehicles ("taxi fleet" scenario). It is clear that electric mobility in Ethiopia needs to focus primarily on public transportation.

Figures and tables start on the next page.

Figures and Tables

FIGURE A.4.1 Advantage of EV adoption in Ethiopia, by type of vehicle

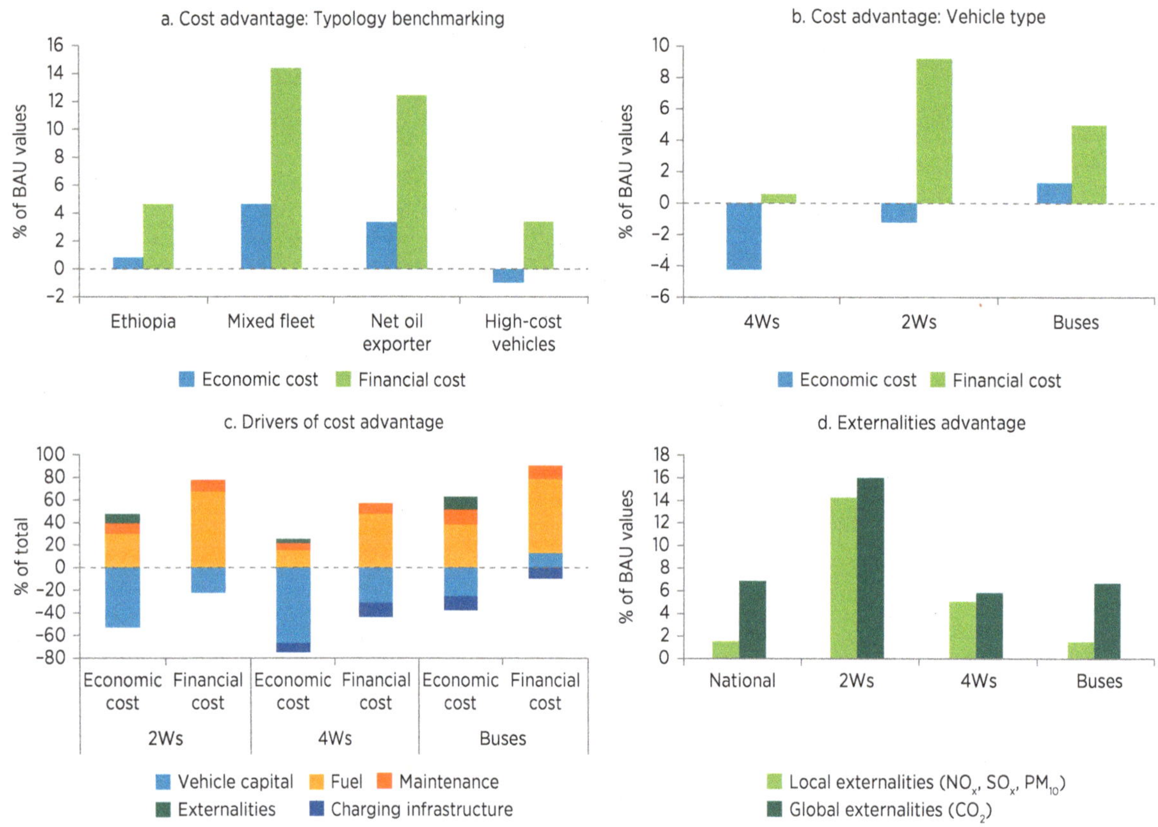

Source: World Bank.
Note: Data in this figure represent the "business as usual" (BAU) scenario minus the 30×30 scenario (averages over fleet additions). The BAU scenario assumes that no policy target will be imposed for electric vehicles and that vehicle purchase decisions will continue to reflect historical trends. The 30×30 scenario assumes that sales of electric cars and buses will reach 30 percent, and of two- and three-wheelers, 70 percent, by 2030. 2W = two-wheeler; 4W = four-wheeler; CO_2 = carbon dioxide; EV = electric vehicle; NO_x = nitrogen oxides; PM_{10} = particulate matter less than 10 microns in diameter; SO_x = sulfur oxides.

TABLE A.4.1 Cost advantage of accelerated EV adoption in Ethiopia, 2030

	US$/vehicle									% of BAU values	
	Charging infrastructure	Vehicle capital cost	Vehicle operating cost	Subtotal	Local externalities	Global externalities	Economic cost advantage	Net taxes and subsidies	Financial cost advantage	Cost advantage	Financial cost advantage including fiscal wedge
	(a)	(b)	(c)	(d) = (a + b + c)	(e)		(f) = (d + e)	(g)	(h) = (d + g)		
Mode											
2Ws	0	(172)	129	(43)	0	23	(20)	223	180	(1.2)	9.2
4Ws	(142)	(1,173)	376	(939)	0	64	(875)	1,093	154	(4.3)	0.6
Buses	(1,545)	(3,375)	6,809	1,890	8	1,320	3,217	10,787	12,676	1.3	5.0

Source: World Bank.
Note: Heading colors: blue = excluding taxes and subsidies, gray = fiscal wedge, green = including taxes and subsidies. 2W = two-wheeler; 4W = four-wheeler; "Local externalities" comprises local (NO_x, PM_{10}, SO_x) air pollution costs. "Global externalities" comprises global (CO_2) air pollution costs. CO_2 = carbon dioxide; NO_x = nitrogen oxides; PM_{10} = particulate matter less than 10 microns in diameter; SO_x = sulfur oxides. Red and parentheses indicate negative value.

FIGURE A.4.2 Investment and financing needs for EV adoption in Ethiopia, 2030

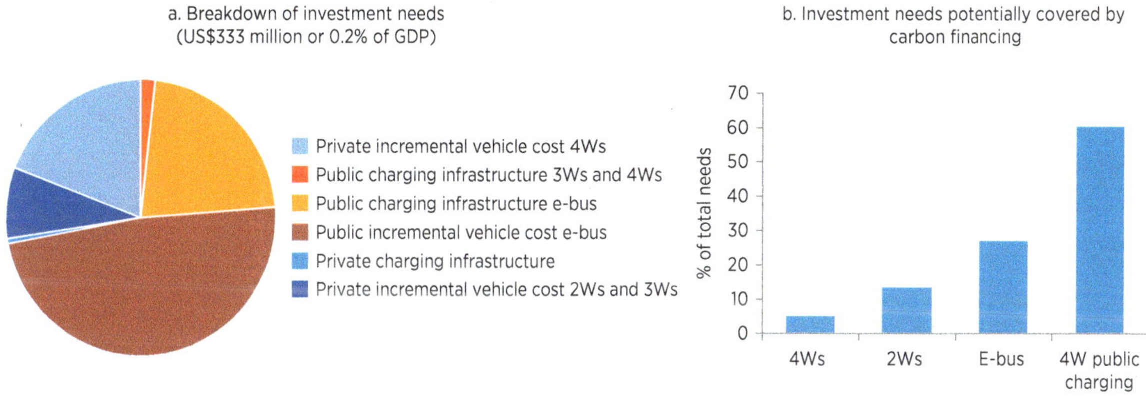

Source: World Bank.

Note: Data in this figure represent the "business as usual" (BAU) scenario minus the 30×30 scenario (averages over fleet additions). The BAU scenario assumes that no policy target will be imposed for electric vehicles and that vehicle purchase decisions will continue to reflect historical trends. The 30×30 scenario assumes that sales of electric cars and buses will reach 30 percent, and of two- and three-wheelers, 70 percent, by 2030. 2W = two-wheeler; 3W = three-wheeler; 4W = four-wheeler; EV = electric vehicle; GDP = gross domestic product.

TABLE A.4.2 Cost advantage of EV adoption in Ethiopia, by scenario, 2030

	National results				Bus only		4W only	
	30×30 scenario	Green grid scenario	Scarce minerals scenario	Fuel efficiency scenario	30×30 scenario	Efficient bus scenario	30×30 scenario	Taxi fleet scenario
	US$/Mpaxvkm				*US$/vehicle*			
Type of cost								
Vehicle capital cost	(4,692)	(4,692)	(6,170)	(4,692)	(3,375)	101	(1,173)	(1,173)
Vehicle maintenance cost	1,838	1,838	1,341	1,838	1,822	1,898	105	(198)
Vehicle fuel cost	5,082	5,082	5,082	3,239	4,987	6,222	271	1,082
Private charging infrastructure	(36)	(36)	(36)	(36)	n.a.	n.a.	(36)	(36)
Public charging infrastructure	(1,476)	(1,476)	(1,476)	(1,476)	(1,545)	(1,545)	(106)	(121)
Subtotal	715	715	(1,260)	(1,128)	1,890	6,677	(939)	(445)
Local externalities (NO_x, SO_x, PM_{10})	7	7	7	7	8	10	0	0
Global externalities (CO_2)	1,323	1,323	1,323	1,114	1,320	1,651	64	263
Economic cost advantage	2,045	2,045	70	(6)	3,217	8,337	(875)	(182)
Fiscal wedge	11,359	11,359	11,295	11,311	10,787	12,289	1,093	1,956
Financial cost advantage	12,074	12,074	10,036	10,183	12,676	18,966	154	1,511
Economic cost advantage, by type of vehicle	*US$/vehicle*							
4Ws	(875)	(875)	(1,147)	(1,001)	n.a.	n.a.	n.a.	n.a.
2Ws	(20)	(20)	(47)	(33)	n.a.	n.a.	n.a.	n.a.
E-buses	3,217	3,217	1,386	1,092	n.a.	n.a.	n.a.	n.a.

Source: World Bank.

Note: Data in this table represent the "business as usual" (BAU) scenario minus the named scenario (averages over fleet additions). The BAU scenario assumes that no policy target will be imposed for electric vehicles and that vehicle purchase decisions will continue to reflect historical trends. The 30×30 scenario assumes that sales of electric cars and buses will reach 30 percent, and of two- and three-wheelers, 70 percent, by 2030. The green grid scenario assumes that countries achieve certain region-specific targets for acceleration of renewable energy, as defined by the International Renewable Energy Agency (IRENA 2020). The scarce minerals scenario assumes that battery cost will decline by approximately 7 percent annually. The fuel efficiency scenario assumes that the rate of improvement of fuel efficiency for the internal combustion engine fleet will double from 15 percent to 30 percent. The efficient bus scenario assumes a capital cost reduction of 35 percent in the procurement of buses as well as optimized bus routes to increase the annual mileage of electric buses. The taxi fleet scenario assumes that the lifetime mileage of intensively used commercial vehicles will increase by four times in each country, that public investment in charging infrastructure will double the fast charger density for cars, and that the maintenance cost for cars will be doubled (assuming two lifetime battery replacements). Results have been normalized by new vehicles entering the market in 2030. The "fiscal wedge" comprises net taxes and subsidies. Red and parentheses indicate negative value. 2W = two-wheeler; 4W = four-wheeler; CO_2 = carbon dioxide; EV = electric vehicle; NO_x = nitrogen oxides; PM_{10} = particulate matter less than 10 microns in diameter; SO_x = sulfur oxides; US$/Mpaxvkm = US dollars per million passenger vehicle-kilometers; n.a.= not applicable.

TABLE A.4.3 Supporting information on parameters and results for EV adoption in Ethiopia

Price (US$/vehicle)

Parameter	Value
Price of ICE 4W	33,232
Price of EV 4W	37,988
Price of ICE 2W	1,129
Price of EV 2W	1,593
Price of ICE bus	164,688
Price of e-bus	135,324

Other parameters

Parameter	Value
Net tax difference on EV 4W (%)	80
Net tax difference on EV 2W (%)	80
Net tax difference on e-bus (%)	80
Price of gasoline (US$/liter)	0.58
Net gasoline tax (US$/liter)	0.16
Price of diesel (US$/liter)	0.73
Net diesel tax (US$/liter)	0.01
Price of electricity (US$/kWh)	0.13
Net electricity tax (US$/kWh)	(0.10)
Electricity carbon intensity (g/kWh)	0.4
Discount rate (%)	6.6

Key characteristics

Parameter	Value
4W mileage (km)	15,224
2W mileage (km)	7,627
Bus mileage (km)	48,092
4W lifetime (years)	22
2W lifetime (years)	17
Bus lifetime (years)	20
4W secondhand (%)	91.8
2W secondhand (%)	91.8
Bus secondhand (%)	91.1
4W share (% paxvkm)	6
2W share (% paxvkm)	4
Bus share (% paxvkm)	85

Efficiency (MJ/km)

Parameter	Value
Efficiency ICE 4W	2.43
Efficiency EV 4W	0.37
Efficiency ICE 2W	0.86
Efficiency EV 2W	0.20
Efficiency ICE bus	16.66
Efficiency EV bus	5.60

Other results for 30×30 scenario

Other results for 30×30 scenario	Value
Overall investment needs (US$, millions)	333
—of which 4W purchase	64
—of which 2W purchase	21
—of which e-bus purchase	160
Fiscal impact (US$, millions)	(609)
—of which vehicle duties	(10)
—of which vehicle taxes/subsidies	(301)
—of which gasoline taxes/subsidies	(11)
—of which diesel taxes/subsidies	(9)
—of which electricity taxes/subsidies	(279)
Implicit carbon price (US$/ton)	(14)
—of which for 4W	380
—of which for 2W	49
—of which for buses	(37)
Pollution reduction (tons)	3
—of which local (SO_x, NO_x, PM_{10})	0
—of which global (CO_2)	3
Affordability of EV 2W (Δ cost % GNI pc)	4.9
Affordability of EV 4W (Δ cost % GNI pc)	23.9

Source: World Bank.

Note: Red and parentheses indicates negative value. 2W = two-wheeler; 4W = four-wheeler; CO_2 = carbon dioxide; EV = electric vehicle; g = gram; GNI pc = gross national income per capita; ICE = internal combustion engine; kWh = kilowatt-hour; km = kilometer; MJ = megajoule; NO_x = nitrogen oxides; paxvkm = passenger vehicle-kilometer; PM_{10} = particulate matter less than 10 microns in diameter; SO_x = sulfur oxides.

Notes

1. Ethiopia Information Communication Technology Directorate.
2. Data from US Energy Information Administration international database and World Bank.

References

2Merkato. 2013. "Nicon PLC. To Establish Electric Bicycles Assembly Plant." *2Merkato.com,* July 1, 2013. https://www.2merkato.com/news/alerts/2378-nicon-plc-to-establish-electric-bicycles-assembly-plant.

Aventa, Jonathan G. 2021. "Africa's Bumpy Road to an EV Future." *Energy Monitor,* January 6, 2021. https://energymonitor.ai/sectors/transport/africas-bumpy-road-to-an-electric-vehicle-future.

Ethiopian Monitor. 2020. "Ministry Pins Hope on Electric Vehicles to Cut Pollution." *Ethiopian Monitor: Daily News from Ethiopia,* October 1, 2020. https://ethiopianmonitor.com/2020/10/01/ministry-pins-hope-on-electric-vehicles-to-cut-pollution/.

Federal Democratic Republic of Ethiopia. 2011. *Ethiopia's Climate-Resilient Green Economy: Green Economy Strategy.* Addis Ababa: Federal Democratic Republic of Ethiopia.

IRENA (International Renewable Energy Agency). 2020. *Global Renewables Outlook: Energy Transformation 2050.* Masdar City: IRENA.

A.5 PASSENGER ELECTRIC MOBILITY IN GHANA

Country Typology

Vehicle fleet composition: Mixed fleet
Net oil trading status: Exporter
Relative cost of vehicles: Low

Country Background

The vehicle fleet in Ghana is diverse. Less than half of the fleet is cars (47.3 percent), followed by buses (37.6 percent), three-wheelers (9.8 percent), and two-wheelers (5.3 percent).[1] Electricity was generated from both renewable sources (50.7 percent) and from fossil fuels (49.3 percent) in 2018. Hydro (50.3 percent) is the largest renewable source for electricity generation, and gas (49.3 percent) is the main fossil fuel source.[2] Ghana does not have any policies that explicitly promote electric vehicles (EVs). The country's National Transport Policy mainly focuses on mass transportation (Ghana Ministry of Transport 2020). However, the government of Ghana, with the assistance of the Climate Technology Centre and Network, started drafting an electric mobility policy in 2020 (CTCN 2020), and adopted several promotional initiatives (Kuhudzai 2020). Ghana's Energy Commission launched the Drive Electric Initiative in 2019 to promote EV uptake. POBAD International partnered with the national power utility company, the Electricity Company of Ghana, to install EV charging stations across Ghana. In the first phase of the project, POBAD is expected to install a total of 200 chargers across southern Ghana. At the same time, Solar Taxi Ghana has started offering EV leasing services and has already established three solar charging stations across the country, with more planned.

Overall Messages

Despite being an oil exporter, Ghana presents some other conditions that are quite favorable to electric mobility, including access to relatively low-cost vehicles and a diversified vehicle fleet (figure A.5.1a). As a result, the overall economics of electric mobility in the country is good (table A.5.1). There is a particularly strong case for adoption of two-wheel electric motorbikes (figure A.5.1b), which present a life-cycle cost advantage of almost 15 percent (almost 20 percent in financial terms), compared with more marginal life-cycle cost advantages of 1–2 percent for electric two-wheelers and buses. The capital cost premiums associated with EVs in Ghana are relatively modest, standing at 20–25 percent for two-wheelers and buses, and as low as 3 percent for four-wheelers (table A.5.3). All things considered, the additional cost of an electric two-wheeler represents no more than 1–2 percent of gross national income per capita and may be affordable with some provision of credit; for four-wheelers the extra vehicle cost represents almost 9 percent of gross national income per capita.

The externality benefits of electric mobility are relatively small (figure A.5.1c), perhaps because of the prevalence of hydro energy and limited urban air quality issues. An important exception is provided by two-wheel EVs, which present much lower externalities than their conventional counterparts (figure A.5.1d). Otherwise, fuel cost savings are the main advantage associated with electric mobility. The fiscal regime is neutral to the purchase of EVs; however, fiscal policies do accentuate the fuel cost advantage of owning them, given that gasoline and diesel are taxed at about 40 percent, whereas electricity is slightly subsidized. Consequently, the overall case for electric mobility in Ghana looks better in financial than in economic terms (figure A.5.1a).

The total investment needs associated with the 30×30 scenario amount to US$192 million per year by 2030 (or 0.18 percent of Ghanaian gross domestic product). Over three-quarters of this investment is associated with the incremental capital cost of electric buses and their charging infrastructure, thus falling on the public sector (figure A.5.2a). Given that implicit carbon prices associated with electric two-wheelers in Ghana are strongly negative (table A.5.3), there is potential to cover a significant part (70 percent for two-wheelers) of the incremental capital cost of such vehicles through carbon financing arrangements (figure A.5.2b).

The overall economic case for electric mobility in Ghana is robust to more conservative assumptions about the cost of batteries ("scarce minerals" scenario) and the fuel efficiency of internal combustion engines ("fuel efficiency" scenario) and only improves as the country's power grid shifts further toward renewable energy ("green grid" scenario) (table A.5.2). On a positive note, the emerging advantage associated with electrification of buses can be as much as tripled through the more efficient procurement and operation of vehicles ("efficient bus" scenario), largely because of the relatively low existing mileage of buses at under 50,000 kilometers per year (table A.5.3). Moreover, the case for electrification of four-wheelers, which does not offer cost advantage for private vehicles, becomes economically attractive for taxi fleets and other intensively used vehicles ("taxi fleet" scenario). In sum, the electrification of two-wheelers in Ghana clearly makes a lot of economic sense, although they represent a relatively small share of the fleet. At the same time, the electrification of buses and commercial four-wheel vehicles also shows promise, as long as it is targeted toward the most intensively used vehicle segments.

Figures and tables start on the next page.

Figures and Tables

FIGURE A.5.1 Advantage of EV adoption in Ghana, by type of vehicle

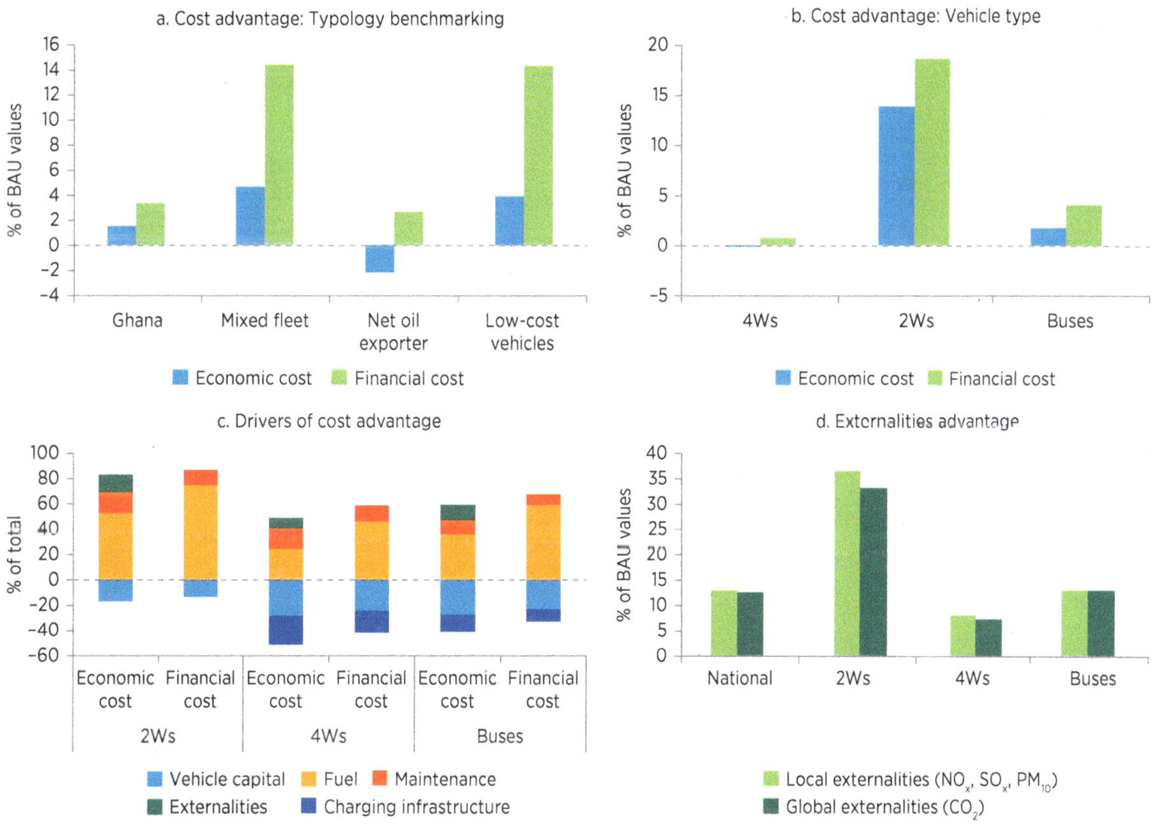

Source: World Bank.
Note: Data in this figure represent the "business as usual" (BAU) scenario minus the 30×30 scenario (averages over fleet additions). The BAU scenario assumes that no policy target will be imposed for electric vehicles and that vehicle purchase decisions will continue to reflect historical trends. The 30×30 scenario assumes that sales of electric cars and buses will reach 30 percent, and of two- and three-wheelers, 70 percent, by 2030. 2W = two-wheeler; 4W = four-wheeler; CO_2 = carbon dioxide; EV = electric vehicle; NO_x = nitrogen oxides; PM_{10} = particulate matter less than 10 microns in diameter; SO_x = sulfur oxides.

TABLE A.5.1 Cost advantage of accelerated EV adoption in Ghana, 2030

	US$/vehicle									% of BAU values	
	Charging infrastructure	Vehicle capital cost	Vehicle operating cost	Subtotal	Local externalities	Global externalities	Economic cost advantage	Net taxes and subsidies	Financial cost advantage	Cost advantage	Financial cost advantage including fiscal wedge
	(a)	(b)	(c)	(d) = (a + b + c)	(e)		(f) = (d + e)	(g)	(h) = (d + g)		
Mode											
2Ws	0	(71)	290	219	7	49	275	220	439	13.9	18.7
4Ws	(232)	(290)	413	(110)	8	72	(30)	332	222	(0.1)	0.8
Buses	(3,675)	(7,738)	13,212	1,800	568	2,681	5,048	11,965	13,765	1.8	4.1

Source: World Bank.
Note: Heading colors: blue = excluding taxes and subsidies, gray = fiscal wedge, green = including taxes and subsidies. 2W = two-wheeler; 4W = four-wheeler; "Local externalities" comprises local (NO_x, PM_{10}, SO_x) air pollution costs. "Global externalities" comprises global (CO_2) air pollution costs. CO_2 = carbon dioxide; NO_x = nitrogen oxides; PM_{10} = particulate matter less than 10 microns in diameter; SO_x = sulfur oxides. Red and parentheses indicate negative value.

FIGURE A.5.2 Investment and financing needs for EV adoption in Ghana, 2030

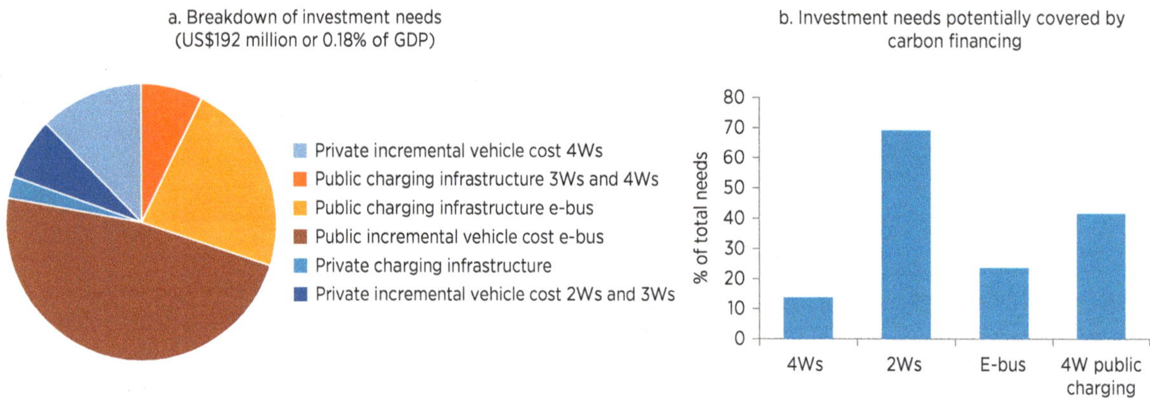

Source: World Bank.
Note: Data in this figure represent the "business as usual" (BAU) scenario minus the 30×30 scenario (averages over fleet additions). The BAU scenario assumes that no policy target will be imposed for electric vehicles and that vehicle purchase decisions will continue to reflect historical trends. The 30×30 scenario assumes that sales of electric cars and buses will reach 30 percent, and of two- and three-wheelers, 70 percent, by 2030. 2W = two-wheeler; 3W = three-wheeler; 4W = four-wheeler; EV = electric vehicle; GDP = gross domestic product.

TABLE A.5.2 Cost advantage of EV adoption in Ghana, by scenario, 2030

	National results				Bus only		4W only	
	30×30 scenario	Green grid scenario	Scarce minerals scenario	Fuel efficiency scenario	30×30 scenario	Efficient bus scenario	30×30 scenario	Taxi fleet scenario
	US$/Mpaxvkm				*US$/vehicle*			
Type of cost								
Vehicle capital cost	(6,241)	(6,241)	(8,741)	(6,241)	(7,738)	(1,367)	(290)	(290)
Vehicle maintenance cost	2,826	2,826	1,772	2,826	3,251	3,649	167	(338)
Vehicle fuel cost	8,020	8,020	8,020	5,589	9,961	12,427	245	981
Private charging infrastructure	(234)	(234)	(234)	(234)	n.a.	n.a.	(59)	(59)
Public charging infrastructure	(2,783)	(2,783)	(2,783)	(2,783)	(3,675)	(3,675)	(172)	(197)
Subtotal	1,587	1,587	(1,966)	(843)	1,800	11,034	(110)	97
Local externalities (NO_x, SO_x, PM_{10})	398	445	398	368	568	708	8	33
Global externalities (CO_2)	2,096	2,302	2,096	1,819	2,681	3,350	72	296
Economic cost advantage	4,081	4,334	528	1,344	5,048	15,093	(30)	427
Fiscal wedge	9,346	9,346	8,944	8,390	11,965	16,341	332	1,447
Financial cost advantage	10,933	10,933	6,978	7,547	13,765	27,375	222	1,544
Economic cost advantage, by type of vehicle	*US$/vehicle*							
4Ws	(30)	(20)	(292)	(183)	n.a.	n.a.	n.a.	n.a.
2Ws	275	278	249	254	n.a.	n.a.	n.a.	n.a.
E-buses	5,048	5,365	879	1,476	n.a.	n.a.	n.a.	n.a.

Source: World Bank.
Note: Data in this table represent the "business as usual" (BAU) scenario minus the named scenario (averages over fleet additions). The BAU scenario assumes that no policy target will be imposed for electric vehicles and that vehicle purchase decisions will continue to reflect historical trends. The 30×30 scenario assumes that sales of electric cars and buses will reach 30 percent, and of two- and three-wheelers, 70 percent, by 2030. The green grid scenario assumes that countries achieve certain region-specific targets for acceleration of renewable energy, as defined by the International Renewable Energy Agency (IRENA 2020). The scarce minerals scenario assumes that battery cost will decline by approximately 7 percent annually. The fuel efficiency scenario assumes that the rate of improvement of fuel efficiency for the internal combustion engine fleet will double from 15 percent to 30 percent. The efficient bus scenario assumes a capital cost reduction of 35 percent in the procurement of buses as well as optimized bus routes to increase the annual mileage of electric buses. The taxi fleet scenario assumes that the lifetime mileage of intensively used commercial vehicles will increase by four times in each country, that public investment in charging infrastructure will double the fast charger density for cars, and that the maintenance cost for cars will be doubled (assuming two lifetime battery replacements). Results have been normalized by new vehicles entering the market in 2030. The "fiscal wedge" comprises net taxes and subsidies. Red and parentheses indicate negative value. 2W = two-wheeler; 4W = four-wheeler; CO_2 = carbon dioxide; EV = electric vehicle; NO_x = nitrogen oxides; PM_{10} = particulate matter less than 10 microns in diameter; SO_x = sulfur oxides; US$/Mpaxvkm = US dollars per million passenger vehicle-kilometers; n.a.= not applicable.

TABLE A.5.3 Supporting information on parameters and results for EV adoption in Ghana

Price (US$/vehicle)

Parameter	Value
Price of ICE 4W	26,183
Price of EV 4W	29,071
Price of ICE 2W	904
Price of EV 2W	1,219
Price of ICE bus	118,214
Price of e-bus	153,085

Other parameters

Parameter	Value
Net tax difference on EV 4W (%)	0
Net tax difference on EV 2W (%)	0
Net tax difference on e-bus (%)	0
Price of gasoline (US$/liter)	0.58
Net gasoline tax (US$/liter)	0.26
Price of diesel (US$/liter)	0.73
Net diesel tax (US$/liter)	0.28
Price of electricity (US$/kWh)	0.14
Net electricity tax (US$/kWh)	(0.01)
Electricity carbon intensity (g/kWh)	203
Discount rate (%)	6.6

Key characteristics

Parameter	Value
4W mileage (km)	15,400
2W mileage (km)	7,627
Bus mileage (km)	48,092
4W lifetime (years)	22
2W lifetime (years)	17
Bus lifetime (years)	20
4W secondhand (%)	93.4
2W secondhand (%)	93.4
Bus secondhand (%)	94.7
4W share (% paxvkm)	24
2W share (% paxvkm)	4
Bus share (% paxvkm)	55

Efficiency (MJ/km)

Parameter	Value
Efficiency ICE 4W	2.41
Efficiency EV 4W	0.43
Efficiency ICE 2W	0.88
Efficiency EV 2W	0.20
Efficiency ICE bus	17.31
Efficiency EV bus	5.91

Other results for 30×30 scenario

Other results for 30×30 scenario	Value
Overall investment needs (US$, millions)	192
—of which 4W purchase	24
—of which 2W purchase	4
—of which e-bus purchase	92
Fiscal impact (US$, millions)	(193)
—of which vehicle duties	6
—of which vehicle taxes/subsidies	17
—of which gasoline taxes/subsidies	(28)
—of which diesel taxes/subsidies	(166)
—of which electricity taxes/subsidies	(23)
Implicit carbon price (US$/ton)	(24)
—of which for 4W	37
—of which for 2W	(119)
—of which for buses	(23)
Pollution reduction (tons)	2
—of which local (SO_x, NO_x, PM_{10})	0
—of which global (CO_2)	2
Affordability of EV 2W (Δ cost % GNI pc)	2.2
Affordability of EV 4W (Δ cost % GNI pc)	9.0

Source: World Bank.
Note: Red and parentheses indicates negative value. 2W = two-wheeler; 4W = four-wheeler; CO_2 = carbon dioxide; EV = electric vehicle; g = gram; GNI pc = gross national income per capita; ICE = internal combustion engine; kWh = kilowatt-hour; km = kilometer; MJ = megajoule; NO_x = nitrogen oxides; paxvkm = passenger vehicle-kilometer; PM_{10} = particulate matter less than 10 microns in diameter; SO_x = sulfur oxides.

Notes

1. Data from Ghana Revenue Authority.
2. Data from US Energy Information Administration international database and World Bank.

References

CTCN (UN Climate Technology Centre & Network). 2020. "CTCN in Ghana: Developing a National Policy on E-mobility." CTCN, Copenhagen, Denmark. https://www.ctc-n.org/news/ctcn-ghana-developing-national-policy-e-mobility.

Ghana Ministry of Transport. 2020. *National Transport Policy.* Revised August 2020. Accra: Ministry of Transport, Republic of Ghana. https://www.bcp.gov.gh/acc/registry/docs/NATIONAL%20TRANSPORT%20POLICY.pdf.

IRENA (International Renewable Energy Agency). 2020. *Global Renewables Outlook: Energy Transformation 2050.* Masdar City: IRENA.

Kuhudzai, Remeredzai Joseph. 2020. "The Electricity Company of Ghana & POBAD International Partner to Install EV Chargin Stations in Ghana." CleanTechnica, December 8, 2020. https://cleantechnica.com/2020/12/08/the-electricity-company-of-ghana-pobad-international-partner-to-install-ev-charging-stations-in-ghana/.

A.6 PASSENGER ELECTRIC MOBILITY IN INDIA

Country Typology

Vehicle fleet composition: Mixed fleet
Net oil trading status: Importer
Relative cost of vehicles: Low

Country Background

The dominant vehicle type in India is two-wheelers (73.0 percent),[1] followed by cars (15.3 percent), three-wheelers (8.5 percent), and buses (3.2 percent) (India Ministry of Road Transport & Highways 2021, 2022). Electricity is primarily generated from fossil fuels (79.5 percent), with the balance of renewable energy coming mostly from hydro (8.6 percent).[2] The electric vehicle industry is growing rapidly, supported by public incentives and financial and industrial policy schemes launched by both central and state governments. The most emblematic program is the Faster Adoption and Manufacturing of Hybrid and Electric Vehicles program (in phase II) that includes explicit policies in support of automakers, innovative practices of procurement and demand aggregation, and the inception of risk mitigation instruments to attract commercial financing. The National Electric Mobility Mission Plan 2020, developed in 2013, addresses the issues of national energy security, vehicular pollution, and growth of domestic manufacturing capabilities (India Press Information Bureau 2015), and emphasizes the use of hybrid and electric vehicles (Drishtiias 2019). The government has plans to make a significant shift to electric vehicles by 2030 (Policy Horizons Canada, n.d.), prompting the Ministry of Power to issue guidelines and standards for charging infrastructure for electric vehicles in 2018 (India Ministry of Power 2019). Moreover, the National Energy Policy aims to increase the share of non-fossil-fuel–based capacity in the electricity mix to more than 40 percent by 2030 (NITI Aayog 2017).

Overall Messages

India presents many of the country characteristics most favorable to the adoption of electric mobility, including relatively low vehicle costs, a highly diversified fleet, and oil-importing status (figure A.6.1a). In addition, the vast scale of the Indian market helps to drive down costs and makes possible domestic production. As a result, the overall case for electric mobility is good (table A.6.1). There is a particularly strong case for adoption of two-wheel electric motorbikes (figure A.6.1b), which present a life-cycle cost advantage of over 20 percent (over 40 percent in financial terms). The case for electrification of buses is also moderately supported, whereas electric four-wheelers are not yet economically attractive (figure A.6.1b). Nevertheless, the capital cost premium for electric two-wheel vehicles in India is about 5 percent and represents as much as 1.2 percent of gross national income per capita, suggesting that provision of credit lines may be important to support adoption.

The externality benefits of electric mobility in India are relatively small (figure A.6.1c), despite the existing prevalence of coal-fired power and serious urban air quality issues. Nevertheless, both electric two-wheelers and buses are able to reduce externalities by about 20 percent, and buses have a particularly large effect on local externalities (figure A.6.1d). Otherwise, fuel cost savings are the main advantage associated with electric mobility in India. Not only does the fiscal regime incentivize the purchase of electric vehicles with a tax differential of minus

32 percent, but it also accentuates the fuel cost savings of electric vehicles, given that gasoline and diesel are heavily taxed by 40–100 percent even as electricity is subsidized by about 40 percent (table A.6.3). Consequently, the overall case for electric mobility in India looks better in financial than in economic terms (figure A.6.1a).

The total investment needs associated with the 30×30 scenario amount to US$22.4 billion per year by 2030 (or 0.44 percent of Indian gross domestic product). Over two-thirds of the required outlay is associated with the incremental capital cost of two-wheel and four-wheel electric vehicles borne by the private sector (figure A.6.2a). In terms of public investment, the most significant item is the provision of charging infrastructure for both buses and private vehicles (figure A.6.2a). Given that implicit carbon prices associated with electric two-wheelers in India are negative (table A.6.3), there is significant scope to cover 26 percent of the incremental capital costs through carbon financing arrangements (figure A.6.2b). Although implicit carbon prices for buses are similarly negative, the potential for carbon financing is quite small relative to incremental capital costs. By contrast, for four-wheel electric vehicles, the implicit carbon price is approaching an exorbitant US$700 per ton.

The overall economic case for electric mobility in India is robust to more conservative assumptions about the cost of batteries ("scarce minerals" scenario) and the fuel efficiency of internal combustion engines ("fuel efficiency" scenario) and improves somewhat under further decarbonization of the power sector ("green grid" scenario) (table A.6.2). On a positive note, the emerging advantage associated with electrification of buses can be as much as doubled through the more efficient procurement and operation of vehicles ("efficient bus" scenario). However, the case for electrification of four-wheelers remains unfavorable even for taxi fleets and other intensively used vehicles ("taxi fleet" scenario). It is clear that electric mobility in India needs to prioritize the massive two-wheel segment of the fleet, which offers so many strong advantages, while working toward further improving the case for electrification of buses.

Figures and tables start on the next page.

Figures and Tables

FIGURE A.6.1 Advantage of EV adoption in India, by type of vehicle

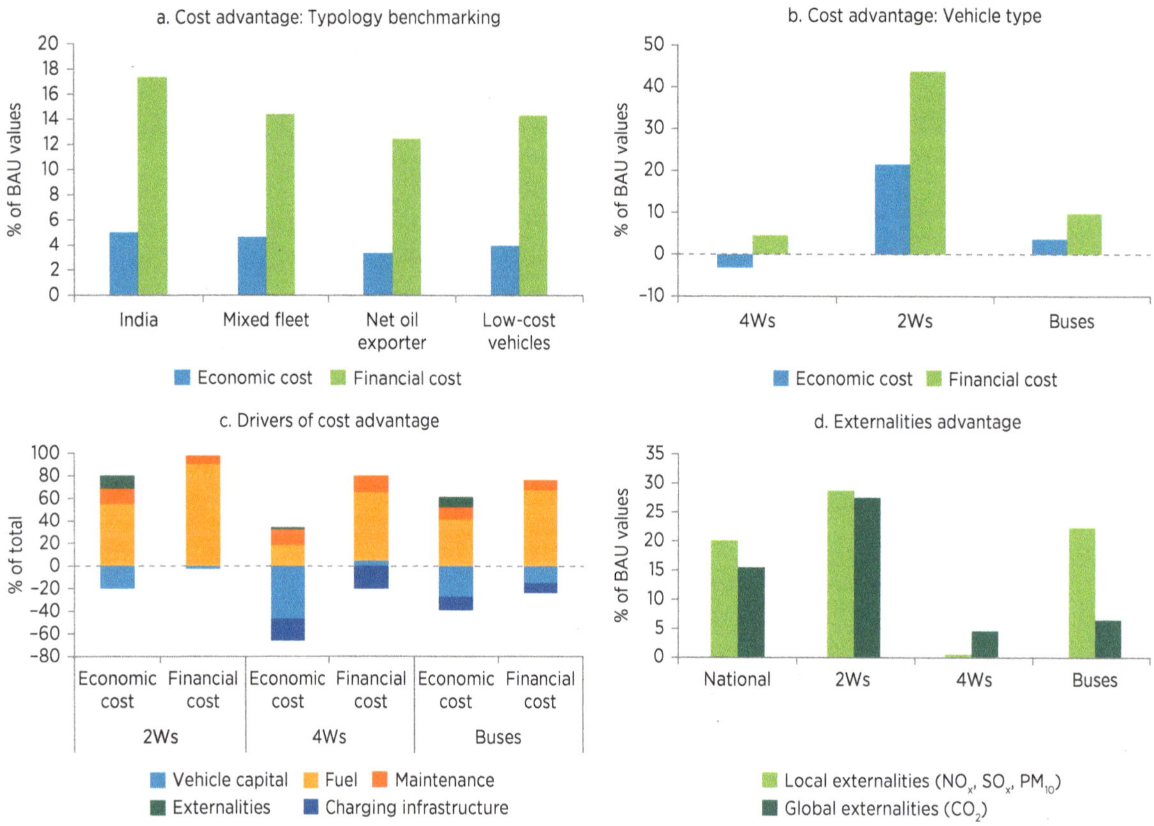

Source: World Bank.
Note: Data in this figure represent the "business as usual" (BAU) scenario minus the 30×30 scenario (averages over fleet additions). The BAU scenario assumes that no policy target will be imposed for electric vehicles and that vehicle purchase decisions will continue to reflect historical trends. The 30×30 scenario assumes that sales of electric cars and buses will reach 30 percent, and of two- and three-wheelers, 70 percent, by 2030. 2W = two-wheeler; 4W = four-wheeler; CO_2 = carbon dioxide; EV = electric vehicle; NO_x = nitrogen oxides; PM_{10} = particulate matter less than 10 microns in diameter; SO_x = sulfur oxides.

TABLE A.6.1 Cost advantage of accelerated EV adoption in India, 2030

	US$/vehicle									% of BAU values	
	Charging infrastructure	Vehicle capital cost	Vehicle operating cost	Subtotal	Local externalities	Global externalities	Economic cost advantage	Net taxes and subsidies	Financial cost advantage	Cost advantage	Financial cost advantage including fiscal wedge
	(a)	(b)	(c)	(d) = (a + b + c)	(e)		(f) = (d + e)	(g)	(h) = (d + g)		
Mode											
2Ws	0	(199)	680	481	54	53	589	1,252	1,733	21.4	43.8
4Ws	(568)	(1,412)	983	(997)	17	33	(947)	2,731	1,733	(3.2)	4.5
Buses	(6,104)	(14,027)	27,370	7,239	3,094	1,310	11,644	29,988	37,227	3.6	9.7

Source: World Bank.
Note: Heading colors: blue = excluding taxes and subsidies, gray = fiscal wedge, green = including taxes and subsidies. 2W = two-wheeler; 4W = four-wheeler; "Local externalities" comprises local (NO_x, PM_{10}, SO_x) air pollution costs. "Global externalities" comprises global (CO_2) air pollution costs. CO_2 = carbon dioxide; NO_x = nitrogen oxides; PM_{10} = particulate matter less than 10 microns in diameter; SO_x = sulfur oxides. Red and parentheses indicate negative value.

FIGURE A.6.2 Investment and financing needs for EV adoption in India, 2030

a. Breakdown of investment needs (US$22,403 million or 0.44% of GDP)

b. Investment needs potentially covered by carbon financing

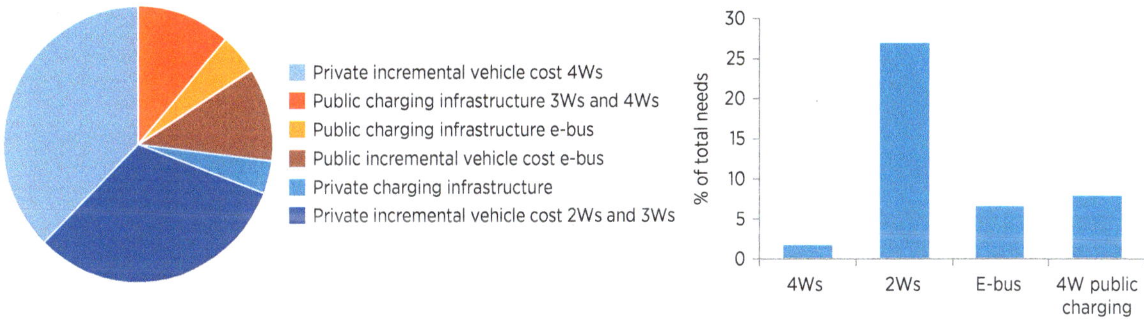

Source: World Bank.
Note: Data in this figure represent the "business as usual" (BAU) scenario minus the 30×30 scenario (averages over fleet additions). The BAU scenario assumes that no policy target will be imposed for electric vehicles and that vehicle purchase decisions will continue to reflect historical trends. The 30×30 scenario assumes that sales of electric cars and buses will reach 30 percent, and of two- and three-wheelers, 70 percent, by 2030. 2W = two-wheeler; 3W = three-wheeler; 4W = four-wheeler; EV = electric vehicle; GDP = gross domestic product.

TABLE A.6.2 Cost advantage of EV adoption in India, by scenario, 2030

	National results				Bus only		4W only	
	30×30 scenario	Green grid scenario	Scarce minerals scenario	Fuel efficiency scenario	30×30 scenario	Efficient bus scenario	30×30 scenario	Taxi fleet scenario
	US$/Mpaxvkm				*US$/vehicle*			
Type of cost								
Vehicle capital cost	(12,207)	(12,207)	(16,662)	(12,207)	(14,027)	(288)	(1,412)	(1,412)
Vehicle maintenance cost	5,465	5,465	5,201	5,465	6,017	6,317	424	(798)
Vehicle fuel cost	17,752	17,752	17,752	14,637	21,353	22,500	559	2,236
Private charging infrastructure	(582)	(582)	(582)	(582)	n.a.	n.a.	(144)	(144)
Public charging infrastructure	(2,441)	(2,441)	(2,441)	(2,441)	(6,104)	(6,104)	(424)	(483)
Subtotal	7,986	7,986	3,268	4,871	7,239	22,426	(997)	(601)
Local externalities (NO_x, SO_x, PM_{10})	1,666	2,141	1,666	1,596	3,094	3,261	17	92
Global externalities (CO_2)	1,549	2,356	1,549	1,168	1,310	1,384	33	161
Economic cost advantage	11,201	12,483	6,483	7,634	11,644	27,071	(947)	(349)
Fiscal wedge	43,109	43,109	42,622	40,804	29,988	32,513	2,731	6,284
Financial cost advantage	51,095	51,095	45,890	45,675	37,227	54,939	1,733	5,683
Economic cost advantage, by type of vehicle	*US$/vehicle*							
4Ws	(947)	(867)	(1,561)	(1,239)	n.a.	n.a.	n.a.	n.a.
2Ws	589	618	528	524	n.a.	n.a.	n.a.	n.a.
E-buses	11,644	13,807	4,408	4,029	n.a.	n.a.	n.a.	n.a.

Source: World Bank.
Note: Data in this table represent the "business as usual" (BAU) scenario minus the named scenario (averages over fleet additions). The BAU scenario assumes that no policy target will be imposed for electric vehicles and that vehicle purchase decisions will continue to reflect historical trends. The 30×30 scenario assumes that sales of electric cars and buses will reach 30 percent, and of two- and three-wheelers, 70 percent, by 2030. The green grid scenario assumes that countries achieve certain region-specific targets for acceleration of renewable energy, as defined by the International Renewable Energy Agency (IRENA 2020). The scarce minerals scenario assumes that battery cost will decline by approximately 7 percent annually. The fuel efficiency scenario assumes that the rate of improvement of fuel efficiency for the internal combustion engine fleet will double from 15 percent to 30 percent. The efficient bus scenario assumes a capital cost reduction of 35 percent in the procurement of buses as well as optimized bus routes to increase the annual mileage of electric buses. The taxi fleet scenario assumes that the lifetime mileage of intensively used commercial vehicles will increase by four times in each country, that public investment in charging infrastructure will double the fast charger density for cars, and that the maintenance cost for cars will be doubled (assuming two lifetime battery replacements). Results have been normalized by new vehicles entering the market in 2030. The "fiscal wedge" comprises net taxes and subsidies. Red and parentheses indicate negative value. 2W = two-wheeler; 4W = four-wheeler; CO_2 = carbon dioxide; EV = electric vehicle; NO_x = nitrogen oxides; PM_{10} = particulate matter less than 10 microns in diameter; SO_x = sulfur oxides; US$/Mpaxvkm = US dollars per million passenger vehicle-kilometers; n.a.= not applicable.

TABLE A.6.3 Supporting information on parameters and results for EV adoption in India

Price (US$/vehicle)

Parameter	Value
Price of ICE 4W	22,275
Price of EV 4W	20,451
Price of ICE 2W	783
Price of EV 2W	843
Price of ICE bus	100,420
Price of e-bus	142,090

Other parameters

Parameter	Value
Net tax difference on EV 4W (%)	32
Net tax difference on EV 2W (%)	33
Net tax difference on e-bus (%)	23
Price of gasoline (US$/liter)	0.57
Net gasoline tax (US$/liter)	0.55
Price of diesel (US$/liter)	0.73
Net diesel tax (US$/liter)	0.29
Price of electricity (US$/kWh)	0.11
Net electricity tax (US$/kWh)	(0.04)
Electricity carbon intensity (g/kWh)	648
Discount rate (%)	6.6

Key characteristics

Parameter	Value
4W mileage (km)	12,200
2W mileage (km)	12,800
Bus mileage (km)	71,175
4W lifetime (years)	22
2W lifetime (years)	17
Bus lifetime (years)	20
4W secondhand (%)	0
2W secondhand (%)	0
Bus secondhand (%)	0
4W share (% paxvkm)	20
2W share (% paxvkm)	56
Bus share (% paxvkm)	17

Efficiency (MJ/km)

Parameter	Value
Efficiency ICE 4W	1.86
Efficiency EV 4W	0.65
Efficiency ICE 2W	0.65
Efficiency EV 2W	0.15
Efficiency ICE bus	10.82
Efficiency EV bus	3.66

Other results for 30×30 scenario

Other results for 30×30 scenario	Value
Overall investment needs (US$, millions)	22,403
—of which 4W purchase	8,410
—of which 2W purchase	6,375
—of which e-bus purchase	2,449
Fiscal impact (US$, millions)	(63,410)
—of which vehicle duties	98
—of which vehicle taxes/subsidies	(14,881)
—of which gasoline taxes/subsidies	(34,687)
—of which diesel taxes/subsidies	(5,178)
—of which electricity taxes/subsidies	(8,761)
Implicit carbon price (US$/ton)	(161)
—of which for 4W	769
—of which for 2W	(259)
—of which for buses	(204)
Pollution reduction (tons)	89
—of which local (SO_x, NO_x, PM_{10})	1
—of which global (CO_2)	88
Affordability of EV 2W (Δ cost % GNI pc)	1.2
Affordability of EV 4W (Δ cost % GNI pc)	(3.6)

Source: World Bank.
Note: Red and parentheses indicates negative value. 2W = two-wheeler; 4W = four-wheeler; CO_2 = carbon dioxide; EV = electric vehicle; g = gram; GNI pc = gross national income per capita; ICE = internal combustion engine; kWh = kilowatt-hour; km = kilometer; MJ = megajoule; NO_x = nitrogen oxides; paxvkm = passenger vehicle-kilometer; PM_{10} = particulate matter less than 10 microns in diameter; SO_x = sulfur oxides.

Notes

1. Two-wheelers cover all motorized two-wheel vehicles registered.
2. Data from US Energy Information Administration international database and World Bank.

References

Drishtiias. 2019. "National Electric Mobility Mission: 2020." Drishtiias, July 10, 2019. https://www.drishtiias.com/daily-updates/daily-news-analysis/national-– electric-mobility-mission-2020.

India Ministry of Power. 2019. "Charging Infrastructure for Electric Vehicles—Revised Guidelines Standards." Ministry of Power, Government of India, New Delhi.

India Ministry of Road Transport & Highways. 2021. *Road Transport Year Book (2017–18 & 2018–19).* New Delhi: Transport Research Wing, Ministry of Road Transport & Highways, Government of India.

India Ministry of Road Transport & Highways. 2022. VAHAN 4.0 Dashboard. Ministry of Road Transport & Highways, Government of India, New Delhi. https://vahan.parivahan.gov.in/vahanservice/vahan/ui/statevalidation/homepage.xhtml.

India Press Information Bureau. 2015. "India Prime Minister Today Unveiled the National Electric Mobility Mission Plan (NEMMP) 2020." Press release, Press Information Bureau, Government of India.

IRENA (International Renewable Energy Agency). 2020. *Global Renewables Outlook: Energy Transformation 2050.* Masdar City: IRENA.

NITI (National Institution for Transforming India) Aayog. 2017. "Draft National Energy Policy." NITI Aayog, Government of India, New Delhi.

Policy Horizons Canada. n.d. "India Is Planning to Reach 100% Electric Vehicles by 2030." Internet Wayback Machine. https://web.archive.org/web/20160916145621/http://www.horizons.gc.ca/eng/content/india-planning-reach-100-electric-vehicles-2030.

A.7 PASSENGER ELECTRIC MOBILITY IN JAMAICA

Country Typology

Vehicle fleet composition:	Car dominant
Net oil trading status:	Importer
Relative cost of vehicles:	High

Country Background

The dominant vehicle type in Jamaica is cars (95.8 percent) (Global Fuel Economy Initiative 2018; IRF 2020; Jamaica Ministry of Economic Growth and Job Creation 2015). As of 2018, electricity was primarily generated from fossil fuels (87.0 percent), essentially oil, with the balance coming from renewable sources (13.0 percent), notably wind (7.2 percent) and hydro (4.2 percent).[1] Jamaica is at an early stage of electric mobility adoption and gradually gaining traction, with the government currently drafting supportive legislation, and several promotional initiatives are under way (Jones 2021). For instance, with assistance from the Inter-American Development Bank, the country is due to introduce 200 electric vehicles and provide training to 400 individuals on maintenance and safety practices. Furthermore, the Jamaica Public Service Company installed a public electric charging station at Drax Hall, St Ann's Bay, with plans for five additional stations by the end of 2021 in the island's two cities, Kingston and Montego Bay, as well as in other urban centers.

Overall Messages

Because of relatively high-cost vehicles and a fleet dominated by cars, Jamaica does not present very favorable conditions for the adoption of electric mobility (figure A.7.1a). Nevertheless, the case for electric mobility is quite strong in the much smaller niches of two-wheelers and buses (table A.7.1). There is a particularly strong case for adoption of two-wheel electric motorbikes (figure A.7.1b), which present a life-cycle cost advantage of 10 percent (16 percent in financial terms). Nevertheless, the capital cost premium for electric two-wheel vehicles in Jamaica is particularly high at almost 40 percent and represents as much as 7 percent of gross national income per capita, suggesting that provision of credit lines would be essential to support adoption. At the same time, electric buses are beginning to offer modest economic advantages on the order of 3 percent of life-cycle cost. By contrast, the economics of electric four-wheel vehicles is consistently negative: the large capital cost premium of such vehicles approaches 6 percent, which is prohibitive, representing almost 37 percent of gross national income per capita. This premium represents a major hurdle to the electrification of transportation in Jamaica, given that four-wheel vehicles represent almost all of the fleet.

The externality benefits of electric mobility in Jamaica are relatively small (figure A.7.1c), despite the prevalence of oil-fired power generation, but may reflect limited urban air quality issues. An important exception is provided by two-wheel electric vehicles, which present much lower externalities than their conventional counterparts (figure A.7.1d). Otherwise, fuel cost savings are the main advantage associated with electric mobility in Jamaica. The fiscal regime neither incentivizes nor disincentivizes the purchase of electric vehicles. However, fiscal policies do accentuate the fuel cost advantage of owning them, given that gasoline and diesel are taxed at 60–80 percent, whereas electricity is not taxed at all. Consequently, the overall case for electric mobility in Jamaica looks better in financial than in economic terms (figure A.7.1a).

The total investment needs associated with the 30×30 scenario amount to US$193 million per year by 2030 (or 1.08 percent of Jamaican gross domestic product). About four-fifths of the required outlay is associated with private investment in the incremental capital cost of four-wheel electric vehicles (figure A.7.2a). In terms of public investment, the most significant item is the provision of public charging infrastructure for private vehicles (figure A.7.2a). Given that implicit carbon prices associated with electric buses in Jamaica are negative (table A.7.3), there is significant scope to cover about 30 percent of incremental public investment costs through carbon financing arrangements (figure A.7.2b). However, for four-wheel electric vehicles, the implicit carbon price is as high as US$288 per ton.

The overall economic case for electric mobility in Jamaica remains negative under more conservative assumptions about the cost of batteries ("scarce minerals" scenario) and the fuel efficiency of internal combustion engines ("fuel efficiency" scenario), and even when some further decarbonization of the power sector is undertaken ("green grid" scenario) (table A.7.2). On a positive note, the emerging advantage associated with electrification of buses can be as much as doubled through the more efficient procurement and operation of vehicles ("efficient bus" scenario). However, the case for electrification of four-wheelers remains unsupportive even for more intensively used commercial four-wheel vehicles, such as taxis ("taxi fleet" scenario). It is clear that electric mobility in Jamaica needs to focus initially on the relatively small two-wheel and bus segments of the fleet, which already offer considerable advantages, while awaiting more favorable cost conditions for the electrification of the bulk of the four-wheel vehicles.

Figures and tables start on the next page.

Figures and Tables

FIGURE A.7.1 Advantage of EV adoption in Jamaica, by type of vehicle

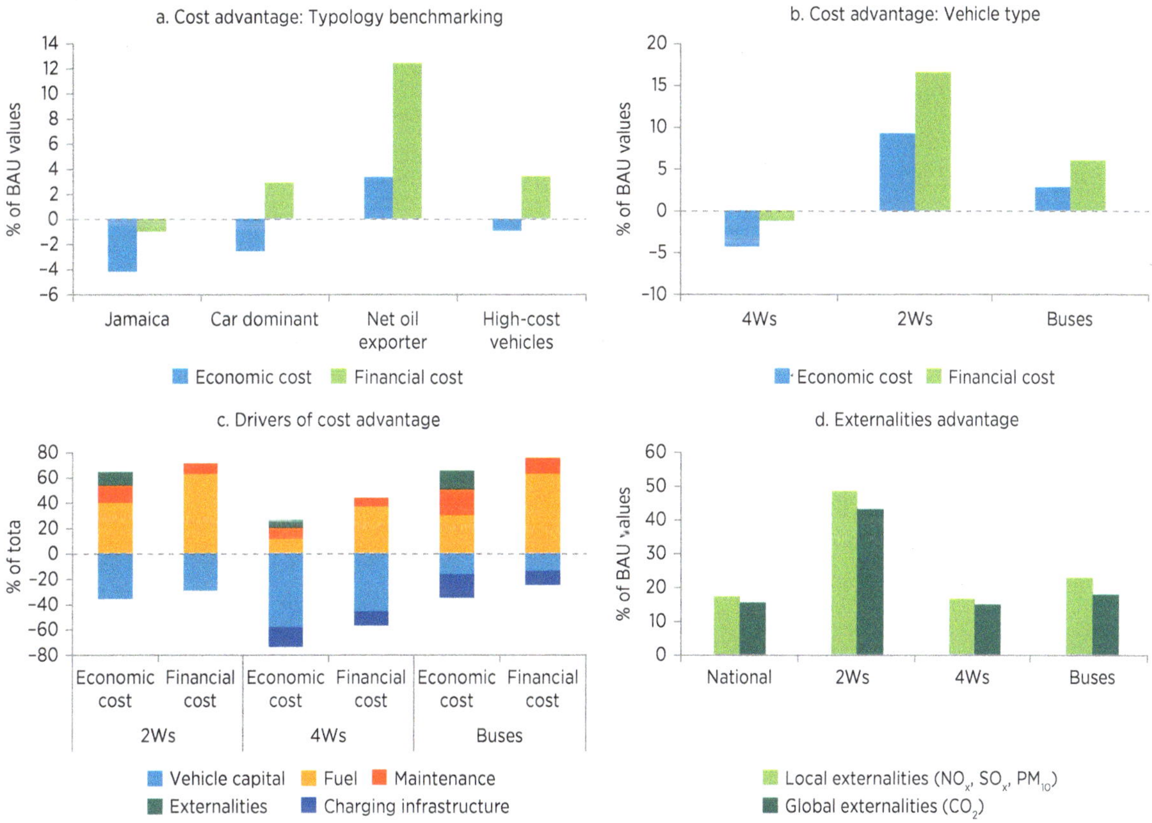

Source: World Bank.
Note: Data in this figure represent the "business as usual" (BAU) scenario minus the 30×30 scenario (averages over fleet additions). The BAU scenario assumes that no policy target will be imposed for electric vehicles and that vehicle purchase decisions will continue to reflect historical trends. The 30×30 scenario assumes that sales of electric cars and buses will reach 30 percent, and of two- and three-wheelers, 70 percent, by 2030. 2W = two-wheeler; 4W = four-wheeler; CO_2 = carbon dioxide; EV = electric vehicle; NO_x = nitrogen oxides; PM_{10} = particulate matter less than 10 microns in diameter; SO_x = sulfur oxides.

TABLE A.7.1 Cost advantage of accelerated EV adoption in Jamaica, 2030

	US$/vehicle									% of BAU values	
	Charging infrastructure	Vehicle capital cost	Vehicle operating cost	Subtotal	Local externalities	Global externalities	Economic cost advantage	Net taxes and subsidies	Financial cost advantage	Cost advantage	Financial cost advantage including fiscal wedge
	(a)	(b)	(c)	(d) = (a + b + c)	(e)		(f) = (d + e)	(g)	(h) = (d + g)		
Mode											
2Ws	0	(305)	458	153	25	66	243	458	611	9.2	16.6
4Ws	(527)	(2,010)	700	(1,837)	29	163	(1,645)	1,184	(652)	(4.3)	(1.2)
Buses	(5,759)	(5,219)	15,966	4,989	998	3,526	9,513	21,756	26,745	2.8	6.0

Source: World Bank.
Note: Heading colors: blue = excluding taxes and subsidies, gray = fiscal wedge, green = including taxes and subsidies. 2W = two-wheeler; 4W = four-wheeler; "Local externalities" comprises local (NO_x, PM_{10}, SO_x) air pollution costs. "Global externalities" comprises global (CO_2) air pollution costs. CO_2 = carbon dioxide; NO_x = nitrogen oxides; PM_{10} = particulate matter less than 10 microns in diameter; SO_x = sulfur oxides. Red and parentheses indicate negative value.

FIGURE A.7.2 Investment and financing needs for EV adoption in Jamaica, 2030

a. Breakdown of investment needs (US$193 million or 1.08% of GDP)

b. Investment needs potentially covered by carbon financing

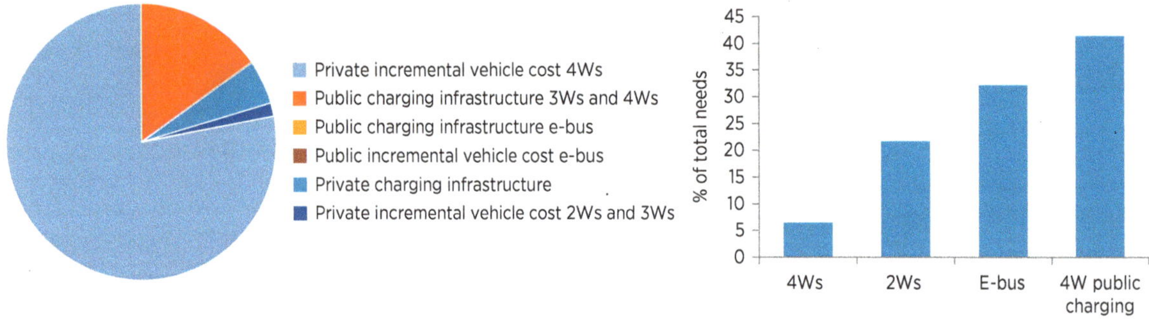

Source: World Bank.
Note: Data in this figure represent the "business as usual" (BAU) scenario minus the 30×30 scenario (averages over fleet additions). The BAU scenario assumes that no policy target will be imposed for electric vehicles and that vehicle purchase decisions will continue to reflect historical trends. The 30×30 scenario assumes that sales of electric cars and buses will reach 30 percent, and of two- and three-wheelers, 70 percent, by 2030. 2W = two-wheeler; 3W = three-wheeler; 4W = four-wheeler; EV = electric vehicle; GDP = gross domestic product.

TABLE A.7.2 Cost advantage of EV adoption in Jamaica, by scenario, 2030

	National results				Bus only		4W only	
	30×30 scenario	Green grid scenario	Scarce minerals scenario	Fuel efficiency scenario	30×30 scenario	Efficient bus scenario	30×30 scenario	Taxi fleet scenario
	US$/Mpaxvkm				*US$/vehicle*			
Type of cost								
Vehicle capital cost	(27,919)	(27,919)	(39,989)	(27,919)	(5,219)	7,124	(2,010)	(2,010)
Vehicle maintenance cost	4,483	4,483	4,478	4,483	6,550	6,877	313	(826)
Vehicle fuel cost	5,895	5,895	5,895	373	9,416	9,416	387	1,548
Private charging infrastructure	(1,826)	(1,826)	(1,826)	(1,826)	n.a.	n.a.	(134)	(134)
Public charging infrastructure	(5,362)	(5,362)	(5,362)	(5,362)	(5,759)	(5,759)	(393)	(448)
Subtotal	(24,729)	(24,729)	(36,804)	(30,251)	4,989	17,658	(1,837)	(1,869)
Local externalities (NO_x, SO_x, PM_{10})	444	605	444	361	998	998	29	119
Global externalities (CO_2)	2,339	2,801	2,339	1,695	3,526	3,526	163	672
Economic cost advantage	(21,947)	(21,323)	(34,021)	(28,194)	9,513	22,182	(1,645)	(1,078)
Fiscal wedge	16,993	16,993	11,898	13,158	21,756	26,866	1,184	5,317
Financial cost advantage	(7,736)	(7,736)	(24,906)	(17,093)	26,745	44,524	(652)	3,447
Economic cost advantage, by type of vehicle	*US$/vehicle*							
4Ws	(1,645)	(1,601)	(2,520)	(2,097)	n.a.	n.a.	n.a.	n.a.
2Ws	243	253	163	197	n.a.	n.a.	n.a.	n.a.
E-buses	9,513	10,325	2,779	2,327	n.a.	n.a.	n.a.	n.a.

Source: World Bank.
Note: Data in this table represent the "business as usual" (BAU) scenario minus the named scenario (averages over fleet additions). The BAU scenario assumes that no policy target will be imposed for electric vehicles and that vehicle purchase decisions will continue to reflect historical trends. The 30×30 scenario assumes that sales of electric cars and buses will reach 30 percent, and of two- and three-wheelers, 70 percent, by 2030. The green grid scenario assumes that countries achieve certain region-specific targets for acceleration of renewable energy, as defined by the International Renewable Energy Agency (IRENA 2020). The scarce minerals scenario assumes that battery cost will decline by approximately 7 percent annually. The fuel efficiency scenario assumes that the rate of improvement of fuel efficiency for the internal combustion engine fleet will double from 15 percent to 30 percent. The efficient bus scenario assumes a capital cost reduction of 35 percent in the procurement of buses as well as optimized bus routes to increase the annual mileage of electric buses. The taxi fleet scenario assumes that the lifetime mileage of intensively used commercial vehicles will increase by four times in each country, that public investment in charging infrastructure will double the fast charger density for cars, and that the maintenance cost for cars will be doubled (assuming two lifetime battery replacements). Results have been normalized by new vehicles entering the market in 2030. The "fiscal wedge" comprises net taxes and subsidies. Red and parentheses indicate negative value. 2W = two-wheeler; 4W = four-wheeler; CO_2 = carbon dioxide; EV = electric vehicle; NO_x = nitrogen oxides; PM_{10} = particulate matter less than 10 microns in diameter; SO_x = sulfur oxides; US$/Mpaxvkm = US dollars per million passenger vehicle-kilometers; n.a.= not applicable.

TABLE A.7.3 Supporting information on parameters and results for EV adoption in Jamaica

Price (US$/vehicle)

Parameter	Value
Price of ICE 4W	34,758
Price of EV 4W	47,069
Price of ICE 2W	1,280
Price of EV 2W	1,994
Price of ICE bus	163,704
Price of e-bus	175,921

Other parameters

Parameter	Value
Net tax difference on EV 4W (%)	1
Net tax difference on EV 2W (%)	0
Net tax difference on e-bus (%)	0
Price of gasoline (US$/liter)	0.64
Net gasoline tax (US$/liter)	0.50
Price of diesel (US$/liter)	0.70
Net diesel tax (US$/liter)	0.41
Price of electricity (US$/kWh)	0.16
Net electricity tax (US$/kWh)	0.00
Electricity carbon intensity (g/kWh)	261
Discount rate (%)	6.6

Key characteristics

Parameter	Value
4W mileage (km)	17,823
2W mileage (km)	7,627
Bus mileage (km)	46,374
4W lifetime (years)	15
2W lifetime (years)	17
Bus lifetime (years)	20
4W secondhand (%)	25.2
2W secondhand (%)	25.2
Bus secondhand (%)	19.7
4W share (% paxvkm)	97
2W share (% paxvkm)	3
Bus share (% paxvkm)	0.2

Efficiency (MJ/km)

Parameter	Value
Efficiency ICE 4W	2.78
Efficiency EV 4W	0.80
Efficiency ICE 2W	0.86
Efficiency EV 2W	0.20
Efficiency ICE bus	16.12
Efficiency EV bus	5.46

Other results for 30×30 scenario

Other results for 30×30 scenario	Value
Overall investment needs (US$, millions)	193
—of which 4W purchase	150
—of which 2W purchase	3
—of which e-bus purchase	0
Fiscal impact (US$, millions)	(93)
—of which vehicle duties	(23)
—of which vehicle taxes/subsidies	39
—of which gasoline taxes/subsidies	(68)
—of which diesel taxes/subsidies	(45)
—of which electricity taxes/subsidies	4
Implicit carbon price (US$/ton)	269
—of which for 4W	288
—of which for 2W	(69)
—of which for buses	(44)
Pollution reduction (tons)	0
—of which local (SO_x, NO_x, PM_{10})	0
—of which global (CO_2)	0
Affordability of EV 2W (Δ cost % GNI pc)	7.3
Affordability of EV 4W (Δ cost % GNI pc)	36.9

Source: World Bank.
Note: Red and parentheses indicates negative value. 2W = two-wheeler; 4W = four-wheeler; CO_2 = carbon dioxide; EV = electric vehicle; g = gram; GNI pc = gross national income per capita; ICE = internal combustion engine; kWh = kilowatt-hour; km = kilometer; MJ = megajoule; NO_x = nitrogen oxides; paxvkm = passenger vehicle-kilometer; PM_{10} = particulate matter less than 10 microns in diameter; SO_x = sulfur oxides.

Note

1. Data from US Energy Information Administration international database and World Bank.

References

Global Fuel Economy Initiative. 2018. "Jamaica Project Overview." Global Fuel Economy Initiative, London.

IRENA (International Renewable Energy Agency). 2020. *Global Renewables Outlook: Energy Transformation 2050.* Masdar City: IRENA.

IRF (International Road Federation). 2020. *IRF World Road Statistics 2020.* Geneva: IRF.

Jamaica Ministry of Economic Growth and Job Creation. 2015. *Biennial Update Report of Jamaica.* Ministry of Economic Growth and Job Creation, Government of Jamaica, Kingston.

Jones, Jonathan Spencer. 2021. "Jamaica's Electric Vehicle Market Set to Take Off." *Smart Energy International,* May 14, 2021. https://www.smart-energy.com/industry-sectors/electric-vehicles/jamaicas-electric-vehicle-market-set-to-take-off/.

A.8 PASSENGER ELECTRIC MOBILITY IN JORDAN

Country Typology

Vehicle fleet composition: Car dominant
Net oil trading status: Importer
Relative cost of vehicles: High

Country Background

The dominant vehicle type in Jordan is cars (84.5 percent), followed by two-wheelers (13.7 percent),[1] and buses (1.8 percent)(CEIC 2020; OICA 2010). Electricity is primarily generated from fossil fuels (88.9 percent), with very limited availability of renewable sources, mainly in the form of solar (7.4 percent) and wind (3.7 percent).[2] The current National Green Growth Plan for Jordan identified fostering electric vehicles as a step toward achieving sustainability. The Intended Nationally Determined Contribution makes sustainability of the sector a main pillar in the Ministry of Transport's National Transport Strategy and includes several targets to green the transportation sector (Hashemite Kingdom of Jordan 2015) such as reducing fuel consumption and emissions (that is, carbon dioxide, particulate matter, and nitrogen oxides); introducing zero-emission electric vehicles; and ensuring inclusion of energy efficiency considerations when purchasing all types of vehicles. In the public sector, the government replaced hundreds of gasoline-powered cars in its fleet with electric ones. The purchase of 151 low-emission buses, including 15 battery-electric buses, is part of the rapid transit project in Amman (Shalalfeh et al. 2021). The central region[3] has a specific advantage for higher uptake because of the availability of charging stations and maintenance centers (Businesswire 2019).

Overall Messages

Jordan's relatively high-cost vehicles, combined with its car-dominated fleet, present a difficult set of conditions for the adoption of electric mobility (figure A.8.1a). As a result, the overall case for electric mobility in the country is not favorable (table A.8.1). Nevertheless, there is a case for adoption of two-wheel electric motorbikes (figure A.8.1b), which present a life-cycle cost advantage of close to 3 percent (approaching 30 percent in financial terms). Nevertheless, the capital cost premium for electric two-wheel vehicles in Jordan is about 20 percent and represents as much as 4 percent of gross national income per capita, suggesting that provision of credit lines may be important to support adoption. At the same time, electric buses are beginning to offer modest economic advantages on the order of 1–2 percent of life-cycle cost. By contrast, the economics of electric four-wheel vehicles is not supportive, although the associated capital cost premium is only 1.5 percent of gross national income per capita.

The externality benefits of electric mobility in Jordan are relatively small (figure A.8.1c), perhaps because of the energy mix and limited urban air quality issues. An important exception is provided by two-wheel electric vehicles, which present much lower externalities than their conventional counterparts, particularly in terms of local air pollution (figure A.8.1d). Otherwise, fuel cost savings are the main advantage associated with electric mobility in Jordan. The fiscal regime significantly incentivizes the purchase of electric vehicles, with a tax differential approaching −60 percent (table A.8.3). Moreover, fiscal policies accentuate the fuel cost advantage of owning them, given that gasoline is heavily taxed at over 100 percent, whereas electricity is slightly subsidized. Consequently, the overall case for electric mobility in Jordan looks marginally favorable in financial terms even though it is negative in economic terms (figure A.8.1a).

The total investment needs associated with the 30×30 scenario amount to US$278 million per year by 2030 (or 0.51 percent of Jordanian gross domestic product). About four-fifths of the required outlay is associated with the incremental capital cost of four-wheel electric vehicles accruing to private individuals (figure A.8.2a). In terms of public investment, the most significant item is the provision of public charging infrastructure for private vehicles (figure A.8.2a). The potential for carbon financing of such investments is minimal (figure A.8.2b). Indeed, the implicit carbon price for four-wheel electric vehicles is more than US$2,000 per ton.

The overall economic case for electric mobility in Jordan is negative, and this result is robust to more conservative assumptions about the cost of batteries ("scarce minerals" scenario) and the fuel efficiency of internal combustion engines ("fuel efficiency" scenario), as well as more optimistic assumptions regarding the further decarbonization of the power sector ("green grid" scenario) (table A.8.2). On a positive note, the emerging advantage associated with electrification of buses can be as much as tripled through the more efficient procurement and operation of vehicles ("efficient bus" scenario). However, the case for electrification of four-wheelers does not improve even when attention focuses exclusively on more intensively used commercial vehicles ("taxi fleet" scenario). The electric mobility strategy in Jordan needs to prioritize the modest two-wheel segment of the fleet, which offers considerable advantages, while also beginning to progress with electric buses. However, when it comes to the dominant four-wheel segment of the fleet, more time (or an improved vehicle procurement strategy) may be needed to allow the prohibitive vehicle costs to come down.

Figures and tables start on the next page.

Figures and Tables

FIGURE A.8.1 Advantage of EV adoption in Jordan, by type of vehicle

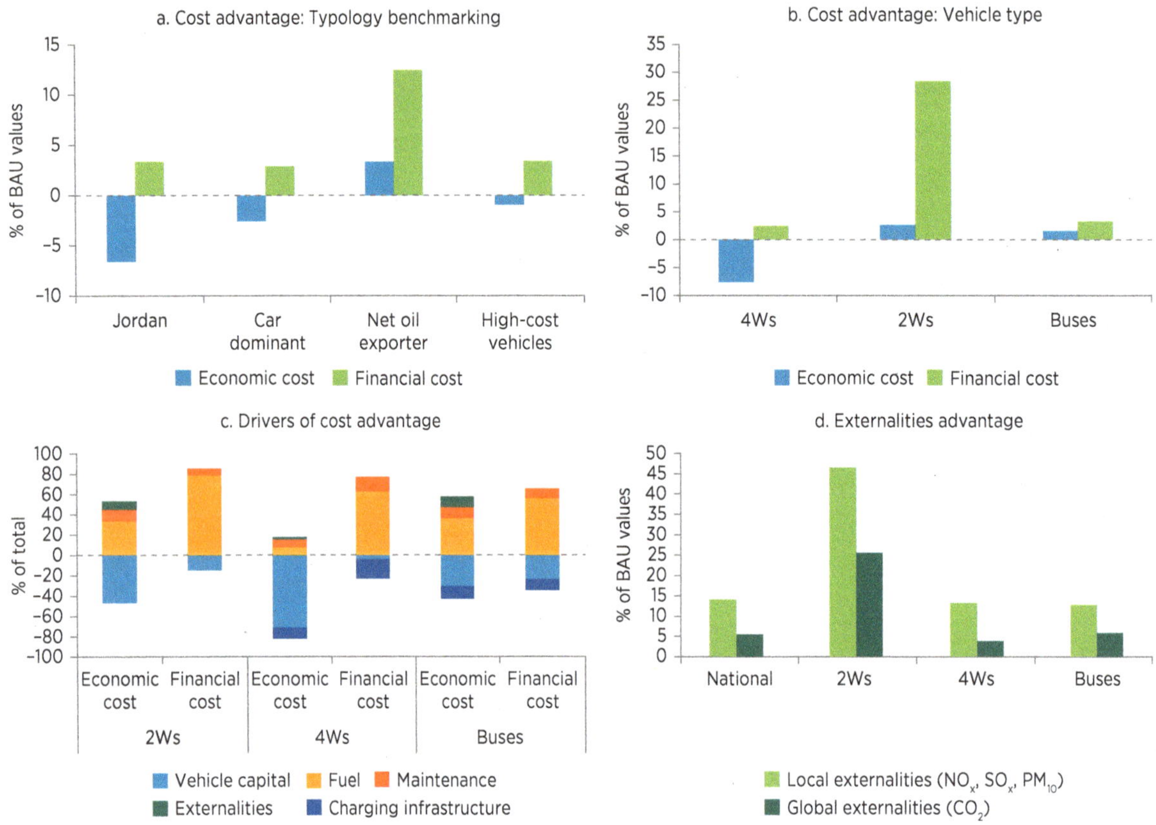

Source: World Bank.

Note: Data in this figure represent the "business as usual" (BAU) scenario minus the 30×30 scenario (averages over fleet additions). The BAU scenario assumes that no policy target will be imposed for electric vehicles and that vehicle purchase decisions will continue to reflect historical trends. The 30×30 scenario assumes that sales of electric cars and buses will reach 30 percent, and of two- and three-wheelers, 70 percent, by 2030. 2W = two-wheeler; 4W = four-wheeler; CO_2 = carbon dioxide; EV = electric vehicle; NO_x = nitrogen oxides; PM_{10} = particulate matter less than 10 microns in diameter; SO_x = sulfur oxides.

TABLE A.8.1 Cost advantage of accelerated EV adoption in Jordan, 2030

	US$/vehicle									% of BAU values	
	Charging infrastructure	Vehicle capital cost	Vehicle operating cost	Subtotal	Local externalities	Global externalities	Economic cost advantage	Net taxes and subsidies	Financial cost advantage	Cost advantage	Financial cost advantage including fiscal wedge
	(a)	(b)	(c)	(d) = (a + b + c)	(e)		(f) = (d + e)	(g)	(h) = (d + g)		
Mode											
2Ws	0	(451)	434	(17)	41	39	63	1,233	1,216	2.6	28.3
4Ws	(441)	(2,895)	633	(2,703)	55	33	(2,615)	3,946	1,243	(7.6)	2.4
Buses	(3,653)	(9,111)	14,088	1,324	1,836	1,177	4,336	9,086	10,409	1.5	3.2

Source: World Bank.

Note: Heading colors: blue = excluding taxes and subsidies, gray = fiscal wedge, green = including taxes and subsidies. 2W = two-wheeler; 4W = four-wheeler; "Local externalities" comprises local (NO_x, PM_{10}, SO_x) air pollution costs. "Global externalities" comprises global (CO_2) air pollution costs. CO_2 = carbon dioxide; NO_x = nitrogen oxides; PM_{10} = particulate matter less than 10 microns in diameter; SO_x = sulfur oxides. Red and parentheses indicate negative value.

FIGURE A.8.2 Investment and financing needs for EV adoption in Jordan, 2030

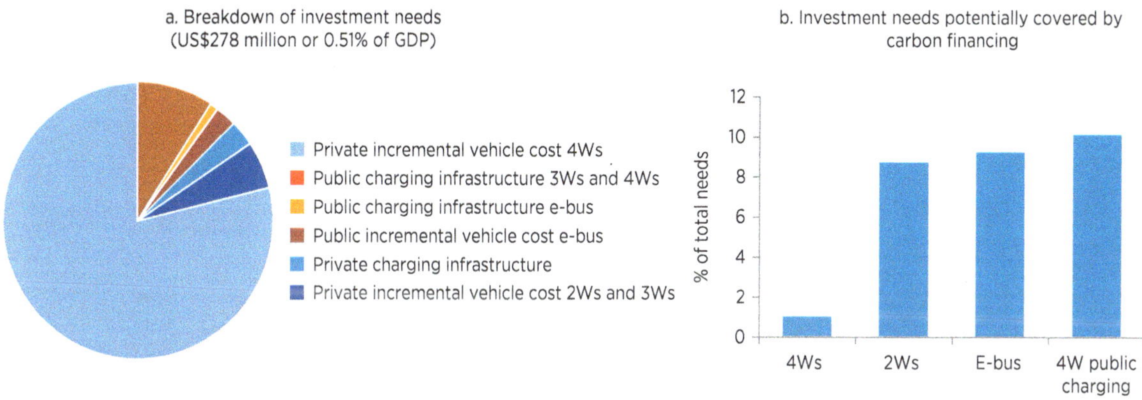

Source: World Bank.
Note: Data in this figure represent the "business as usual" (BAU) scenario minus the 30×30 scenario (averages over fleet additions). The BAU scenario assumes that no policy target will be imposed for electric vehicles and that vehicle purchase decisions will continue to reflect historical trends. The 30×30 scenario assumes that sales of electric cars and buses will reach 30 percent, and of two- and three-wheelers, 70 percent, by 2030. 2W = two-wheeler; 3W = three-wheeler; 4W = four-wheeler; EV = electric vehicle; GDP = gross domestic product.

TABLE A.8.2 Cost advantage of EV adoption in Jordan, by scenario, 2030

	National results				Bus only		4W only	
	30×30 scenario	Green grid scenario	Scarce minerals scenario	Fuel efficiency scenario	30×30 scenario	Efficient bus scenario	30×30 scenario	Taxi fleet scenario
	US$/Mpaxvkm				US$/vehicle			
Type of cost								
Vehicle capital cost	(41,124)	(41,124)	(51,711)	(41,124)	(9,111)	(2,806)	(2,895)	(2,895)
Vehicle maintenance cost	5,356	5,356	5,114	5,356	3,216	3,614	332	(615)
Vehicle fuel cost	7,187	7,187	7,187	3,540	10,872	13,564	300	1,201
Private charging infrastructure	(1,436)	(1,436)	(1,436)	(1,436)	n.a.	n.a.	(111)	(111)
Public charging infrastructure	(4,722)	(4,722)	(4,722)	(4,722)	(3,653)	(3,653)	(329)	(375)
Subtotal	(34,739)	(34,739)	(45,568)	(38,386)	1,324	10,719	(2,703)	(2,795)
Local externalities (NO_x, SO_x, PM_{10})	1,193	2,148	1,193	959	1,836	2,293	55	265
Global externalities (CO_2)	813	1,133	813	385	1,177	1,474	33	153
Economic cost advantage	(32,733)	(31,458)	(43,562)	(37,041)	4,336	14,486	(2,615)	(2,377)
Fiscal wedge	59,233	59,233	58,022	56,328	9,086	13,750	3,946	7,370
Financial cost advantage	24,494	24,494	12,454	17,942	10,409	24,469	1,243	4,575
Economic cost advantage, by type of vehicle	US$/vehicle							
4Ws	(2,615)	(2,537)	(3,377)	(2,893)	n.a.	n.a.	n.a.	n.a.
2Ws	63	77	(18)	19	n.a.	n.a.	n.a.	n.a.
E-buses	4,336	5,813	194	718	n.a.	n.a.	n.a.	n.a.

Source: World Bank.
Note: Data in this table represent the "business as usual" (BAU) scenario minus the named scenario (averages over fleet additions). The BAU scenario assumes that no policy target will be imposed for electric vehicles and that vehicle purchase decisions will continue to reflect historical trends. The 30×30 scenario assumes that sales of electric cars and buses will reach 30 percent, and of two- and three-wheelers, 70 percent, by 2030. The green grid scenario assumes that countries achieve certain region-specific targets for acceleration of renewable energy, as defined by the International Renewable Energy Agency (IRENA 2020). The scarce minerals scenario assumes that battery cost will decline by approximately 7 percent annually. The fuel efficiency scenario assumes that the rate of improvement of fuel efficiency for the internal combustion engine fleet will double from 15 percent to 30 percent. The efficient bus scenario assumes a capital cost reduction of 35 percent in the procurement of buses as well as optimized bus routes to increase the annual mileage of electric buses. The taxi fleet scenario assumes that the lifetime mileage of intensively used commercial vehicles will increase by four times in each country, that public investment in charging infrastructure will double the fast charger density for cars, and that the maintenance cost for cars will be doubled (assuming two lifetime battery replacements). Results have been normalized by new vehicles entering the market in 2030. The "fiscal wedge" comprises net taxes and subsidies. Red and parentheses indicate negative value. 2W = two-wheeler; 4W = four-wheeler; CO_2 = carbon dioxide; EV = electric vehicle; NO_x = nitrogen oxides; PM_{10} = particulate matter less than 10 microns in diameter; SO_x = sulfur oxides; US$/Mpaxvkm = US dollars per million passenger vehicle-kilometers; n.a.= not applicable.

TABLE A.8.3 Supporting information on parameters and results for EV adoption in Jordan

Price (US$/vehicle)

Parameter	Value
Price of ICE 4W	39,329
Price of EV 4W	40,865
Price of ICE 2W	1,225
Price of EV 2W	1,713
Price of ICE bus	157,274
Price of e-bus	148,856

Other parameters

Parameter	Value
Net tax difference on EV 4W (%)	58
Net tax difference on EV 2W (%)	58
Net tax difference on e-bus (%)	58
Price of gasoline (US$/liter)	0.60
Net gasoline tax (US$/liter)	0.86
Price of diesel (US$/liter)	0.74
Net diesel tax (US$/liter)	0.13
Price of electricity (US$/kWh)	0.14
Net electricity tax (US$/kWh)	(0.02)
Electricity carbon intensity (g/kWh)	598
Discount rate (%)	6.6

Key characteristics

Parameter	Value
4W mileage (km)	15,224
2W mileage (km)	7,627
Bus mileage (km)	48,092
4W lifetime (years)	22
2W lifetime (years)	17
Bus lifetime (years)	20
4W secondhand (%)	24.6
2W secondhand (%)	24.6
Bus secondhand (%)	66.9
4W share (% paxvkm)	78
2W share (% paxvkm)	9
Bus share (% paxvkm)	13

Efficiency (MJ/km)

Parameter	Value
Efficiency ICE 4W	2.16
Efficiency EV 4W	0.60
Efficiency ICE 2W	0.86
Efficiency EV 2W	0.20
Efficiency ICE bus	17.03
Efficiency EV bus	5.69

Other results for 30×30 scenario

Other results for 30×30 scenario	Value
Overall investment needs (US$, millions)	278
—of which 4W purchase	219
—of which 2W purchase	16
—of which e-bus purchase	7
Fiscal impact (US$, millions)	(348)
—of which vehicle duties	(37)
—of which vehicle taxes/subsidies	(183)
—of which gasoline taxes/subsidies	(102)
—of which diesel taxes/subsidies	(13)
—of which electricity taxes/subsidies	(14)
Implicit carbon price (US$/ton)	1,067
—of which for 4W	2,058
—of which for 2W	(15)
—of which for buses	(69)
Pollution reduction (tons)	0
—of which local (SO_x, NO_x, PM_{10})	0
—of which global (CO_2)	0
Affordability of EV 2W (Δ cost % GNI pc)	4.3
Affordability of EV 4W (Δ cost % GNI pc)	1.5

Source: World Bank.
Note: Red and parentheses indicates negative value. 2W = two-wheeler; 4W = four-wheeler; CO_2 = carbon dioxide; EV = electric vehicle; g = gram; GNI pc = gross national income per capita; ICE = internal combustion engine; kWh = kilowatt-hour; km = kilometer; MJ = megajoule; NO_x = nitrogen oxides; paxvkm = passenger vehicle-kilometer; PM_{10} = particulate matter less than 10 microns in diameter; SO_x = sulfur oxides.

Notes

1. Two-wheelers cover all motorized two-wheel vehicles registered.
2. Data from US Energy Information Administration international database and World Bank.
3. Central region consists of Balqa, Amman, Zarqa, and Madaba.

References

Businesswire. 2019. "Jordan Electric Vehicle Market Analysis & Outlook, 2019–2025: Vehicle Types, Regions, Competitive Landscape—ResearchAndMarkets.com." Businesswire, September 6, 2019. https://www.businesswire.com/news/home/20190906005441/en/Jordan-Electric-Vehicle-Market-Analysis-Outlook-2019-2025.

CEIC. 2020. "Jordan Number of Registered Vehicles, 1970–2020." CEIC Data, New York. https://www.ceicdata.com/en/indicator/jordan/number-of-registered-vehicles.

Hashemite Kingdom of Jordan. 2015. "Intended Nationally Determined Contribution (INDC)." Nationally Determined Contribution under Paris Agreement. https://unfccc.int/NDCREG.

IRENA (International Renewable Energy Agency). 2020. *Global Renewables Outlook: Energy Transformation 2050*. Masdar City: IRENA.

OICA (Organisation Internationale des Constructeurs d'Automobiles [International Organization of Motor Vehicle Manufacturers]). 2021. "Global Sales Statistics, 2019–2021." OICA, Paris. https://www.oica.net/global-sales-statistics-2019-2021/.

Shalalfeh, Laith, Ashraf AlShalalfeh, Khaled Alkaradsheh, Mahmoud Alhamarneh, and Ahmad Bashaireh. 2021. "Electric Vehicles in Jordan: Challenges and Limitations." *Sustainability* 13 (6): 3199. https://doi.org/10.3390/su13063199.

A.9 PASSENGER ELECTRIC MOBILITY IN KAZAKHSTAN

Country Typology

Vehicle fleet composition:	Car dominant
Net oil trading status:	Exporter
Relative cost of vehicles:	Low

Country Background

The dominant vehicle type in Kazakhstan is cars (92.1 percent), followed by buses (7.9 percent).[1] Electricity is primarily generated from fossil fuels (89.1 percent), and hydropower (10.1 percent)[2] is the lead renewable energy source. Two of the top priorities of the Kazakhstan 2050 Strategy are to make the country's public transportation system more eco-friendly and to invest in charging infrastructure across the country. The City of Almaty Sustainable Transport project recommends the use of electricity produced from local gas to power electric vehicles (ETC Transport Consultants 2017). In the absence of domestic manufacturing capability, Kazakhstan imports most of its vehicle fleet (Gadimova 2019). And although, according to Kazakhstan's industry and infrastructure development ministry, most of the 200 electric cars in operation in 2018 were imported, the target is to produce about 2,000 units of electric cars locally by the end of 2022 (Yergaliyeva 2020). The government is already advancing an aggressive investment in charging infrastructure, having in place more than 50 charging stations in Astana in 2020 (Yergaliyeva 2020).

Overall Messages

Although vehicle costs are relatively low, Kazakhstan's car-dominated fleet and oil-exporting status create some countervailing challenges for the scale-up of electric mobility (figure A.9.1a). On balance, the overall case for electric mobility in the country is somewhat positive (table A.9.1). There is a particularly strong case for adoption of two-wheel electric motorbikes (figure A9.1b), despite the low number in the fleet, because these present a life-cycle cost advantage of about 22 percent (almost 30 percent in financial terms). Moreover, the capital cost premium for electric two-wheel vehicles is moderate at about 17 percent, representing an affordable 0.6 percent of gross national income per capita. The electrification of four-wheelers does not offer life-cycle cost advantage, but four-wheelers are eminently affordable with a capital cost premium of less than 2 percent, equivalent to a little more than 2 percent of gross national income per capita. By contrast, the capital cost premium associated with electric buses is particularly high at about 51 percent, and a life-cycle cost analysis shows a modest advantage of about 2 percent.

The externality benefits of electric mobility in Kazakhstan are particularly significant in absolute value in the case of electric buses (figure A.9.1c), whereas two-wheel electric vehicles present much lower externalities than their conventional counterparts in percentage terms (figure A.9.1d). Otherwise, fuel cost savings are the main advantage associated with electric mobility. The fiscal regime neither incentivizes nor disincentivizes the purchase of electric vehicles. However, fiscal policies do accentuate the fuel cost advantage of owning them. Although fuel taxes are not particularly high—about 25 percent for gasoline—electricity benefits from a 50 percent subsidy. Consequently, the overall case for electric mobility in Kazakhstan looks better in financial than in economic terms (figure A.9.1c) for two-wheelers and four-wheelers.

The total investment needs associated with the 30×30 scenario amount to US$251 million per year by 2030 (or 0.11 percent of Kazakhstan gross domestic product). About 70 percent of the required outlay is associated with public investment in charging infrastructure (figure A.9.2a). Implicit carbon prices associated with electric vehicles in Kazakhstan are negative for two-wheelers and buses (table A.9.3). However, only in the case of electric two-wheelers is there a potential for carbon financing to cover a substantial share of the incremental cost of vehicle purchase (figure A.9.2b). The implicit carbon prices for four-wheelers are about US$93/ton.

The overall economic case for electric mobility in Kazakhstan is positive and improves substantially with further decarbonization of the power sector ("green grid" scenario) (table A.9.2). However, this result is not robust to more conservative assumptions about the cost of batteries ("scarce minerals" scenario) or the fuel efficiency of internal combustion engines ("fuel efficiency" scenario), both of which tip the balance against electric mobility (table A.9.2). On a positive note, the emerging advantage associated with electrification of buses can be as much as doubled through the more efficient procurement and operation of vehicles ("efficient bus" scenario). Moreover, the case for electrification of four-wheelers improves and offers cost advantages in the case of taxi fleets and other intensively used vehicles ("taxi fleet" scenario). Ironically, almost nonexistent two-wheelers are the most attractive segment for electrification in Kazakhstan. However, there is scope to advance with electrification of buses and four-wheelers, as long as efforts are targeted toward more intensively used vehicles.

Figures and tables start on the next page.

Figures and Tables

FIGURE A.9.1 **Advantage of EV adoption in Kazakhstan, by type of vehicle**

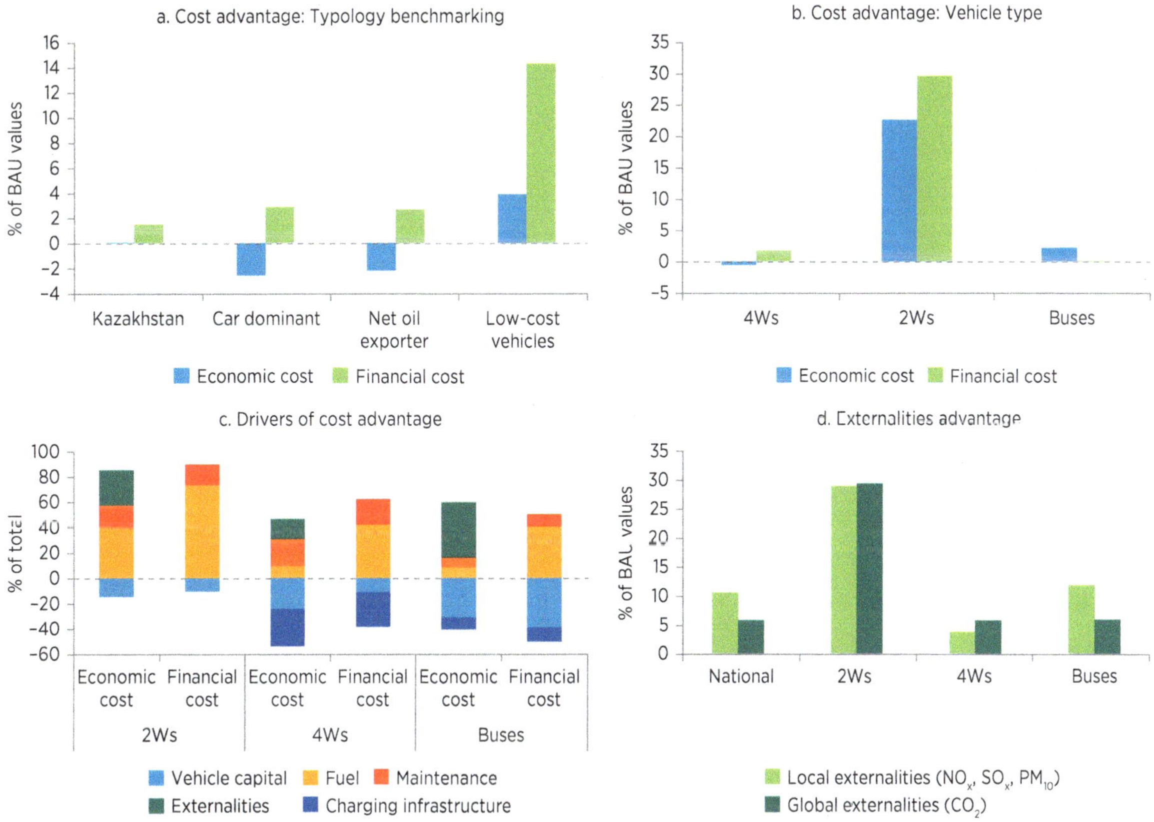

Source: World Bank.
Note: Data in this figure represent the "business as usual" (BAU) scenario minus the 30×30 scenario (averages over fleet additions). The BAU scenario assumes that no policy target will be imposed for electric vehicles and that vehicle purchase decisions will continue to reflect historical trends. The 30×30 scenario assumes that sales of electric cars and buses will reach 30 percent, and of two- and three-wheelers, 70 percent, by 2030. 2W = two-wheeler; 4W = four-wheeler; CO_2 = carbon dioxide; EV = electric vehicle; NO_x = nitrogen oxides; PM_{10} = particulate matter less than 10 microns in diameter; SO_x = sulfur oxides.

TABLE A.9.1 **Cost advantage of accelerated EV adoption in Kazakhstan, 2030**

	US$/vehicle									% of BAU values	
	Charging infrastructure	Vehicle capital cost	Vehicle operating cost	Subtotal	Local externalities	Global externalities	Economic cost advantage	Net taxes and subsidies	Financial cost advantage	Cost advantage	Financial cost advantage including fiscal wedge
	(a)	(b)	(c)	(d) = (a + b + c)	(e)		(f) = (d + e)	(g)	(h) = (d + g)		
Mode											
2Ws	0	(107)	413	306	152	46	504	311	618	22.6	29.6
4Ws	(540)	(459)	572	(427)	230	55	(142)	895	468	(0.5)	1.7
Buses	(3,516)	(11,639)	6,043	(9,112)	14,662	1,458	7,008	8,952	(160)	2.2	(0.1)

Source: World Bank.
Note: Heading colors: blue = excluding taxes and subsidies, gray = fiscal wedge, green = including taxes and subsidies. 2W = two-wheeler; 4W = four-wheeler; "Local externalities" comprises local (NO_x, PM_{10}, SO_x) air pollution costs. "Global externalities" comprises global (CO_2) air pollution costs. CO_2 = carbon dioxide; NO_x = nitrogen oxides; PM_{10} = particulate matter less than 10 microns in diameter; SO_x = sulfur oxides. Red and parentheses indicate negative value.

FIGURE A.9.2 Investment and financing needs for EV adoption in Kazakhstan, 2030

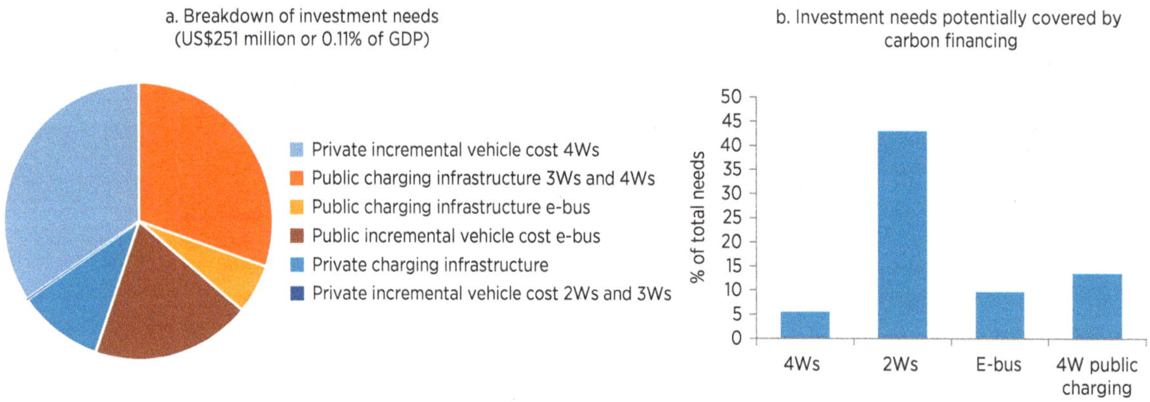

Source: World Bank.

Note: Data in this figure represent the "business as usual" (BAU) scenario minus the 30×30 scenario (averages over fleet additions). The BAU scenario assumes that no policy target will be imposed for electric vehicles and that vehicle purchase decisions will continue to reflect historical trends. The 30×30 scenario assumes that sales of electric cars and buses will reach 30 percent, and of two- and three-wheelers, 70 percent, by 2030. 2W = two-wheeler; 3W = three-wheeler; 4W = four-wheeler; EV = electric vehicle; GDP = gross domestic product.

TABLE A.9.2 Cost advantage of EV adoption in Kazakhstan, by scenario, 2030

	National results				Bus only		4W only	
	30×30 scenario	Green grid scenario	Scarce minerals scenario	Fuel efficiency scenario	30×30 scenario	Efficient bus scenario	30×30 scenario	Taxi fleet scenario
	US$/Mpaxvkm				*US$/vehicle*			
Type of cost								
Vehicle capital cost	(8,347)	(8,347)	(13,378)	(8,347)	(11,639)	(5,749)	(459)	(459)
Vehicle maintenance cost	5,448	5,448	4,982	5,448	2,993	3,397	400	(756)
Vehicle fuel cost	2,834	2,834	2,834	(492)	3,049	3,258	172	688
Private charging infrastructure	(1,587)	(1,587)	(1,587)	(1,587)	n.a.	n.a.	(136)	(136)
Public charging infrastructure	(5,605)	(5,605)	(5,605)	(5,605)	(3,516)	(3,516)	(404)	(459)
Subtotal	(7,257)	(7,257)	(12,754)	(10,584)	(9,112)	(2,610)	(427)	(1,122)
Local externalities (NO_x, SO_x, PM_{10})	6,459	11,620	6,459	5,645	14,662	15,666	230	1,090
Global externalities (CO_2)	1,017	1,568	1,017	435	1,458	1,559	55	244
Economic cost advantage	219	5,932	(5,278)	(4,504)	7,008	14,615	(142)	212
Fiscal wedge	12,773	12,773	12,167	12,251	8,952	10,168	895	2,896
Financial cost advantage	5,516	5,516	(586)	1,668	(160)	7,558	468	1,774
Economic cost advantage, by type of vehicle	*US$/vehicle*							
4Ws	(142)	188	(526)	(482)	n.a.	n.a.	n.a.	n.a.
2Ws	504	547	466	458	n.a.	n.a.	n.a.	n.a.
E-buses	7,008	14,272	3,038	4,075	n.a.	n.a.	n.a.	n.a.

Source: World Bank.

Note: Data in this table represent the "business as usual" (BAU) scenario minus the named scenario (averages over fleet additions). The BAU scenario assumes that no policy target will be imposed for electric vehicles and that vehicle purchase decisions will continue to reflect historical trends. The 30×30 scenario assumes that sales of electric cars and buses will reach 30 percent, and of two- and three-wheelers, 70 percent, by 2030. The green grid scenario assumes that countries achieve certain region-specific targets for acceleration of renewable energy, as defined by the International Renewable Energy Agency (IRENA 2020). The scarce minerals scenario assumes that battery cost will decline by approximately 7 percent annually. The fuel efficiency scenario assumes that the rate of improvement of fuel efficiency for the internal combustion engine fleet will double from 15 percent to 30 percent. The efficient bus scenario assumes a capital cost reduction of 35 percent in the procurement of buses as well as optimized bus routes to increase the annual mileage of electric buses. The taxi fleet scenario assumes that the lifetime mileage of intensively used commercial vehicles will increase by four times in each country, that public investment in charging infrastructure will double the fast charger density for cars, and that the maintenance cost for cars will be doubled (assuming two lifetime battery replacements). Results have been normalized by new vehicles entering the market in 2030. The "fiscal wedge" comprises net taxes and subsidies. Red and parentheses indicate negative value. 2W = two-wheeler; 4W = four-wheeler; CO_2 = carbon dioxide; EV = electric vehicle; NO_x = nitrogen oxides; PM_{10} = particulate matter less than 10 microns in diameter; SO_x = sulfur oxides; US$/Mpaxvkm = US dollars per million passenger vehicle-kilometers; n.a.= not applicable.

TABLE A.9.3 Supporting information on parameters and results for EV adoption in Kazakhstan

Price (US$/vehicle)

Parameter	Value
Price of ICE 4W	14,924
Price of EV 4W	14,525
Price of ICE 2W	499
Price of EV 2W	609
Price of ICE bus	66,052
Price of e-bus	135,324

Other parameters

Parameter	Value
Net tax difference on EV 4W (%)	12
Net tax difference on EV 2W (%)	12
Net tax difference on e-bus (%)	12
Price of gasoline (US$/liter)	0.46
Net gasoline tax (US$/liter)	0.12
Price of diesel (US$/liter)	0.43
Net diesel tax (US$/liter)	0.02
Price of electricity (US$/kWh)	0.10
Net electricity tax (US$/kWh)	(0.05)
Electricity carbon intensity (g/kWh)	556
Discount rate (%)	6.6

Key characteristics

Parameter	Value
4W mileage (km)	15,224
2W mileage (km)	7,627
Bus mileage (km)	56,162
4W lifetime (years)	22
2W lifetime (years)	17
Bus lifetime (years)	20
4W secondhand (%)	11.4
2W secondhand (%)	11.4
Bus secondhand (%)	84.1
4W share (% paxvkm)	71
2W share (% paxvkm)	0.3
Bus share (% paxvkm)	29

Efficiency (MJ/km)

Parameter	Value
Efficiency ICE 4W	2.21
Efficiency EV 4W	0.75
Efficiency ICE 2W	0.85
Efficiency EV 2W	0.20
Efficiency ICE bus	17.84
Efficiency EV bus	6.24

Other results for 30×30 scenario

Other results for 30×30 scenario	Value
Overall investment needs (US$, millions)	251
—of which 4W purchase	87
—of which 2W purchase	0
—of which e-bus purchase	48
Fiscal impact (US$, millions)	(207)
—of which vehicle duties	18
—of which vehicle taxes/subsidies	(58)
—of which gasoline taxes/subsidies	(31)
—of which diesel taxes/subsidies	(11)
—of which electricity taxes/subsidies	(125)
Implicit carbon price (US$/ton)	20
—of which for 4W	93
—of which for 2W	(259)
—of which for buses	(98)
Pollution reduction (tons)	1
—of which local (SO_x, NO_x, PM_{10})	0
—of which global (CO_2)	1
Affordability of EV 2W (Δ cost % GNI pc)	0.7
Affordability of EV 4W (Δ cost % GNI pc)	2.0

Source: World Bank.
Note: Red and parentheses indicates negative value. 2W = two-wheeler; 4W = four-wheeler; CO_2 = carbon dioxide; EV = electric vehicle; g = gram; GNI pc = gross national income per capita; ICE = internal combustion engine; kWh = kilowatt-hour; km = kilometer; MJ = megajoule; NO_x = nitrogen oxides; paxvkm = passenger vehicle-kilometer; PM_{10} = particulate matter less than 10 microns in diameter; SO_x = sulfur oxides.

Notes

1. Data from the World Bank.
2. Data from US Energy Information Administration international database and World Bank.

References

ETC Transport Consultants. 2017. "Policy Review of the Development of the Public Transport Sector in Kazakhstan." United Nations Development Program and Global Environment Facility, Washington, DC.

Gadimova, Nazrin. 2019. "Electric Cars Could Soon Be Mass-Produced in Kazakhstan." *Caspian News*, July 12, 2019. https://caspiannews.com/news-detail/electric-cars-could-soon-be-mass-produced-in-kazakhstan-2019-7-11-9/.

IRENA (International Renewable Energy Agency). 2020. *Global Renewables Outlook: Energy Transformation 2050.* Masdar City: IRENA.

Yergaliyeva, Aidana. 2020. "Kazakhstan Plans to Launch Electric Car Production by 2021." *Astana Times*, October 28, 2020. https://astanatimes.com/2020/10/kazakhstan-plans-to-launch-electric-car-production-in-kazakhstan-by-2021/.

A.10 PASSENGER ELECTRIC MOBILITY IN MALDIVES

Country Typology

Vehicle fleet composition: Mixed fleet
Net oil trading status: Importer
Relative cost of vehicles: High

Country Background

The dominant vehicle type in Maldives is two-wheelers (78.4 percent),[1] followed by cars (16.7 percent) (Maldives National Bureau of Statistics 2020). Electricity is primarily generated from fossil fuels, essentially oil (99.6 percent), with very limited generation from renewable sources (0.4 percent), mainly wind.[2] The latest National Action Plan on Air Pollutants places emphasis on the adoption of electric vehicles in the islands (Hameed and Ajmal 2019), and includes formulating and adopting enforceable national requirements on emission limits and standards; implementing effective programs for permitting and enforcement; developing a strategy to deploy electric vehicles, including financial mechanisms to support implementation and potential for using solar photovoltaic power for charging facilities; and implementing a demonstration project comprising 75 electric motorcycles and 200 electric bicycles. Several international entities are supporting the national government to address air pollution issues. The United Nations Environment Programme is providing technical assistance to the government in adopting an integrated transportation system that prioritizes nonmotorized transportation and the introduction of electric vehicles powered by renewable energy. In addition, Maldives is one of the countries under the Global Environment Facility support program to shift toward electric vehicles, benefiting from a trust-funded Integrated and Low Emissions Transport project.[3]

Overall Messages

Maldives faces exceptionally high vehicle purchase costs that present a formidable barrier for the adoption of electric mobility, despite other favorable conditions, such as the country's diversified fleet and status as an oil importer (figure A.10.1a). As a result, there is no case for the adoption of electric mobility in the horizon to 2030 across any of the three vehicle types considered (table A.10.1). Although two-wheel electric vehicles are economically attractive in most countries, this is not true for Maldives given that these vehicles cost over US$3,000, which represents a cost premium more than 76 percent over conventional counterparts before tax (although the cost gap shrinks because Maldives relies heavily on secondhand vehicles and offers sizable tax advantages to electric vehicles). Other vehicle categories are also exceptionally expensive (figure A.10.1b).

The externality benefits of electric mobility in Maldives are quite substantial for buses and two-wheel electric vehicles (figure A.10.1c), and are predominantly associated with reductions in local air pollution (figure A.10.1d). In economic terms, there is no fuel cost advantage for electric vehicles because of the exceptionally high cost of electricity on the islands (figure A.10.1c), approaching US$0.50 per kilowatt-hour (table A.10.3). However, because transportation fuel is (modestly) taxed and electricity is heavily subsidized at over 50 percent, the story changes completely in financial terms, bringing a significant operating cost advantage—albeit not sufficient to offset the substantial capital cost premium (figure A.10.1c).

The total investment needs associated with the 30×30 scenario amount to US$10 million per year by 2030 (or 0.13 percent of gross domestic product). About four-fifths of the required outlay is associated with the incremental capital cost of private electric vehicles (figure A.10.2a). Given that implicit carbon prices for electric mobility in Maldives are over US$2,700 per ton for four-wheel electric vehicles and US$300–400 per ton for two-wheelers and buses, the scope for carbon financing is relatively modest (figure A.10.2b), and the country may be better-off seeking more cost-effective means of decarbonizing the transport sector.

In sum, there is no overall economic case for electric mobility in Maldives over the time horizon to 2030, even under a scenario of further decarbonization of the power sector ("green grid" scenario) (table A.10.2). Moreover, the case deteriorates further under more conservative assumptions about the cost of batteries ("scarce minerals" scenario) and the fuel efficiency of internal combustion engines ("fuel efficiency" scenario) (table A.10.2). Even achieving greater efficiency in the procurement and operation of electric buses fails to reverse the negative conclusion ("efficient bus" scenario), and the outcome is similar for more intensive use of four-wheel vehicles ("taxi fleet" scenario) (table A.10.2). The results strongly suggest that rapid adoption of electric mobility in Maldives would be premature, across all vehicle types, and the country may be best advised to wait until capital cost premiums can be brought down further.

Figures and tables start on the next page.

Figures and Tables

FIGURE A.10.1 Advantages of EV adoption in Maldives, by type of vehicle

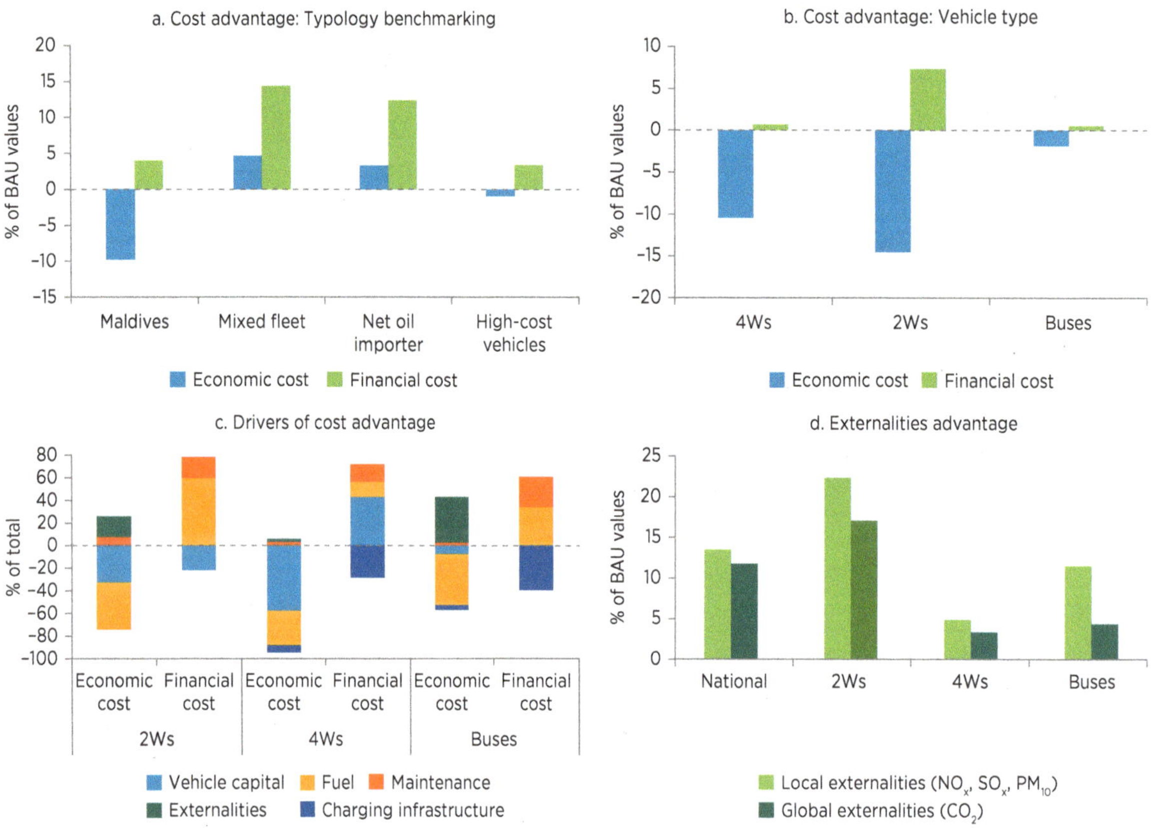

Source: World Bank.
Note: Data in this figure represent the "business as usual" (BAU) scenario minus the 30×30 scenario (averages over fleet additions). The BAU scenario assumes that no policy target will be imposed for electric vehicles and that vehicle purchase decisions will continue to reflect historical trends. The 30×30 scenario assumes that sales of electric cars and buses will reach 30 percent, and of two- and three-wheelers, 70 percent, by 2030. 2W = two-wheeler; 4W = four-wheeler; CO_2 = carbon dioxide; EV = electric vehicle; NO_x = nitrogen oxides; PM_{10} = particulate matter less than 10 microns in diameter; SO_x = sulfur oxides.

TABLE A.10.1 Cost advantage of accelerated EV adoption in Maldives, 2030

	US$/vehicle									% of BAU values	
	Charging infrastructure	Vehicle capital cost	Vehicle operating cost	Subtotal	Local externalities	Global externalities	Economic cost advantage	Net taxes and subsidies	Financial cost advantage	Cost advantage	Financial cost advantage including fiscal wedge
	(a)	(b)	(c)	(d) = (a + b + c)	(e)		(f) = (d + e)	(g)	(h) = (d + g)		
Mode											
2Ws	0	(231)	(234)	(465)	102	24	(338)	627	162	(14.5)	7.3
4Ws	(211)	(2,011)	(948)	(3,170)	54	29	(3,087)	3,496	326	(10.4)	0.7
Buses	(2,871)	(5,501)	(29,435)	(37,807)	27,502	909	(9,397)	39,411	1,604	(1.8)	0.5

Source: World Bank.
Note: Heading colors: blue = excluding taxes and subsidies, gray = fiscal wedge, green = including taxes and subsidies. 2W = two-wheeler; 4W = four-wheeler; "Local externalities" comprises local (NO_x, PM_{10}, SO_x) air pollution costs. "Global externalities" comprises global (CO_2) air pollution costs. CO_2 = carbon dioxide; NO_x = nitrogen oxides; PM_{10} = particulate matter less than 10 microns in diameter; SO_x = sulfur oxides. Red and parentheses indicate negative value.

FIGURE A.10.2 Investment and financing needs for EV adoption in Maldives, 2030

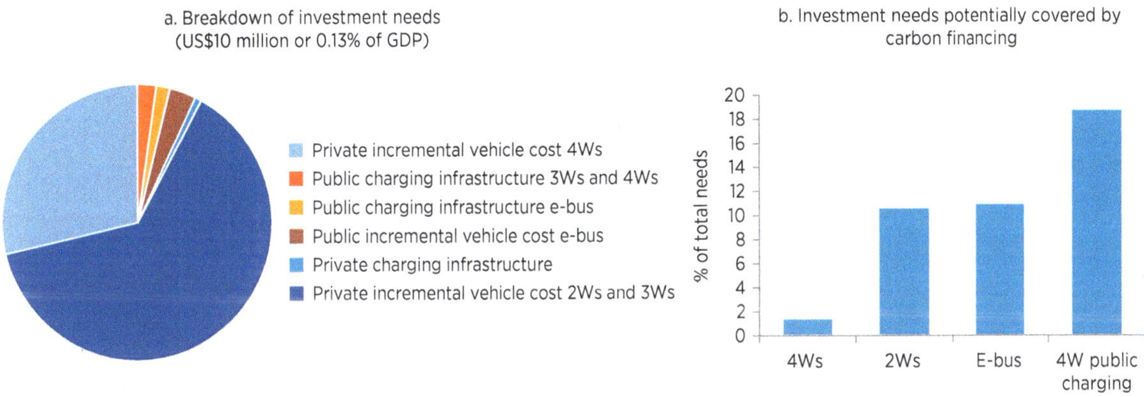

Source: World Bank.

Note: Data in this figure represent the "business as usual" (BAU) scenario minus the 30×30 scenario (averages over fleet additions). The BAU scenario assumes that no policy target will be imposed for electric vehicles and that vehicle purchase decisions will continue to reflect historical trends. The 30×30 scenario assumes that sales of electric cars and buses will reach 30 percent, and of two- and three-wheelers, 70 percent, by 2030. 2W = two-wheeler; 3W = three-wheeler; 4W = four-wheeler; EV = electric vehicle; GDP = gross domestic product.

TABLE A.10.2 Cost advantage of EV adoption in Maldives, by scenario, 2030

	National results				Bus only		4W only	
	30×30 scenario	Green grid scenario	Scarce minerals scenario	Fuel efficiency scenario	30×30 scenario	Efficient bus scenario	30×30 scenario	Taxi fleet scenario
	US$/Mpaxvkm				US$/vehicle			
Type of cost								
Vehicle capital cost	(9,370)	(9,370)	(11,104)	(9,370)	(5,501)	(1,570)	(2,011)	(2,011)
Vehicle maintenance cost	1,784	1,784	1,686	1,784	1,943	2,373	114	(353)
Vehicle fuel cost	(13,074)	(13,074)	(13,074)	(13,610)	(31,379)	(31,379)	(1,062)	(4,249)
Private charging infrastructure	(77)	(77)	(77)	(77)	n.a.	n.a.	(55)	(55)
Public charging infrastructure	(386)	(386)	(386)	(386)	(2,871)	(2,871)	(156)	(178)
Subtotal	(21,123)	(21,123)	(22,955)	(21,658)	(37,807)	(33,446)	(3,170)	(6,846)
Local externalities (NO_x, SO_x, PM_{10})	4,702	5,722	4,702	4,660	27,502	27,502	54	232
Global externalities (CO_2)	928	1,253	928	864	909	909	29	120
Economic cost advantage	(15,492)	(14,148)	(17,325)	(16,134)	(9,397)	(5,035)	(3,087)	(6,494)
Fiscal wedge	27,540	27,540	27,436	27,485	39,411	39,647	3,496	6,979
Financial cost advantage	6,417	6,417	4,481	5,827	1,604	6,201	326	133
Economic cost advantage, by type of vehicle	US$/vehicle							
4Ws	(3,087)	(2,935)	(3,497)	(3,181)	n.a.	n.a.	n.a.	n.a.
2Ws	(338)	(314)	(377)	(351)	n.a.	n.a.	n.a.	n.a.
E-buses	(9,397)	(6,056)	(12,552)	(11,331)	n.a.	n.a.	n.a.	n.a.

Source: World Bank.

Note: Data in this table represent the "business as usual" (BAU) scenario minus the named scenario (averages over fleet additions). The BAU scenario assumes that no policy target will be imposed for electric vehicles and that vehicle purchase decisions will continue to reflect historical trends. The 30×30 scenario assumes that sales of electric cars and buses will reach 30 percent, and of two- and three-wheelers, 70 percent, by 2030. The green grid scenario assumes that countries achieve certain region-specific targets for acceleration of renewable energy, as defined by the International Renewable Energy Agency (IRENA 2020). The scarce minerals scenario assumes that battery cost will decline by approximately 7 percent annually. The fuel efficiency scenario assumes that the rate of improvement of fuel efficiency for the internal combustion engine fleet will double from 15 percent to 30 percent. The efficient bus scenario assumes a capital cost reduction of 35 percent in the procurement of buses as well as optimized bus routes to increase the annual mileage of electric buses. The taxi fleet scenario assumes that the lifetime mileage of intensively used commercial vehicles will increase by four times in each country, that public investment in charging infrastructure will double the fast charger density for cars, and that the maintenance cost for cars will be doubled (assuming two lifetime battery replacements). Results have been normalized by new vehicles entering the market in 2030. The "fiscal wedge" comprises net taxes and subsidies. Red and parentheses indicate negative value. 2W = two-wheeler; 4W = four-wheeler; CO_2 = carbon dioxide; EV = electric vehicle; NO_x = nitrogen oxides; PM_{10} = particulate matter less than 10 microns in diameter; SO_x = sulfur oxides; US$/Mpaxvkm = US dollars per million passenger vehicle-kilometers; n.a.= not applicable.

TABLE A.10.3 Supporting information on parameters and results for EV adoption in Maldives

Price (US$/vehicle)

Parameter	Value
Price of ICE 4W	35,187
Price of EV 4W	82,998
Price of ICE 2W	1,584
Price of EV 2W	3,173
Price of ICE bus	162,258
Price of e-bus	143,443

Other parameters

Parameter	Value
Net tax difference on EV 4W (%)	3
Net tax difference on EV 2W (%)	12
Net tax difference on e-bus (%)	0
Price of gasoline (US$/liter)	0.60
Net gasoline tax (US$/liter)	0.09
Price of diesel (US$/liter)	0.74
Net diesel tax (US$/liter)	0.01
Price of electricity (US$/kWh)	0.47
Net electricity tax (US$/kWh)	(0.28)
Electricity carbon intensity (g/kWh)	609
Discount rate (%)	6.6

Key characteristics

Parameter	Value
4W mileage (km)	15,224
2W mileage (km)	7,627
Bus mileage (km)	48,092
4W lifetime (years)	22
2W lifetime (years)	17
Bus lifetime (years)	20
4W secondhand (%)	88.0
2W secondhand (%)	88.0
Bus secondhand (%)	93.6
4W share (% paxvkm)	9
2W share (% paxvkm)	38
Bus share (% paxvkm)	6

Efficiency (MJ/km)

Parameter	Value
Efficiency ICE 4W	2.39
Efficiency EV 4W	0.33
Efficiency ICE 2W	0.88
Efficiency EV 2W	0.20
Efficiency ICE bus	17.81
Efficiency EV bus	6.10

Other results for 30×30 scenario

Other results for 30×30 scenario	Value
Overall investment needs (US$, millions)	10.0
—of which 4W purchase	3
—of which 2W purchase	6
—of which e-bus purchase	0
Fiscal impact (US$, millions)	(28)
—of which vehicle duties	(8)
—of which vehicle taxes/subsidies	(1)
—of which gasoline taxes/subsidies	(2)
—of which diesel taxes/subsidies	(0.1)
—of which electricity taxes/subsidies	(18)
Implicit carbon price (US$/ton)	458
—of which for 4W	2,774
—of which for 2W	387
—of which for buses	293
Pollution reduction (tons)	0
—of which local (SO_x, NO_x, PM_{10})	0
—of which global (CO_2)	0
Affordability of EV 2W (Δ cost % GNI pc)	0.5
Affordability of EV 4W (Δ cost % GNI pc)	(2.8)

Source: World Bank.
Note: Red and parentheses indicates negative value. 2W = two-wheeler; 4W = four-wheeler; CO_2 = carbon dioxide; EV = electric vehicle; g = gram; GNI pc = gross national income per capita; ICE = internal combustion engine; kWh = kilowatt-hour; km = kilometer; MJ = megajoule; NO_x = nitrogen oxides; paxvkm = passenger vehicle-kilometer; PM_{10} = particulate matter less than 10 microns in diameter; SO_x = sulfur oxides.

Notes

1. Two-wheelers cover all motorized two-wheel vehicles registered.
2. Data from US Energy Information Administration international database and World Bank.
3. Global Environment Facility, "Integrated, Sustainable, and Low Emissions Transport in the Maldives." https://www.thegef.org/projects-operations/projects/10301.

References

Hameed, Aminath Maiha, and Ismail Ajmal. 2019. *National Action Plan on Air Pollutants: Determining Nationally Avoided Emissions*. Maafannu, Maldives: Ministry of Environment.

IRENA (International Renewable Energy Agency). 2020. *Global Renewables Outlook: Energy Transformation 2050*. Masdar City: IRENA.

Maldives National Bureau of Statistics. 2020. *Statistical Pocketbook of Maldives 2020*. Malé, Maldives: National Bureau of Statistics, Ministry of National Planning, Housing & Infrastructure. http://statisticsmaldives.gov.mv/nbs/wp-content/uploads/2020/12/Statistical-Pocketbook-2020-updated-12820.pdf.

A.11 PASSENGER ELECTRIC MOBILITY IN NEPAL

Country Typology

Vehicle fleet composition:	Mixed fleet
Net oil trading status:	Importer
Relative cost of vehicles:	High

Country Background

The dominant vehicle type in Nepal is two-wheelers (61.4 percent),[1] followed by three-wheelers (17.3 percent), cars (11.3 percent), and buses (10.0 percent) (CEIC 2020). Moreover, 100 percent of the electricity produced in Nepal is from renewable sources, primarily hydro (98.1 percent).[2] Nepal is quite advanced in creating a supportive policy framework for the adoption of electric mobility. The government has developed its National Action Plan for electric mobility in 2018, which identified three priority actions: (1) delivery of a National Program for Electric Mobility to facilitate electric vehicles purchase, invest in supporting infrastructure, and fast-track operational progress and refine legislation; (2) creation of a centralized regulatory and promotional unit, responsible for oversight of financial and program initiatives; and (3) establishment of a "National Financing Vehicle" for effective management and disbursement of financial support to promote infrastructure, innovation, and entrepreneurship for electric mobility (Government of Nepal 2018).

These actions are reflected in the latest 2021 budget, which includes some key incentives to support electric mobility adoption in the country (Nepali Times 2021), a complete repeal of excise duties on electric vehicle imports, and reducing custom duties down to 10 percent. The current number of electric vehicles in Nepal is very limited; less than 100 electric cars are in the Kathmandu Valley. There is a pilot project by Hulas Motors to produce small electric cars in the country. Otherwise, most of the electric vehicles are imported from China, the Republic of Korea, and India (Shrestha 2018). The Global Green Growth Institute conceptualized several investment projects for Nepal to upscale electric mobility in the country: deploying an electric trolley bus system in Kathmandu Valley; upscaling electric vehicle battery leasing for three-wheelers; upscaling and monetizing public access charging stations; establishing battery recycling; and converting fossil fuel taxis to electric taxis (Government of Nepal 2018).

Overall Messages

Although Nepal has several conditions that are favorable toward electric mobility, notably its oil-importing status and the predominance of two- and three-wheelers in the vehicle fleet, these advantages are overwhelmed by the exceptionally high cost of vehicles in the country (figure A.11.1a). In fact, electric two-wheelers and four-wheelers remain at a substantial economic disadvantage relative to their conventional counterparts, and it is only in the bus segment that electrification brings modest advantages on the order of 3–4 percent of life-cycle costs (figure A.11.1b).

Underlying these findings is the fact that electric two-wheelers and four-wheelers have exceptionally high capital costs, more than three times those of conventional alternatives (table A.11.3). Indeed, the incremental capital cost of an electric two-wheeler is already enough to absorb almost 80 percent of gross national income per capita, making such vehicles completely unaffordable for the population. Although electric buses are also expensive by global standards, the cost differential compared with diesel buses is less than double (figure A.11.1c).

The externality benefits of electric mobility in Nepal are relatively small (figure A.11.1d), making fuel cost savings the main advantage associated with electric mobility. Given a fiscal regime that taxes gasoline almost three times as heavily as electricity, these fuel cost savings are further accentuated in financial terms (figure A.11.1a).

The total investment needs associated with the 30×30 scenario amount to US$739 million per year by 2030 (or 1.75 percent of Nepalese gross domestic product). About two-thirds of the required outlay is associated with the incremental capital cost of electric vehicles, particularly two- and three-wheelers (figure A.11.2a). In terms of public investment, the most significant item is the additional capital cost associated with electric buses (figure A.11.2a). Implicit carbon prices associated with electric mobility in Nepal are negative for buses, but otherwise very high—above US$100 per ton for two-wheelers and US$700 per ton for four-wheelers (table A.11.3). The scope for carbon financing is therefore limited, except in the case of public provision of charging infrastructure for private vehicles (figure A.11.2b).

The overall economic case for electric mobility in Nepal is quite negative, with the notable exception of buses (table A.11.1). The economics of electric two-wheelers and four-wheelers certainly do not improve under more conservative assumptions about the cost of batteries ("scarce minerals" scenario) and the fuel efficiency of internal combustion engines ("fuel efficiency" scenario), nor is there any scope to further decarbonize a power sector that is already entirely renewable ("green grid" scenario) (table A.11.2). On a positive note, the emerging advantage associated with electrification of buses can be hugely increased through the more efficient procurement and operation of vehicles ("efficient bus" scenario). However, there is no real case for electrification of four-wheelers even when it comes to taxi fleets and other intensively used vehicles ("taxi fleet" scenario). It is clear that electric mobility in Nepal, for the time being, needs to prioritize the bus segment of the fleet, pending measures to reduce the capital costs of private vehicles.

Figures and tables start on the next page.

Figures and Tables

FIGURE A.11.1 Advantage of EV adoption in Nepal, by type of vehicle

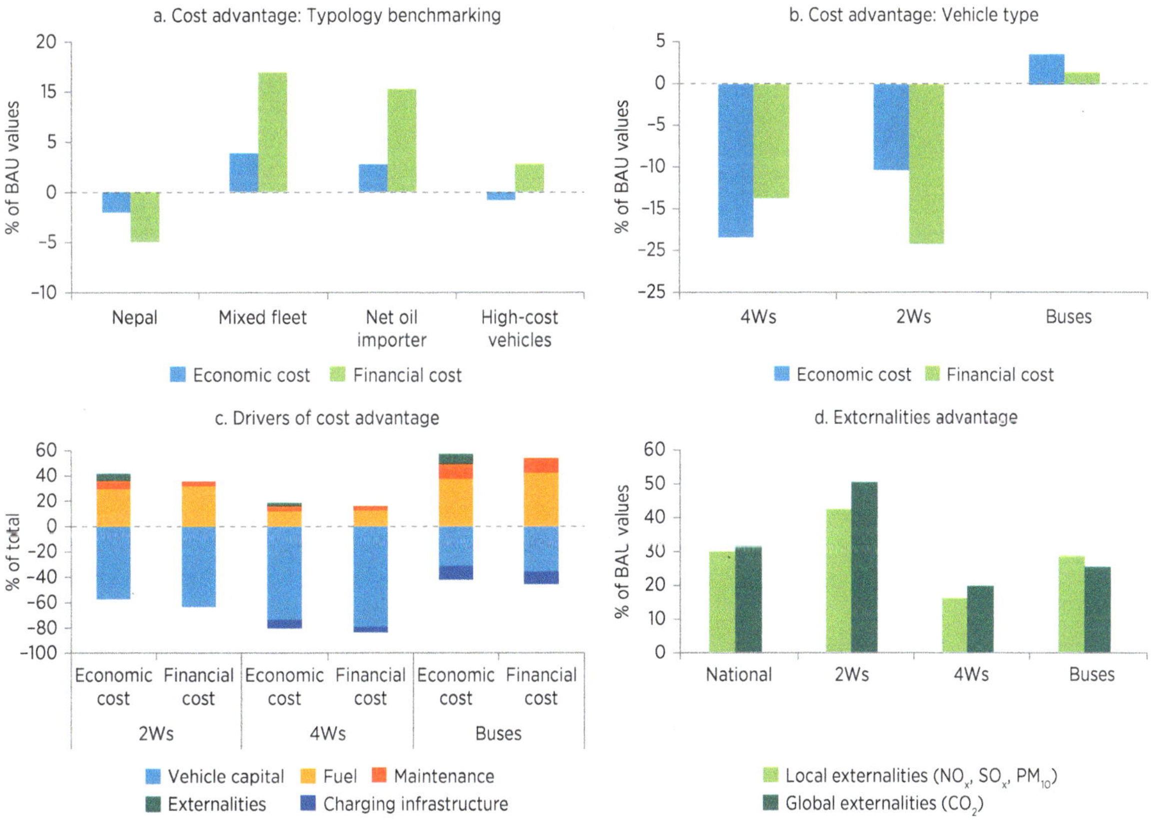

Source: World Bank.
Note: Data in this figure represent the "business as usual" (BAU) scenario minus the 30×30 scenario (averages over fleet additions). The BAU scenario assumes that no policy target will be imposed for electric vehicles and that vehicle purchase decisions will continue to reflect historical trends. The 30×30 scenario assumes that sales of electric cars and buses will reach 30 percent, and of two- and three-wheelers, 70 percent, by 2030. 2W = two-wheeler; 4W = four-wheeler; CO_2 = carbon dioxide; EV = electric vehicle; NO_x = nitrogen oxides; PM_{10} = particulate matter less than 10 microns in diameter; SO_x = sulfur oxides.

TABLE A.11.1 Cost advantage of accelerated EV adoption in Nepal, 2030

	US$/vehicle									% of BAU values	
	Charging infrastructure	Vehicle capital cost	Vehicle operating cost	Subtotal	Local externalities	Global externalities	Economic cost advantage	Net taxes and subsidies	Financial cost advantage	Cost advantage	Financial cost advantage including fiscal wedge
	(a)	(b)	(c)	(d) = (a + b + c)	(e)		(f) = (d + e)	(g)	(h) = (d + g)		
Mode											
2Ws	0	(694)	449	(245)	3	59	(183)	(344)	(589)	(10.3)	(19.3)
4Ws	(504)	(5,593)	1,276	(4,820)	1	170	(4,649)	(3,063)	(7,884)	(18.5)	(13.8)
Buses	(6,102)	(18,705)	29,789	4,981	637	3,848	9,467	681	5,663	3.6	1.4

Source: World Bank.
Note: Heading colors: blue = excluding taxes and subsidies, gray = fiscal wedge, green = including taxes and subsidies. 2W = two-wheeler; 4W = four-wheeler; "Local externalities" comprises local (NO_x, PM_{10}, SO_x) air pollution costs. "Global externalities" comprises global (CO_2) air pollution costs. CO_2 = carbon dioxide; NO_x = nitrogen oxides; PM_{10} = particulate matter less than 10 microns in diameter; SO_x = sulfur oxides. Red and parentheses indicate negative value.

FIGURE A.11.2 Investment and financing needs for EV adoption in Nepal, 2030

a. Breakdown of investment needs (US$739 million or 1.75% of GDP)

b. Investment needs potentially covered by carbon financing

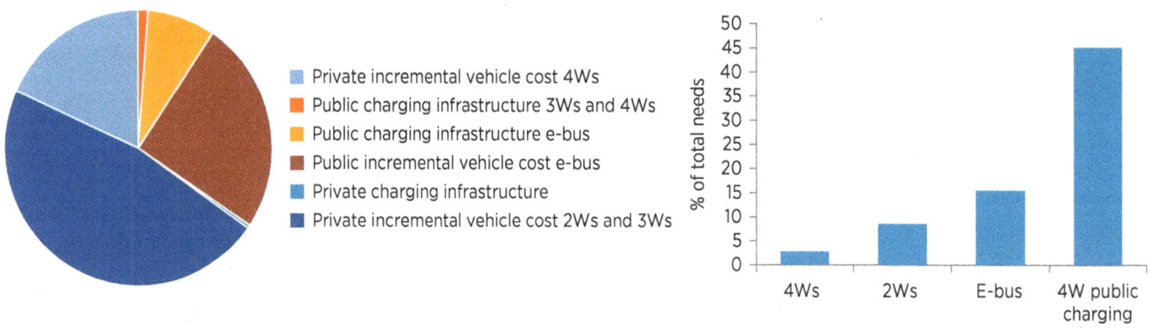

Source: World Bank.

Note: Data in this figure represent the "business as usual" (BAU) scenario minus the 30×30 scenario (averages over fleet additions). The BAU scenario assumes that no policy target will be imposed for electric vehicles and that vehicle purchase decisions will continue to reflect historical trends. The 30×30 scenario assumes that sales of electric cars and buses will reach 30 percent, and of two- and three-wheelers, 70 percent, by 2030. 2W = two-wheeler; 3W = three-wheeler; 4W = four-wheeler; EV = electric vehicle; GDP = gross domestic product.

TABLE A.11.2 Cost advantage of EV adoption in Nepal, by scenario, 2030

	National results				Bus only		4W only	
	30×30 scenario	Green grid scenario	Scarce minerals scenario	Fuel efficiency scenario	30×30 scenario	Efficient bus scenario	30×30 scenario	Taxi fleet scenario
	US$/Mpaxvkm				*US$/vehicle*			
Type of cost								
Vehicle capital cost	(39,111)	(39,111)	(46,449)	(39,111)	(18,705)	(4,970)	(5,593)	(5,593)
Vehicle maintenance cost	7,174	7,174	5,887	7,174	7,200	7,500	358	(742)
Vehicle fuel cost	25,545	25,545	25,545	21,012	22,589	38,680	919	3,674
Private charging infrastructure	(182)	(182)	(182)	(182)	n.a.	n.a.	(130)	(130)
Public charging infrastructure	(4,070)	(4,070)	(4,070)	(4,070)	(6,102)	(6,102)	(374)	(427)
Subtotal	(10,644)	(10,644)	(19,269)	(15,177)	4,981	35,107	(4,820)	(3,218)
Local externalities (NO_x, SO_x, PM_{10})	456	456	456	456	637	1,091	1	5
Global externalities (CO_2)	4,253	4,253	4,253	3,734	3,848	6,637	170	704
Economic cost advantage	(5,935)	(5,935)	(14,560)	(10,987)	9,467	42,835	(4,649)	(2,509)
Fiscal wedge	(13,928)	(13,928)	(22,303)	(15,420)	681	18,797	(3,063)	(1,367)
Financial cost advantage	(24,572)	(24,572)	(41,571)	(30,597)	5,663	53,905	(7,884)	(4,585)
Economic cost advantage, by type of vehicle	*US$/vehicle*							
4Ws	(4,649)	(4,649)	(5,684)	(4,982)	n.a.	n.a.	n.a.	n.a.
2Ws	(183)	(183)	(285)	(215)	n.a.	n.a.	n.a.	n.a.
E-buses	9,467	9,467	2,233	3,209	n.a.	n.a.	n.a.	n.a.

Source: World Bank.

Note: Data in this table represent the "business as usual" (BAU) scenario minus the named scenario (averages over fleet additions). The BAU scenario assumes that no policy target will be imposed for electric vehicles and that vehicle purchase decisions will continue to reflect historical trends. The 30×30 scenario assumes that sales of electric cars and buses will reach 30 percent, and of two- and three-wheelers, 70 percent, by 2030. The green grid scenario assumes that countries achieve certain region-specific targets for acceleration of renewable energy, as defined by the International Renewable Energy Agency (IRENA 2020). The scarce minerals scenario assumes that battery cost will decline by approximately 7 percent annually. The fuel efficiency scenario assumes that the rate of improvement of fuel efficiency for the internal combustion engine fleet will double from 15 percent to 30 percent. The efficient bus scenario assumes a capital cost reduction of 35 percent in the procurement of buses as well as optimized bus routes to increase the annual mileage of electric buses. The taxi fleet scenario assumes that the lifetime mileage of intensively used commercial vehicles will increase by four times in each country, that public investment in charging infrastructure will double the fast charger density for cars, and that the maintenance cost for cars will be doubled (assuming two lifetime battery replacements). Results have been normalized by new vehicles entering the market in 2030. The "fiscal wedge" comprises net taxes and subsidies. Red and parentheses indicate negative value. 2W = two-wheeler; 4W = four-wheeler; CO_2 = carbon dioxide; EV = electric vehicle; NO_x = nitrogen oxides; PM_{10} = particulate matter less than 10 microns in diameter; SO_x = sulfur oxides; US$/Mpaxvkm = US dollars per million passenger vehicle-kilometers; n.a.= not applicable.

TABLE A.11.3 Supporting information on parameters and results for EV adoption in Nepal

Price (US$/vehicle)

Parameter	Value
Price of ICE 4W	26,744
Price of EV 4W	84,356
Price of ICE 2W	1,250
Price of EV 2W	3,537
Price of ICE bus	145,423
Price of e-bus	270,647

Other parameters

Parameter	Value
Net tax difference on EV 4W (%)	0
Net tax difference on EV 2W (%)	0
Net tax difference on e-bus (%)	0
Price of gasoline (US$/liter)	0.60
Net gasoline tax (US$/liter)	0.43
Price of diesel (US$/liter)	0.74
Net diesel tax (US$/liter)	0.16
Price of electricity (US$/kWh)	0.08
Net electricity tax (US$/kWh)	0.02
Electricity carbon intensity (g/kWh)	0
Discount rate (%)	6.6

Key characteristics

Parameter	Value
4W mileage (km)	15,224
2W mileage (km)	7,627
Bus mileage (km)	35,040
4W lifetime (years)	20
2W lifetime (years)	10
Bus lifetime (years)	20
4W secondhand (%)	16.4
2W secondhand (%)	16.4
Bus secondhand (%)	0.0
4W share (% paxvkm)	9
2W share (% paxvkm)	44
Bus share (% paxvkm)	41

Efficiency (MJ/km)

Parameter	Value
Efficiency ICE 4W	2.12
Efficiency EV 4W	0.64
Efficiency ICE 2W	0.86
Efficiency EV 2W	0.20
Efficiency ICE bus	15.63
Efficiency EV bus	5.19

Other results for 30×30 scenario

Other results for 30×30 scenario	Value
Overall investment needs (US$, millions)	739
—of which 4W purchase	134
—of which 2W purchase	338
—of which e-bus purchase	185
Fiscal impact (US$, millions)	237
—of which vehicle duties	(198)
—of which vehicle taxes/subsidies	666
—of which gasoline taxes/subsidies	(195)
—of which diesel taxes/subsidies	(80)
—of which electricity taxes/subsidies	44
Implicit carbon price (US$/ton)	62
—of which for 4W	734
—of which for 2W	107
—of which for buses	(38)
Pollution reduction (tons)	3
—of which local (SO_x, NO_x, PM_{10})	0
—of which global (CO_2)	3
Affordability of EV 2W (Δ cost % GNI pc)	78.7
Affordability of EV 4W (Δ cost % GNI pc)	527.6

Source: World Bank.
Note: Red and parentheses indicates negative value. 2W = two-wheeler; 4W = four-wheeler; CO_2 = carbon dioxide; EV = electric vehicle; g = gram; GNI pc = gross national income per capita; ICE = internal combustion engine; kWh = kilowatt-hour; km = kilometer; MJ = megajoule; NO_x = nitrogen oxides; paxvkm = passenger vehicle-kilometer; PM_{10} = particulate matter less than 10 microns in diameter; SO_x = sulfur oxides.

Notes

1. Two-wheelers cover all motorized two-wheel vehicles registered.
2. Data from US Energy Information Administration international database and World Bank.

References

CEIC. 2020. "Nepal Number of Vehicles: Registered." CEIC Data, New York. https://www.ceicdata.com/en/nepal/motor-vehicles-registration/number-of-motor-vehicles-registered.

Government of Nepal. 2018. *Investment Projects for Electric Mobility: Accelerating Implementation of Nepal's Nationally Determined Contribution.* Kathmandu: Government of Nepal. https://gggi.org/wp-content/uploads/2020/02/GGGI_Nepal_Investment-Projects-for-Electric-Mobility_Final.pdf.

IRENA (International Renewable Energy Agency). 2020. *Global Renewables Outlook: Energy Transformation 2050.* Masdar City: IRENA.

Nepali Times. 2021. "New Nepal Budget Sparks Electric Comeback." *Nepali Times,* May 30, 2021. https://www.nepalitimes.com/latest/new-nepal-budget-sparks-electric-comeback/.

Shrestha, Shritu. 2018. *EV Readiness Assessment.* Berlin: UEMI Solutions. https://www.uemi.net/_files/ugd/de12cd_c0a6e24b27bd41a7aba2bb70b2557fe1.pdf.

A.12 PASSENGER ELECTRIC MOBILITY IN NIGERIA

Country Typology

Vehicle fleet composition:	Mixed fleet
Net oil trading status:	Exporter
Relative cost of vehicles:	High

Country Background

The vehicle fleet in Nigeria is quite mixed, though slightly over half is cars (51.8 percent), followed by buses (26.6 percent), and two-wheelers[1] (21.7 percent) (Nigeria National Bureau of Statistics 2020; OICA 2021). Electricity is primarily generated from gas (81.3 percent), with most of the remainder being hydro (18.5 percent).[2] There are no electric mobility policies and strategies developed for the country. The Public-Private Infrastructure Advisory Facility is supporting the country to develop an integrated electric mobility strategy and pilot models. The key components of that support include (1) development of an integrated e-mobility strategy, using renewable energy solutions; (2) design of a pilot integrated e-mobility model for using clean-powered electric public transportation (along bus rapid transit corridors) in the city of Lagos for subsequent replication in other parts of the country; (3) development of an integrated e-mobility strategy and plan for rural areas of Nigeria; and (4) assessment of market opportunities and investment barriers for private sector investment and operation of electric transportation services and charging infrastructure (PPIAF 2020). The government is receiving support from the United Nations Environment Programme's Climate Technology Centre and Network to assess the market readiness for electric vehicles, develop policy recommendations, create a business case for electric vehicle deployment and capacity building and an awareness program for stakeholders (CTCN 2020). Nigeria's first locally assembled electric car, the Hyundai Kona, was officially unveiled by the federal government through the National Automotive Design and Development Council in 2021 (Ajayi 2021). Additionally, the Council installed a fully solar-powered electric vehicle charging station in the country (Cable 2021).

Overall Messages

Despite having a relatively diversified fleet, Nigeria faces many conditions that are less favorable toward electric mobility, including relatively high-cost vehicles and energy-exporting status (figure A.12.1a). Although electrifying transportation looks to be economically favorable as a national strategy (table A.12.1), this favorability is driven entirely by private vehicles—particularly two-wheelers, which present a life-cycle cost advantage of as much as 15 percent (figure A.12.1b). Underlying these results are relatively low capital cost differentials for private electric vehicles of about 10 percent for four-wheelers and 30 percent for two-wheelers. Not only are these capital cost differentials low in absolute terms, but they are also relatively affordable for the population. An important reason for this is the fact that Nigeria relies heavily on imported secondhand vehicles. Thus, it is relevant to note that electric vehicles depreciate more rapidly than conventional ones, to a point at which they may be cheaper to buy on a secondhand basis. Electric buses, by contrast, remain marginally unattractive in economic terms, despite very low capital cost differentials of just 5 percent.

The externality benefits of electric mobility in Nigeria are relatively small (figure A.12.1, panels c and d), with fuel cost savings representing the main advantage associated with electric mobility. However, given a fiscal regime that, unusually, taxes electricity more heavily than either gasoline or diesel, these fuel cost savings are eroded, which is why the overall case for electric mobility in Nigeria looks better in economic than in financial terms (figure A.12.1a).

The total investment needs associated with the 30×30 scenario amount to US$438 million per year by 2030 (or 0.08 percent of Nigerian gross domestic product). About four-fifths of the required outlay is associated with the incremental public investment in electric buses and associated charging infrastructure (figure A.12.2a). Given that implicit carbon prices associated with electric two-wheelers and four-wheelers in Nigeria are strongly negative (table A.12.3), there is ample scope to cover incremental investment costs in private vehicles through carbon financing arrangements (figure A.12.2b). However, in the case of electric buses, the implicit carbon price exceeds US$100 per ton.

The overall positive economic case for electric mobility in Nigeria only improves when further action is taken to decarbonize the electricity sector ("green grid" scenario) and can also withstand a scenario in which internal combustion engine vehicles become more efficient ("fuel efficiency" scenario) (table A.12.2). However, the case for electric mobility is reversed under more conservative assumptions about the cost of batteries ("scarce minerals" scenario). On a positive note, the negative balance for electric buses can be turned positive through the more efficient procurement and operation of vehicles ("efficient bus" scenario), but the case for electric four-wheelers improves only in the case of intensively used commercial vehicles ("taxi fleet" scenario). Thus, electric mobility in Nigeria is likely to proceed with private vehicles, pending measures to make buses more efficient.

Figures and tables start on the next page.

Figures and Tables

FIGURE A.12.1 Advantage of EV adoption in Nigeria, by type of vehicle

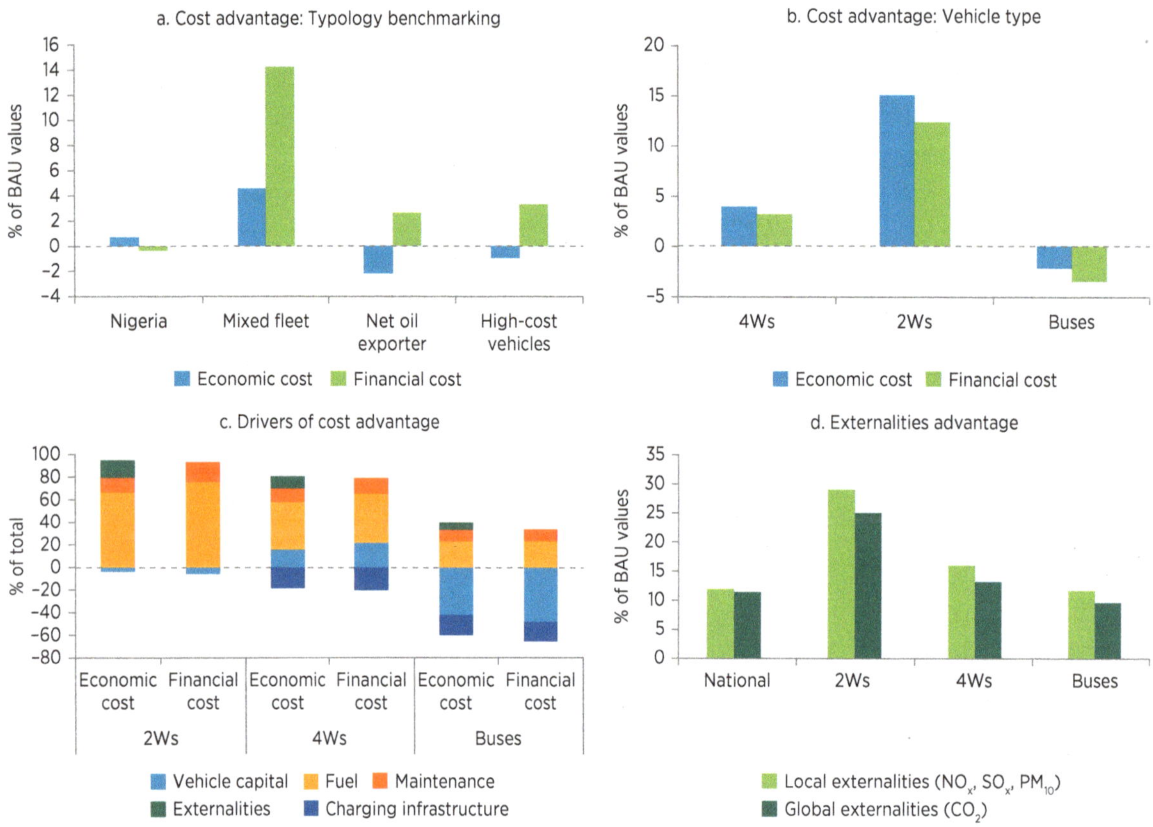

Source: World Bank.
Note: Data in this figure represent the "business as usual" (BAU) scenario minus the 30×30 scenario (averages over fleet additions). The BAU scenario assumes that no policy target will be imposed for electric vehicles and that vehicle purchase decisions will continue to reflect historical trends. The 30×30 scenario assumes that sales of electric cars and buses will reach 30 percent, and of two- and three-wheelers, 70 percent, by 2030. 2W = two-wheeler; 4W = four-wheeler; CO_2 = carbon dioxide; EV = electric vehicle; NO_x = nitrogen oxides; PM_{10} = particulate matter less than 10 microns in diameter; SO_x = sulfur oxides.

TABLE A.12.1 Cost advantage of accelerated EV adoption in Nigeria, 2030

	US$/vehicle									% of BAU values	
	Charging infrastructure	Vehicle capital cost	Vehicle operating cost	Subtotal	Local externalities	Global externalities	Economic cost advantage	Net taxes and subsidies	Financial cost advantage	Cost advantage	Financial cost advantage including fiscal wedge
	(a)	(b)	(c)	(d) = (a + b + c)	(e)		(f) = (d + e)	(g)	(h) = (d + g)		
Mode											
2Ws	0	(12)	254	243	5	42	290	(27)	216	15.0	12.3
4Ws	(342)	308	1,043	1,009	20	178	1,206	29	1,038	3.9	3.2
Buses	(2,668)	(6,418)	5,222	(3,863)	126	764	(2,973)	(938)	(4,801)	(2.2)	(3.5)

Source: World Bank.
Note: Heading colors: blue = excluding taxes and subsidies, gray = fiscal wedge, green = including taxes and subsidies. 2W = two-wheeler; 4W = four-wheeler; "Local externalities" comprises local (NO_x, PM_{10}, SO_x) air pollution costs. "Global externalities" comprises global (CO_2) air pollution costs. CO_2 = carbon dioxide; NO_x = nitrogen oxides; PM_{10} = particulate matter less than 10 microns in diameter; SO_x = sulfur oxides. Red and parentheses indicate negative value.

FIGURE A.12.2 Investment and financing needs for EV adoption in Nigeria, 2030

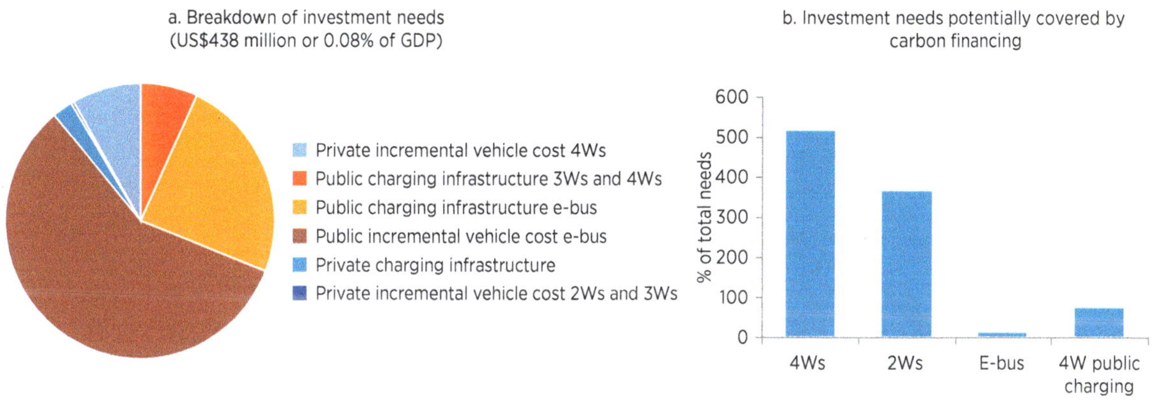

Source: World Bank.
Note: Data in this figure represent the "business as usual" (BAU) scenario minus the 30×30 scenario (averages over fleet additions). The BAU scenario assumes that no policy target will be imposed for electric vehicles and that vehicle purchase decisions will continue to reflect historical trends. The 30×30 scenario assumes that sales of electric cars and buses will reach 30 percent, and of two- and three-wheelers, 70 percent, by 2030. 2W = two-wheeler; 3W = three-wheeler; 4W = four-wheeler; EV = electric vehicle; GDP = gross domestic product.

TABLE A.12.2 Cost advantage of EV adoption in Nigeria, by scenario, 2030

	National results				Bus only		4W only	
	30×30 scenario	Green grid scenario	Scarce minerals scenario	Fuel efficiency scenario	30×30 scenario	Efficient bus scenario	30×30 scenario	Taxi fleet scenario
	US$/Mpaxvkm				US$/vehicle			
Type of cost								
Vehicle capital cost	(6,511)	(6,511)	(8,612)	(6,511)	(6,418)	(3,102)	308	308
Vehicle maintenance cost	2,888	2,888	905	2,888	1,613	2,051	233	(523)
Vehicle fuel cost	7,962	7,962	7,962	6,732	3,609	9,040	810	3,242
Private charging infrastructure	(311)	(311)	(311)	(311)	n.a.	n.a.	(89)	(89)
Public charging infrastructure	(4,018)	(4,018)	(4,018)	(4,018)	(2,668)	(2,668)	(253)	(289)
Subtotal	9	9	(4,074)	(1,222)	(3,863)	5,322	1,009	2,647
Local externalities (NO_x, SO_x, PM_{10})	240	261	240	228	126	317	20	79
Global externalities (CO_2)	1,695	1,874	1,695	1,552	764	1,919	178	712
Economic cost advantage	1,944	2,145	(2,139)	558	(2,973)	7,558	1,206	3,439
Fiscal wedge	(1,112)	(1,112)	(1,484)	(1,187)	(938)	(248)	29	(112)
Financial cost advantage	(1,103)	(1,103)	(5,559)	(2,409)	(4,801)	5,074	1,038	2,536
Economic cost advantage, by type of vehicle	US$/vehicle							
4Ws	1,206	1,226	1,018	995	n.a.	n.a.	n.a.	n.a.
2Ws	290	293	286	283	n.a.	n.a.	n.a.	n.a.
E-buses	(2,973)	(2,874)	(5,872)	(3,496)	n.a.	n.a.	n.a.	n.a.

Source: World Bank.
Note: Data in this table represent the "business as usual" (BAU) scenario minus the named scenario (averages over fleet additions). The BAU scenario assumes that no policy target will be imposed for electric vehicles and that vehicle purchase decisions will continue to reflect historical trends. The 30×30 scenario assumes that sales of electric cars and buses will reach 30 percent, and of two- and three-wheelers, 70 percent, by 2030. The green grid scenario assumes that countries achieve certain region-specific targets for acceleration of renewable energy, as defined by the International Renewable Energy Agency (IRENA 2020). The scarce minerals scenario assumes that battery cost will decline by approximately 7 percent annually. The fuel efficiency scenario assumes that the rate of improvement of fuel efficiency for the internal combustion engine fleet will double from 15 percent to 30 percent. The efficient bus scenario assumes a capital cost reduction of 35 percent in the procurement of buses as well as optimized bus routes to increase the annual mileage of electric buses. The taxi fleet scenario assumes that the lifetime mileage of intensively used commercial vehicles will increase by four times in each country, that public investment in charging infrastructure will double the fast charger density for cars, and that the maintenance cost for cars will be doubled (assuming two lifetime battery replacements). Results have been normalized by new vehicles entering the market in 2030. The "fiscal wedge" comprises net taxes and subsidies. Red and parentheses indicate negative value. 2W = two-wheeler; 4W = four-wheeler; CO_2 = carbon dioxide; EV = electric vehicle; NO_x = nitrogen oxides; PM_{10} = particulate matter less than 10 microns in diameter; SO_x = sulfur oxides; US$/Mpaxvkm = US dollars per million passenger vehicle-kilometers; n.a.= not applicable.

TABLE A.12.3 Supporting information on parameters and results for EV adoption in Nigeria

Price (US$/vehicle)

Parameter	Value
Price of ICE 4W	29,885
Price of EV 4W	32,730
Price of ICE 2W	1,038
Price of EV 2W	1,372
Price of ICE bus	137,037
Price of e-bus	145,473

Other parameters

Parameter	Value
Net tax difference on EV 4W (%)	0
Net tax difference on EV 2W (%)	0
Net tax difference on e-bus (%)	0
Price of gasoline (US$/liter)	0.58
Net gasoline tax (US$/liter)	(0.00)
Price of diesel (US$/liter)	0.73
Net diesel tax (US$/liter)	0.06
Price of electricity (US$/kWh)	0.12
Net electricity tax (US$/kWh)	0.02
Electricity carbon intensity (g/kWh)	215
Discount rate (%)	6.6

Key characteristics

Parameter	Value
4W mileage (km)	17,000
2W mileage (km)	7,000
Bus mileage (km)	29,940
4W lifetime (years)	22
2W lifetime (years)	17
Bus lifetime (years)	20
4W secondhand (%)	97.9
2W secondhand (%)	97.9
Bus secondhand (%)	95.7
4W share (% paxvkm)	24
2W share (% paxvkm)	6
Bus share (% paxvkm)	70

Efficiency (MJ/km)

Parameter	Value
Efficiency ICE 4W	3.08
Efficiency EV 4W	0.34
Efficiency ICE 2W	1.13
Efficiency EV 2W	0.25
Efficiency ICE bus	10.86
Efficiency EV bus	3.70

Other results for 30×30 scenario

Other results for 30×30 scenario	Value
Overall investment needs (US$, millions)	438
—of which 4W purchase	(43)
—of which 2W purchase	2
—of which e-bus purchase	305
Fiscal impact (US$, millions)	45
—of which vehicle duties	20
—of which vehicle taxes/subsidies	20
—of which gasoline taxes/subsidies	1
—of which diesel taxes/subsidies	(50)
—of which electricity taxes/subsidies	55
Implicit carbon price (US$/ton)	(4)
—of which for 4W	(150)
—of which for 2W	(153)
—of which for buses	127
Pollution reduction (tons)	3
—of which local (SO_x, NO_x, PM_{10})	0
—of which global (CO_2)	3
Affordability of EV 2W (Δ cost % GNI pc)	0.5
Affordability of EV 4W (Δ cost % GNI pc)	(13.8)

Source: World Bank.

Note: Red and parentheses indicates negative value. 2W = two-wheeler; 4W = four-wheeler; CO_2 = carbon dioxide; EV = electric vehicle; g = gram; GNI pc = gross national income per capita; ICE = internal combustion engine; kWh = kilowatt-hour; km = kilometer; MJ = megajoule; NO_x = nitrogen oxides; paxvkm = passenger vehicle-kilometer; PM_{10} = particulate matter less than 10 microns in diameter; SO_x = sulfur oxides.

Notes

1. Two-wheelers cover all motorized two-wheel vehicles registered.
2. Data from US Energy Information Administration international database and World Bank.

References

Ajayi, Omokolade. 2021. "NADDC Moves to Unveil Nigeria's First Electric Vehicle." *Nairametrics*, February 5, 2021. https://nairametrics.com/2021/02/05/naddc-moves-to-unveil-nigerias-first-electric-vehicle/.

Cable. 2021. "Nigeria Launches First Solar-Powered Charging Station for Electric Vehicles." *The Cable*, April 9, 2021. https://www.thecable.ng/nigeria-launches-first-solar-powered-charging-station-for-electric-vehicles.

CTCN (UN Climate Technology Centre & Network). 2020. "Developing a National eMobility Policy and Framework for Deploying and Scaling Up e-Mobility in Nigeria." CTCN, Copenhagen, Denmark. https://www.ctc-n.org/technical-assistance/projects/developing-national-emobility-policy-and-framework-deploying-and.

IRENA (International Renewable Energy Agency). 2020. *Global Renewables Outlook: Energy Transformation 2050*. Masdar City: IRENA.

Nigeria National Bureau of Statistics. 2020. *Road Transport Data (Q4 2018)*. Abuja, Nigeria: National Bureau of Statistics.

OICA (Organisation Internationale des Constructeurs d'Automobiles [International Organization of Motor Vehicle Manufacturers]). 2021. "Global Sales Statistics, 2019–2021." OICA, Paris. https://www.oica.net/global-sales-statistics-2019-2021/.

PPIAF (Public–Private Infrastructure Advisory Facility). 2020. "Nigeria: Sustainable Green e-Mobility Solutions." PPIAF, World Bank Group, Washington, DC. https://ppiaf.org/activity/nigeria-sustainable-green-e-mobility-solutions-0.

A.13 PASSENGER ELECTRIC MOBILITY IN POLAND

Country Typology

Vehicle fleet composition:	Car dominant
Net oil trading status:	Importer
Relative cost of vehicles:	Low

Country Background

The dominant vehicle type in Poland is cars (91.5 percent), followed by two-wheelers (7.5 percent),[1] and buses (1.0 percent) (Statistics Poland 2021). Electricity is primarily generated from fossil fuels (86.5 percent), notably coal (81.3 percent). When it comes to renewable energy, the main sources are wind (7.8 percent) and biomass and waste (4.3 percent).[2] The Polish national government has adopted a variety of policies to drive the electrification of its vehicle fleet (Wappelhorst and Pniewska 2020) with a target to deploy 600,000 electric vehicles by 2030 ("Sustainable Transport Development Strategy until 2030") that also includes a strategy for electric vehicle and charging infrastructure deployment. The strategy is complemented by various incentive schemes such as (1) the "Green Car" scheme to incentivize private individuals and support the purchase of a new battery electric vehicle; (2) the "eVAN" incentive scheme to provide one-time incentives for businesses purchasing or leasing zero-emission delivery vans; and (3) the "Koliber" incentive scheme to support the purchase or lease of an electric car, benefiting micro, small, and medium businesses. Poland has also instituted an electric vehicle registration tax benefit and electric vehicle usage tax benefits. About 20,181 electric cars were registered at the end 2020, of which 48.3 percent were battery powered and 51.7 percent were hybrid electric (FirstNews 2021). The domestic manufacturing market is set to start production of electric vehicles in 2024 (Randall 2020). Moreover, the draft Energy Policy of Poland until 2040 has set a target to increase its existing share of renewables to 21 percent by 2030. Offshore wind firms are expected to play a major role in reaching that target (Poland Ministry of Energy 2018).

Overall Messages

Poland enjoys several conditions favorable toward electric mobility, such as oil-importing status and relatively low-cost vehicles, but these are largely offset by the country's almost exclusive reliance on cars for transportation (figure A.13.1a). Only in the very minor two-wheel segment of the fleet is the economic balance favorable to electric mobility, with a life-cycle cost advantage exceeding 10 percent (table A.13.1). Nevertheless, strongly supportive government policy means that electric mobility is financially advantageous across all types of vehicles (figure A.13.1b). Indeed, tax differentials in favor of the purchase of electric vehicles are as high as 23 percent for buses, 46 percent for four-wheelers, and 106 percent for two-wheelers (table A.13.3).

The externality benefits of electric mobility in Poland are quite modest (figure A.13.1c), except in the case of electric buses, which bring sizable local externality benefits (figure A.13.1d). Otherwise, fuel cost savings are the main advantage associated with electric mobility in Poland. Given a fiscal regime that taxes gasoline and diesel three to four times as heavily as electricity, these fuel cost savings are further accentuated in financial terms, which is another reason why the overall case for electric mobility in Poland looks better in financial than in economic terms (figure A.13.1a).

The total investment needs associated with the 30×30 scenario amount to US$2.2 billion per year by 2030 (or 0.3 percent of Polish gross domestic product). About two-thirds of the required outlay is associated with the incremental capital of private four-wheel vehicles (figure A.13.2a). In terms of public investment, the most significant item is the provision of public charging infrastructure for private vehicles (figure A.13.2a). Given that implicit carbon prices associated with electric two-wheelers in Poland are highly negative (table A.13.3), there is significant scope to cover 30 percent of the incremental capital costs through carbon financing arrangements (figure A.13.2b). However, for four-wheel electric vehicles, the implicit carbon price exceeds US$1,000 per ton.

The overall negative economic case for electric mobility in Poland certainly does not improve under more conservative assumptions about the cost of batteries ("scarce minerals" scenario) and the fuel efficiency of internal combustion engines ("fuel efficiency" scenario), nor under further decarbonization of the power sector ("green grid" scenario) (table A.13.2). On a positive note, the negative balance for electric buses can be very substantially reversed through the adoption of more efficient procurement and operation of vehicles ("efficient bus" scenario). However, there is no real case for electrification of four-wheelers even when it comes to taxi fleets and other intensively used vehicles ("taxi fleet" scenario). Although electrification of two-wheelers in Poland is attractive, their limited role in the vehicle fleet suggests that a more important priority is to focus on improving the efficiency of electric buses, particularly in view of the significant externality benefits they bring.

Figures and tables start on the next page.

Figures and Tables

FIGURE A.13.1 Advantage of EV adoption in Poland, by type of vehicle

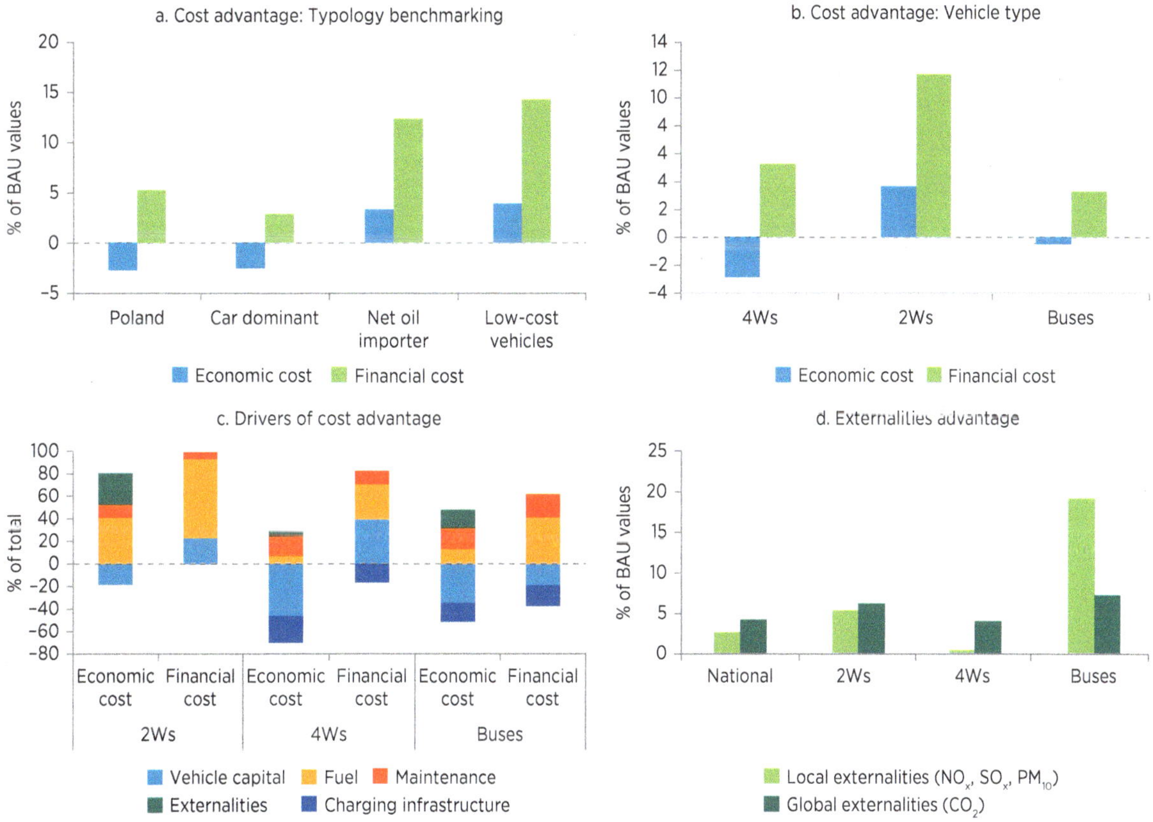

Source: World Bank.
Note: Data in this figure represent the "business as usual" (BAU) scenario minus the 30×30 scenario (averages over fleet additions). The BAU scenario assumes that no policy target will be imposed for electric vehicles and that vehicle purchase decisions will continue to reflect historical trends. The 30×30 scenario assumes that sales of electric cars and buses will reach 30 percent, and of two- and three-wheelers, 70 percent, by 2030. 2W = two-wheeler; 4W = four-wheeler; CO_2 = carbon dioxide; EV = electric vehicle; NO_x = nitrogen oxides; PM_{10} = particulate matter less than 10 microns in diameter; SO_x = sulfur oxides.

TABLE A.13.1 Cost advantage of accelerated EV adoption in Poland, 2030

	US$/vehicle									% of BAU values	
	Charging infrastructure	Vehicle capital cost	Vehicle operating cost	Subtotal	Local externalities	Global externalities	Economic cost advantage	Net taxes and subsidies	Financial cost advantage	Cost advantage	Financial cost advantage including fiscal wedge
	(a)	(b)	(c)	(d) = (a + b + c)	(e)		(f) = (d + e)	(g)	(h) = (d + g)		
Mode											
2Ws	0	(29)	82	53	34	9	96	263	316	3.7	11.8
4Ws	(460)	(886)	470	(876)	63	20	(793)	2,725	1,848	(2.9)	5.3
Buses	(5,911)	(12,412)	11,529	(6,794)	5,156	500	(1,138)	15,011	8,217	(0.5)	3.3

Source: World Bank.
Note: Heading colors: blue = excluding taxes and subsidies, gray = fiscal wedge, green = including taxes and subsidies. 2W = two-wheeler; 4W = four-wheeler; "Local externalities" comprises local (NO_x, PM_{10}, SO_x) air pollution costs. "Global externalities" comprises global (CO_2) air pollution costs. CO_2 = carbon dioxide; NO_x = nitrogen oxides; PM_{10} = particulate matter less than 10 microns in diameter; SO_x = sulfur oxides. Red and parentheses indicate negative value.

FIGURE A.13.2 Investment and financing needs for EV adoption in Poland, 2030

a. Breakdown of investment needs (US$2,26 million or 0.31% of GDP)

b. Investment needs potentially covered by carbon financing

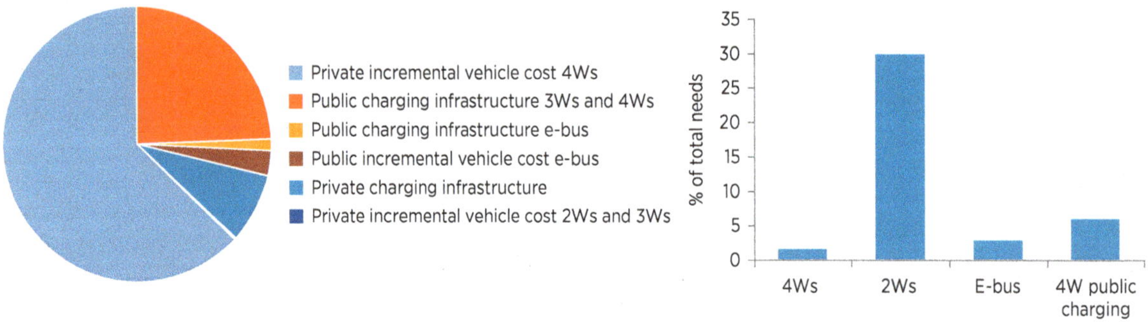

Source: World Bank.

Note: Data in this figure represent the "business as usual" (BAU) scenario minus the 30×30 scenario (averages over fleet additions). The BAU scenario assumes that no policy target will be imposed for electric vehicles and that vehicle purchase decisions will continue to reflect historical trends. The 30×30 scenario assumes that sales of electric cars and buses will reach 30 percent, and of two- and three-wheelers, 70 percent, by 2030. 2W = two-wheeler; 3W = three-wheeler; 4W = four-wheeler; EV = electric vehicle; GDP = gross domestic product.

TABLE A.13.2 Cost advantage of EV adoption in Poland, by scenario, 2030

	National results				Bus only		4W only	
	30×30 scenario	Green grid scenario	Scarce minerals scenario	Fuel efficiency scenario	30×30 scenario	Efficient bus scenario	30×30 scenario	Taxi fleet scenario
	US$/Mpaxvkm				*US$/vehicle*			
Type of cost								
Vehicle capital cost	(26,712)	(26,712)	(41,506)	(26,712)	(12,412)	742	(886)	(886)
Vehicle maintenance cost	10,379	10,379	10,170	10,379	6,888	7,196	337	(651)
Vehicle fuel cost	4,460	4,460	4,460	636	4,641	19,555	134	534
Private charging infrastructure	(3,338)	(3,338)	(3,338)	(3,338)	n.a.	n.a.	(116)	(116)
Public charging infrastructure	(10,435)	(10,435)	(10,435)	(10,435)	(5,911)	(5,911)	(344)	(391)
Subtotal	(25,646)	(25,646)	(40,649)	(29,470)	(6,794)	21,582	(876)	(1,511)
Local externalities (NO_x, SO_x, PM_{10})	2,408	5,832	2,408	1,880	5,156	21,965	63	351
Global externalities (CO_2)	652	1,024	652	174	500	2,307	20	101
Economic cost advantage	(22,586)	(18,790)	(37,589)	(27,415)	(1,138)	45,854	(793)	(1,059)
Fiscal wedge	80,405	80,405	79,980	75,252	15,011	43,903	2,725	4,951
Financial cost advantage	54,759	54,759	39,331	45,782	8,217	65,485	1,848	3,440
Economic cost advantage, by type of vehicle	*US$/vehicle*							
4Ws	(793)	(668)	(1,291)	(952)	n.a.	n.a.	n.a.	n.a.
2Ws	96	131	86	86	n.a.	n.a.	n.a.	n.a.
E-buses	(1,138)	(2)	(8,130)	(3,582)	n.a.	n.a.	n.a.	n.a.

Source: World Bank.

Note: Data in this table represent the "business as usual" (BAU) scenario minus the named scenario (averages over fleet additions). The BAU scenario assumes that no policy target will be imposed for electric vehicles and that vehicle purchase decisions will continue to reflect historical trends. The 30×30 scenario assumes that sales of electric cars and buses will reach 30 percent, and of two- and three-wheelers, 70 percent, by 2030. The green grid scenario assumes that countries achieve certain region-specific targets for acceleration of renewable energy, as defined by the International Renewable Energy Agency (IRENA 2020). The scarce minerals scenario assumes that battery cost will decline by approximately 7 percent annually. The fuel efficiency scenario assumes that the rate of improvement of fuel efficiency for the internal combustion engine fleet will double from 15 percent to 30 percent. The efficient bus scenario assumes a capital cost reduction of 35 percent in the procurement of buses as well as optimized bus routes to increase the annual mileage of electric buses. The taxi fleet scenario assumes that the lifetime mileage of intensively used commercial vehicles will increase by four times in each country, that public investment in charging infrastructure will double the fast charger density for cars, and that the maintenance cost for cars will be doubled (assuming two lifetime battery replacements). Results have been normalized by new vehicles entering the market in 2030. The "fiscal wedge" comprises net taxes and subsidies. Red and parentheses indicate negative value. 2W = two-wheeler; 4W = four-wheeler; CO_2 = carbon dioxide; EV = electric vehicle; NO_x = nitrogen oxides; PM_{10} = particulate matter less than 10 microns in diameter; SO_x = sulfur oxides; US$/Mpaxvkm = US dollars per million passenger vehicle-kilometers; n.a.= not applicable.

TABLE A.13.3 **Supporting information on parameters and results for EV adoption in Poland**

Price (US$/vehicle)

Parameter	Value
Price of ICE 4W	26,080
Price of EV 4W	18,599
Price of ICE 2W	890
Price of EV 2W	174
Price of ICE bus	116,312
Price of e-bus	135,324

Other parameters

Parameter	Value
Net tax difference on EV 4W (%)	46
Net tax difference on EV 2W (%)	106
Net tax difference on e-bus (%)	23
Price of gasoline (US$/liter)	0.58
Net gasoline tax (US$/liter)	0.81
Price of diesel (US$/liter)	0.73
Net diesel tax (US$/liter)	0.67
Price of electricity (US$/kWh)	0.13
Net electricity tax (US$/kWh)	0.04
Electricity carbon intensity (g/kWh)	546
Discount rate (%)	6.6

Key characteristics

Parameter	Value
4W mileage (km)	8,029
2W mileage (km)	7,627
Bus mileage (km)	17,799
4W lifetime (years)	22
2W lifetime (years)	17
Bus lifetime (years)	20
4W secondhand (%)	62.0
2W secondhand (%)	0.0
Bus secondhand (%)	10.7
4W share (% paxvkm)	92
2W share (% paxvkm)	4
Bus share (% paxvkm)	3

Efficiency (MJ/km)

Parameter	Value
Efficiency ICE 4W	2.13
Efficiency EV 4W	0.58
Efficiency ICE 2W	1.08
Efficiency EV 2W	0.25
Efficiency ICE bus	11.53
Efficiency EV bus	3.91

Other results for 30×30 scenario

Other results for 30×30 scenario	Value
Overall investment needs (US$, millions)	2,226
—of which 4W purchase	1,399
—of which 2W purchase	5
—of which e-bus purchase	65
Fiscal impact (US$, millions)	(4,422)
—of which vehicle duties	(61)
—of which vehicle taxes/subsidies	(3,117)
—of which gasoline taxes/subsidies	(1,457)
—of which diesel taxes/subsidies	(79)
—of which electricity taxes/subsidies	292
Implicit carbon price (US$/ton)	921
—of which for 4W	1,041
—of which for 2W	(263)
—of which for buses	85
Pollution reduction (tons)	1
—of which local (SO_x, NO_x, PM_{10})	0
—of which global (CO_2)	1
Affordability of EV 2W (Δ cost % GNI pc)	(0.4)
Affordability of EV 4W (Δ cost % GNI pc)	(5.6)

Source: World Bank.
Note: Red and parentheses indicates negative value. 2W = two-wheeler; 4W = four-wheeler; CO_2 = carbon dioxide; EV = electric vehicle; g = gram; GNI pc = gross national income per capita; ICE = internal combustion engine; kWh = kilowatt-hour; km = kilometer; MJ = megajoule; NO_x = nitrogen oxides; paxvkm = passenger vehicle-kilometer; PM_{10} = particulate matter less than 10 microns in diameter; SO_x = sulfur oxides.

Notes

1. Two-wheelers cover all motorized two-wheel vehicles registered.
2. Data from US Energy Information Administration international database and World Bank.

References

FirstNews. 2021. "Popularity of Electric Cars in Poland Continues to Grow." *TheFirstNews*, January 14, 2021. https://www.thefirstnews.com/article/popularity-of-electric-cars-in-poland-continues-to-grow-19060.

IRENA (International Renewable Energy Agency). 2020. *Global Renewables Outlook: Energy Transformation 2050*. Masdar City: IRENA.

Poland Ministry of Energy. 2018. "Energy Policy of Poland until 2040." Draft, Ministry of Energy, Warsaw.

Randall, Chris. 2020. "Poland's First Electric Car Factory to Be Built in Jaworzno." Electrive.com, December 21, 2020. https://www.electrive.com/2020/12/21/polands-first-electric-car-factory-is-being-built-in-jaworzno/.

Statistics Poland. 2021. *Road Transport in Poland in the Years 2018 and 2019*. Warsaw: Statistics Poland. https://stat.gov.pl/en/topics/transport-and-communications/transport/road-transport-in-poland-in-the-years-2018-and-2019,5,6.htm.l

Wappelhorst, Sandra, and Izabela Pniewska. 2020. "Emerging Electric Passenger Car Markets in Europe: Can Poland Lead the Way?" Working Paper 2020-19, International Council on Clean Transportation, Washington, DC.

A.14 PASSENGER ELECTRIC MOBILITY IN RWANDA

Country Typology

Vehicle fleet composition:	Mixed fleet
Net oil trading status:	Importer
Relative cost of vehicles:	High

Country Background

The vehicle fleet in Rwanda is quite mixed. The leading share goes to two-wheelers (46.6 percent),[1] followed by cars (29.4 percent), and buses (23.9 percent) (NISR 2019). In 2018, electricity was generated almost equally from renewable sources (53.4 percent), primarily hydro (45.6 percent), and from fossil fuels (46.6 percent). The government has recently approved a very aggressive electric mobility strategy (Mwai 2021) that includes preferential electricity tariffs for charging stations (at industrial tariff level); exemptions in import and excise duties on electric vehicles, spare parts, batteries, and charging station equipment; and rent-free land for charging stations for land owned by the government. In addition, companies manufacturing and assembling electric vehicles will see a reduced 15 percent corporate income tax and a tax holiday; and there will be ease of market entry by providing free license and authorization for commercial electric vehicles. Several locally operated firms are already successfully rolling out electric motorbikes. In partnership with Siemens and the government of Rwanda, the car manufacturing company Volkswagen introduced a fleet of four electric cars and one charging station in Kigali in October 2019. The fleet has since expanded to 20 electric cars and an additional charging station (Venter 2021). The International Finance Corporation is supporting an "Electric Bus Concept Validation in Kigali" study, and the World Bank is supporting a "Rwanda: Inclusive and Electric Last Mile Connectivity Study" in Rwanda.[2] Rwanda's Energy Sector Strategic Plan (2017/18–2023/24) set a target of increasing the renewable share in the power generation mix to 52 percent by 2024 (Rwanda, Ministry of Infrastructure 2018), which has already been exceeded, and further benefit will be derived from accelerating electric mobility adoption.

Overall Messages

Rwanda faces many conditions that are favorable toward electric mobility, including net oil-importing status and a relatively diversified vehicle fleet; however, they are somewhat offset by relatively high-cost vehicles (figure A.14.1a). Electrification of transportation is only marginally economical as a national strategy (table A.14.1). Nevertheless, there is a strong case for adoption of electrification of two-wheelers, which represent close to half of the fleet (figure A.14.1b), because they carry a life-cycle cost advantage approaching 10 percent (and over 20 percent in financial terms). In addition, the 30 percent capital cost differential associated with electric two-wheelers looks relatively affordable, representing no more than 1 percent of gross national income per capita (table A.14.3). By contrast, the economic case for electric four-wheelers is only marginally positive, and for electric buses it is marginally negative—despite minimal differences in purchase prices due to a sizable 28 percent tax advantage for electric mobility.

The externality benefits of electric mobility in Rwanda are relatively small (figure A.14.1c), except for the global externality savings associated with electric buses, which are quite sizable (figure A.14.1d). Otherwise, fuel cost savings are the main advantage associated with electric mobility in Rwanda, primarily due to a fiscal regime that taxes gasoline and diesel at 60–90 percent, while subsidizing electricity at 25 percent. Combining the fiscal incentives for vehicle purchase with those affecting operating costs means that electric mobility in Rwanda is much more attractive in financial than in economic terms (figure A.14.1a).

The total investment needs associated with the 30×30 scenario amount to US$20 million per year by 2030 (or 0.1 percent of Rwandese gross domestic product). About half of the required outlay is associated with the incremental capital cost of electric buses, and the remainder relates to public investment in charging infrastructure (figure A.14.2a). Given that the implicit carbon price associated with electric two-wheelers is strongly negative (table A.14.3), there is significant scope to cover as much as 90 percent of the incremental capital cost through carbon financing arrangements (figure A.14.2b). However, for electric buses, the implicit carbon price is almost US$70 per ton.

The overall economic case for electric mobility in Rwanda is quite marginal (table A.14.2). Although it improves somewhat under further decarbonization of the power sector ("green grid" scenario), it is not robust to more conservative assumptions about the cost of batteries ("scarce minerals" scenario) or the improved fuel efficiency of internal combustion engines ("fuel efficiency" scenario). On a positive note, the negative economic balance for electrification of buses can be reversed through the more efficient procurement and operation of vehicles ("efficient bus" scenario). However, there is no real case for electrification of four-wheelers even when it comes to taxi fleets and other intensively used vehicles ("taxi fleet" scenario). It is clear that electric mobility in Rwanda needs to prioritize the two-wheel segment of the fleet, while working to improve the efficiency of electric buses.

Figures and tables start on the next page.

Figures and Tables

FIGURE A.14.1 Advantage of EV adoption in Rwanda, by type of vehicle

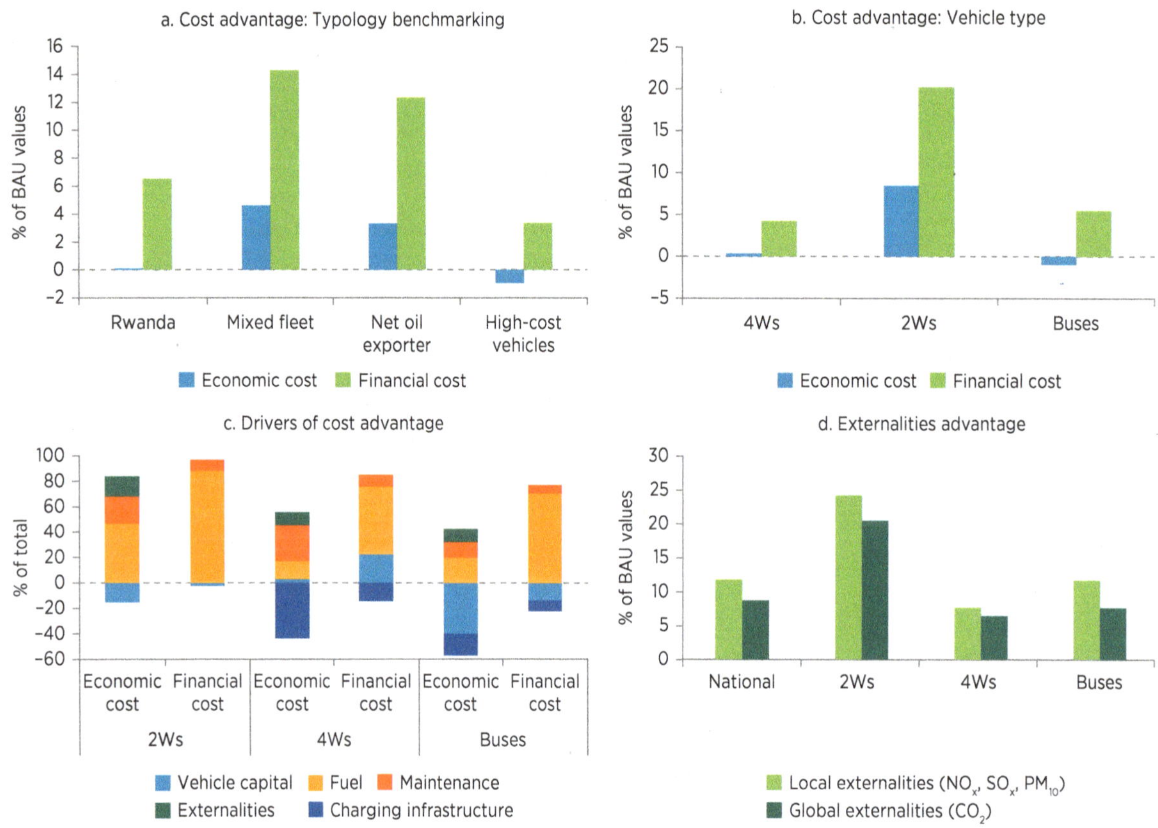

Source: World Bank.

Note: Data in this figure represent the "business as usual" (BAU) scenario minus the 30×30 scenario (averages over fleet additions). The BAU scenario assumes that no policy target will be imposed for electric vehicles and that vehicle purchase decisions will continue to reflect historical trends. The 30×30 scenario assumes that sales of electric cars and buses will reach 30 percent, and of two- and three-wheelers, 70 percent, by 2030. 2W = two-wheeler; 4W = four-wheeler; CO_2 = carbon dioxide; EV = electric vehicle; NO_x = nitrogen oxides; PM_{10} = particulate matter less than 10 microns in diameter; SO_x = sulfur oxides.

TABLE A.14.1 Cost advantage of accelerated EV adoption in Rwanda, 2030

	US$/vehicle									% of BAU values	
	Charging infrastructure	Vehicle capital cost	Vehicle operating cost	Subtotal	Local externalities	Global externalities	Economic cost advantage	Net taxes and subsidies	Financial cost advantage	Cost advantage	Financial cost advantage including fiscal wedge
	(a)	(b)	(c)	(d) = (a + b + c)	(e)		(f) = (d + e)	(g)	(h) = (d + g)		
Mode											
2Ws	0	(32)	148	115	3	30	149	425	540	8.5	20.4
4Ws	(249)	18	246	15	4	55	74	1,268	1,283	0.3	4.3
Buses	(3,054)	(7,116)	5,825	(4,346)	259	1,531	(2,556)	24,523	20,178	(1.0)	5.5

Source: World Bank.

Note: Heading colors: blue = excluding taxes and subsidies, gray = fiscal wedge, green = including taxes and subsidies. 2W = two-wheeler; 4W = four-wheeler; "Local externalities" comprises local (NO_x, PM_{10}, SO_x) air pollution costs. "Global externalities" comprises global (CO_2) air pollution costs. CO_2 = carbon dioxide; NO_x = nitrogen oxides; PM_{10} = particulate matter less than 10 microns in diameter; SO_x = sulfur oxides. Red and parentheses indicate negative value.

FIGURE A.14.2 Investment and financing needs for EV adoption in Rwanda, 2030

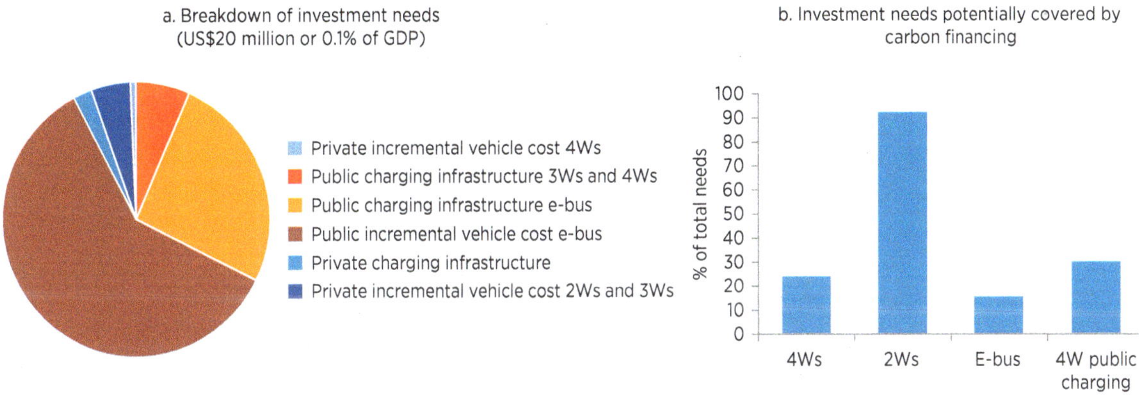

Source: World Bank.
Note: Data in this figure represent the "business as usual" (BAU) scenario minus the 30×30 scenario (averages over fleet additions). The BAU scenario assumes that no policy target will be imposed for electric vehicles and that vehicle purchase decisions will continue to reflect historical trends. The 30×30 scenario assumes that sales of electric cars and buses will reach 30 percent, and of two- and three-wheelers, 70 percent, by 2030. 2W = two-wheeler; 3W = three-wheeler; 4W = four-wheeler; EV = electric vehicle; GDP = gross domestic product.

TABLE A.14.2 Cost advantage of EV adoption in Rwanda, by scenario, 2030

	National results				Bus only		4W only	
	30×30 scenario	Green grid scenario	Scarce minerals scenario	Fuel efficiency scenario	30×30 scenario	Efficient bus scenario	30×30 scenario	Taxi fleet scenario
	US$/Mpaxvkm				US$/vehicle			
Type of cost								
Vehicle capital cost	(5,112)	(5,112)	(6,701)	(5,112)	(7,116)	(2,628)	18	18
Vehicle maintenance cost	2,523	2,523	1,348	2,523	2,242	2,664	163	(389)
Vehicle fuel cost	3,833	3,833	3,833	2,290	3,583	4,470	83	330
Private charging infrastructure	(185)	(185)	(185)	(185)	n.a.	n.a.	(65)	(65)
Public charging infrastructure	(2,577)	(2,577)	(2,577)	(2,577)	(3,054)	(3,054)	(184)	(211)
Subtotal	(1,518)	(1,518)	(4,282)	(3,061)	(4,346)	1,452	15	(317)
Local externalities (NO_x, SO_x, PM_{10})	225	411	225	218	259	323	4	15
Global externalities (CO_2)	1,535	1,886	1,535	1,359	1,531	1,913	55	222
Economic cost advantage	243	779	(2,522)	(1,484)	(2,556)	3,688	74	(79)
Fiscal wedge	25,110	25,110	25,110	24,073	24,523	30,064	1,268	3,910
Financial cost advantage	23,592	23,592	20,828	21,012	20,178	31,516	1,283	3,594
Economic cost advantage, by type of vehicle	US$/vehicle							
4Ws	74	97	(63)	2	n.a.	n.a.	n.a.	n.a.
2Ws	149	155	140	140	n.a.	n.a.	n.a.	n.a.
E-buses	(2,556)	(1,961)	(5,942)	(4,672)	n.a.	n.a.	n.a.	n.a.

Source: World Bank.
Note: Data in this table represent the "business as usual" (BAU) scenario minus the named scenario (averages over fleet additions). The BAU scenario assumes that no policy target will be imposed for electric vehicles and that vehicle purchase decisions will continue to reflect historical trends. The 30×30 scenario assumes that sales of electric cars and buses will reach 30 percent, and of two- and three-wheelers, 70 percent, by 2030. The green grid scenario assumes that countries achieve certain region-specific targets for acceleration of renewable energy, as defined by the International Renewable Energy Agency (IRENA 2020). The scarce minerals scenario assumes that battery cost will decline by approximately 7 percent annually. The fuel efficiency scenario assumes that the rate of improvement of fuel efficiency for the internal combustion engine fleet will double from 15 percent to 30 percent. The efficient bus scenario assumes a capital cost reduction of 35 percent in the procurement of buses as well as optimized bus routes to increase the annual mileage of electric buses. The taxi fleet scenario assumes that the lifetime mileage of intensively used commercial vehicles will increase by four times in each country, that public investment in charging infrastructure will double the fast charger density for cars, and that the maintenance cost for cars will be doubled (assuming two lifetime battery replacements). Results have been normalized by new vehicles entering the market in 2030. The "fiscal wedge" comprises net taxes and subsidies. Red and parentheses indicate negative value. 2W = two-wheeler; 4W = four-wheeler; CO_2 = carbon dioxide; EV = electric vehicle; NO_x = nitrogen oxides; PM_{10} = particulate matter less than 10 microns in diameter; SO_x = sulfur oxides; US$/Mpaxvkm = US dollars per million passenger vehicle-kilometers; n.a.= not applicable.

TABLE A.14.3 Supporting information on parameters and results for EV adoption in Rwanda

Price (US$/vehicle)

Parameter	Value
Price of ICE 4W	31,202
Price of EV 4W	31,005
Price of ICE 2W	1,060
Price of EV 2W	1,300
Price of ICE bus	137,108
Price of e-bus	135,324

Other parameters

Parameter	Value
Net tax difference on EV 4W (%)	28
Net tax difference on EV 2W (%)	28
Net tax difference on e-bus (%)	28
Price of gasoline (US$/liter)	0.58
Net gasoline tax (US$/liter)	0.53
Price of diesel (US$/liter)	0.73
Net diesel tax (US$/liter)	0.47
Price of electricity (US$/kWh)	0.19
Net electricity tax (US$/kWh)	(0.05)
Electricity carbon intensity (g/kWh)	441
Discount rate (%)	6.6

Key characteristics

Parameter	Value
4W mileage (km)	15,224
2W mileage (km)	7,627
Bus mileage (km)	48,092
4W lifetime (years)	22
2W lifetime (years)	17
Bus lifetime (years)	20
4W secondhand (%)	96.4
2W secondhand (%)	96.4
Bus secondhand (%)	87.6
4W share (% paxvkm)	17
2W share (% paxvkm)	18
Bus share (% paxvkm)	65

Efficiency (MJ/km)

Parameter	Value
Efficiency ICE 4W	2.34
Efficiency EV 4W	0.28
Efficiency ICE 2W	0.89
Efficiency EV 2W	0.20
Efficiency ICE bus	16.92
Efficiency EV bus	5.44

Other results for 30×30 scenario

Other results for 30×30 scenario	Value
Overall investment needs (US$, millions)	20
—of which 4W purchase	(0.1)
—of which 2W purchase	1
—of which e-bus purchase	12
Fiscal impact (US$, millions)	(64)
—of which vehicle duties	(2)
—of which vehicle taxes/subsidies	(5)
—of which gasoline taxes/subsidies	(13)
—of which diesel taxes/subsidies	(30)
—of which electricity taxes/subsidies	(14)
Implicit carbon price (US$/ton)	22
—of which for 4W	(9)
—of which for 2W	(104)
—of which for buses	69
Pollution reduction (tons)	0
—of which local (SO_x, NO_x, PM_{10})	0
—of which global (CO_2)	0
Affordability of EV 2W (Δ cost % GNI pc)	0.9
Affordability of EV 4W (Δ cost % GNI pc)	(29.7)

Source: World Bank.
Note: Red and parentheses indicates negative value. 2W = two-wheeler; 4W = four-wheeler; CO_2 = carbon dioxide; EV = electric vehicle; g = gram; GNI pc = gross national income per capita; ICE = internal combustion engine; kWh = kilowatt-hour; km = kilometer; MJ = megajoule; NO_x = nitrogen oxides; paxvkm = passenger vehicle-kilometer; PM_{10} = particulate matter less than 10 microns in diameter; SO_x = sulfur oxides.

Notes

1. Two-wheelers cover all motorized two-wheel vehicles registered.
2. From the World Bank Group.

References

IRENA (International Renewable Energy Agency). 2020. *Global Renewables Outlook: Energy Transformation 2050*. Masdar City: IRENA.

Mwai, Collins. 2021. "Rwanda Unveils New Incentives to Drive Electric Vehicle Uptake." *New Times*, April 16, 2021. https://www.newtimes.co.rw/article/185379/News/rwanda-unveils-new-incentives-to-drive-electric-vehicle-uptake.

NISR (National Institute of Statistics of Rwanda). 2019. *Rwanda Statistical Yearbook 2019*. Kigali: Republic of Rwanda.

Rwanda, *Ministry* of Infrastructure. 2018. Energy Sector Strategic Plan 2018/19–2023/24. Kigali: Republic of Rwanda.

Venter, Irma. 2021. "Volkswagen Mobility Solutions Rwanda (VWMSR) Has Unveiled Its Second Charging Station for Electric Vehicles (EVs) in the Capital of Rwanda." Engineering News, April 15, 2021. https://www.engineeringnews.co.za/article/volkswagen-rwanda-unveils-second-charging-station-for-electric-vehicles-2021-04-15.

A.15 PASSENGER ELECTRIC MOBILITY IN TAJIKISTAN

Country Typology

Vehicle fleet composition: Car dominant
Net oil trading status: Importer
Relative cost of vehicles: Low

Country Background

The transportation system in Tajikistan is dominated by cars (OICA 2020). Electricity is primarily generated from renewable sources of energy, notably hydropower (93.5 percent), with the balance coming from coal (6.5 percent).[1] The country has yet to develop an electric vehicle road map and policy incentives to foster electric vehicle adoption (Grütter and Kim 2019). Tajikistan will need specific policy incentives to address the issues of high up-front cost, limited charging infrastructure, and lack of awareness (Development Asia 2019). The power sector in Tajikistan is highly subsidized. As a result, electricity tariffs are low, leading to excessive usage of electricity and other inefficiencies (UNECE 2017). Recently, the government approved exemptions on value added tax and import duties for electric vehicles, for a limited allowance of 100 units of passenger electric vehicles during 2020.[2] With international support, the government is gradually implementing some electric mobility projects in the country. The European Bank for Reconstruction and Development has provided an investment grant for the introduction of an electric off-wire electric trolleybus for a 15-kilometer route (Leeder et al. 2021).

Overall Messages

Unusually for a car-dominated country, Tajikistan presents quite favorable conditions for electric mobility, particularly because of the very low cost of vehicles, as well as the country's status as an oil importer (figure A.15.1a). Electrification of transportation looks to be economically viable overall (table A.15.1) because of the fact that electric four-wheel vehicles are already *cheaper* (and thus more affordable) to purchase than their conventional counterparts (table A.15.3), offering modest life-cycle cost advantages of almost 3 percent (figure A.15.1b). Electric buses, by contrast, still cost about twice as much to purchase as diesel buses (table A.15.3), with life-cycle cost advantages closer to 2 percent (figure A.15.1b).

The externality benefits of electric mobility in Tajikistan are relatively modest for four-wheelers, but quite substantial for buses (figures A.15.1c and A.15.1d). Otherwise, fuel cost savings are the main advantage associated with electric mobility. Given a fiscal regime that taxes gasoline and diesel by 20–40 percent, while subsidizing electricity by 80 percent, these fuel cost savings are further accentuated in financial terms (figure A.15.1c). This makes the overall case for electric mobility in Tajikistan much better in financial than in economic terms (figure A.15.1a).

The total investment needs associated with the 30×30 scenario amount to US$3.2 million per year by 2030 (or 0.03 percent of Tajik gross domestic product). Close to half of the investment relates to the incremental capital cost of vehicles and charging infrastructure incurred by the private sector, and much of the remainder is public investment in public infrastructure charging stations (figure A.15.2a). Given that implicit carbon prices associated with electric four-wheelers in Tajikistan are strongly negative (table A.15.3), there is significant scope to cover 60–80 percent of the incremental private and public investments associated with electric four-wheelers through carbon financing arrangements (figure A.15.2b).

The overall economic case for electric mobility in Tajikistan is favorable (table A.15.2). This finding is robust to more conservative assumptions about the cost of batteries ("scarce minerals" scenario) and the fuel efficiency of internal combustion engines ("fuel efficiency" scenario), and only improves with further decarbonization of the power sector ("green grid" scenario). On a positive note, the emerging advantage associated with electrification of buses can be as much as doubled through the more efficient procurement and operation of vehicles ("efficient bus" scenario), and the case for electric four-wheelers is greatly strengthened when it comes to taxi fleets and other intensively used vehicles ("taxi fleet" scenario). Tajikistan is unusual in that the case for electric mobility is primarily driven by four-wheelers, with potential for electric buses to also play a role.

Figures and tables start on the next page.

Figures and Tables

FIGURE A.15.1 Advantage of EV adoption in Tajikistan, by type of vehicle

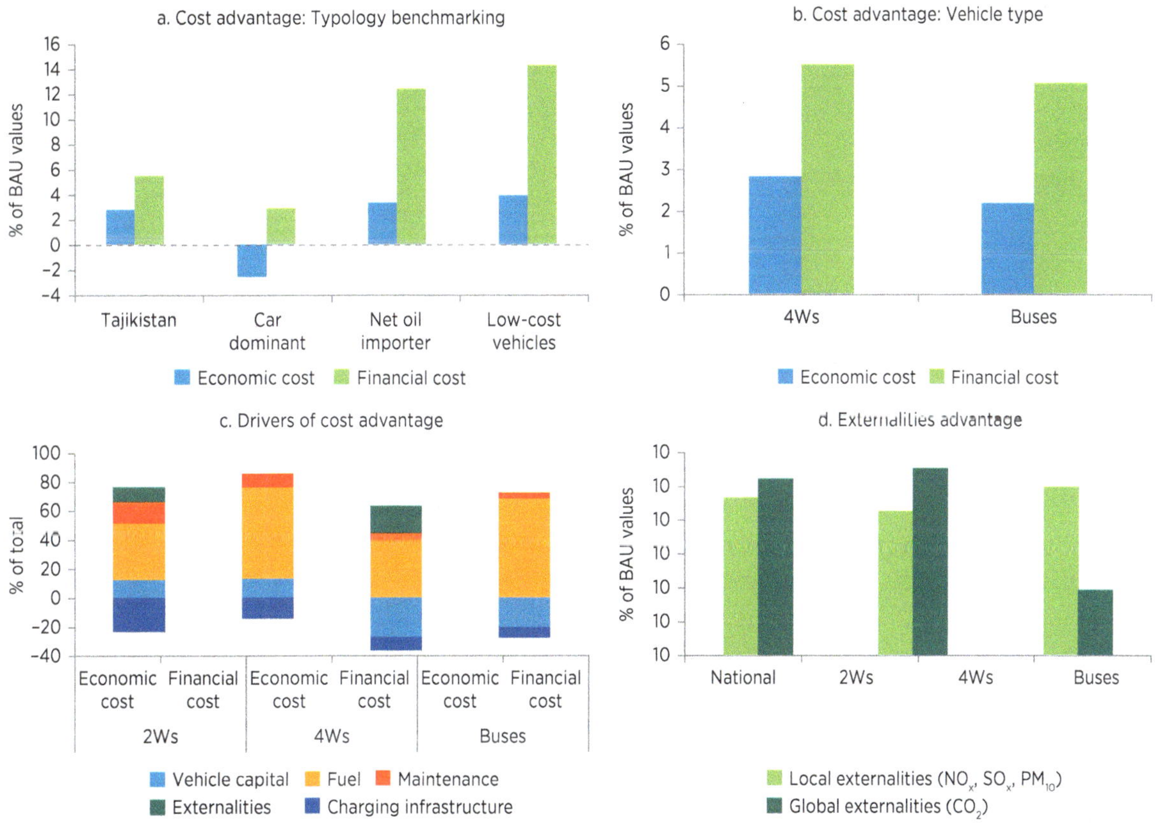

Source: World Bank.
Note: Data in this figure represent the "business as usual" (BAU) scenario minus the 30×30 scenario (averages over fleet additions). The BAU scenario assumes that no policy target will be imposed for electric vehicles and that vehicle purchase decisions will continue to reflect historical trends. The 30×30 scenario assumes that sales of electric cars and buses will reach 30 percent, and of two- and three-wheelers, 70 percent, by 2030. 2W = two-wheeler; 4W = four-wheeler; CO_2 = carbon dioxide; EV = electric vehicle; NO_x = nitrogen oxides; PM_{10} = particulate matter less than 10 microns in diameter; SO_x = sulfur oxides.

TABLE A.15.1 Cost advantage of accelerated EV adoption in Tajikistan, 2030

	US$/vehicle									% of BAU values	
	Charging infrastructure	Vehicle capital cost	Vehicle operating cost	Subtotal	Local externalities	Global externalities	Economic cost advantage	Net taxes and subsidies	Financial cost advantage	Cost advantage	Financial cost advantage including fiscal wedge
	(a)	(b)	(c)	(d) = (a + b + c)	(e)		(f) = (d + e)	(g)	(h) = (d + g)		
Mode											
4Ws	(221)	115	505	399	3	92	494	677	1,077	2.8	5.5
Buses	(2,098)	(6,226)	10,114	1,790	2,206	1,987	5,983	11,437	13,227	2.2	5.1

Source: World Bank.
Note: Heading colors: blue = excluding taxes and subsidies, gray = fiscal wedge, green = including taxes and subsidies. 2W = two-wheeler; 4W = four-wheeler; "Local externalities" comprises local (NO_x, PM_{10}, SO_x) air pollution costs. "Global externalities" comprises global (CO_2) air pollution costs. CO_2 = carbon dioxide; NO_x = nitrogen oxides; PM_{10} = particulate matter less than 10 microns in diameter; SO_x = sulfur oxides. Red and parentheses indicate negative value.

FIGURE A.15.2 Investment and financing needs for EV adoption in Tajikistan, 2030

a. Breakdown of investment needs (US$3.2 million or 0.03% of GDP)

b. Investment needs potentially covered by carbon financing

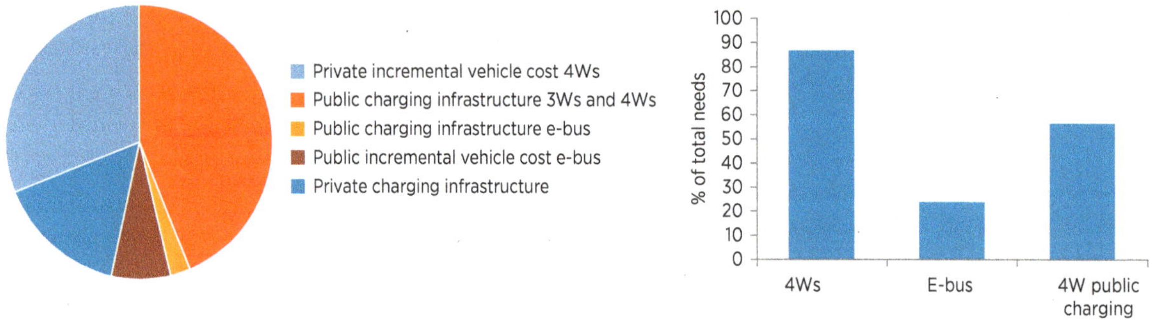

Source: World Bank.

Note: Data in this figure represent the "business as usual" (BAU) scenario minus the 30×30 scenario (averages over fleet additions). The BAU scenario assumes that no policy target will be imposed for electric vehicles and that vehicle purchase decisions will continue to reflect historical trends. The 30×30 scenario assumes that sales of electric cars and buses will reach 30 percent, and of two- and three-wheelers, 70 percent, by 2030. 2W = two-wheeler; 3W = three-wheeler; 4W = four-wheeler; EV = electric vehicle; GDP = gross domestic product.

TABLE A.15.2 Cost advantage of EV adoption in Tajikistan, by scenario, 2030

	National results				Bus only		4W only	
	30×30 scenario	Green grid scenario	Scarce minerals scenario	Fuel efficiency scenario	30×30 scenario	Efficient bus scenario	30×30 scenario	Taxi fleet scenario
	US$/Mpaxvkm				*US$/vehicle*			
Type of cost								
Vehicle capital cost	1,351	1,351	818	1,351	(6,226)	(3,860)	115	115
Vehicle maintenance cost	2,228	2,228	2,136	2,228	1,145	1,517	140	(353)
Vehicle fuel cost	6,209	6,209	6,209	5,540	8,969	11,190	365	1,461
Private charging infrastructure	(892)	(892)	(892)	(892)	n.a.	n.a.	(58)	(58)
Public charging infrastructure	(2,638)	(2,638)	(2,638)	(2,638)	(2,098)	(2,098)	(163)	(186)
Subtotal	6,258	6,258	5,633	5,589	1,790	6,749	399	979
Local externalities (NO_x, SO_x, PM_{10})	192	192	192	190	2,206	2,752	3	12
Global externalities (CO_2)	1,542	1,542	1,542	1,462	1,987	2,480	92	367
Economic cost advantage	7,991	7,991	7,366	7,240	5,983	11,980	494	1,358
Fiscal wedge	11,174	11,174	11,174	10,987	11,437	14,245	677	2,459
Financial cost advantage	17,431	17,431	16,807	16,576	13,227	20,994	1,077	3,438
Economic cost advantage, by type of vehicle	*US$/vehicle*							
4Ws	494	494	463	449	n.a.	n.a.	n.a.	n.a.
2Ws	5,983	5,983	3,727	5,115	n.a.	n.a.	n.a.	n.a.

Source: World Bank.

Note: Data in this table represent the "business as usual" (BAU) scenario minus the named scenario (averages over fleet additions). The BAU scenario assumes that no policy target will be imposed for electric vehicles and that vehicle purchase decisions will continue to reflect historical trends. The 30×30 scenario assumes that sales of electric cars and buses will reach 30 percent, and of two- and three-wheelers, 70 percent, by 2030. The green grid scenario assumes that countries achieve certain region-specific targets for acceleration of renewable energy, as defined by the International Renewable Energy Agency (IRENA 2020). The scarce minerals scenario assumes that battery cost will decline by approximately 7 percent annually. The fuel efficiency scenario assumes that the rate of improvement of fuel efficiency for the internal combustion engine fleet will double from 15 percent to 30 percent. The efficient bus scenario assumes a capital cost reduction of 35 percent in the procurement of buses as well as optimized bus routes to increase the annual mileage of electric buses. The taxi fleet scenario assumes that the lifetime mileage of intensively used commercial vehicles will increase by four times in each country, that public investment in charging infrastructure will double the fast charger density for cars, and that the maintenance cost for cars will be doubled (assuming two lifetime battery replacements). Results have been normalized by new vehicles entering the market in 2030. The "fiscal wedge" comprises net taxes and subsidies. Red and parentheses indicate negative value. 2W = two-wheeler; 4W = four-wheeler; CO_2 = carbon dioxide; EV = electric vehicle; NO_x = nitrogen oxides; PM_{10} = particulate matter less than 10 microns in diameter; SO_x = sulfur oxides; US$/Mpaxvkm = US dollars per million passenger vehicle-kilometers; n.a.= not applicable.

TABLE A.15.3 Supporting information on parameters and results for EV adoption in Tajikistan

Price (US$/vehicle)

Parameter	Value
Price of ICE 4W	14,975
Price of EV 4W	13,966
Price of ICE 2W	486
Price of EV 2W	586
Price of ICE bus	67,994
Price of e-bus	135,324

Other parameters

Parameter	Value
Net tax difference on EV 4W (%)	18
Net tax difference on EV 2W (%)	18
Net tax difference on e-bus (%)	18
Price of gasoline (US$/liter)	0.58
Net gasoline tax (US$/liter)	0.22
Price of diesel (US$/liter)	0.73
Net diesel tax (US$/liter)	0.13
Price of electricity (US$/kWh)	0.11
Net electricity tax (US$/kWh)	(0.09)
Electricity carbon intensity (g/kWh)	65
Discount rate (%)	6.6

Key characteristics

Parameter	Value
4W mileage (km)	15,224
2W mileage (km)	7,627
Bus mileage (km)	48,092
4W lifetime (years)	22
2W lifetime (years)	17
Bus lifetime (years)	20
4W secondhand (%)	99.8
2W secondhand (%)	99.8
Bus secondhand (%)	98.2
4W share (% paxvkm)	94
2W share (% paxvkm)	0
Bus share (% paxvkm)	6

Efficiency (MJ/km)

Parameter	Value
Efficiency ICE 4W	2.50
Efficiency EV 4W	0.26
Efficiency ICE 2W	0.89
Efficiency EV 2W	0.20
Efficiency ICE bus	18.11
Efficiency EV bus	6.24

Other results for 30×30 scenario

Other results for 30×30 scenario	Value
Overall investment needs (US$, millions)	3.2
—of which 4W purchase	(3)
—of which 2W purchase	0
—of which e-bus purchase	1
Fiscal impact (US$, millions)	(17)
—of which vehicle duties	(0.5)
—of which vehicle taxes/subsidies	(1)
—of which gasoline taxes/subsidies	(3)
—of which diesel taxes/subsidies	(2)
—of which electricity taxes/subsidies	(9)
Implicit carbon price (US$/ton)	(108)
—of which for 4W	(113)
—of which for 2W	n.a.
—of which for buses	(52)
Pollution reduction (tons)	0
—of which local (SO_x, NO_x, PM_{10})	0
—of which global (CO_2)	0
Affordability of EV 2W (Δ cost % GNI pc)	n.a.
Affordability of EV 4W (Δ cost % GNI pc)	(12.9)

Source: World Bank.
Note: Red and parentheses indicates negative value. 2W = two-wheeler; 4W = four-wheeler; CO_2 = carbon dioxide; EV = electric vehicle; g = gram; GNI pc = gross national income per capita; ICE = internal combustion engine; kWh = kilowatt-hour; km = kilometer; MJ = megajoule; NO_x = nitrogen oxides; paxvkm = passenger vehicle-kilometer; PM_{10} = particulate matter less than 10 microns in diameter; SO_x = sulfur oxides.

Notes

1. Data from US Energy Information Administration international database and World Bank.
2. "Order of the Government of the Republic of Tajikistan of June 25, 2020, No. 393." https://cis-legislation.com/document.fwx?rgn=126129.

References

Development Asia. 2019. "Insight: How Electric Vehicles Can Make Tajikistan Emissions-Free." Insight, December 12, 2019. https://development.asia/insight/how-electric-vehicles-can-make-tajikistan-emissions-free.

Grütter, Jürg M., and Ki-Joon Kim. 2019. "E-Mobility Options for ADB Developing Member Countries." ADB Sustainable Development Working Paper Series 60, Asian Development Bank, Manila. http://dx.doi.org/10.22617/WPS190075-2.

IRENA (International Renewable Energy Agency). 2020. *Global Renewables Outlook: Energy Transformation 2050.* Masdar City: IRENA.

Leeder, David, Alok Jain, Ian Jennings, Xiaolu Wang, and Kjetil Tvedt. 2021. "Going Electric: A Pathway to Zero-Emission Buses." Policy paper, European Bank for Reconstruction and Development, London.

OICA (Organisation Internationale des Constructeurs d'Automobiles [International Organization of Motor Vehicle Manufacturers]). 2020. "Global Sales Statistics, 2019–2021." OICA, Paris. https://www.oica.net/global-sales-statistics-2019-2021/.

UNECE (United Nations Economic Commission for Europe). 2017. *Tajikistan: Environmental Performance Reviews; Third Review.* Environmental Performance Reviews Series 45. New York and Geneva: United Nations. https://unece.org/environment-policy/publications/3rd-environmental-performance-review-tajikistan.

A.16 PASSENGER ELECTRIC MOBILITY IN TÜRKIYE

Country Typology

Vehicle fleet composition: Car dominant
Net oil trading status: Importer
Relative cost of vehicles: High

Country Background

The dominant vehicle type in Türkiye is cars (80.3 percent), followed by buses (13.4 percent), and two-wheelers[1] (6.3 percent) (OICA 2020; Turkish Statistical Institute 2020). Electricity is primarily generated from fossil fuels (66.7 percent), including gas (37.3 percent) and coal (28.6 percent), and to a lesser extent from renewable sources (33.3 percent), notably hydro (20.5 percent) and wind (6.8 percent).[2] The national policies and plans related to electric vehicle uptake include an automotive support program to improve domestic production capabilities in sensors, batteries, fuel cells, and software; development of a workforce capable of adapting digitalization and technological development; development of national production and research and development activities in the automotive industries; establishment of effective infrastructure for vehicles with alternative power systems; increased investment in the battery sector for electrical automotive production; and the increased use of domestically manufactured electrical buses in urban and suburban transportation (Presidency of Strategy and Budget, Presidency of Republic of Turkey 2020). From the power sector perspective, the electric vehicle strategy includes the adoption of cost-based pricing practices in the electricity and natural gas markets; introduction of nuclear-based power plants in the country; reduction in imported sources of electricity generation; integration of renewable energy generation facilities into the grid; and reducing the use of natural gas in electricity generation and increasing the use of renewable sources from 33 percent to 39 percent by 2023. A series of incentives were introduced (Saygin et al. 2019): reductions in Special Consumption Tax rates were introduced in 2016 for electric vehicles with electric engine power of greater than 50 kilowatts (and cylinder volume greater than 1,800 square centimeters) and greater than 100 kilowatts (and cylinder volume greater than 2,500 square centimeters), from 90 percent to 45 percent and from 145 percent to 90 percent, respectively. According to the Turkish Statistical Institute, the number of electric vehicles registered in Türkiye reached 15,000 in 2019 (TRTWorld 2021). The domestic electric vehicle manufacturing industries are growing in Türkiye. A factory in Gemlik that has an annual capacity of 175,000 units launched production in 2022 (Wikipedia 2023). The domestic car project named Automotive Joint Venture Group (TOGG), which is a joint venture between Anadolu Group, BMC, Kök Group, Turkcell, Zorlu Holding, and TOBB, kick-started in 2019 (TRTWorld 2021).

Overall Messages

Türkiye faces many conditions that are less favorable toward electric mobility, including a car-dominated fleet and relatively high-cost vehicles, notwithstanding oil-importing status (figure A.16.1a). Although electrification of transportation does not yet look economically favorable as a national strategy (table A.16.2), this is largely driven by the fact that the electrification of four-wheel vehicles is not attractive under current conditions, given significant (and unaffordable capital) cost differentials (table A.16.1). By contrast, there is a strong case for adoption of two-wheel electric motorbikes (figure A.16.1b), which present a life-cycle cost advantage of about 7 percent (or 17 percent in financial terms). However, the percentage capital cost differential for electric two-wheelers is relatively high at over 40 percent and represents almost 3 percent of gross national income per capita, suggesting an affordability barrier in the absence of finance. Furthermore, electric buses also offer modest economic advantages on the order of 4 percent of life-cycle cost and are only 20 percent more expensive in capital cost terms. Across all vehicle categories, the fiscal regime offers a 21 percent reduced tax incentive for the purchase of electric vehicles.

The externality benefits of electric mobility in Türkiye are relatively small (figure A.16.1c), except for local externalities associated with buses that are very large (figure A.16.1d). Otherwise, fuel cost savings are the main advantage associated with electric mobility in Türkiye, further accentuated in financial terms by a fiscal regime that taxes gasoline and diesel at 50–100 percent. Thus, the overall case for electric mobility in Türkiye looks better in financial than in economic terms (figure A.16.1a).

The total investment needs associated with the 30×30 scenario amount to US$3.4 billion per year by 2030 (or 0.3 percent of Turkish gross domestic product). About two-thirds of the required outlay is associated with the incremental capital cost of four-wheel electric vehicles (figure A.16.2a). In terms of public investment, the most significant items are the additional capital cost associated with electric buses, as well as the provision of public charging infrastructure for private vehicles (figure A.16.2a). Implicit carbon prices associated with electric two-wheelers and buses in Türkiye are negative, but that price exceeds US$4,000 for four-wheelers (table A.16.3). As a result, there is little scope to cover investment needs through carbon financing arrangements (figure A.16.2b).

The overall economic case for electric mobility in Türkiye is negative, and this does not change even with further decarbonization of the power grid ("green grid" scenario), let alone under more conservative assumptions about the cost of batteries ("scarce minerals" scenario) and the fuel efficiency of internal combustion engines ("fuel efficiency" scenario). On a positive note, the emerging advantage associated with electrification of buses can be hugely increased through the more efficient procurement and operation of vehicles ("efficient bus" scenario). However, there is no real case for electrification of four-wheelers, even when it comes to taxi fleets and other intensively used vehicles ("taxi fleet" scenario). It is clear that electric mobility in Türkiye needs to prioritize the two-wheel segment of the fleet and work to further enhance the advantages of electric buses.

Figures and tables start on the next page.

Figures and Tables

FIGURE A.16.1 Advantage of EV adoption in Türkiye, by type of vehicle

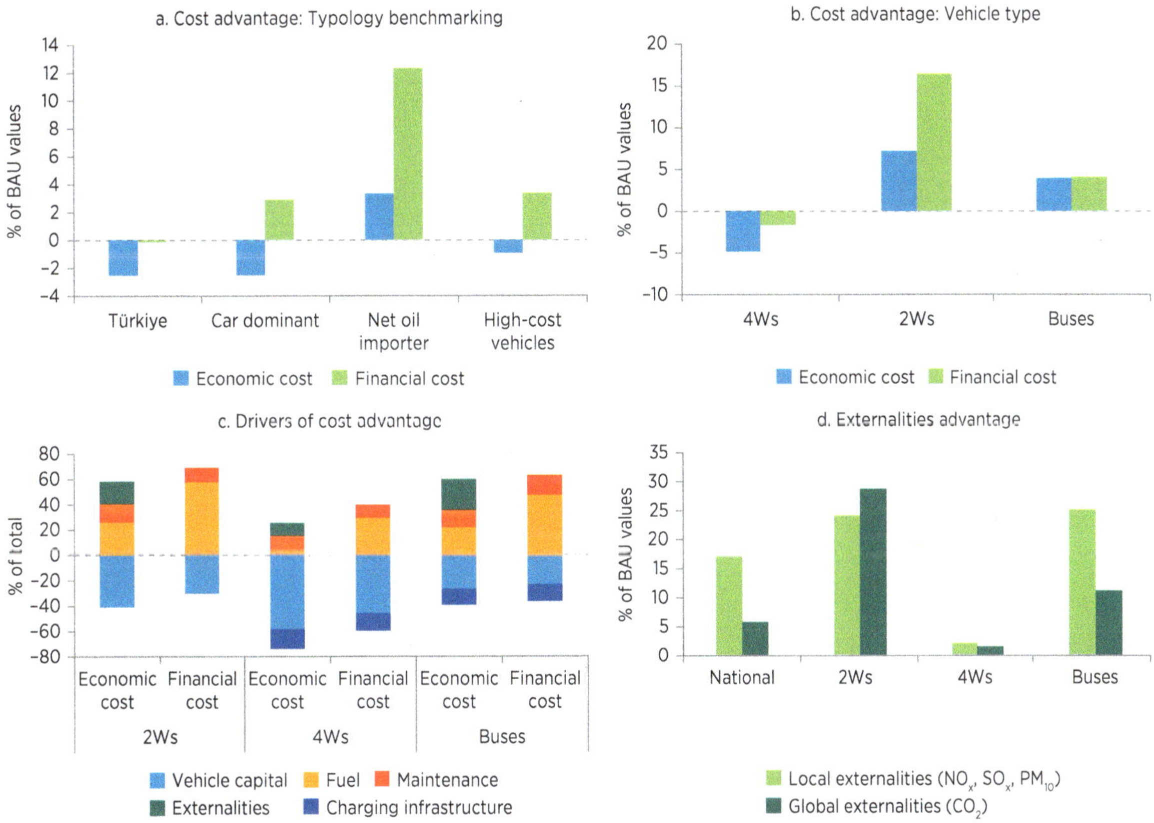

Source: World Bank.
Note: Data in this figure represent the "business as usual" (BAU) scenario minus the 30×30 scenario (averages over fleet additions). The BAU scenario assumes that no policy target will be imposed for electric vehicles and that vehicle purchase decisions will continue to reflect historical trends. The 30×30 scenario assumes that sales of electric cars and buses will reach 30 percent, and of two- and three-wheelers, 70 percent, by 2030. 2W = two-wheeler; 4W = four-wheeler; CO_2 = carbon dioxide; EV = electric vehicle; NO_x = nitrogen oxides; PM_{10} = particulate matter less than 10 microns in diameter; SO_x = sulfur oxides.

TABLE A.16.1 Cost advantage of accelerated EV adoption in Türkiye, 2030

	US$/vehicle									% of BAU values	
	Charging infrastructure	Vehicle capital cost	Vehicle operating cost	Subtotal	Local externalities	Global externalities	Economic cost advantage	Net taxes and subsidies	Financial cost advantage	Cost advantage	Financial cost advantage including fiscal wedge
	(a)	(b)	(c)	(d) = (a + b + c)	(e)		(f) = (d + e)	(g)	(h) = (d + g)		
Mode											
2Ws	0	(368)	376	8	132	26	166	461	469	7.2	16.6
4Ws	(574)	(2,172)	583	(2,163)	360	11	(1,792)	1,338	(825)	(4.9)	(1.7)
Buses	(6,088)	(12,982)	17,814	(1,256)	10,536	1,090	10,370	13,684	12,428	3.9	4.1

Source: World Bank.
Note: Heading colors: blue = excluding taxes and subsidies, gray = fiscal wedge, green = including taxes and subsidies. 2W = two-wheeler; 4W = four-wheeler; "Local externalities" comprises local (NO_x, PM_{10}, SO_x) air pollution costs. "Global externalities" comprises global (CO_2) air pollution costs. CO_2 = carbon dioxide; NO_x = nitrogen oxides; PM_{10} = particulate matter less than 10 microns in diameter; SO_x = sulfur oxides. Red and parentheses indicate negative value.

FIGURE A.16.2 Investment and financing needs for EV adoption in Türkiye, 2030

a. Breakdown of investment needs (US$3,402 million or 0.3% of GDP)

b. Investment needs potentially covered by carbon financing

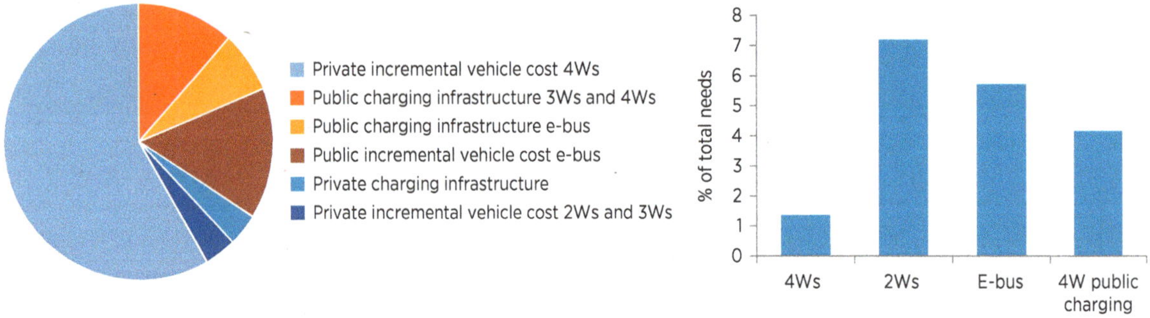

Source: World Bank.
Note: Data in this figure represent the "business as usual" (BAU) scenario minus the 30×30 scenario (averages over fleet additions). The BAU scenario assumes that no policy target will be imposed for electric vehicles and that vehicle purchase decisions will continue to reflect historical trends. The 30×30 scenario assumes that sales of electric cars and buses will reach 30 percent, and of two- and three-wheelers, 70 percent, by 2030. 2W = two-wheeler; 3W = three-wheeler; 4W = four-wheeler; EV = electric vehicle; GDP = gross domestic product.

TABLE A.16.2 Cost advantage of EV adoption in Türkiye, by scenario, 2030

	National results				Bus only		4W only	
	30×30 scenario	Green grid scenario	Scarce minerals scenario	Fuel efficiency scenario	30×30 scenario	Efficient bus scenario	30×30 scenario	Taxi fleet scenario
	US$/Mpaxvkm				*US$/vehicle*			
Type of cost								
Vehicle capital cost	(31,494)	(31,494)	(43,733)	(31,494)	(12,982)	710	(2,172)	(2,172)
Vehicle maintenance cost	8,699	8,699	7,633	8,699	7,176	7,477	429	(792)
Vehicle fuel cost	7,824	7,824	7,824	3,150	10,638	21,022	154	618
Private charging infrastructure	(1,568)	(1,568)	(1,568)	(1,568)	n.a.	n.a.	(144)	(144)
Public charging infrastructure	(7,630)	(7,630)	(7,630)	(7,630)	(6,088)	(6,088)	(431)	(489)
Subtotal	(24,169)	(24,169)	(37,475)	(28,842)	(1,256)	23,121	(2,163)	(2,979)
Local externalities (NO_x, SO_x, PM_{10})	9,551	14,662	9,551	7,774	10,536	21,056	360	1,874
Global externalities (CO_2)	754	1,041	754	208	1,090	2,217	11	72
Economic cost advantage	(13,865)	(8,465)	(27,171)	(20,860)	10,370	46,394	(1,792)	(1,033)
Fiscal wedge	23,127	23,127	19,050	19,754	13,684	29,388	1,338	4,588
Financial cost advantage	(1,042)	(1,042)	(18,426)	(9,089)	12,428	52,509	(825)	1,609
Economic cost advantage, by type of vehicle	*US$/vehicle*							
4Ws	(1,792)	(1,444)	(2,660)	(2,208)	n.a.	n.a.	n.a.	n.a.
2Ws	166	204	81	130	n.a.	n.a.	n.a.	n.a.
E-buses	10,370	13,362	3,154	5,583	n.a.	n.a.	n.a.	n.a.

Source: World Bank.
Note: Data in this table represent the "business as usual" (BAU) scenario minus the named scenario (averages over fleet additions). The BAU scenario assumes that no policy target will be imposed for electric vehicles and that vehicle purchase decisions will continue to reflect historical trends. The 30×30 scenario assumes that sales of electric cars and buses will reach 30 percent, and of two- and three-wheelers, 70 percent, by 2030. The green grid scenario assumes that countries achieve certain region-specific targets for acceleration of renewable energy, as defined by the International Renewable Energy Agency (IRENA 2020). The scarce minerals scenario assumes that battery cost will decline by approximately 7 percent annually. The fuel efficiency scenario assumes that the rate of improvement of fuel efficiency for the internal combustion engine fleet will double from 15 percent to 30 percent. The efficient bus scenario assumes a capital cost reduction of 35 percent in the procurement of buses as well as optimized bus routes to increase the annual mileage of electric buses. The taxi fleet scenario assumes that the lifetime mileage of intensively used commercial vehicles will increase by four times in each country, that public investment in charging infrastructure will double the fast charger density for cars, and that the maintenance cost for cars will be doubled (assuming two lifetime battery replacements). Results have been normalized by new vehicles entering the market in 2030. The "fiscal wedge" comprises net taxes and subsidies. Red and parentheses indicate negative value. 2W = two-wheeler; 4W = four-wheeler; CO_2 = carbon dioxide; EV = electric vehicle; NO_x = nitrogen oxides; PM_{10} = particulate matter less than 10 microns in diameter; SO_x = sulfur oxides; US$/Mpaxvkm = US dollars per million passenger vehicle-kilometers; n.a.= not applicable.

TABLE A.16.3 Supporting information on parameters and results for EV adoption in Türkiye

Price (US$/vehicle)

Parameter	Value
Price of ICE 4W	32,156
Price of EV 4W	38,111
Price of ICE 2W	1,104
Price of EV 2W	1,598
Price of ICE bus	136,866
Price of e-bus	170,959

Other parameters

Parameter	Value
Net tax difference on EV 4W (%)	21
Net tax difference on EV 2W (%)	21
Net tax difference on e-bus (%)	21
Price of gasoline (US$/liter)	0.58
Net gasoline tax (US$/liter)	0.64
Price of diesel (US$/liter)	0.73
Net diesel tax (US$/liter)	0.40
Price of electricity (US$/kWh)	0.10
Net electricity tax (US$/kWh)	(0)
Electricity carbon intensity (g/kWh)	451
Discount rate (%)	6.6

Key characteristics

Parameter	Value
4W mileage (km)	13,776
2W mileage (km)	3,960
Bus mileage (km)	37,952
4W lifetime (years)	22
2W lifetime (years)	17
Bus lifetime (years)	20
4W secondhand (%)	1.5
2W secondhand (%)	1.5
Bus secondhand (%)	0.7
4W share (% paxvkm)	60
2W share (% paxvkm)	3
Bus share (% paxvkm)	37

Efficiency (MJ/km)

Parameter	Value
Efficiency ICE 4W	1.75
Efficiency EV 4W	1.02
Efficiency ICE 2W	0.85
Efficiency EV 2W	0.20
Efficiency ICE bus	8.42
Efficiency EV bus	2.83

Other results for 30×30 scenario

Other results for 30×30 scenario	Value
Overall investment needs (US$, millions)	3,402
—of which 4W purchase	1,981
—of which 2W purchase	130
—of which e-bus purchase	522
Fiscal impact (US$, millions)	(1,934)
—of which vehicle duties	85
—of which vehicle taxes/subsidies	(414)
—of which gasoline taxes/subsidies	(704)
—of which diesel taxes/subsidies	(844)
—of which electricity taxes/subsidies	(58)
Implicit carbon price (US$/ton)	501
—of which for 4W	4,319
—of which for 2W	(137)
—of which for buses	(220)
Pollution reduction (tons)	2
—of which local (SO_x, NO_x, PM_{10})	0
—of which global (CO_2)	2
Affordability of EV 2W (Δ cost % GNI pc)	2.9
Affordability of EV 4W (Δ cost % GNI pc)	15.8

Source: World Bank.

Note: Red and parentheses indicates negative value. 2W = two-wheeler; 4W = four-wheeler; CO_2 = carbon dioxide; EV = electric vehicle; g = gram; GNI pc = gross national income per capita; ICE = internal combustion engine; kWh = kilowatt-hour; km = kilometer; MJ = megajoule; NO_x = nitrogen oxides; paxvkm = passenger vehicle-kilometer; PM_{10} = particulate matter less than 10 microns in diameter; SO_x = sulfur oxides.

Notes

1. Two-wheelers cover all motorized two-wheel vehicles registered.
2. Data from US Energy Information Administration international database and World Bank.

References

IRENA (International Renewable Energy Agency). 2020. *Global Renewables Outlook: Energy Transformation 2050*. Masdar City: IRENA.

OICA (Organisation Internationale des Constructeurs d'Automobiles [International Organization of Motor Vehicle Manufacturers]). 2020. "Global Sales Statistics, 2019–2021." OICA, Paris. https://www.oica.net/global-sales-statistics-2019-2021/.

Presidency of Strategy and Budget, Presidency of Republic of Turkey. 2020. *Turkey Eleventh Development Plan (2019–2023)*. Ankara: Division of Knowledge Management and Documentation, General Directorate of Administrative Services, Presidency of Strategy and Budget, Presidency of the Republic of Turkey. https://policy.thinkbluedata.com/node/4364.

Saygin, Değer, Osman Bülent Tor, Saeed Teimourzadeh, Mehmet Koc, Julia Hildermeier, and Christos Kolokathis. 2019. *Transport Sector Transformation: Integrating Electric Vehicles into Turkey's Distribution Grids*. Istanbul: SHURA Energy Transition Center.

Turkish Statistical Institute. 2020. Transportation summary tables. Turkish Statistical Institute, Ankara. https://data.tuik.gov.tr/Bulten/Index?p=Road-Motor-Vehicles-December-2020-37410.

TRTWorld. 2021. "Electric Car Use in Turkey Rises by 150 Percent." *TRTWorld*, March 29, 2021. https://www.trtworld.com/magazine/electric-car-use-in-turkey-rises-by-150-percent-45425.

Wikipedia. 2023. "Togg C-SUV." January 5, 2023. https://en.wikipedia.org/wiki/TOGG_Turkish_national_car.

A.17 PASSENGER ELECTRIC MOBILITY IN UKRAINE

Country Typology

Vehicle fleet composition: Car dominant
Net oil trading status: Importer
Relative cost of vehicles: Low

Country Background

The dominant vehicle type in Ukraine is cars (87.0 percent), followed by buses (8.5 percent), and two-wheelers[1] (4.5 percent) (OICA 2020).[2] Electricity is primarily generated from nuclear power (53.4 percent), followed by fossil fuels (38.0 percent)—mainly coal (31.9 percent)—and much less from renewable sources (8.6 percent)—mainly hydropower (6.9 percent).[3] Ukraine's electric car market has shown significant growth in recent years. The Ministry of Infrastructure of Ukraine has developed strategies to foster electric vehicle adoption that include the inception of tax incentives such as introducing no corporate income tax on lithium extraction and battery production for the next 15 years to promote industries for domestic electric vehicles and battery production (Ozeran, n.d.). The strategy also calls for reducing the cost of ownership of electric vehicles through tax incentives such as a value added tax reduction, income tax discounts, and no registration fee for the next 5 years; and nonmonetary policies such as free parking and free bus lane usage for the next 15 years. The government expects to reduce electric vehicle costs by up to 40 percent through these tax incentives combined. The strategy also incorporates targets to increase the share of renewable sources for power generation to 15 percent by 2035.[4] One of the main challenges for the electric vehicle market is developing a suitable regulatory framework for charging infrastructure. According to Ukraine's legal code, those who install charging stations don't have the right to take payment, as electrical energy can only officially be sold by the large state companies who are licensed to do so.[5] The European Investment Bank provided a €200 million loan to modernize the public transportation system, including through the purchase of electric buses.

Overall Messages

Despite having a car-dominated fleet, Ukraine faces other conditions more favorable to electric mobility, such as relatively low-cost vehicles and oil-importing status (figure A.17.1a). Electrification of transportation does not yet look economically favorable as a national strategy (table A.17.2) largely because of the fact that the electrification of four-wheelers is not attractive under current conditions. Although the capital cost differential for electric four-wheelers is relatively small, it is not fully compensated by operating cost advantages (table A.17.1). By contrast, there is a strong case for adoption of two-wheel electric motorbikes (figure A.17.1b), which present a life-cycle cost advantage of almost 12 percent (and over 30 percent in financial terms). In addition, the 12 percent capital cost differential associated with electric two-wheelers looks relatively affordable, representing no more than 1–2 percent of gross national income per capita. Furthermore, electric buses are only 20 percent more expensive and are beginning to offer modest economic advantages on the order of 3 percent of life-cycle cost.

The externality benefits of electric mobility in Ukraine are substantial in the case of buses, but relatively small for private vehicles (figure A.17.1d). Fuel cost savings present the main operating cost advantage of electric vehicles and are substantial in the case of two-wheelers and buses (figure A.17.1c). Given a fiscal regime that taxes gasoline and diesel at 50–100 percent, while subsidizing electricity by 70 percent, these fuel cost savings are further accentuated in financial terms. Thus, the overall case for electric mobility in Ukraine looks better in financial than in economic terms (figure A.17.1a).

The total investment needs associated with the 30×30 scenario amount to US$537 million per year by 2030 (or 0.33 percent of Ukrainian gross domestic product). About half the required outlay is associated with the incremental capital cost of private electric vehicles—mainly four-wheelers (figure A.17.2a). In terms of public investment, the most significant items are the additional cost of acquiring electric buses and the provision of public charging infrastructure for private vehicles (figure A.17.2a). The implicit carbon prices associated with electric two-wheelers and buses in Ukraine are negative, whereas that for electric four-wheelers exceeds US$150 (table A.17.3). Consequently, the most promising areas for pursuing carbon financing arrangements are electric two-wheelers and public charging infrastructure: approximately 30–40 percent of investment costs could be covered from this source (figure A.17.2b).

The overall economic case for electric mobility in Ukraine is negative, even considering the prospect for further decarbonization of the power sector ("green grid" scenario), let alone under more conservative assumptions about the cost of batteries ("scarce minerals" scenario) and the fuel efficiency of internal combustion engines ("fuel efficiency" scenario). On a positive note, the emerging advantage associated with electrification of buses can be as much as tripled through the more efficient procurement and operation of vehicles ("efficient bus" scenario). However, there is no real case for electrification of four-wheelers even when it comes to taxi fleets and other intensively used vehicles ("taxi fleet" scenario). It is clear that electric mobility in Ukraine needs to prioritize buses and two-wheelers, until such time as the case for four-wheelers further improves.

Figures and tables start on the next page.

Figures and Tables

FIGURE A.17.1 Advantage of EV adoption in Ukraine, by type of vehicle

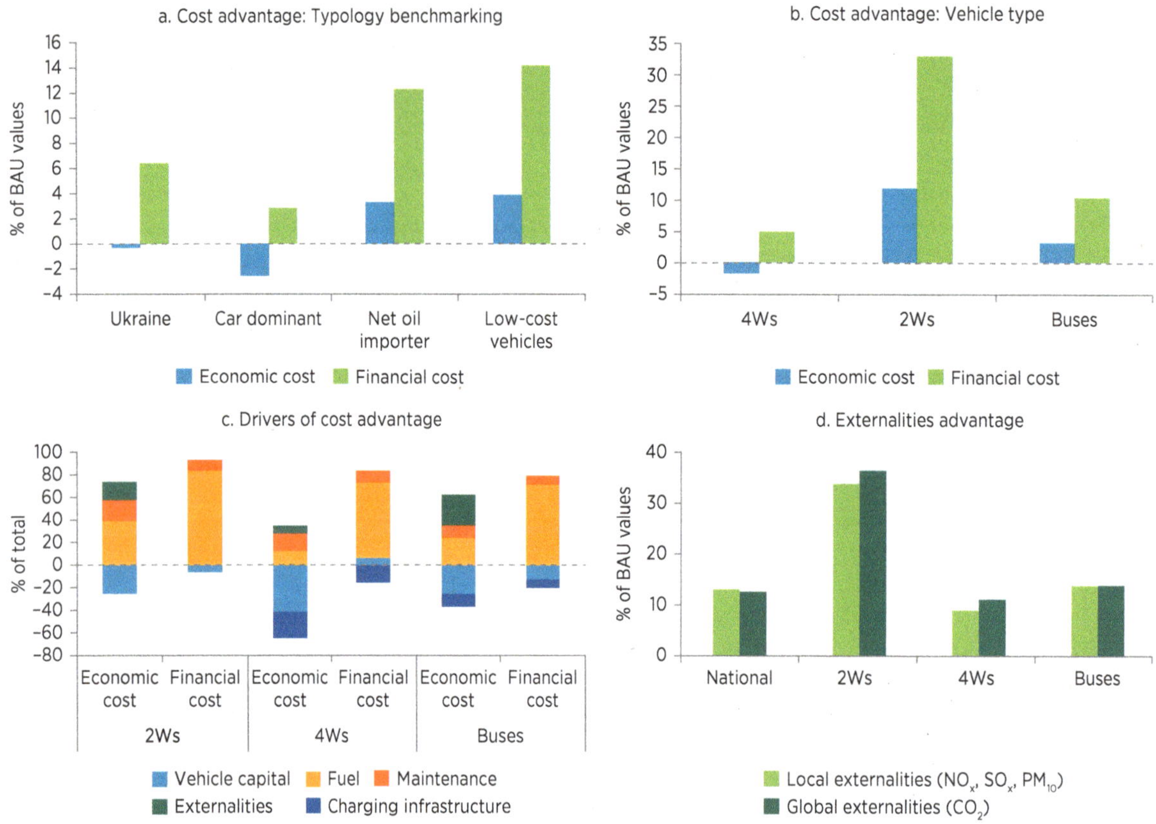

Source: World Bank.
Note: Data in this figure represent the "business as usual" (BAU) scenario minus the 30×30 scenario (averages over fleet additions). The BAU scenario assumes that no policy target will be imposed for electric vehicles and that vehicle purchase decisions will continue to reflect historical trends. The 30×30 scenario assumes that sales of electric cars and buses will reach 30 percent, and of two- and three-wheelers, 70 percent, by 2030. 2W = two-wheeler; 4W = four-wheeler; CO_2 = carbon dioxide; EV = electric vehicle; NO_x = nitrogen oxides; PM_{10} = particulate matter less than 10 microns in diameter; SO_x = sulfur oxides.

TABLE A.17.1 Cost advantage of accelerated EV adoption in Ukraine, 2030

	US$/vehicle									% of BAU values	
	Charging infrastructure	Vehicle capital cost	Vehicle operating cost	Subtotal	Local externalities	Global externalities	Economic cost advantage	Net taxes and subsidies	Financial cost advantage	Cost advantage	Financial cost advantage including fiscal wedge
	(a)	(b)	(c)	(d) = (a + b + c)	(e)		(f) = (d + e)	(g)	(h) = (d + g)		
Mode											
2Ws	0	(128)	301	173	25	56	253	789	961	11.9	33.1
4Ws	(393)	(712)	491	(615)	11	100	(503)	2,396	1,781	(1.7)	4.9
Buses	(4,525)	(10,558)	14,748	(334)	8,363	2,882	10,911	37,988	37,653	3.1	10.4

Source: World Bank.
Note: Heading colors: blue = excluding taxes and subsidies, gray = fiscal wedge, green = including taxes and subsidies. 2W = two-wheeler; 4W = four-wheeler; "Local externalities" comprises local (NO_x, PM_{10}, SO_x) air pollution costs. "Global externalities" comprises global (CO_2) air pollution costs. CO_2 = carbon dioxide; NO_x = nitrogen oxides; PM_{10} = particulate matter less than 10 microns in diameter; SO_x = sulfur oxides. Red and parentheses indicate negative value.

FIGURE A.17.2 Investment and financing needs for EV adoption in Ukraine, 2030

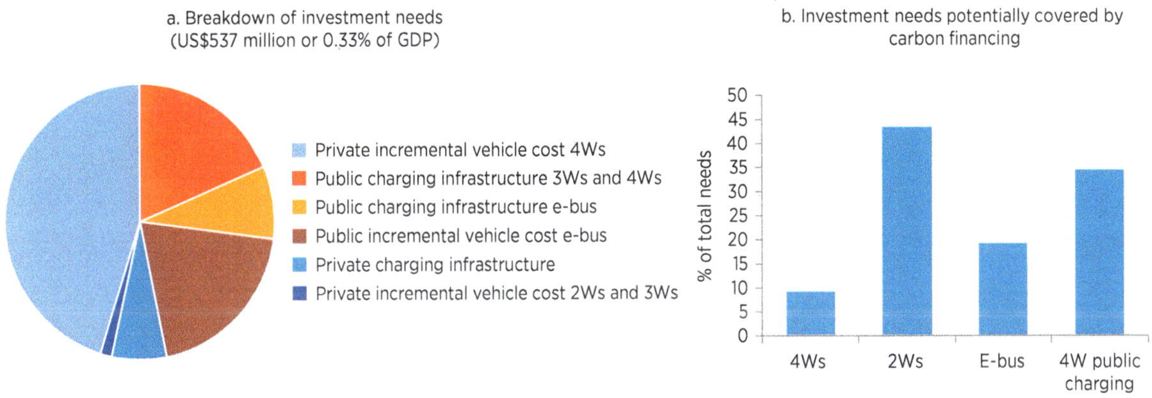

Source: World Bank.

Note: Data in this figure represent the "business as usual" (BAU) scenario minus the 30×30 scenario (averages over fleet additions). The BAU scenario assumes that no policy target will be imposed for electric vehicles and that vehicle purchase decisions will continue to reflect historical trends. The 30×30 scenario assumes that sales of electric cars and buses will reach 30 percent, and of two- and three-wheelers, 70 percent, by 2030. 2W = two-wheeler; 3W = three-wheeler; 4W = four-wheeler; EV = electric vehicle; GDP = gross domestic product.

TABLE A.17.2 Cost advantage of EV adoption in Ukraine, by scenario, 2030

	National results				Bus only		4W only	
	30×30 scenario	Green grid scenario	Scarce minerals scenario	Fuel efficiency scenario	30×30 scenario	Efficient bus scenario	30×30 scenario	Taxi fleet scenario
	US$/Mpaxvkm				*US$/vehicle*			
Type of cost								
Vehicle capital cost	(11,376)	(11,376)	(17,040)	(11,376)	(10,558)	(1,606)	(712)	(712)
Vehicle maintenance cost	4,628	4,628	3,992	4,628	4,635	4,998	272	(590)
Vehicle fuel cost	6,008	6,008	6,008	2,113	10,114	15,772	219	875
Private charging infrastructure	(1,104)	(1,104)	(1,104)	(1,104)	n.a.	n.a.	(102)	(102)
Public charging infrastructure	(4,633)	(4,633)	(4,633)	(4,633)	(4,525)	(4,525)	(292)	(333)
Subtotal	(6,478)	(6,478)	(12,776)	(10,372)	(334)	14,638	(615)	(862)
Local externalities (NO_x, SO_x, PM_{10})	2,862	3,033	2,862	2,834	8,363	13,044	11	50
Global externalities (CO_2)	2,119	2,318	2,119	1,652	2,882	4,515	100	417
Economic cost advantage	(1,497)	(1,127)	(7,796)	(5,887)	10,911	32,198	(503)	(395)
Fiscal wedge	39,734	39,734	39,614	37,604	37,988	58,132	2,396	6,937
Financial cost advantage	33,256	33,256	26,837	27,232	37,653	72,770	1,781	6,074
Economic cost advantage, by type of vehicle	*US$/vehicle*							
4Ws	(503)	(483)	(920)	(743)	n.a.	n.a.	n.a.	n.a.
2Ws	253	258	210	222	n.a.	n.a.	n.a.	n.a.
E-buses	10,911	11,346	5,667	5,569	n.a.	n.a.	n.a.	n.a.

Source: World Bank.

Note: Data in this table represent the "business as usual" (BAU) scenario minus the named scenario (averages over fleet additions). The BAU scenario assumes that no policy target will be imposed for electric vehicles and that vehicle purchase decisions will continue to reflect historical trends. The 30×30 scenario assumes that sales of electric cars and buses will reach 30 percent, and of two- and three-wheelers, 70 percent, by 2030. The green grid scenario assumes that countries achieve certain region-specific targets for acceleration of renewable energy, as defined by the International Renewable Energy Agency (IRENA 2020). The scarce minerals scenario assumes that battery cost will decline by approximately 7 percent annually. The fuel efficiency scenario assumes that the rate of improvement of fuel efficiency for the internal combustion engine fleet will double from 15 percent to 30 percent. The efficient bus scenario assumes a capital cost reduction of 35 percent in the procurement of buses as well as optimized bus routes to increase the annual mileage of electric buses. The taxi fleet scenario assumes that the lifetime mileage of intensively used commercial vehicles will increase by four times in each country, that public investment in charging infrastructure will double the fast charger density for cars, and that the maintenance cost for cars will be doubled (assuming two lifetime battery replacements). Results have been normalized by new vehicles entering the market in 2030. The "fiscal wedge" comprises net taxes and subsidies. Red and parentheses indicate negative value. 2W = two-wheeler; 4W = four-wheeler; CO_2 = carbon dioxide; EV = electric vehicle; NO_x = nitrogen oxides; PM_{10} = particulate matter less than 10 microns in diameter; SO_x = sulfur oxides; US$/Mpaxvkm = US dollars per million passenger vehicle-kilometers; n.a.= not applicable.

TABLE A.17.3 Supporting information on parameters and results for EV adoption in Ukraine

Price (US$/vehicle)

Parameter	Value
Price of ICE 4W	26,219
Price of EV 4W	24,581
Price of ICE 2W	887
Price of EV 2W	1,031
Price of ICE bus	110,826
Price of e-bus	135,324

Other parameters

Parameter	Value
Net tax difference on EV 4W (%)	20
Net tax difference on EV 2W (%)	20
Net tax difference on e-bus (%)	20
Price of gasoline (US$/liter)	0.54
Net gasoline tax (US$/liter)	0.46
Price of diesel (US$/liter)	0.73
Net diesel tax (US$/liter)	0.31
Price of electricity (US$/kWh)	0.15
Net electricity tax (US$/kWh)	(0.11)
Electricity carbon intensity (g/kWh)	274
Discount rate (%)	6.6

Key characteristics

Parameter	Value
4W mileage (km)	15,224
2W mileage (km)	7,627
Bus mileage (km)	48,092
4W lifetime (years)	22
2W lifetime (years)	17
Bus lifetime (years)	20
4W secondhand (%)	65.8
2W secondhand (%)	65.8
Bus secondhand (%)	71.9
4W share (% paxvkm)	66
2W share (% paxvkm)	3
Bus share (% paxvkm)	31

Efficiency (MJ/km)

Parameter	Value
Efficiency ICE 4W	2.21
Efficiency EV 4W	0.55
Efficiency ICE 2W	0.87
Efficiency EV 2W	0.20
Efficiency ICE bus	16.84
Efficiency EV bus	5.74

Other results for 30×30 scenario

Other results for 30×30 scenario	Value
Overall investment needs (US$, millions)	537
—of which 4W purchase	243
—of which 2W purchase	7
—of which e-bus purchase	107
Fiscal impact (US$, millions)	(1,247)
—of which vehicle duties	(22)
—of which vehicle taxes/subsidies	(310)
—of which gasoline taxes/subsidies	(176)
—of which diesel taxes/subsidies	(268)
—of which electricity taxes/subsidies	(470)
Implicit carbon price (US$/ton)	44
—of which for 4W	156
—of which for 2W	(92)
—of which for buses	(72)
Pollution reduction (tons)	3
—of which local (SO_x, NO_x, PM_{10})	0
—of which global (CO_2)	3
Affordability of EV 2W (Δ cost % GNI pc)	1.4
Affordability of EV 4W (Δ cost % GNI pc)	(3.7)

Source: World Bank.
Note: Red and parentheses indicates negative value. 2W = two-wheeler; 4W = four-wheeler; CO_2 = carbon dioxide; EV = electric vehicle; g = gram; GNI pc = gross national income per capita; ICE = internal combustion engine; kWh = kilowatt-hour; km = kilometer; MJ = megajoule; NO_x = nitrogen oxides; paxvkm = passenger vehicle-kilometer; PM_{10} = particulate matter less than 10 microns in diameter; SO_x = sulfur oxides.

Notes

1. Two wheelers cover all motorized two-wheel vehicles registered.
2. Passenger cars sales from UKrAutoprom (2020).
3. Data from US Energy Information Administration international database and World Bank.
4. Energy Policy Master Plan for Ukraine, Ministry of Economy, Trade and Industry, 2015.
5. From Kiev Check-In, "Is Ukraine entering the era of the electric car? Here's everything you need to know..." https://www.kievcheckin.com/discover-kiev/are-we-entering-the-era-of-the-electric-car-heres-everything-you-need-to-know.

References

IRENA (International Renewable Energy Agency). 2020. *Global Renewables Outlook: Energy Transformation 2050*. Masdar City: IRENA.

OICA (Organisation Internationale des Constructeurs d'Automobiles [International Organization of Motor Vehicle Manufacturers]). 2020. "Global Sales Statistics, 2019–2021." OICA, Paris. https://www.oica.net/global-sales-statistics-2019-2021/.

Ozeran, Alexander. n.d. "Electric Mobility: Global Trends and What We Do in Ukraine." Ministry of Infrastructure of Ukraine. https://www.globalfueleconomy.org/media/460888/gfei-alexander-ozeran-global-trends.pdf.

UKrAutoprom (Ukrainian Motor Vehicle Manufacturers Association). 2020. "First Registrations of New Buses and Minibuses in Ukraine by Brands (in Units)." https://ukrautoprom.com.ua/wp-content/uploads/2020/07/2019-12-market.x90683.pdf.

A.18 PASSENGER ELECTRIC MOBILITY IN URUGUAY

Country Typology

Vehicle fleet composition: Mixed fleet
Net oil trading status: Importer
Relative cost of vehicles: High

Country Background

Uruguay has a mixed vehicle fleet, though cars dominate the mix (57.6 percent), followed by two-wheelers (40.2 percent),[1] and buses (2.2 percent) (OICA 2020).[2] Electricity is primarily generated from renewable sources (97.6 percent), including hydro (44.7 percent), wind (32.5 percent), and biomass and waste (17.5 percent).[3] The national government has taken several steps to foster e-mobility. Measures encouraging bus operators to transition to electric vehicles include establishing tax breaks and subsidies for bus purchases. As a result of tax incentives and subsidies, the price difference between an electric bus and a diesel bus has become marginal to an operator (Bnamericas 2020). There is also an awareness program to encourage private operators to take up electric buses.[4] In 2019, the first call for subsidies for the purchase of e-buses was launched under a specific e-bus subsidy regulation to replace 4 percent of the total bus fleet.[5] There are several plans and ongoing programs: The MOVÉS project promotes the use of electric vehicles, helps banks develop green credits for the purchase of electric vehicles, and gives specific credits for medium enterprises.[6] A vehicle manufacturing facility planned for Uruguay is scheduled to go into operation in 2024 with a product line of small electric cars and electric delivery vans (Randall 2021). The United Nations Development Programme is supporting the national government in developing sustainable and efficient urban mobility systems in Uruguay. The program focuses partly on reforming the current regulations and incentives for promoting electric vehicles in the public transport sector (MIEM, n.d.)

Overall Messages

Despite facing relatively high vehicle costs, Uruguay presents many conditions that are more favorable toward electric mobility, including a mixed fleet and oil-importing status (figure A.18.1a). Electrification of transportation does not yet look economically favorable as a national strategy, largely because of the fact that the electrification of four-wheel vehicles is not attractive under current conditions (table A.18.1). By contrast, there is a strong case for adoption of two-wheel electric motorbikes (figure A.18.1b), which present a life-cycle cost advantage of almost 16 percent (over 30 percent in financial terms) and are relatively affordable with incremental capital costs representing no more than 1 percent of gross national income per capita. The case for electric buses is also good, offering life-cycle cost advantages of 7–8 percent, against an incremental capital cost under 30 percent, and these are more relevant to Uruguay given that they represent a much larger share of transportation than two-wheelers (figures A.18.1c).

The main externality benefits of electric mobility in Uruguay are associated with the reduced carbon emissions of buses (figure A.18.1d). Fuel cost savings are also important, despite the fact that electricity is taxed almost as heavily as petroleum at close to 140 percent. Considering also a 20 percent tax advantage in favor of the purchase of electric vehicles, the overall case for electric mobility in Uruguay looks significantly better in financial than in economic terms (figure A.18.1a).

The total investment needs associated with the 30×30 scenario amount to US$352 million per year by 2030 (or 0.45 percent of Uruguayan gross domestic product). About four-fifths of the required outlay is associated with the incremental capital cost of private electric vehicles (figure A.18.2a). In terms of public investment, the most significant item is the provision of public charging infrastructure for private vehicles (figure A.18.2a). Given that implicit carbon prices associated with electric buses in Uruguay are quite negative (table A.18.3), there is significant scope to cover almost 80 percent of the incremental capital cost of bus procurement through carbon financing arrangements (figure A.18.2b). However, for four-wheel electric vehicles, the implicit carbon price exceeds US$260 per ton.

The overall economic case for electric mobility in Uruguay is negative in economic terms, although—because of government incentives—strongly positive in financial terms. This outcome is further accentuated under more conservative assumptions about the cost of batteries ("scarce minerals" scenario) and the fuel efficiency of internal combustion engines ("fuel efficiency" scenario), and there is not much scope for further decarbonization of the power sector ("green grid" scenario) (table A.18.2). On a positive note, the significant advantage associated with electrification of buses can be further increased through the more efficient procurement and operation of vehicles ("efficient bus" scenario). However, even when it comes to taxi fleets and other intensively used vehicles, the case for electric four-wheelers remains marginal ("taxi fleet" scenario). It is clear that electric mobility in Uruguay needs to prioritize the bus segment of the fleet, in view of the many advantages offered.

Figures and tables start on the next page.

Figures and Tables

FIGURE A.18.1 Advantage of EV adoption in Uruguay, by type of vehicle

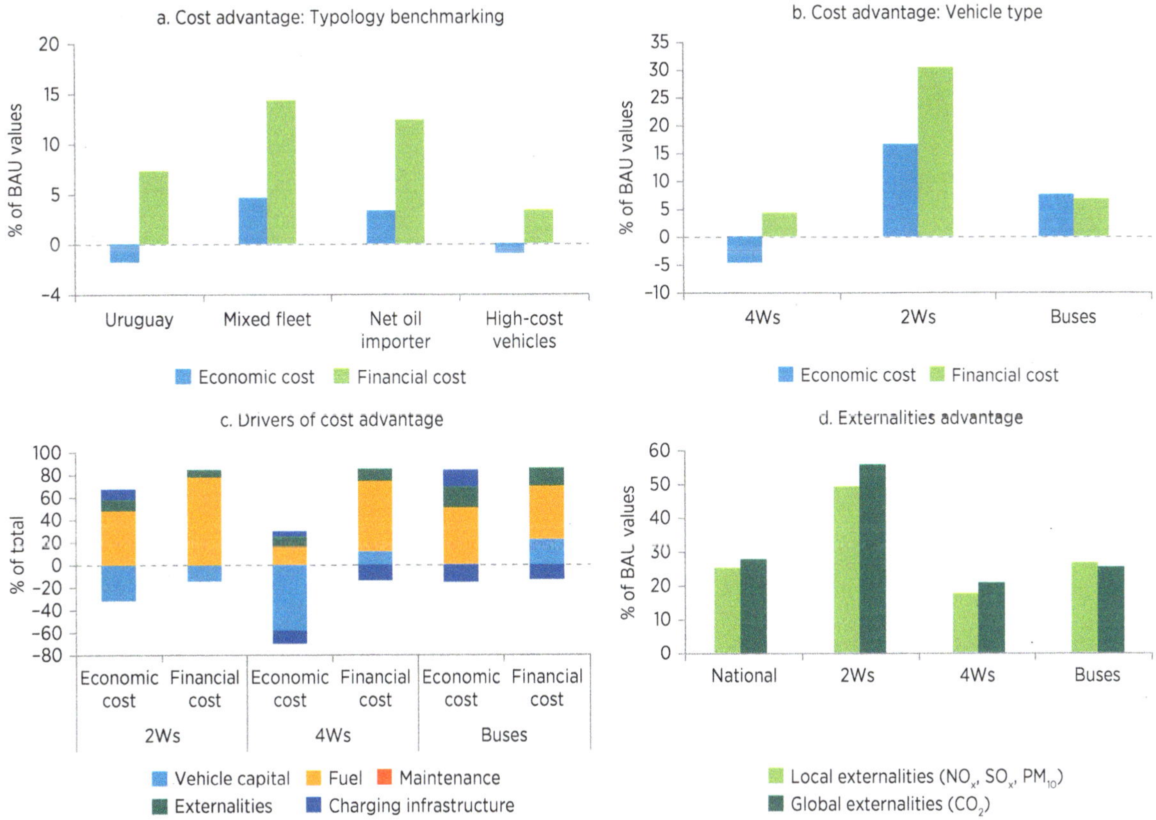

Source: World Bank.

Note: Data in this figure represent the "business as usual" (BAU) scenario minus the 30×30 scenario (averages over fleet additions). The BAU scenario assumes that no policy target will be imposed for electric vehicles and that vehicle purchase decisions will continue to reflect historical trends. The 30×30 scenario assumes that sales of electric cars and buses will reach 30 percent, and of two- and three-wheelers, 70 percent, by 2030. 2W = two-wheeler; 4W = four-wheeler; CO_2 = carbon dioxide; EV = electric vehicle; NO_x = nitrogen oxides; PM_{10} = particulate matter less than 10 microns in diameter; SO_x = sulfur oxides.

TABLE A.18.1 Cost advantage of accelerated EV adoption in Uruguay, 2030

	US$/vehicle									% of BAU values	
	Charging infrastructure	Vehicle capital cost	Vehicle operating cost	Subtotal	Local externalities	Global externalities	Economic cost advantage	Net taxes and subsidies	Financial cost advantage	Cost advantage	Financial cost advantage including fiscal wedge
	(a)	(b)	(c)	(d) = (a + b + c)	(e)		(f) = (d + e)	(g)	(h) = (d + g)		
Mode											
2Ws	0	(404)	751	347	30	88	466	1,156	1,503	16.7	30.7
4Ws	(555)	(2,866)	1,250	(2,171)	6	214	(1,951)	5,085	2,914	(4.7)	4.4
Buses	(6,013)	249	27,870	22,106	859	5,096	28,060	11,764	33,869	7.7	6.8

Source: World Bank.

Note: Heading colors: blue = excluding taxes and subsidies, gray = fiscal wedge, green = including taxes and subsidies. 2W = two-wheeler; 4W = four-wheeler; "Local externalities" comprises local (NO_x, PM_{10}, SO_x) air pollution costs. "Global externalities" comprises global (CO_2) air pollution costs. CO_2 = carbon dioxide; NO_x = nitrogen oxides; PM_{10} = particulate matter less than 10 microns in diameter; SO_x = sulfur oxides. Red and parentheses indicate negative value.

FIGURE A.18.2 Investment and financing needs for EV adoption in Uruguay, 2030

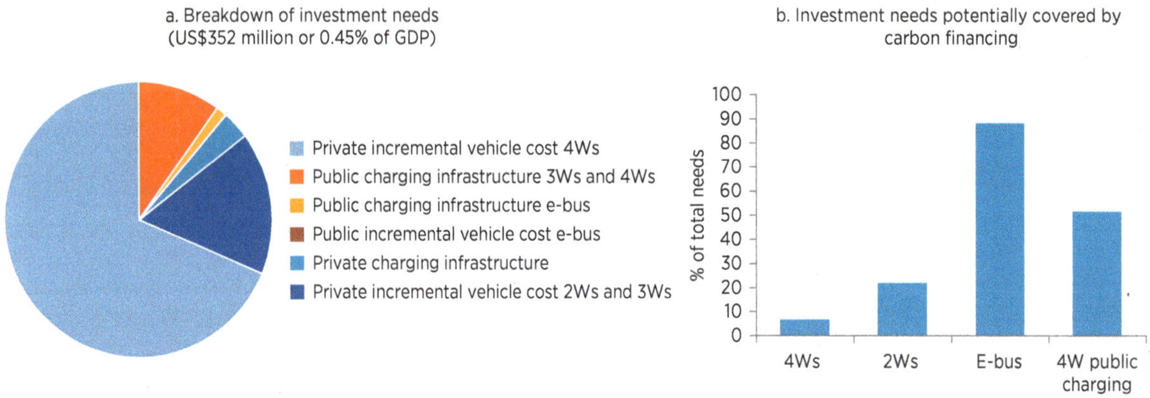

Source: World Bank.

Note: Data in this figure represent the "business as usual" (BAU) scenario minus the 30×30 scenario (averages over fleet additions). The BAU scenario assumes that no policy target will be imposed for electric vehicles and that vehicle purchase decisions will continue to reflect historical trends. The 30×30 scenario assumes that sales of electric cars and buses will reach 30 percent, and of two- and three-wheelers, 70 percent, by 2030. 2W = two-wheeler; 3W = three-wheeler; 4W = four-wheeler; EV = electric vehicle; GDP = gross domestic product.

TABLE A.18.2 Cost advantage of EV adoption in Uruguay, by scenario, 2030

	National results				Bus only		4W only	
	30×30 scenario	Green grid scenario	Scarce minerals scenario	Fuel efficiency scenario	30×30 scenario	Efficient bus scenario	30×30 scenario	Taxi fleet scenario
	US$/Mpaxvkm				*US$/vehicle*			
Type of cost								
Vehicle capital cost	(37,121)	(37,121)	(50,012)	(37,121)	249	13,729	(2,866)	(2,866)
Vehicle maintenance cost	7,251	7,251	7,046	7,251	7,218	7,519	407	(771)
Vehicle fuel cost	21,964	21,964	21,964	15,837	20,652	25,766	843	3,370
Private charging infrastructure	(1,445)	(1,445)	(1,445)	(1,445)	n.a.	n.a.	(139)	(139)
Public charging infrastructure	(4,897)	(4,897)	(4,897)	(4,897)	(6,013)	(6,013)	(416)	(473)
Subtotal	(14,247)	(14,247)	(27,343)	(20,375)	22,106	41,001	(2,171)	(879)
Local externalities (NO_x, SO_x, PM_{10})	687	687	687	678	859	1,071	6	23
Global externalities (CO_2)	4,300	4,300	4,300	3,585	5,096	6,372	214	885
Economic cost advantage	(9,260)	(9,260)	(22,356)	(16,112)	28,060	48,444	(1,951)	30
Fiscal wedge	74,957	74,957	74,567	65,733	11,764	12,975	5,085	10,294
Financial cost advantage	60,710	60,710	47,223	45,358	33,869	53,976	2,914	9,415
Economic cost advantage, by type of vehicle	*US$/vehicle*							
4Ws	(1,951)	(1,951)	(2,971)	(2,447)	n.a.	n.a.	n.a.	n.a.
2Ws	466	466	365	414	n.a.	n.a.	n.a.	n.a.
E-buses	28,060	28,060	20,937	20,025	n.a.	n.a.	n.a.	n.a.

Source: World Bank.

Note: Data in this table represent the "business as usual" (BAU) scenario minus the named scenario (averages over fleet additions). The BAU scenario assumes that no policy target will be imposed for electric vehicles and that vehicle purchase decisions will continue to reflect historical trends. The 30×30 scenario assumes that sales of electric cars and buses will reach 30 percent, and of two- and three-wheelers, 70 percent, by 2030. The green grid scenario assumes that countries achieve certain region-specific targets for acceleration of renewable energy, as defined by the International Renewable Energy Agency (IRENA 2020). The scarce minerals scenario assumes that battery cost will decline by approximately 7 percent annually. The fuel efficiency scenario assumes that the rate of improvement of fuel efficiency for the internal combustion engine fleet will double from 15 percent to 30 percent. The efficient bus scenario assumes a capital cost reduction of 35 percent in the procurement of buses as well as optimized bus routes to increase the annual mileage of electric buses. The taxi fleet scenario assumes that the lifetime mileage of intensively used commercial vehicles will increase by four times in each country, that public investment in charging infrastructure will double the fast charger density for cars, and that the maintenance cost for cars will be doubled (assuming two lifetime battery replacements). Results have been normalized by new vehicles entering the market in 2030. The "fiscal wedge" comprises net taxes and subsidies. Red and parentheses indicate negative value. 2W = two-wheeler; 4W = four-wheeler; CO_2 = carbon dioxide; EV = electric vehicle; NO_x = nitrogen oxides; PM_{10} = particulate matter less than 10 microns in diameter; SO_x = sulfur oxides; US$/Mpaxvkm = US dollars per million passenger vehicle-kilometers; n.a.= not applicable.

TABLE A.18.3 Supporting information on parameters and results for EV adoption in Uruguay

Price (US$/vehicle)

Parameter	Value
Price of ICE 4W	34,261
Price of EV 4W	37,429
Price of ICE 2W	1,193
Price of EV 2W	1,569
Price of ICE bus	171,910
Price of e-bus	135,324

Other parameters

Parameter	Value
Net tax difference on EV 4W (%)	23
Net tax difference on EV 2W (%)	23
Net tax difference on e-bus (%)	23
Price of gasoline (US$/liter)	0.63
Net gasoline tax (US$/liter)	1.02
Price of diesel (US$/liter)	0.70
Net diesel tax (US$/liter)	0.51
Price of electricity (US$/kWh)	0.11
Net electricity tax (US$/kWh)	0.15
Electricity carbon intensity (g/kWh)	23
Discount rate (%)	6.6

Key characteristics

Parameter	Value
4W mileage (km)	15,224
2W mileage (km)	7,627
Bus mileage (km)	48,092
4W lifetime (years)	22
2W lifetime (years)	17
Bus lifetime (years)	20
4W secondhand (%)	6.5
2W secondhand (%)	6.5
Bus secondhand (%)	1.9
4W share (% paxvkm)	63
2W share (% paxvkm)	28
Bus share (% paxvkm)	9

Efficiency (MJ/km)

Parameter	Value
Efficiency ICE 4W	2.40
Efficiency EV 4W	0.78
Efficiency ICE 2W	0.85
Efficiency EV 2W	0.11
Efficiency ICE bus	15.52
Efficiency EV bus	5.08

Other results for 30×30 scenario

Other results for 30×30 scenario	Value
Overall investment needs (US$, millions)	352
—of which 4W purchase	242
—of which 2W purchase	59
—of which e-bus purchase	(0.2)
Fiscal impact (US$, millions)	(607)
—of which vehicle duties	(123)
—of which vehicle taxes/subsidies	(182)
—of which gasoline taxes/subsidies	(466)
—of which diesel taxes/subsidies	(21)
—of which electricity taxes/subsidies	185
Implicit carbon price (US$/ton)	82
—of which for 4W	261
—of which for 2W	(111)
—of which for buses	(117)
Pollution reduction (tons)	1
—of which local (SO_x, NO_x, PM_{10})	0
—of which global (CO_2)	1
Affordability of EV 2W (Δ cost % GNI pc)	1.4
Affordability of EV 4W (Δ cost % GNI pc)	(2.3)

Source: World Bank.
Note: Red and parentheses indicates negative value. 2W = two-wheeler; 4W = four-wheeler; CO_2 = carbon dioxide; EV = electric vehicle; g = gram; GNI pc = gross national income per capita; ICE = internal combustion engine; kWh = kilowatt-hour; km = kilometer; MJ = megajoule; NO_x = nitrogen oxides; paxvkm = passenger vehicle-kilometer; PM_{10} = particulate matter less than 10 microns in diameter; SO_x = sulfur oxides.

Notes

1. Two wheelers cover all motorized two-wheel vehicles registered.
2. Passenger cars sales from Uruguay Instituto Nacional de Estadistica (2020).
3. Data from US Energy Information Administration international database and World Bank.
4. http://www.uemi.net/montevideo---uruguay.html.
5. Information from The World Bank Group.
6. Information from The World Bank Group.

References

Bnamericas. 2020. "Spotlight: The Future of Electric Vehicles in the Southern Cone." Feature article, January 22, 2020. https://www.bnamericas.com/en/features/spotlight-the-future-of-electric-vehicles-in-the-southern-cone.

IRENA (International Renewable Energy Agency). 2020. *Global Renewables Outlook: Energy Transformation 2050*. Masdar City: IRENA.

MIEM (Uruguay, Ministry of Industry, Energy, and Mining). n.d. "Towards a Sustainable and Efficient Urban Mobility System in Uruguay." Annotated Project Document template, Global Environment Facility and United Nations Development Programme. http://www.eficienciaenergetica.gub.uy/documents/20182/32151/pad_towards_a_sustainable_and_efficient_urban_mobility_system_in_uruguay.pdf/e828843e-3cba-4c67-aaed-0ddec3002774.

OICA (Organisation Internationale des Constructeurs d'Automobiles [International Organization of Motor Vehicle Manufacturers]). 2020. "Global Sales Statistics, 2019–2021." OICA, Paris. https://www.oica.net/global-sales-statistics-2019-2021/.

Randall, Chris. 2021. "Spanish EV Startup Plans Plant in Uruguay." Electrive.com, February 24, 2021. https://www.electrive.com/2021/02/24/spanish-ev-startup-plans-plant-in-uruguay/.

Uruguay Instituto Nacional de Estadistica. 2020. Parque automotor del país según tipo de vehículo utilizado. https://www.ine.gub.uy/transporte-y-comunicaciones.

A.19 PASSENGER ELECTRIC MOBILITY IN VANUATU

Country Typology

Vehicle fleet composition: Mixed fleet
Net oil trading status: Importer
Relative cost of vehicles: High

Country Background

Vanuatu has a mixed vehicle fleet with the largest share being buses (60.5 percent), followed by cars (35.6 percent), and two-wheelers[1] (3.9 percent).[2] Electricity is primarily generated from fossil fuels (85.6 percent)—mainly coal (85.6 percent)—and less from renewable sources (14.4 percent)—notably solar (7.6 percent) and wind (6.8 percent). There are no current transportation policies to promote the adoption of electric vehicles. The Intended Nationally Determined Contribution plan has set an ambitious target to increase to 100 percent the share of renewable energy by 2030.[3] The plan targets reducing greenhouse gases by 100 percent in the power generation subsector and by 30 percent for the whole energy sector. A recent update of the plan (2020) has set the following target for electric vehicle adoption in the country by 2030: 10 percent of the public transport buses to be electric; 10 percent of the government fleet to be electric; and the number of electric two- and three-wheelers to be increased to 1,000.[4] Electric vehicle penetration in the country has been extremely low. Recently, some private initiatives have taken place to introduce electric vehicles.

Overall Messages

Despite having some conditions favorable to electric mobility, such as a mixed fleet and oil-importing status, Vanuatu is held back by relatively high-cost vehicles (figure A.19.1a). Electrification of transportation does not yet look economically favorable as a national strategy. Even with buses, the economic case for electric mobility is only marginally favorable and turns substantially negative in financial terms (table A.19.1). For two-wheelers, the opposite occurs, with electric mobility being uneconomic, yet financially attractive (figure A.19.1b). In any case, the capital cost differentials associated with electric two- and four-wheelers, at about 30 percent, are unaffordable, representing 10–20 percent of gross national income per capita.

The externality benefits of electric mobility in Vanuatu are substantial only in the case of buses, which yield important carbon savings (figure A.19.1d). Otherwise, maintenance cost savings are the main advantage associated with electric mobility. Fuel costs do *not* typically present savings, because electricity is very costly and additionally taxed much more heavily than gasoline at 110 percent. This accounts for the unusual finding that the case for electric mobility in Vanuatu looks substantially worse in financial than in economic terms (figure A.19.1c).

The total investment needs associated with the 30×30 scenario amount to US$2.5 million per year by 2030 (or 0.21 percent of Vanuatu's gross domestic product). Over half of the required outlay is associated with the incremental cost of public charging infrastructure for buses (figure A.19.2a). In terms of private investment, the most significant item is the incremental capital cost of electric four-wheelers (figure A.19.2a). Given that implicit carbon prices associated with electric buses in Vanuatu are negative (table A.19.3), there is significant scope to cover 40 percent of the incremental cost of electric buses through carbon financing arrangements (figure A.19.2b). However, for four-wheel electric vehicles, the implicit carbon price approaches US$1,150 per ton.

The overall economic case for electric mobility in Vanuatu is negative and certainly does not improve under more conservative assumptions about the cost of batteries ("scarce minerals" scenario) and the fuel efficiency of internal combustion engines ("fuel efficiency" scenario); however, it does become marginally positive with further decarbonization of the power sector ("green grid" scenario) (table A.19.2). On a positive note, the emerging advantage associated with electrification of buses can be as much as tripled through the more efficient procurement and operation of vehicles ("efficient bus" scenario). However, there is no real case for electrification of four-wheelers, even when it comes to taxi fleets and other intensively used vehicles ("taxi fleet" scenario). It is clear that electric mobility in Vanuatu needs to prioritize the bus segment of the fleet.

Figures and tables start on the next page.

Figures and Tables

FIGURE A.19.1 Advantage of EV adoption in Vanuatu, by type of vehicle

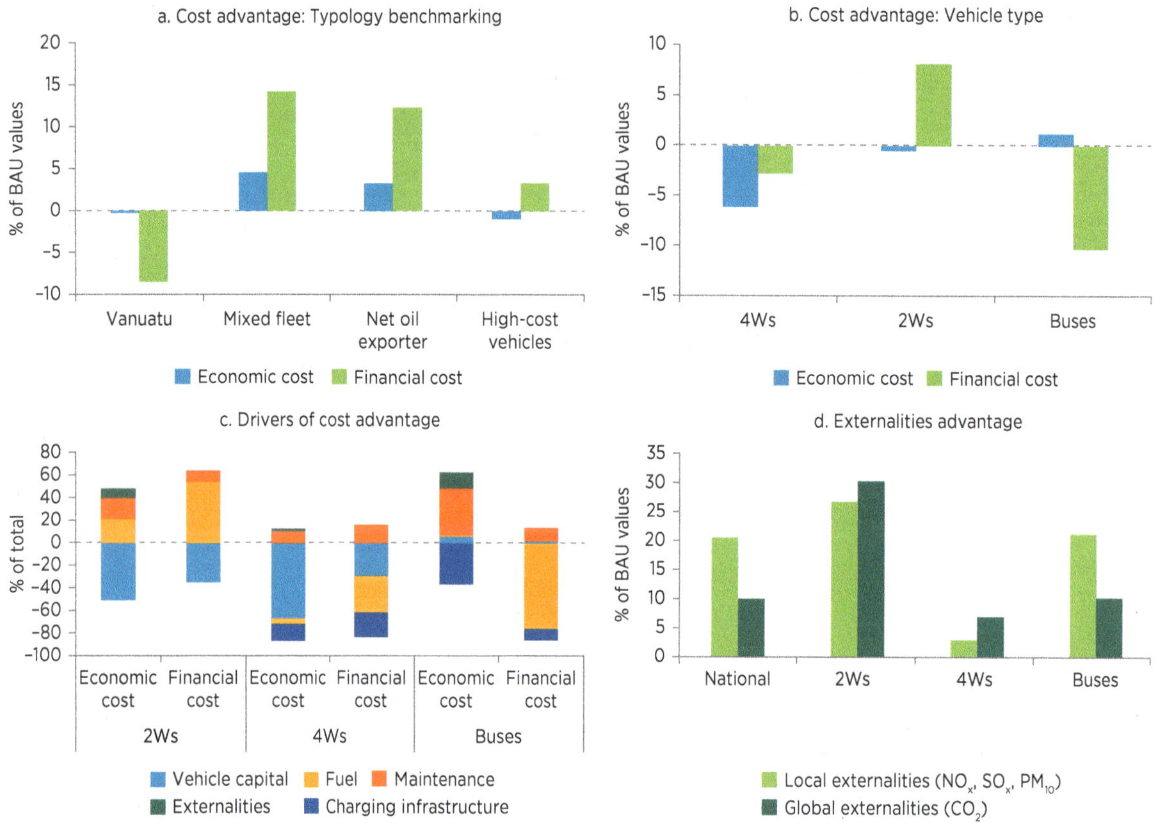

Source: World Bank.

Note: Data in this figure represent the "business as usual" (BAU) scenario minus the 30×30 scenario (averages over fleet additions). The BAU scenario assumes that no policy target will be imposed for electric vehicles and that vehicle purchase decisions will continue to reflect historical trends. The 30×30 scenario assumes that sales of electric cars and buses will reach 30 percent, and of two- and three-wheelers, 70 percent, by 2030. 2W = two-wheeler; 4W = four-wheeler; CO_2 = carbon dioxide; EV = electric vehicle; NO_x = nitrogen oxides; PM_{10} = particulate matter less than 10 microns in diameter; SO_x = sulfur oxides.

TABLE A.19.1 Cost advantage of accelerated EV adoption in Vanuatu, 2030

	US$/vehicle									% of BAU values	
	Charging infrastructure	Vehicle capital cost	Vehicle operating cost	Subtotal	Local externalities	Global externalities	Economic cost advantage	Net taxes and subsidies	Financial cost advantage	Cost advantage	Financial cost advantage including fiscal wedge
	(a)	(b)	(c)	(d) = (a + b + c)	(e)		(f) = (d + e)	(g)	(h) = (d + g)		
Mode											
2Ws	0	(351)	283	(68)	6	48	(15)	469	401	(0.5)	8.3
4Ws	(550)	(2,473)	227	(2,796)	0	63	(2,733)	1,094	(1,702)	(6.1)	(2.8)
Buses	(6,082)	996	7,367	2,281	228	2,084	4,594	(46,122)	(43,840)	1.2	(10.4)

Source: World Bank.

Note: Heading colors: blue = excluding taxes and subsidies, gray = fiscal wedge, green = including taxes and subsidies. 2W = two-wheeler; 4W = four-wheeler; "Local externalities" comprises local (NO_x, PM_{10}, SO_x) air pollution costs. "Global externalities" comprises global (CO_2) air pollution costs. CO_2 = carbon dioxide; NO_x = nitrogen oxides; PM_{10} = particulate matter less than 10 microns in diameter; SO_x = sulfur oxides. Red and parentheses indicate negative value.

FIGURE A.19.2 Investment and financing needs for EV adoption in Vanuatu, 2030

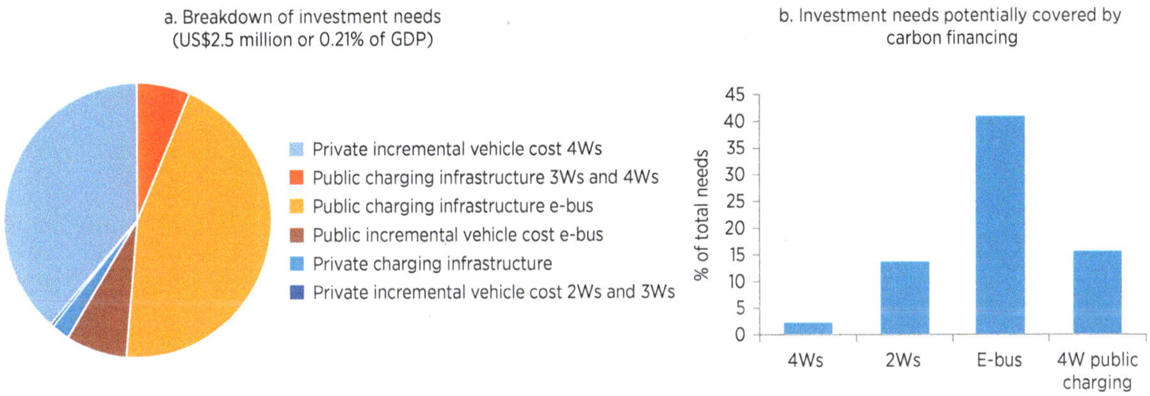

Source: World Bank.
Note: Data in this figure represent the "business as usual" (BAU) scenario minus the 30×30 scenario (averages over fleet additions). The BAU scenario assumes that no policy target will be imposed for electric vehicles and that vehicle purchase decisions will continue to reflect historical trends. The 30×30 scenario assumes that sales of electric cars and buses will reach 30 percent, and of two- and three-wheelers, 70 percent, by 2030. 2W = two-wheeler; 3W = three-wheeler; 4W = four-wheeler; EV = electric vehicle; GDP = gross domestic product.

TABLE A.19.2 Cost advantage of EV adoption in Vanuatu, by scenario, 2030

	National results				Bus only		4W only	
	30×30 scenario	Green grid scenario	Scarce minerals scenario	Fuel efficiency scenario	30×30 scenario	Efficient bus scenario	30×30 scenario	Taxi fleet scenario
	US$/Mpaxvkm				*US$/vehicle*			
Type of cost								
Vehicle capital cost	(3,915)	(3,915)	(10,604)	(3,915)	996	14,670	(2,473)	(2,473)
Vehicle maintenance cost	7,386	7,386	5,359	7,386	7,167	7,467	418	(788)
Vehicle fuel cost	(165)	(165)	(165)	(7,968)	200	200	(191)	(764)
Private charging infrastructure	(274)	(274)	(274)	(274)	n.a.	n.a.	(142)	(142)
Public charging infrastructure	(6,354)	(6,354)	(6,354)	(6,354)	(6,082)	(6,082)	(408)	(466)
Subtotal	(3,322)	(3,322)	(12,039)	(11,126)	2,281	16,256	(2,796)	(4,634)
Local externalities (NO_x, SO_x, PM_{10})	210	236	210	208	228	228	0	2
Global externalities (CO_2)	2,036	3,274	2,036	1,160	2,084	2,084	63	281
Economic cost advantage	(1,076)	187	(9,792)	(9,758)	4,594	18,568	(2,733)	(4,351)
Fiscal wedge	(40,029)	(40,029)	(41,823)	(41,568)	(46,122)	(41,712)	1,094	(808)
Financial cost advantage	(43,352)	(43,352)	(53,862)	(52,694)	(43,840)	(25,456)	(1,702)	(5,442)
Economic cost advantage, by type of vehicle	*US$/vehicle*							
4Ws	(2,733)	(2,682)	(3,822)	(3,133)	n.a.	n.a.	n.a.	n.a.
2Ws	(15)	2	(122)	(66)	n.a.	n.a.	n.a.	n.a.
E-buses	4,594	5,864	(2,615)	(4,041)	n.a.	n.a.	n.a.	n.a.

Source: World Bank.
Note: Data in this table represent the "business as usual" (BAU) scenario minus the named scenario (averages over fleet additions). The BAU scenario assumes that no policy target will be imposed for electric vehicles and that vehicle purchase decisions will continue to reflect historical trends. The 30×30 scenario assumes that sales of electric cars and buses will reach 30 percent, and of two- and three-wheelers, 70 percent, by 2030. The green grid scenario assumes that countries achieve certain region-specific targets for acceleration of renewable energy, as defined by the International Renewable Energy Agency (IRENA 2020). The scarce minerals scenario assumes that battery cost will decline by approximately 7 percent annually. The fuel efficiency scenario assumes that the rate of improvement of fuel efficiency for the internal combustion engine fleet will double from 15 percent to 30 percent. The efficient bus scenario assumes a capital cost reduction of 35 percent in the procurement of buses as well as optimized bus routes to increase the annual mileage of electric buses. The taxi fleet scenario assumes that the lifetime mileage of intensively used commercial vehicles will increase by four times in each country, that public investment in charging infrastructure will double the fast charger density for cars, and that the maintenance cost for cars will be doubled (assuming two lifetime battery replacements). Results have been normalized by new vehicles entering the market in 2030. The "fiscal wedge" comprises net taxes and subsidies. Red and parentheses indicate negative value. 2W = two-wheeler; 4W = four-wheeler; CO_2 = carbon dioxide; EV = electric vehicle; NO_x = nitrogen oxides; PM_{10} = particulate matter less than 10 microns in diameter; SO_x = sulfur oxides; US$/Mpaxvkm = US dollars per million passenger vehicle-kilometers; n.a.= not applicable.

TABLE A.19.3 Supporting information on parameters and results for EV adoption in Vanuatu

Price (US$/vehicle)

Parameter	Value
Price of ICE 4W	34,719
Price of EV 4W	44,329
Price of ICE 2W	1,282
Price of EV 2W	1,859
Price of ICE bus	163,189
Price of e-bus	155,622

Other parameters

Parameter	Value
Net tax difference on EV 4W (%)	0
Net tax difference on EV 2W (%)	0
Net tax difference on e-bus (%)	0
Price of gasoline (US$/liter)	0.60
Net gasoline tax (US$/liter)	0.97
Price of diesel (US$/liter)	0.74
Net diesel tax (US$/liter)	0.09
Price of electricity (US$/kWh)	0.21
Net electricity tax (US$/kWh)	0.23
Electricity carbon intensity (g/kWh)	551
Discount rate (%)	6.6

Key characteristics

Parameter	Value
4W mileage (km)	15,224
2W mileage (km)	7,627
Bus mileage (km)	48,092
4W lifetime (years)	22
2W lifetime (years)	17
Bus lifetime (years)	20
4W secondhand (%)	2.7
2W secondhand (%)	2.7
Bus secondhand (%)	0.6
4W share (% paxvkm)	12
2W share (% paxvkm)	0.2
Bus share (% paxvkm)	88

Efficiency (MJ/km)

Parameter	Value
Efficiency ICE 4W	2.08
Efficiency EV 4W	0.71
Efficiency ICE 2W	0.85
Efficiency EV 2W	0.20
Efficiency ICE bus	15.80
Efficiency EV bus	5.31

Other results for 30×30 scenario

Other results for 30×30 scenario	Value
Overall investment needs (US$, millions)	2.5
—of which 4W purchase	1
—of which 2W purchase	0
—of which e-bus purchase	(0.2)
Fiscal impact (US$, millions)	9
—of which vehicle duties	(1.0)
—of which vehicle taxes/subsidies	0
—of which gasoline taxes/subsidies	(0.7)
—of which diesel taxes/subsidies	(1.4)
—of which electricity taxes/subsidies	12
Implicit carbon price (US$/ton)	40
—of which for 4W	1,142
—of which for 2W	34
—of which for buses	(31)
Pollution reduction (tons)	0
—of which local (SO_x, NO_x, PM_{10})	0
—of which global (CO_2)	0
Affordability of EV 2W (Δ cost % GNI pc)	10.5
Affordability of EV 4W (Δ cost % GNI pc)	16.9

Source: World Bank.
Note: Red and parentheses indicates negative value. 2W = two-wheeler; 4W = four-wheeler; CO_2 = carbon dioxide; EV = electric vehicle; g = gram; GNI pc = gross national income per capita; ICE = internal combustion engine; kWh = kilowatt-hour; km = kilometer; MJ = megajoule; NO_x = nitrogen oxides; paxvkm = passenger vehicle-kilometer; PM_{10} = particulate matter less than 10 microns in diameter; SO_x = sulfur oxides.

Notes

1. Two wheelers cover all motorized two-wheel vehicles registered.
2. From Pacific Datahub, https://pacificdata.org/data/dataset/vanuatu-2000-2011-registered-vehicle.
3. Intended National Determined Contribution (INDC), Ministry of Energy, Vanuatu, 2020.
4. Vanuatu's First Nationally Determined Contribution (NDC) (Updated Submission 2020).

Reference

IRENA (International Renewable Energy Agency). 2020. *Global Renewables Outlook: Energy Transformation 2050*. Masdar City: IRENA.

A.20 PASSENGER ELECTRIC MOBILITY IN VIETNAM

Country Typology

Vehicle fleet composition: Mixed fleet
Net oil trading status: Importer
Relative cost of vehicles: High

Country Background

The dominant vehicle type in Vietnam is the two-wheeler (82.9 percent), followed by cars (9.1 percent), three-wheelers (6.2 percent), and buses (1.8 percent). Electricity is primarily generated from fossil fuels (63.6 percent)—mainly gas (33.4 percent) and coal (29.7 percent)—plus a significant contribution from renewable sources (36.4 percent)—almost exclusively hydro (36.1 percent).[1] The government has targeted increasing the electric vehicle stock (a combination of hybrid and electric cars) to 6 million by 2020,[2] from a low starting point of about 306,000.[3] Vietnam is second only to China as a leader in electric two-wheelers, with an established high market share that reached 14 percent in 2020 (McKerracher 2021). VinFast, a part of Vietnam's biggest private enterprise Vingroup, is spearheading domestic electric vehicle manufacturing. It plans to produce electric motorbikes, electric buses, and electric cars in their production plants in the country. VinFast is expecting to invest US$1.0–1.5 billion with a target to produce 100,000–200,000 vehicles per year, including five-seat sedans, SUVs and electric motorbikes (Pastoor 2018). The United Nations Environment Programme is supporting the introduction of electric two- and three-wheelers in Vietnam, along with some other Asian countries.[4] GIZ has a major technical assistance program to support transport initiatives under Vietnam's Nationally Determined Contribution. The program includes building mechanisms, policies, and road maps to advance e-mobility development at national and city levels.[5] The World Bank Group is developing an e-mobility road map for the country and an operational plan for a pilot city (Cheung 2021).

Overall Messages

Vietnam faces many conditions that are favorable toward electric mobility, including a mixed fleet and oil-importing status, but vehicle costs are relatively high (figure A.20.1a). Electrification of transportation looks to be viable as a national strategy (table A.20.1), with the exception of the four-wheel segment, because of significant (and unaffordable) capital cost differentials (table A.20.1). By contrast, there is a strong case for adoption of two-wheel electric motorbikes (figure A.20.1b), which present a life-cycle cost advantage of about 13 percent (almost 20 percent in financial terms). However, a significant barrier to uptake is the 50 percent capital cost differential associated with electric two-wheelers, which represents 8.7 percent of gross national income per capita and looks unaffordable even with consumer finance. Furthermore, electric buses also offer significant economic advantages on the order of 6 percent of life-cycle cost, against a capital cost differential of just over 10 percent.

The externality benefits of electric mobility in Vietnam are particularly significant for buses, in terms of both local air quality and savings in carbon emissions (figure A.20.1d).

Otherwise, fuel cost savings are the main advantage associated with electric mobility in Vietnam, given that gasoline is taxed at 60 percent and electricity is tax exempt (table A.20.3). Furthermore, electric buses and four-wheelers enjoy a tax differential of 45 percent. As a result, the overall case for electric mobility in Vietnam looks even better in financial than in economic terms (figure A.20.1c).

The total investment needs associated with the 30×30 scenario amount to US$3.8 billion per year by 2030 (or 0.85 percent of Vietnamese gross domestic product). About four-fifths of the required outlay is associated with the incremental capital of private electric vehicles, mainly two-wheelers (figure A.20.2a). In terms of public investment, the most significant item is the incremental capital cost of electric buses (figure A.20.2a). Given that implicit carbon prices associated with electric two-wheelers and buses in Vietnam are negative (table A.20.3), there is scope to cover 20 percent of incremental investments associated with these vehicle categories through carbon financing arrangements (figure A.20.2b). However, for four-wheel electric vehicles, the implicit carbon price is approaching US$700 per ton.

The overall economic case for electric mobility is very positive in Vietnam, even under more conservative assumptions about the cost of batteries ("scarce minerals" scenario) and the fuel efficiency of internal combustion engines ("fuel efficiency" scenario), and only improves with further decarbonization of the power sector ("green grid" scenario) (table A.20.2). On a positive note, the important advantage associated with electrification of buses is substantially increased through the more efficient procurement and operation of vehicles ("efficient bus" scenario). However, there is not yet any case for electrification of four-wheelers, even when it comes to taxi fleets and other intensively used vehicles ("taxi fleet" scenario). It is clear that electric mobility in Vietnam needs to prioritize the bus and two-wheel segments of the fleet, with efforts needed to reduce the capital cost.

Figures and tables start on the next page.

Figures and Tables

FIGURE A.20.1 **Advantage of EV adoption in Vietnam, by type of vehicle**

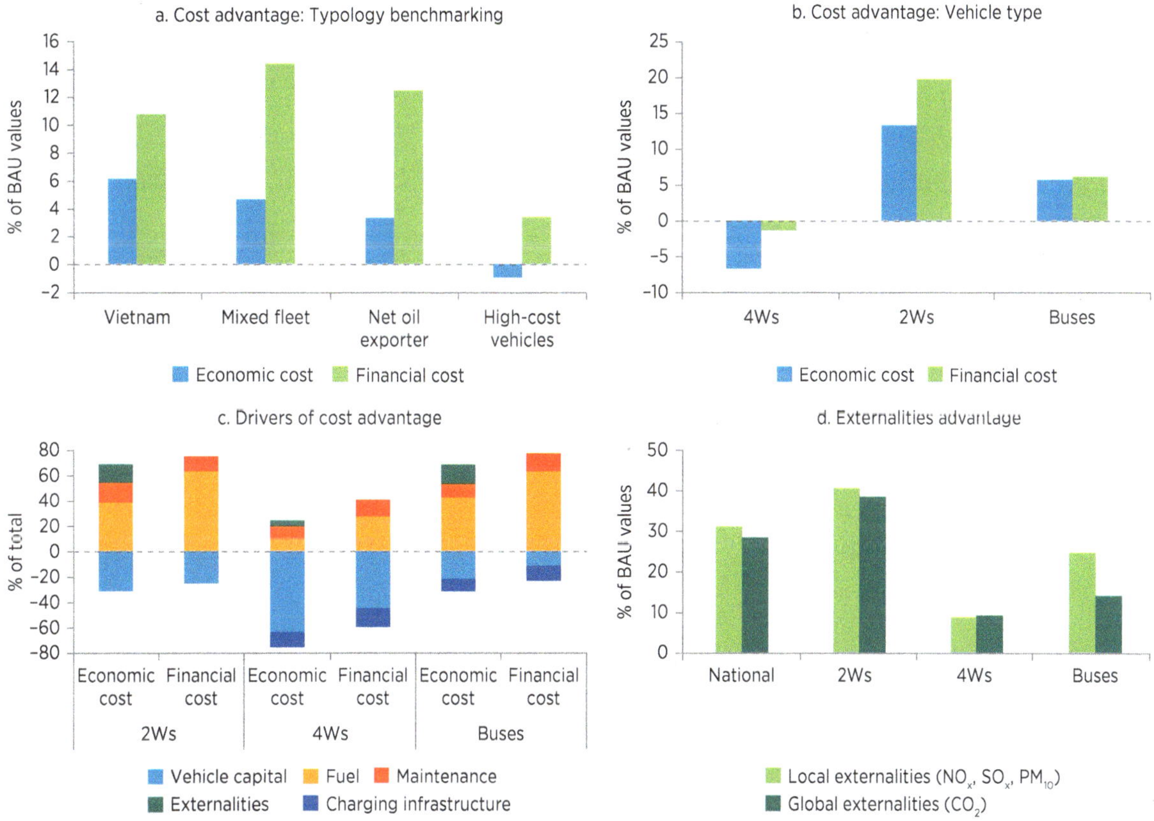

Source: World Bank.

Note: Data in this figure represent the "business as usual" (BAU) scenario minus the 30×30 scenario (averages over fleet additions). The BAU scenario assumes that no policy target will be imposed for electric vehicles and that vehicle purchase decisions will continue to reflect historical trends. The 30×30 scenario assumes that sales of electric cars and buses will reach 30 percent, and of two- and three-wheelers, 70 percent, by 2030. 2W = two-wheeler; 4W = four-wheeler; CO_2 = carbon dioxide; EV = electric vehicle; NO_x = nitrogen oxides; PM_{10} = particulate matter less than 10 microns in diameter; SO_x = sulfur oxides.

TABLE A.20.1 **Cost advantage of accelerated EV adoption in Vietnam, 2030**

	US$/vehicle									% of BAU values	
	Charging infrastructure	Vehicle capital cost	Vehicle operating cost	Subtotal	Local externalities	Global externalities	Economic cost advantage	Net taxes and subsidies	Financial cost advantage	Cost advantage	Financial cost advantage including fiscal wedge
	(a)	(b)	(c)	(d) = (a + b + c)	(e)		(f) = (d + e)	(g)	(h) = (d + g)		
Mode											
2Ws	0	(348)	605	258	80	76	413	506	764	13.3	19.7
4Ws	(569)	(3,004)	942	(2,631)	110	93	(2,427)	1,872	(759)	(6.7)	(1.4)
Buses	(6,102)	(14,234)	34,576	14,239	5,257	4,457	23,953	13,784	28,023	5.7	6.2

Source: World Bank.

Note: Red and parentheses indicate negative value. 2W = two-wheeler; 4W = four-wheeler; CO_2 = carbon dioxide; EV = electric vehicle; NO_x = nitrogen oxides; PM_{10} = particulate matter less than 10 microns in diameter; SO_x = sulfur oxides.

FIGURE A.20.2 Investment and financing needs for EV adoption in Vietnam, 2030

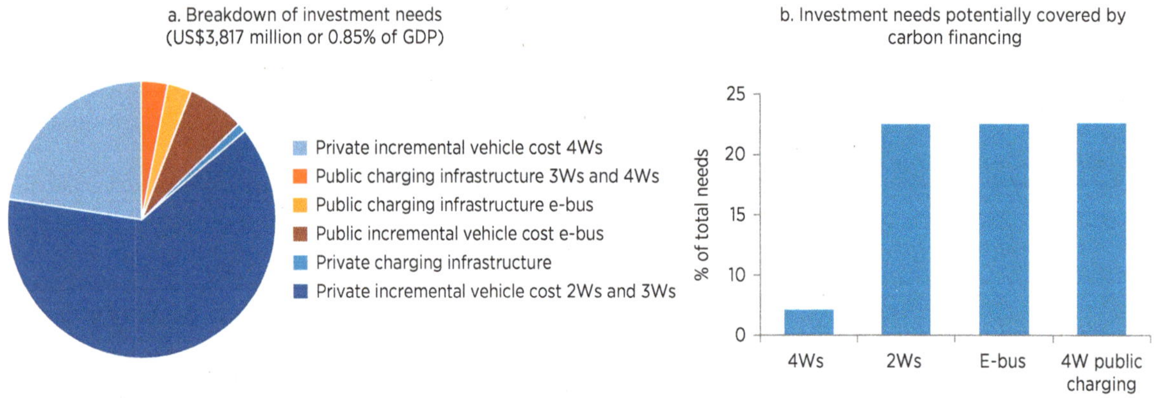

Source: World Bank.
Note: Data in this figure represent the "business as usual" (BAU) scenario minus the 30×30 scenario (averages over fleet additions). The BAU scenario assumes that no policy target will be imposed for electric vehicles and that vehicle purchase decisions will continue to reflect historical trends. The 30×30 scenario assumes that sales of electric cars and buses will reach 30 percent, and of two- and three-wheelers, 70 percent, by 2030. 2W = two-wheeler; 3W = three-wheeler; 4W = four-wheeler; EV = electric vehicle; GDP = gross domestic product.

TABLE A.20.2 Cost advantage of EV adoption in Vietnam, by scenario, 2030

	National results				Bus only		4W only	
	30×30 scenario	Green grid scenario	Scarce minerals scenario	Fuel efficiency scenario	30×30 scenario	Efficient bus scenario	30×30 scenario	Taxi fleet scenario
	US$/Mpaxvkm				*US$/vehicle*			
Type of cost								
Vehicle capital cost	(22,595)	(22,595)	(28,694)	(22,595)	(14,234)	(499)	(3,004)	(3,004)
Vehicle maintenance cost	9,186	9,186	8,929	9,186	7,200	7,500	504	(722)
Vehicle fuel cost	21,892	21,892	21,892	17,876	27,376	27,376	438	1,751
Private charging infrastructure	(265)	(265)	(265)	(265)	n.a.	n.a.	(144)	(144)
Public charging infrastructure	(1,490)	(1,490)	(1,490)	(1,490)	(6,102)	(6,102)	(425)	(484)
Subtotal	6,728	6,728	374	2,712	14,239	28,274	(2,631)	(2,603)
Local externalities (NO_x, SO_x, PM_{10})	4,195	5,602	4,195	3,847	5,257	5,257	110	520
Global externalities (CO_2)	3,916	4,604	3,916	3,355	4,457	4,457	93	403
Economic cost advantage	14,839	16,935	8,484	9,914	23,953	37,988	(2,427)	(1,681)
Fiscal wedge	26,451	26,451	24,579	24,826	13,784	17,795	1,872	3,739
Financial cost advantage	33,179	33,179	24,953	27,538	28,023	46,070	(759)	1,135
Economic cost advantage, by type of vehicle	*US$/vehicle*							
4Ws	(2,427)	(2,244)	(3,367)	(2,825)	n.a.	n.a.	n.a.	n.a.
2Ws	413	443	321	350	n.a.	n.a.	n.a.	n.a.
E-buses	23,953	28,562	16,720	10,688	n.a.	n.a.	n.a.	n.a.

Source: World Bank.
Note: Data in this table represent the "business as usual" (BAU) scenario minus the named scenario (averages over fleet additions). The BAU scenario assumes that no policy target will be imposed for electric vehicles and that vehicle purchase decisions will continue to reflect historical trends. The 30×30 scenario assumes that sales of electric cars and buses will reach 30 percent, and of two- and three-wheelers, 70 percent, by 2030. The green grid scenario assumes that countries achieve certain region-specific targets for acceleration of renewable energy, as defined by the International Renewable Energy Agency (IRENA 2020). The scarce minerals scenario assumes that battery cost will decline by approximately 7 percent annually. The fuel efficiency scenario assumes that the rate of improvement of fuel efficiency for the internal combustion engine fleet will double from 15 percent to 30 percent. The efficient bus scenario assumes a capital cost reduction of 35 percent in the procurement of buses as well as optimized bus routes to increase the annual mileage of electric buses. The taxi fleet scenario assumes that the lifetime mileage of intensively used commercial vehicles will increase by four times in each country, that public investment in charging infrastructure will double the fast charger density for cars, and that the maintenance cost for cars will be doubled (assuming two lifetime battery replacements). Results have been normalized by new vehicles entering the market in 2030. The "fiscal wedge" comprises net taxes and subsidies. Red and parentheses indicate negative value. 2W = two-wheeler; 4W = four-wheeler; CO_2 = carbon dioxide; EV = electric vehicle; NO_x = nitrogen oxides; PM_{10} = particulate matter less than 10 microns in diameter; SO_x = sulfur oxides; US$/Mpaxvkm = US dollars per million passenger vehicle-kilometers; n.a.= not applicable.

TABLE A.20.3 Supporting information on parameters and results for EV adoption in Vietnam

Price (US$/vehicle)

Parameter	Value
Price of ICE 4W	32,230
Price of EV 4W	37,262
Price of ICE 2W	1,051
Price of EV 2W	1,562
Price of ICE bus	141,332
Price of e-bus	155,622

Other parameters

Parameter	Value
Net tax difference on EV 4W (%)	45
Net tax difference on EV 2W (%)	5
Net tax difference on e-bus (%)	45
Price of gasoline (US$/liter)	0.50
Net gasoline tax (US$/liter)	0.31
Price of diesel (US$/liter)	0.64
Net diesel tax (US$/liter)	0.04
Price of electricity (US$/kWh)	0.11
Net electricity tax (US$/kWh)	(0.00)
Electricity carbon intensity (g/kWh)	441
Discount rate (%)	6.6

Key characteristics

Parameter	Value
4W mileage (km)	15,330
2W mileage (km)	7,373
Bus mileage (km)	77,380
4W lifetime (years)	35
2W lifetime (years)	34
Bus lifetime (years)	20
4W secondhand (%)	0
2W secondhand (%)	0
Bus secondhand (%)	0
4W share (% paxvkm)	11
2W share (% paxvkm)	55
Bus share (% paxvkm)	18

Efficiency (MJ/km)

Parameter	Value
Efficiency ICE 4W	2.08
Efficiency EV 4W	0.73
Efficiency ICE 2W	0.85
Efficiency EV 2W	0.20
Efficiency ICE bus	15.85
Efficiency EV bus	5.35

Other results for 30×30 scenario

Other results for 30×30 scenario	Value
Overall investment needs (US$, millions)	3,817
—of which 4W purchase	863
—of which 2W purchase	2,047
—of which e-bus purchase	258
Fiscal impact (US$, millions)	(4,146)
—of which vehicle duties	261
—of which vehicle taxes/subsidies	(463)
—of which gasoline taxes/subsidies	(3,716)
—of which diesel taxes/subsidies	(89)
—of which electricity taxes/subsidies	(138)
Implicit carbon price (US$/ton)	(72)
—of which for 4W	698
—of which for 2W	(115)
—of which for buses	(113)
Pollution reduction (tons)	24
—of which local (SO_x, NO_x, PM_{10})	0
—of which global (CO_2)	24
Affordability of EV 2W (Δ cost % GNI pc)	8.7
Affordability of EV 4W (Δ cost % GNI pc)	38.6

Source: World Bank.
Note: Red and parentheses indicates negative value. 2W = two-wheeler; 4W = four-wheeler; CO_2 = carbon dioxide; EV = electric vehicle; g = gram; GNI pc = gross national income per capita; ICE = internal combustion engine; kWh = kilowatt-hour; km = kilometer; MJ = megajoule; NO_x = nitrogen oxides; paxvkm = passenger vehicle-kilometer; PM_{10} = particulate matter less than 10 microns in diameter; SO_x = sulfur oxides.

Notes

1. Generation mix comes from a combination of US EIA international database and World Bank Group data.
2. Data from the Global Electric Vehicle Policy Database.
3. Power train mix comes from country-specific sources. Additional data on EVs come from separate data provided by the World Bank. Otherwise, if data are still missing, we assume 100 percent internal combustion engine vehicles and a 50:50 split for gasoline and diesel for cars, 100 percent gasoline for two-wheelers and 100 percent diesel for buses. For three wheelers, the shares are used from India data because it is one of the largest markets for three-wheelers in the world.
4. From the United Nations Environment Programme web page, "Electric mobility projects in Asia and the Pacific," https://www.unep.org/explore-topics/transport/what-we-do/electric-mobility/electric-mobility-projects-asia-and-pacific
5. Information from the World Bank.

References

Cheung, Jerman. 2021. "Accelerating E-mobility in Vietnam." News release, March 2, 2021. https://www.arup.com/news-and-events/accelerating-e-mobility-in-vietnam.

IRENA (International Renewable Energy Agency). 2020. *Global Renewables Outlook: Energy Transformation 2050.* Masdar City: IRENA.

McKerracher, Colin. 2021. "Hyperdrive Daily: The EV Revolution Rides on Two Wheels." Bloomberg, April 20, 2021. https://www.bloomberg.com/news/newsletters/2021-04-20/hyperdrive-daily-the-ev-revolution-rides-on-two-wheels.

ECO-AUDIT
Environmental Benefits Statement

The World Bank Group is committed to reducing its environmental footprint. In support of this commitment, we leverage electronic publishing options and print-on-demand technology, which is located in regional hubs worldwide. Together, these initiatives enable print runs to be lowered and shipping distances decreased, resulting in reduced paper consumption, chemical use, greenhouse gas emissions, and waste.

We follow the recommended standards for paper use set by the Green Press Initiative. The majority of our books are printed on Forest Stewardship Council (FSC)–certified paper, with nearly all containing 50–100 percent recycled content. The recycled fiber in our book paper is either unbleached or bleached using totally chlorine-free (TCF), processed chlorine–free (PCF), or enhanced elemental chlorine–free (EECF) processes.

More information about the Bank's environmental philosophy can be found at http://www.worldbank.org/corporateresponsibility.

green press INITIATIVE